Kenya's Past as Prologue: Voters, Violence and the 2013 General Election

EDITED BY

Christian Thibon   Marie-Aude Fouéré
Mildred Ndeda   Susan Mwangi

TWAWEZA
COMMUNICATIONS
"Working Towards a Better World"

Published in 2014 by:
Twaweza Communications Ltd.
P.O. Box 66872 - 00800 Westlands
Twaweza House, Parklands Road
Mpesi Lane, Nairobi Kenya
website: www.twawezacommunications.org
Tel: +(254) 020 269 4409

Design and Layout: Centrepress Media
Email: info@centrepressmedia.com

Cover Photo: Boniface Mwangi

With the support of French Institute for Research in Africa (IFRA); Heinrich Böll Stiftung, East and Horn of Africa; Agence Française de Développement (AFD); and Afrique Contemporaine

ISBN: 978-9966-028-51-8

Printed by: Modern Lithographic
Email: sales@modernlithographic.co.ke

TABLE OF CONTENTS

Foreword

General elections in Kenya have been moments of great expectations and social anxiety. They are tension packed, conflict-ridden and passionate-driven processes not only because they offer the prospect of ushering in new sets of leaders and political visions but more so because they confer power and control over economic resources and social opportunities. They have the potential to facilitate transition to more democracy and economic transformation or, on the contrary, undermine social, political and economic change through patronage, corruption and autocratic governance. Academics can contribute to our understanding of such transformative moments through deep reflection and knowledge sharing as has been done in this volume.

This book is a multi-disciplinary approach to the 2013 general election in Kenya. It carries research undertaken by Kenyan and French academics and seeks to provide insight into the event itself as well as factors and circumstances that shaped it. Methodologically, most of the papers adopted an ethnographic approach and relied on in-depth interviews and on-site participant observation. These approaches, combined with field studies and extensive literature review, provide the writers with the tools they require to share their reflections on the key issues facing Kenyan politics. The volume builds on the growing body of literature on Kenyan general elections especially since the reintroduction of multiparty political engagement in 1991. The research project shows how voting is linked to identity, cooptation and patronage, power struggles and economic challenges.

The organizations involved in the production of this book – French Institute for Research in Africa, Afrique Contemporaine, Agence Française de Développement, Heinrich Böll Stiftung, De Boeck, and Twaweza Communications share the belief that although regular free and fair elections are not a sufficient condition for the evolution of a democratic state, they are a necessary condition. They pave the way for the strengthening of governance institutions that buttress democratic practices.

Another volume on the 2013 general election will be released in 2015 through a partnership involving Twaweza Communications, the Heinrich Böll Stiftung and the Goethe-Institut. The book comprises of multi-disciplinary reflections by scholars based in Kenya. It looks at the drivers of the general election, sources of the mandate to lead and what needs to be done to make Kenyan electoral politics free, fair, inclusive and democratic. Taken together, the two volumes greatly enhance perspectives of the 2013 general election. We believe that this volume will open up important discussions on general elections in Kenya. It provides analyses and insights on the country's history and increases our understanding of the political trajectory necessary for greater democracy.

Marie-Emmanuelle Pommerolle

IFRA

Katrin Seidel

Heinrich Böll Stiftung

Kimani Njogu

Twaweza Communications

Acknowledgment

IFRA wishes to thank the French Embassy in Nairobi for supporting its research project on Kenya's 2013 elections, notably fieldwork, seminars and publication. Former Cultural and Co-operation Counselor Jérémie Blin and Co-operation Attaché Sarah Ayito Nguema are deeply thanked for their continuous support. IFRA owes a great debt to the Heinrich Böll Stiftung in Nairobi and its head Katrin Seidel, as well as to the French journal *Afrique Contemporaine* through the Agence Française de Développement (AFD) for supporting this publication. Five articles of this edited volume were originally published in French in *Afrique Contemporaine* (2013/3, no. 247) and translated to English by the journal's translators. Raphaël Jozan and Nicolas Court in greatly contributed to the journal's editorial and scientific work, and this edited volumebenefitted from their continuous help and advice. IFRA is indebted to De Boeck Supérieur for licensing the rights on these five articles. This project would not have been possible without the commitment of Prof. Christian Thibon, IFRA's former director, and Dr. Marie-Aude Fouéré, IFRA's former deputy director. The project owes, too, a debt of gratitude to Prof. Mildred Ndeda from Jaramogi Oginga Odinga University of Science and Technology and Dr. Susan Waiyego from Kenyatta University for their involvement. IFRA wishes to express their sincere thanks to the Director of Twaweza Communications, Kimani Njogu, for his enthusiastic and enduring support since the beginning of this project, as well as to all members of the Twaweza team. Finally, all the contributors to this book are thanked for their commitment, diligence and patience since the inception of the project.

Introduction

Kenya's 2013 General Election: A National Event Set Between 'The Inescapable' and 'The Unforeseeable'

Christian Thibon   Marie-Aude Fouéré   Mildred Ndeda   Susan Mwangi

This volume is the fruit of joint research carried out by a group of academics drawn from the research network of the *Institut français de recherche en Afrique* or IFRA (French Institute for Research in Africa). Most of them work in major Kenyan and French universities: some are doctoral students while others are junior or experienced scholars in the humanities and social sciences, mainly political science, history and anthropology. All of them were aware of the tremendous civic issues that were likely to arise during the March 2013 general election. They had also participated in research on the 2007 general elections and post-election violence, or witnessed them as Kenyan citizens or foreign observers. Questions such as whether past mistakes could be avoided this time and what new faces might emerge after the presidential election results were foremost in their minds. They were therefore convinced that a national event of such significance in Kenya's history and political life was a crucial research topic that needed to be both explored and explained.[1] Their research was completed a few weeks after the vote and thus does not take into account the impact of the Westgate terrorist attack in September 2013 on the Kenyan political scene.

This publication testifies to the desire to build a research program capable of offering insight into the recent past – by definition a complex past that calls for an approach at once narrative and explanatory. Exploring the recent past requires understanding the event – or its "momentum" – without, however, being able to view events from the distance normally demanded of the researcher or simply adopting a linear historical, cultural and structural perspective. Integrating all the necessary explanatory factors into an historical analysis can indeed be difficult at times. And in giving primacy to these explanatory factors, one tends to lose sight of the possibility of accidental trends, disruptions and discontinuities, commonly regarded as deceptive or delusive. All in all, the approach adopted in this volume situates the contingency of the event between the inescapable and the unforeseeable (Rémond, 1984). The general election, by nature a conflicting and passionate process, took place in a heated environment characterised by attempts to make political, partisan, ideological, media and even academic headway. At the same time, they sought to rectify previous political mistakes and justify the need to forgive and forget, a discussion that was – and still is – indispensable for the country as a whole.

The approach and methodologies used in this work are undeniably academic: researchers collected data on the successive phases of the electoral process (the campaign, the political debate, the post-election period) and on the various actors involved. They have undertaken an analysis of the election and its outcome from multiple points of view, paying special attention to their different – though usually intermingled – national, regional and local dimensions. Most of the contributions in this volume draw extensively on findings obtained with ethnographic methods – in-depth interviews and on-site participant observation. They combine or compare these findings with data from nationwide field studies and data-collection techniques such as polls and surveys as well as scholarly literature on the historical and political scene since Kenya's independence, particularly the 1992 and 2007 general elections. Reflections on colonial memory, especially as it relates to the land question and its attendant tensions, are also part of our understanding of the central issues at stake in Kenya.

Against electoral doom-mongering

The breaking news that constantly punctuated the election period together with the unknown factors and worrying scenarios that were widely discussed – notably the polarisation of Kenyan society – prompted the academic community and even more civil society, the government and the international community to focus their attention on the places and populations that were prone to radicalisation. These "hotspots", as they are often called, were targeted as areas in which potential political and ethnic violence had to be managed or controlled. These shared pessimistic scenarios were partly grounded in the trend towards electoral violence and its crescendo since 1992 as well as the workings of the political system and problems implementing the new national constitution. Due to the urgency and risks of the political situation, everyone, including the universities, felt compelled to take part in electoral monitoring. This broad-based engagement had its flaws, however: it mostly resulted in a restrained, consensual interpretation of some situations and the distortion of others, as if they were viewed through a magnifying glass.

As a general rule, the sampling of observations gathered in this volume was made randomly. Despite insights into electoral sociology, the analysis lacks a representative sample of places and spaces of the various electoral constituencies, though this could still be done. Such a sample might have served as a useful database for estimating voting patterns based on early electoral results rather than on the results gathered at the polling stations after all the ballots had been cast. In other words, the assessment of voter choices and the electoral process, including electoral irregularities, could make use of other data besides the information obtained from nationwide exit polls (Ferree, Gibson and Long, 2014). We were aware of this gap and did not wish to fall into the trap of catastrophism that had characterised the predominant view of Kenya in the media and among academics during the previous election. More often than not, elections in Kenya and in Africa generally tend to bring out and intensify latent political crises rather than opportunities to overcome them. The research presented here set out to look at the elections differently, tracking the events in two distinct yet complementary directions.

Navigating the inescapable and the unforeseeable

Firstly, the researchers adopted a critical approach that some readers may find a bit cynical and pessimistic, in the sense that it tried to identify what we call "the inescapable" in the elections. This approach, which distinguishes between the objectives of academic research and political expertise, was focused on assessing the expected fault lines and disputes of the electoral campaign. It examines these issues at the local level in everyday practices, taking a close look at corruption, fraud, manipulation, etc., and at the national level through political actors (e.g. the ethnicising and politicising of identity, the use of violence to achieve strategic electoral goals, etc.). This second level could be called "the prisons of *longue durée*", to borrow the words of Fernand Braudel (1958: 31).[2] As explorers of electoral political life with its political elites and dynasties as well as its political entrepreneurs, researchers are familiar with the structural factors – defined as stable elements over the long term – that weigh on the course of the electoral event, limiting and shaping the ways it unfolds.

Secondly, the approach took a more optimistic turn by paying attention to the overall trend and attempted to grasp what we call here "the unforeseeable". It investigated the appeasing, or at least moderating, factors and hypotheses that might promise a happier election outcome. These factors include: cosmopolitan or mono-ethnic spaces, whether urban or rural; the crucial role of civil society; the significance of new, emerging actors – social actors such as the middle class and institutional actors; information and communication technologies, notably social media like Twitter, Facebook and blogs; and lastly, the institutional or practical capacity to manage an election requiring voters to cast six separate ballots on the same day. This approach was pursued against the backdrop of a broad reflection on whether Kenyan society could be considered an "electoral civilisation", i.e. a civilisation featuring electoral civic practices and knowledge, in which voting is a peaceful act resulting from a historical process of self-restraint. Past experience and memory, particularly of 2007-2008 post-election violence, played a crucial role during the 2013 electoral year.

These choices did not preclude an interest in exploring the specific challenges facing certain sensitive places ("hotspots") of the country. The sensitive areas are mostly peripheral, both in the geographical sense, i.e. the pastoral areas and semi-arid regions of the North and the Indian Ocean coast, and in terms of socio-cultural patterns (including in particular the marginalized populations, peoples and ethnic groups of Kenya). They also encompass historically identified ethno-political conflict areas. This was especially the case of the Rift Valley. In view of the new ethno-political Jubilee alliance between Uhuru Kenyatta and William Ruto, a Kikuyu and a Kalenjin respectively, most of these hotspots *de facto* lost their potential for conflict.

The two-faceted approach being implemented by the IFRA research team became obvious at two interim programme meetings in January and February 2013. The first meeting was devoted to mapping the electorate and determining the relevance of opinion polls; the second centred on the ability of "soft power" to influence the conduct of the elections. The group discussed the increasing concerted efforts in December 2012 and January 2013 to mobilise citizens in the central areas of Kenya on the issue of land policy (which had already been the case for the 2010 referendum), whereas the peripheral areas remained poorly mobilised. This joint reflection enabled the research team to revise opinion poll projections that took only demographic data into account. The conclusions from the second meeting were more enigmatic. They addressed the likelihood of a calm election scenario under the management of civil society and several stakeholders. All these players seemed to tacitly agree that election-related ethnic and political violence loomed large over the election process and that it was crucial to avoid replaying the disputed electoral competition of 2007-2008 that had torn the country apart.[3]

But this half-hearted analysis suggested a certain interpretation of Election Day and the post-election period as the country awaited the validation of the results by the Supreme Court. Indeed, the peaceful conduct of the elections, the absence of political confrontation which might well have arisen in such a highly polarised electoral campaign, the voting itself and the settlement of post-election disputes all came as a surprise to many observers and analysts – particularly in light of numerous reports of electoral fraud and the malfunctioning of election-related technology. The questions guiding the group's collective observation therefore changed in the course of events, confirming or rejecting the hypotheses formulated at the beginning of the electoral process. This book brings together these observations-cum-analyses,[4] written from July to October 2013, when the terrorist attack on Westgate and its management by the Kenyan government brought the electoral period to a close in an apparent movement of national unity that cut across party allegiances.

Exploring the particular to reach the general

Readers will encounter two different types of texts here. The first could be described as "impressionist". These essays take stock of general or topical issues and highlight the structural factors underlying elections and voting in Kenya, as well as Kenya's political system, culture and political transition process. They also examine new structural and short-term trends and the core issues at stake in the new political order. The second type of texts could be called "pointillist". These chapters offer insights into specific case studies, situations and contexts and bring nuances and diversity into focus against the background of more systemic analyses in the "impressionist" texts.

The introductory contribution to the volume presents a broad overview of the elections, seen from a middle- or long-term perspective. It provides keys to understand the combination of factors that shaped the specific patterns of the 2013 general elections in Kenyan electoral history since 1963. The other contributions focus on specific, localised topics. They seek to explore the role of electoral strategies – of individuals, political parties or alliances – at the domestic level but also with regard to international stakes; political loyalties and routine patronage practices; the sense of belonging instilled along clan, ethnic or regional lines; generational and gender dynamics; and patterns of inclusion in and exclusion or marginalisation from the political system. At this stage, such an event-focused, locally grounded approach to the elections may not show how these last elections fit into the broader perspective of Kenya's long-term electoral and political history. Nevertheless, they do provide us with rich empirical findings that can serve as a basis for further – and later – theoretical reflection on the significance of the 2013 Kenyan elections – whether as a turning point, a mere continuation of the past, or a slight but real change – in Kenya's history.

The research collection nevertheless remains incomplete, both in terms of the topics covered and perhaps even more in its monographic section. A number of books, special issues and articles published to date (notably Cheeseman, Lynch and Willis, 2014) can serve as a useful complements to make up for the lack of studies on certain issues, areas and stakeholders. This does not mean, however, that the aim and general pattern of this volume come under the heading of applied research, like reports on how to manage and prevent electoral violence (Adenauer Foundation, 2013), let alone political expertise or consultancy. Nor does it fit entirely into broader, highly conceptualised theoretical discussions on elections in Africa. It explores specific case studies and topics mainly to give readers the empirical tools and alternative analyses they need to achieve a better grasp of Kenyan history and the country's current political, economic and social situation. When the research presented here is compared to other national situations in neighbouring African countries, it can indirectly, and where applicable, satisfy the expectations of readers looking for usable, operational information as well as those seeking an entry to general discussions of elections in Africa.

The scope and limits of democratisation

There are three main topics that cut across all the contributions, implicitly or explicitly. The first of these topics is violence. As indicated above, most scenarios indeed predicted, or at least feared, renewed violence in 2013. Yet, unlike 2007-2008, the 2013 general election in Kenya did not result in mass violence, though violent actions and turmoil were not totally absent. Clashes took place between and within communities in several regions of the country, especially in Kenya's peripheral areas, resulting in more than 500 deaths and nearly 120,000 internally displaced persons, thus revealing ongoing latent tensions and contained violence. Deterring election-related violence – whether actual or symbolic – was a tremendous challenge and it turned out to be relatively successful, testifying to the growing ability of Kenya's "soft power" to make a difference. A "virtuous environment" was introduced and politicians, civil society and the media were mobilised to prevent potential low or high levels of violence. In the run-up to the 2013 elections, the leading presidential candidates made a systematic, collective appeal for peace and stepped up their calls for tolerance; CSOs and NGOs – both secular and religious – launched programmes for civic education and peace strongly imbued with violence-prevention messages and engaged in election monitoring and conflict management; the media worked with government institutions to broadcast messages of peace and stifle "hate speech", which had been a major trigger in previous violence and turmoil; and lastly, a dissuasive climate was fostered by the security forces and the judiciary. The 2013 election appears to have been exceptional in the sense that it contradicted the scenario anticipated by the international community and Kenya's media. Hopefully it illustrated a step forward in the construction of public space, civil society and the rule of law, in other words, in political maturity and progress towards democratisation in Kenyan society.

A second theme that structured the research team's questioning had to do with the reliability and credibility of the electoral process driven by the state. The organisation of free and fair elections that reflected the choice of the majority was a major concern throughout Kenyan society. It reflected underlying expectations that these elections could be a turning point in opening up a new democratic space. However, as in 2007-2008, manifest electoral irregularities point to a flawed electoral process, challenging once again assumptions about the maturity of Kenyan democracy and thus undermining the enormous hopes placed in Kenya's 2010 constitution and national institutions. The legitimacy and reliability of the Independent Elections and Boundaries Commission (IEBC) to supervise the electoral process was called into question at a very early stage: delays in organising the election, hiring Election Day workers and determining the number of polling places eroded its credibility; technical malfunctions and multiple pressures in the form of intimidation and non-compliance with the rules were observed;[5] and after the vote, the ballot-counting and compiling phase was marred by lack of transparency and inefficiency. The declaration of the results on 9 March 2013,[6] and their validation on 30 March by the Supreme Court following a ballot recount for 22 polling places, did not convince the Kenyan citizenry of the integrity of the electoral process. Political strategies and manoeuvres adopted by political parties and politicians to garner votes, such as intimidation and vote-buying, were also crucial in assessing the solidity and reliability of national electoral institutions such as the IEBC and of the electoral process in general.

Lastly, a topic that cut across the reflections of the research team was the ability of Kenyan society to prompt democratic political change. Central to this concern is the state's ability to perform the tasks assigned to it – the last election showed that unpreparedness and urgency were the rule – and to counter manipulation or strategies of manipulation. It is crucial to avoid "diabolic causalities" (Rémond, 1984) or fears of plots and conspiracies, as they may skew the interpretation of electoral results and distort the picture of the political situation. It is also essential to question the capabilities of the elite before, during and after the elections. The elite may be able to mobilise through "democratic" persuasion – notably through the media – and thus offset the use of violence or the ethnic vote, which are no longer enough to win. Such new strategies work well in countries like Kenya where media coverage is high, while lack of control over electoral campaign funds enables their use. This means, however, that financial patronage remains at the centre of the post-electoral political configuration. The role of religion, as a belief but also as a political resource, is also one among such political strategies for gaining legitimacy and holding power.

This concern intersects with the question of ethnic-driven voting behaviour and ethnic manipulation by the political class, which brings the researcher back to the debate on moral ethnicity (Berman and Lonsdale, 1992) in Kenya. It also relates to new social and economic dynamics, particularly the emergence of a Kenyan middle class that votes less and less along ethnic lines, but instead to protect its class interests, or to the position of women in Kenyan society set between domination and agency. The difficult position of marginalised communities and minorities whose voice remains muted or silenced at the national level reveals how voting is not simply a result of belonging, but is essentially the outcome of social, economic and political interests. And finally, further inquiry is needed regarding the less visible mechanisms used to reproduce and renew the political elite in Kenya; among them the revival of past loyalties based on family networks and transmission, which could be termed "dynastic". The emerging aspect of coalition building among ethnic groups, especially for or against the ICC, is also highlighted.

Questioning whether a given election should be viewed as a decisive turning point in a country's electoral history, or on the contrary reveals the resilience of voting patterns and electoral functioning, is central to analysing its current political dynamics and foreshadowing its political trajectory. Undeniably, such questioning is highly relevant in the case of Kenya, where the possibilities for opening up a democratic space seem so great, but where, thus far, people's hopes and expectations have seldom been fulfilled.

Notes

1   This undertaking follows a similar initiative launched during the 2007 Kenyan election by the French political scientist Jérôme Lafargue in the framework of the IFRA programme "The Election Observatory in East Africa", resulting in *The General Election in Kenya, 2007* (2008).

2   *Longue durée* history is defined by French historian Fernand Braudel as "a history to be measured in centuries", "the history of the long, even of the very long, time span" as opposed to the *histoire événementielle* approach (the history of events), concerned with a short time span, investigating the moment and the event, and characterised by the "headlong, dramatic, breathless rush of its narrative" (Braudel, 1958: 27).

3   The need to prevent violence was on everyone's mind in 2012 and 2013, as the debates in the media and popular discussions reveal. The ethnically-targeted violence that broke out in 2007-2008 in various parts of Kenya after the announcement of President Kibaki's electoral victory in December 2007, was directed first at Kikuyu supporters of Kibaki's Party of National Unity (PNU) in the North Rift, then Luo and other allies of Raila Odinga's Orange Democratic Movement (ODM) in the Central Rift. It had been a national trauma, leaving more than 1,100 dead, 300,000 injured and about 600,000 forcibly displaced.

4   Some research and case studies not covered in this book are still in progress in individual doctoral research, such as that of Joyce Kaguta, Christine Adongo, or Charles Khamala.

5   In the end, the electoral administration reached nearly 80% of its voter target. On the other hand, 44% of one voter age group remained excluded from the voter registration list (a significant unregistered population). This group corresponded to spaces and societies located in peripheral pastoral and rural marginalised areas with the highest poverty levels and the lowest human development indicators (including young potential voters and women).

6   While most observers expected a run-off between Raila Odinga (Cord) and Uhuru Kenyatta (Jubilee), Kenyatta was declared the winner of the presidential election with 6,173,422 votes (50.07%). Odinga received only 5,340,546 votes, about 830,000 fewer.

Bibliography

Konrad Adenauer Stiftung. 'Summary Report on the Outlook of the Kenya Situation after the Election 2013' (http://www.kas.de/wf/doc/kas_33842-1522-2-30.pdf?130319104216).

Braudel, F. "History and the Social Science: The Longue Durée." In *On History* (trans. Sarah Matthew): 25-54. Chicago: University of Chicago Press, 1982. Originally published in *Annales ESC*, no. 4 (Oct.-Dec. 1958): 725-753.

Cheesman, N., G. Lynch and J. Willis. "Democracy and Its Discontent: Understanding Kenya's 2013 Elections." *Journal of Eastern African Studies* 1, no. 8 (2014): 2-24.

Ferree, K. E., C.C. Gibson and J.D. Lang. "Voting behavior and electoral irregularities in Kenya's 2013 Election." *Journal of Eastern African Studies* 1, no. 8 (2014): 153-172.

Rémond, R. "Le siècle de la contingence ?" *Vingtième siècle* 1, no. 1 (1984): 97-104.

Kenyan Elections: When Does History Repeat Itself and Does Not Repeat Itself?

Christian Thibon [*]

With regard to most other African elections seen as liberating moments or crisis resolution and, more often, as periods of conflict or endless crises, the 2013 Kenyan elections appeared exceptional, at least atypical. The scenario retained by the international community and by some Kenyan media was not realised. This scenario was double. On the one hand, a closely contested election race with violent excesses was feared (or a conflagration that some feared), thus following the conflictingelectoral history of the country (1997, 2002, 2007-2008). On the other hand, in view of existing structural social tensions, it was expected that the outgoing Prime Minister Raila Odinga would win in the second round against Uhuru Kenyatta and his running mate William Ruto, who were both de-legitimised internationally due to their indictment by the International Criminal Court (ICC). It has become a constant that, in Kenyan elections and since 1997, observers who are bent to perceive Kenyan politics as a pre-written Greek tragedy are frequently mistaken.

At first glance, two essential ambivalent facts – unforeseen though predictable – marked these recent elections. One the one hand, with these peaceful elections, history was not repeated but it stutters, seeing that beyond a symbolic Kenyatta-Odinga confrontation of the sons of the two Fathers of Independence, the polarisation and ethnic manipulation replayed the Kikuyu/Luo contention that has undergirded Kenya's history.

[*] Professor of history at the University of Pau and Pays de l'Adour (UPPA). This article was originally published in French under the title "Les élections générales de 2013 au Kenya : Les bégaiements de l'histoire politique kényane" DOI: 10.3917/afco.247.0015 (*Afrique Contemporaine*, n° 247, Élections Kenya, © De Boeck Supérieur s.a., 2013 1re édition, Fond Jean-Pâques 4, B-1348 Louvain-la-Neuve).

Paradoxically, this scenario raises many unknown issues about the nature of the observed events and expected changes. First, might the peaceful conduct of the elections as a structural and structuring effect herald the future? Or is it just an accident, a short-term"effect of grace", a combination of factors or circumstances? Unless it is a "turning point" in Kenyan politics, is the end of a political cycle a guarantee of change and a balanced transition? This turning point, partly resulting from the new Constitution, would be based on a *de facto* two-party system (with a government marked by a strong majority and opposition), the renewal of elites either affiliated to the old one or newly promoted, and the expected constitutional reforms, notably the devolution which, in the background, is imbued with a liberal and developmental consensus shared by almost all political actors. Secondly and beyond appearances, the results and the outcome of elections as well as the unknown issues raised by the electoral data are destabilising. This is due to germs of ethnic tensions and a game of fragile alliances which are maybe more circumstantial than real. This would be the case of the victorious Kikuyu/Kalenjin coalition and their respective parties TNA/URP, and of a legitimate power that has a deficit in international or internal credibility andcould re-establish past authoritarian practices, unless this new domestic and geopolitical order opens new political perspectives which are reflected by projects under constructionand visions through which a country aims to emerge.

History does not repeat itself: Peaceful elections

Elections, in their different phases – that is: the official election campaign, a heavy electoral process consisting of six polls in one day (presidential, parliamentary, senatorial, gubernatorial, and for women and county ward representatives), then a long period of announcement of the results with an appeal to the Supreme Court, all shortened to one round – took place peacefully with the exception of two incidences of violence: during the party primaries in Nairobi in the Mathare Valley slum and on the eve of the elections in Mombasa when several police stations were attacked at night. The media, as well as official observers, international, national and local NGOs, and Internet monitoring, attest to the peaceful atmosphere.[1]

There were certainly, during the campaign and on Election Day, technical malfunctions and multiple pressures in form of intimidation and non-compliance with the rules. Such practices were not systemically used, but rather put in place locally.[2] The same usual petty corruption practices were also seen, such as dispensation of "presents" like small notes of money. These are practices accepted by all, and manipulated by both the givers, who are from various political parties,and the beneficiaries who take advantage of such practices.[3] Yet these issues are incommensurate with the previous pre-election violence that had terrorised and destabilised the populations of Kenya. It explains, among other things, the record electoral turnout of 85.9%[4] and the electoral registration of 55.6 %.[5] Furthermore, inter-ethnic and religious-regionalist violence which repeated in 2012 in the border regions of Somalia – in the North or on the Coast – and which had little to do with pre-election issues as such, or were not manipulated in such a way, did not have any disruptive effect on registration, except in the north-eastern county of Mandera. They reveal the existence of different societies and time-spaces faced with land and pastoral conflicts in under-populated peripheral areas compared to densely populated electoral strongholds. Finally, while militias had a tremendous role in the previous election crisis of 2007-2008, they were not to be seen this time, even though political parties mobilised the youth and students. Universities too had no such political fever.

There are many reasons for this peaceful election. First, the significance and efficiency of "soft power", thus pointing to the growth of an"electoral civilization"[6] and the moralisation of public life, as summed by the head of the Anglican Church of Kenya, Eliud Wabukala, saying that "We've learnt our lesson".[7] This virtuous environment is explained by the strong peace-making investment of churches and religions, educational institutions and implementation of peace programs through the engagement of civil society in election monitoring, conflict management and the media in a modern and fair media campaign[8] – even seen by some as overly consensual – and finally in a dissuasive climate of the security forces, the judiciary and the "management" by these institutions (the Electoral Commission, the Supreme Court). All this was in line with the awareness, if not the maturity or capacity of an increasing educated, even globalised, literate population with access to the media, but also with a society particularly affected and traumatised by the violence of 2007-2008 that longed for peace above all.

This "self-control" that led to a more "relaxed" national campaign atmosphere was also the result of the moderation and caution of political leaders. Both losers and winners seemed confident in their success without using violence. Was it due to the moral pressure of the ICC? There were few ideological excesses in public while delicate subjects, including the land issue, were not discussed until the end of the campaign. Neither were there festive excesses among the winners but appeals for calm by the defeated, nor excessive mass enthusiasm when Kenyans watched Uhuru Kenyatta's presidential inauguration on TV.[9] Moreover, an anecdotal fact suggests that the piecemeal proclamation of results prepared public opinion to digest announcements that were unfavourable to half of them. In fact, resorting to justice has become a common practice since the first single-party and multi-party elections, thus contributing to the integration of various disputes – numerous on every level – in the institution.

These successful elections in their moderate progress could reflect a step in the construction of a public and civil society and the rule of law. At least, this positive analysis, made more by observers than by experts or academics, deserves to be questioned through the lens of the role and power of the key actors who have emerged with democratisation, such as the civil society and churches, the media, institutions and a dynamic public opinion.[10]

The electoral appeasement is also explained by structural factors of a "moyenne durée" (medium duration),[11] perhaps corresponding to a generational period. Since 2000, with the rebound in economic growth, the rise (and the future) of a bourgeois business and middle class weighs on political life. This elite is increasingly associated with the market and less with administrative and direction positions, in the sense that it is less dependent on political fallout and political corruption – in reference to the 1990s or what is called "the Goldenberg era" named after the main scandal of that decade. Although it is still marked by ethnic resentment, this elite aspires for a moderate transition or succession. As in 2007-2008, any open crisis would have jeopardised its gains, its investments and its property savings in a Kenyan economy dependent on the service and tourism industry. The choice of the election date, during the low tourist season, illustrates this calculation. And well before the results were announced, the Nairobi Stock Exchange and the strength of the national currency in their way praised the event. It is the same for Kenyan society, at least a dominant part of it.[12] Although benefits from growth have been unevenly distributed, living conditions have improved and the benefits of an emerging economy and some public redistribution have been anticipated and expected by many, as evident during a campaign in which issues regarding education, public health, security or access to basic services were prominent. This is a request and a claim that social movements (nurses and hospital staff, teachers on strike), or scandals in the health services, had already put in the public space in the second half of 2012. At least this hope, rather than frustration, is true for a part of the Kenyan society.

However there remains, beyond the normal abstention, a significant unregistered population.[13] Abstention corresponded to 44% of a voter-age population living in spaces and societies that are peripheral, often pastoral, and to marginalised rural time-spaces where poverty levels are the highest and levels of the human development indicator the lowest.[14] A symptomatic fact is that the two realities of low electoral registration and low registration of newborns look alike.

Finally, the last explanation for the peaceful conduct of the last election is difficult to quantify but was noticeable during the campaign. Kenyan society lives a double trauma. The first trauma, introverted, relates to the HIV/AIDS epidemic from the 1990s; the second, extroversive, has to do with violence, which was highly publicised during the 2007-2008, and with a latent moral crisis partly associated with socio-cultural changes. In these conditions, it resorts to and displays public, societal and familial moralisation supported by churches and religions, educational institutions and moral authorities – the elders.[15] This is true in everyday life in the condemnation of drugs, alcohol, tobacco and corruption. It translated during the campaign into a discourse highlighting the value of integrity, the redemptive efforts of candidates, and normative collective behaviours greatly sanctified and dramatised through collective prayers and blessing of the candidates, or highly ritualised performancesat the request of elders and councils of the wise in each community. This peace education was all the more possible because the most violent actors in the light of recent history, i.e. the Kikuyu and the Kalenjin, were united this time in the same political alliance, Jubilee. This alliance served as a pact which the militant protocol of the Jubilee coalition was keen on respecting with a fraternal balance between the two candidates – which the patronymic slogan fusion "Uhuruto" reflects – and the logo of a dove with a strong, subliminal connotation.[16]

In contrast, history stutters

Will the Kenya of 2013 find itself facing challenges similar to those of the time of independence, being prisoner of the same exclusive and regressive identity logics, with its "small countries" or "small nations", if not its internal nationalisms?[17] The results of the presidential election and the electoral geography reveal the print of such logics based upon multi-ethnic polarisation in the three-quarters of the country. This draws two Kenyas: the central Kenya made of Mount Kenya and the Rift Valley, supportive of the Uhuru Kenyatta/William Ruto ticket, and the Kenya of the peripheries, with the West and the East, all acquired by the Raila Odinga/Kalonzo Musyoka ticket. They reflect two ethno-political blocs. The city of Nairobi partly escapes this logic even though the politico-ethnic fragmentation makes its mark on this area. Such cleavages are also reflected at the local level in some territories, constituencies, or wards, but in these cases, there are small ethnic groups or clans sufficiently concentrated to influence the results in the western and northern counties like Marsabit and Narok.

The ethnic vote, which confirms the relevance of rival, strategic multi-ethnic alliances manipulating ethnic advantage, is not new. It is part of a political culture or political grammar maintained for fifty years by different political generations so as to win and to stay in power. It is rooted in implicit mobilisation, through two dimensions: the ethnic "unspoken" which profits from accumulated contentions and frustrations, and moral ethnicity, this sense of honor associated with territorial and cultural identity. But this time, the thresholds of intensity and politico-ethnic membership were high, with worrying electoral agreement of 85% to 95% in the two main candidates' strongholds, so much so that these non-violent elections were based, for a large part of the electorate, on a "symbolic violence" that locks up the mind.

Partisan strategies and political ambitions have once again used this leverage, especially since the new constitution. This constitution, which is presidential with a President and a Deputy President and a two-round election, justified the creation of multi-ethnic duos which the candidates intended to be "winners" by ensuring maximum demographic weight. This was the case of the Jubilee[18] coalition of Uhuru Kenyatta and William Ruto (champions of the Kikuyu and the Kalenjin) and the CORD coalition of Raila Odinga and Kalonzo Musyoka (champions of the Luo and the Kamba). These four main ethnic groups[19] represent nearly 51% of the population, and slightly more of the electorate – and even more of the electorate registered on the basis of provincial populations, which are not completely homogeneous. The battle of numbers implicitly weighed on political strategies and calculations seeing that the census data or the data of the electoral registration are used to justify the chosen ethnic lines. Thus, the calculation of the ethnic audience following the 2009 census inclined to Jubilee (30%), while CORD could only count on 21%. On the other hand, the central provinces (Kikuyu and Kalenjin) aligned to the Jubilee coalition only brought together 38% of the population and 41% of registered Kenyans while the eastern and western provinces aligned to CORD brought together 53% of the population and 47% of registered Kenyans, though the total of peripheral ethnic groups (Luo/Kisii/Luhya/Kamba/Mijikenda) more favourable to CORD covered many internal divisions as in the case of the Luhya.

However, in a diverse multi-ethnic society and given the new electoral system of two rounds, the winning strategy could not be exclusively ethnic because it was based on two challenges: the ability to maximally harness community voters, and the obligation to win beyond successful binary alliances. Therefore, unlike the previous elections in which the violence used to strengthen ethnic ranks should theoretically have secured a victory with a simple majority, this time – and to the extent that the "rule of numbers" could not mathematically ensure victory of either of the two coalitions – the attraction of undecided electorates coming from small ethnic groups and emanating from all major ethnic groups and of the cosmopolitan urban electorate was necessary in a democratic process. Yet the ethnic reference continued to weigh on the winning momentum of the two main coalitions, giving them some popularity and a reservoir of votes that favourable opinion polls confirmed and reinforced. This in practice brought about the rallying and co-option of allies or of "representatives" from ethnic minorities. Like "matatus" or "horses",[20] the two main partisan alliances or presidential aspirants reaped maximum converts or returnees from minority ethnic groups. In this exercise, Jubilee was more efficient in winning the votes of the Meru and the Embu, formerly associated with the Kikuyu (ex GEMA) and turning Raila Odinga's leading ex-allies coming from peripheral areas. This ethnic logic was at the expense of "independent" candidates who rejected this rule or those like Musalia Mudavadi who, relying only on the Luhya vote, did not manage to create such a strategy.

In this context, it is not surprising that the tensest phase of the elections was the primaries[21] in December 2012 when the coalitions and the parties they were comprised of decided who would pursue the electoral adventure. This was due to the fact that the ethnic vote – as the polls had already revealed – would act as a bonus to the victory but also as an assurance of an honourable defeat especially because the new constitution had led to a considerable increase in political seats with the new position of senator, governor, women and county ward representatives and nominees.

The results confirmed this ethnic polarisation. Uhuru Kenyatta and Jubilee narrowly won the presidential election in the first round with 50.07% but with a gap of over 800,000 votes as well as the parliamentary, senatorial, and county elections. Raila Odinga and CORD (43.28% in the presidential elections) accrued seats (20 out of 47 senators, 20 governors of 47, and 132 MPs of 337) in the richest counties (Nairobi, Mombasa, Kisumu). The campaign and its financial challenges favoured national parties and strong coalitions to the detriment of the independent aspirants. A comparison of the maps of the different polls somewhat qualifies this political dichotomy, but in local elections, the criteria for recognition, popularity or even age played an important role, showing in some counties the combination of favourable votes in the elections for candidates of opposing coalitions. It is the same in elections for the county committees. The composition of county committees reveals the presence of the big national parties (ODM 26.8% of elected members, TNA and GNU 26.3%, URP 15.7%) and the regional presence of their allies (Wiper 6.3%, UDF 3.8%, Ford Kenya 3% and KANU 3%) but independent representatives or small regional parties still account for nearly 18% whilst they have virtually disappeared from the national political arena.[22]

This political change – if we can speak of "change" seeing that, since 2008, political compromise on a transition basis has been the rule – gives the impression of a rotation of power. But this embryonic two-party system, built on alliances between parties and especially between ethnic champions or heroes, reveals many shortcomings: a divided political class, anchored on new political territories, though united in the defence of its privileges, individual political strategies steeped in the "big men" tradition. It reveals, above all, an exclusive membership of electorates in the respective strongholds of the two alliances and a partisan geography since the five major parties are concentrated in homogeneous ethnic territories: for Jubilee, TNA and GNU in the Central Kikuyu Province, URP in the Kalenjin Rift Valley, for CORD, ODM in the Western Luo Provinces, Wiper in the Kamba Provinces and UDF, the third alliance, in the Luhya area. This identity voting, which was "emotional" but not passionate, aroused fears fuelled by post-election rumours including a return to authoritarian practices associated with the regime of President Daniel arap Moi who had already presented the Kenyatta/Ruto ticket in the 2002 presidential election, with the risk of seeing the centre/peripheral divide widen – a dialectic difficult to achieve yet indispensable for national construction, Kenyanism.

However, these historical perspectives situated between, in the "moyenne durée" the confirmation of "state building" and the rule of law and, in the "longue durée" (long term), the fragility of national construction and "nation building", must be specified if not exceeded. The Kenyan paradox lies in the conduct of peaceful elections along symbolically violent political behaviour, and gives way to binary analyses that underpin the assumptions of an assumed modernity, or on the contrary to ethnic tensions. It conceals a complexity that should be explored by following several steps or by using certain keys. To do so, once must resort to a short time approach and look at both the "election momentum", to use a term in vogue, and the incidentals of an unofficial campaign, stemming from the 2008 crisis, as well as the new directions arising from the event. Three unknown issues are worth interrogation concerning the limits of the electoral process, the fragility of the electoral scenario and new political and geopolitical orders.

Unknown post-election issues

Imperfections of the electoral process, the fragility of the electoral scene and the risk of a third post-election round?

On 30 March 2013, the day after Good Friday and the eve of Easter (in a religious country, this date is not neutral), the Supreme Court upheld the official results by rejecting the appeal by CORD.The international, regional, national observer missions, after congratulating the people of Kenya and questioning the nature of discrepancies and malfunctions, acknowledged quickly on 9 March, following the ELOG consortium example,[23] the compliance of results and, on 4 April, like the Carter Center, that the elections had offered all the guarantees to respect the political will of the Kenyan people. However, using diplomatic and politically correct language, the national and international civil society supported by the press raised a range of problems from cases and representative samples.[24] In addition, delays in the publication of results and audits increased doubts that independent statistics could not dispel: parallel computing by ELOG gives a range of 47% to 52% for Uhuru Kenyatta and 41% to 46% for Raila Odinga and opinion polls in the exit polls place the two candidates side by side.[25] In August, the audit by Mars group, an NGO rather suspected of obliging the powers, confirmed the results with minimal error for the benefit of both camps.[26]

The audit concerned with the official reports of the polling stations (form 34) prior to aggregated data (form 36) and which re-calculated the results gives them as follows for 32,095 out of 34,680 official reports. Of these 32,095 officially checked documents: 2,180 reports i.e. 6.7 % reveal discrepancies between the re-calculated and officially reported data (mainly concerning rejected votes), 848 reports i.e. 2.7 % difference between votes cast and those reported. These differences, however, are minimal to the benefit and expense of all the candidates. With regard to the audited data, Uhuru Kenyatta's total is 5,831,000 votes and Raila Odinga garnered 4,887,000 votes. Official data from 2,585 missing or lost reports which is 7.4 % of cast votes reflects partisan territorial trends; out of 943,520 "lost" votes, 360,370 votes were attributed to Uhuru Kenyatta and 467,305 to Raila Odinga. The mapping of these lost documents reveals that they are generally few (less than 2%) except in certain counties (10%) which were either acquired through a coalition (Kilifi, Siaya, Homa Bay, Migori, Machakos, Kitui for CORD and Kiambu, Nyeri for Jubilee) or trilateral counties (Vihiga, Bungoma) where a high turnout in electoral participation is observed.

But questions remain concerning the record between the original data of November and the final document (due to corrections imposed by the electronic registration method and additions regarding some categories of the population), the consideration or not of rejected votes for calculating the eligibility threshold in the first round and finally, the gap between voters in the first elections (presidential) compared to subsequent ones (parliamentary) of about 26,491 ballots. Moreover, pleas and petitions increased locally for the other elections (parliamentary, senatorial and for counties) in a now classic fashion,[27] as in the 103 pleas for a total of 469 elections in the case of the constituency election.

If political realism and political calculations prevailed to recognise the outcome of the polls and validate a peaceful change in power – indeed, a potential second round would have confirmed the results of the first round – suspicion remained high for two reasons: the incomplete transparency including the lack of access to the final results of the various elections, and the significance of the systemic or accidental malfunctions of the electoral process. Yet the electoral process was presented, similarly to the country, as a global system and a high-tech package. It allowed for an electronic registration and distribution of voter cards and the compilation of electoral lists (file and paper) displaying the voter and their fingerprints, then for identification in the same way during the elections, and last the live transmission of the results that were to appear on the official website of the electoral commission, the IEBC, and television channels. These logistics added to administrative tasks and equally ambitious communication components (services via internet). For increased objectivity, the system was sectioned to independent operators and markets, but put in place late in a hurry. The two main elements, identification and transmission, did not function well for multiple reasons, including the failure of batteries! So much, so that, there was a recourse to the manual method for official reports and calculation of results.

Furthermore, consolidating six polls in one day, even if this method avoided a long electoral calendar often disturbed by the withdrawal of the losers in the first election, was as much a challenge of delay for voters who braved it stoically and a logistics burden that the independent commission discovered in an emergency. But in a sensitive election period as is the case for all bipolar elections with differences in limited votes for eligibility in the first round, the sum of malfunctions and conflicting interpretations contribute to undermining the political field and to maintaining in an interactive way the tensions between the two camps and post-election disputes.

However, the risk of this third legal round is not comparable to previous post-election crises with their string of victims,of violence, and of internally displaced persons (IDPs). Moreover, all the actors, be they winners and losers, gave pledges of peace whether in their speech, their political actions and their initial trips in the country, notably the President's visit to Kisumu, where his father Jomo Kenyatta had been violently challenged during his last presidential visit in 1969, and Mombasa, a region that had voted for his rival.

Furthermore, the terrorist attack at Westgate mall on 21 September 2013 reunited a divided political class through national emotion and a mature mobilisation, renewed national unity. This event *de facto* closes the post-election period, which until this tragedy was still marked by disputes on the legitimacy of the results of the last elections, and strengthens the authority of the new government of President Uhuru Kenyatta and his Deputy President William Ruto.

The victory of Uhuru Kenyatta and the defeat of Raila Odinga, beyond ethnic burdens? A generational change?

The mapping of election results in a somewhat simplified way and the narrow victory of Uhuru Kenyatta in the first round mask a significant difference in vote and thenational distribution of electoral support. With regard to the results, the victory of Uhuru Kenyatta/William Ruto was only partly due to massive assurance of their respective community electorates. It resulted also from their ability to win over outsider ethnic groups and populations, composed of the many undecided voters in populous counties who were campaign stakes, from conquering new positions in the north-east, from having almost equal footing with CORD in "cosmopolitan" regions (inter-ethnic cities) including the capital Nairobi and finally from winning comfortable minorities in the regions of their two main competitors in the West and on the coast. The double objective of ensuring utmost result in their community electorates and at least a minority in the rest of the country was "tricky" because trying too hard to maintain their community affiliation chips away their national image; but it was achieved. These gains, beyond their electoral base (a constant trend described by the polls from November 2012 with a domino effect in the last weeks that the opinion polls boosted), came from the undecided votes. These undecided voters (from 12% to 20% in December 2012) were mostly composed of supporters of the tickets of the third way. In December 2012, political circumstances worked in favour of Jubilee. Among such circumstances were the failure of Musalia Mudavadi's candidature and his missed alliance with Jubilee, the difficulty of independent candidates to present local candidates and the good choices made in local candidates.

Following the example of the Western campaigns, the last two months of the campaign were important and beneficial to the Jubilee coalition for the following reasons. They relied on an investment in a mediatised and modern campaign more in line with a young population and a generational society, used better political communication (audiovisual), resorted to political marketing and to a seductive "double-discourse" to many population segments such as pastoralists, Asian and Arab-Swahili populations, and to an Internet battle, at least a battle of reputation, won in January when on social networks quotes by Uhuru Kenyatta outnumbered those of his rival.[28] This was supported by logistics that appeared limitless.[29]

Equally key to the campaign was Jubilee's ability to turn around negative images they were labelled with as ICC suspects, as candidates of the establishment or of the past, even seen as "bad boys". Rather, their images, through "story telling" built thanks to spin-doctors or simply experienced political flair delivered in a piecemeal way and throughout the unofficial campaign that began in 2011, presented them as victims of the ICC. This was the result of skilled rhetoric that did not openly challenge international engagement but followed a redemptive religious approach asking for forgiveness in each field visit. This position was particularly dramatic as the two candidates represented the two contending ethnic groups in 2008. Moreover, this approach exaggerated public opinion that favours a return of the ICC to Kenya,[30] a solution that politicians had previously challenged. Furthermore, the ICC procedure (notably excluding some key officials) as well as the delay of local procedures for victims (IDPs) gave the impression of manipulation of this issue for political purposes only, even interference, while still pursuing the lawsuit of nationalist veterans of the 1950s against the British government.

Finally, isolated from power, both Jubilee candidates could appear not only as the young men they are but as "new men", estranged or otherwise falling out with their political fathers, former Presidents Mwai Kibaki for Uhuru Kenyatta and Daniel arap Moi for William Ruto who had rather inclined to a candidature of the third way.[31] At least they were presented and represented as "digital leaders", popular in light shirts and caps and comfortable with the new populist leaders of popular neighbourhoods. Given the generational anthropological culture in which the senior/junior conflict underlie most Kenyan ethnic groups, the fact that they sometimes appeared as distant with Kikuyu or Kalenjin notables, was a bonus. In addition to a better mobilisation of their community electorate after a powerful electoral registration in November 2012 of the populations in Central and Rift Valley provinces – a level of participation already observed during the 2010 constitutional referendum – the candidates benefitted from these two self-defence actions: firstly an action of national pride, and secondly an action of identification which took the form of a useful vote in the first round at the expense of "independent" candidates whose electoral scores were well below the satisfaction ratings achieved in the polls. From the first round, this shift of the electorate of independent Kikuyu candidates benefitted Uhuru Kenyatta whereas the maintenance of the third alliance led by Musalia Mudavadi weakened Raila Odinga's score in the Western region.

In contrast, Raila Odinga's campaign, by default expecting the errors of its rivals, and having a more "established" image through its successful candidates, was less incisive in terms of electoral marketing, political communication and program. It was not based on achievements, merited only by the outgoing President, and only tackled at the end of the campaign – but too late – critical socio-economic, land and even ideological issues. Perhaps in anticipation of a second round, it relied on the assurance of a multi-ethnic peripheral vote and on the process of de-legitimisation of Uhuru Kenyatta by the international community supported by the civil society. However, this moral conviction was counterproductive as his image depreciated following media campaigns and criticism of his family control over the political life of the western regions, while his returning support[32] only served to reinforce the image of a party of "big men" and notables.

The last two major moments were the two debates televised in February 2013, a first in the country. It closed a campaign in favour of Uhuru Kenyatta, more adept at this exercise of audio-visual communication at the expense of Raila Odinga, a candidate who appeared worn, while in the opinion polls, the candidates were neck and neck. This novel exercise, which had a significant impact, formalised a generational change and revealed the national dimension of the candidates, who during the debate on the most sensitive issues, used Swahili in preference to English. The campaign, just like the election results, points to the importance to add nuances to the exclusive ethnic analysis of Uhuru Kenyatta's victory. National identification and a young electorate also mattered while setbacks with the ICC have served and will continue to serve him in the future in this national situation. But the risk of such a withdrawal exists in so far as the political scene remains fragile.

The complexity of behaviour and political strategies? A new political order?

Far more than the imperfections of the electoral process, it is the fragility, or at least the originality of the new and open political scene, that raises questions. Thus, the ruling coalition appears to be a circumstantial agreement which began at the ICC when William Ruto and Uhuru Kenyatta were tried. This common destiny brings together two men who, despite being allies in 2002 during the presidential elections, opposed violently in 2007-2008 when William Ruto then an ally of Raila Odinga and Uhuru Kenyatta of Mwai Kibaki symbolised the historical Kalenjin/Kikuyu dispute.[33] This was initially a circumstance, or a line of defence in the face of adversity which has become a plan of a victorious political conquest and can be a political exit, rather than an electoral pact, for a social crisis that plagues the Rift Valley. The popular reception when they returned to Nairobi[34] certainly influenced their presidential strategy, which was originally their best defence against a global government of judges that William Ruto recalled on the day of the announcement of the results as "Vox populi, Vox Dei". The duo worked well during the campaign and in the "moments of grace" that marked a post-campaign victory. In addition, the composition of the winning ticket (the former ticket of the 2002 elections sponsored by President Daniel arap Moi), the reappearance of KANU, the former ruling party[35], and of leadership issues in a two-headed state or during the composition of ministerial teams as well as of counties[36] brings fears, among some columnists, of a reaction, if not a return to the practices of a hated regime of racketeering.

But even if the affiliation with the former regime remains symbolic and circumstances influenced the course of events, the context has changed, thus suggesting a new deal. This would be confirmed at different levels, from voters to politicians. Thus, an examination of votes in the various elections does not reveal a blocked vote. Political behaviours appear to be more "rational" at intermediate levels (governors, senators, MPs and county representatives). Many outgoing candidates were not re-elected and local standards or reputation contributing as much as party accreditation. This paradox of an emotional presidential vote and local rational choices is explained differently by the defence of local interests including management which now depends on decentralised authorities, the tiredness of some historical leaders, or "big men", and the emergence of new territorial or opinion leaders. Moreover, this renewal from the bottom, which was common in every election including under the ruling party, is less dramatic than in the past. On the one hand, the private sector can hire those leaving the political world – a private/public rotation thus seems to be established in the biography of the new elites – while on the other hand, the expansion of the political life benefits the political class. This modernity is reflected in local political strategies: the positions of governors and senators have been at stake while decentralisation will, if it goes as planned, split large ethnic regional entities, maintain internal rivalries with more social or territorial than identity motivations.

Beyond the generational renewal of the political class, the new institutional rules including devolution, a balanced and divided distribution policy (behind the two coalitions, 3 if not 4 national parties are present in the political national arena confirmed by the news of party financing first with the losing party ODM and the two "government" parties TNA and URP), and *de facto* an emergent two-party system, shapes the foundations of a new system on which the new government can build, while policy programmes, hardly different, are part of a pragmatic modernisation whose matrix is Vision 2030 and ideological references. Moreover, the democratic impulse is present; media pluralism is enhanced while democratisation is underway as evidenced by the release of the Report of the Truth, Justice and Reconciliation Commission in May 2013. However the challenges of land, IDPs, and poverty still remain.

Does the economic context account for this orientation? The real and expected growth margins, such as financial and monetary stability, offer the capacity for redistribution and regulation with regard to social issues and expectations raised during the campaign. These issues, which remained discreet during the campaign, are significant. Even if the situation has changed considerably, Kenya is still the land of millionaires and millions of poor people.[37] While the new classes have urgent aspirations, the long teachers' strike in the aftermath of the elections reminded them of this. This transfer of power and the social transformation appear as a historic opportunity for the new government that resembles neither Marcos nor Lula! But President Uhuru Kenyatta has the historic opportunity to transform Kenya, and to preside over the transfer of power to citizens.[38]

The New Geopolitical Deal

With the ICC pitfall, the international community (UN, AU) and Kenya were trapped in the management of the 2007-2008 crisis by the process of political compromise imposed in 2008 which reclassified all current political actors although disqualified by the 2007-2008 crisis (the ICC defendants and others). In the name of peace, the international justice calendar has been delayed and is now in front of the accused who, at the time of their hearing, were the losers on the path of political marginalisation but who today can lay claim to democratic legitimacy. This situation is awkward for the three parties: the international justice, the countries (including Kenya), which by having signed the Rome Statute support this process, and Kenya whose exemplary policy is tarnished. In the name of realism and mutual interests, strategic and economic geopolitics imposes its rules in a sensitive environment. Indeed, Kenya experiences a post-colonial crisis of low intensity, the first in its history, while independent attitudes of its East African Community (EAC) partners, the Kenyatta-Museveni-Kagame axis, the geopolitical and strategic situation with a competitive advantage for Asian powers arepushing the new authorities to a hardening on an issue tied with memorybecause of the particular circumstances of the fiftieth anniversary of Independence: the son of the Father of the Nation is accused!

Notes

1 Reports on elections are numerous. They comprise the official documents of the IEBC, petitions and decisions of the Supreme Court, reports and press documents of international organisations and NGOs, as well as, among others, those of the EEC (European Economic Community), the AU (African Union), the Carter Center, the NCCK (National Council of Churches of Kenya), AGLI (African Great Lakes Initiative), ICG (International Crisis Group), ELOG (Elections Observation Group, a civil society consortium for election observation), and finally monitoring sites including Usalama Forum, platforms such as Uchaguzi, and blogs on the Internet.

2 Reports by Uchaguzi, an ICT platform that monitors electoral incidents, are very efficient in central and urban places but less efficient in peripheral areas.

3 These practices would usefully be put into perspective with the analyses of historians and historical sociology of politics on the entry of rural societies into politics in the 19th century in Europe.

4 Participation in presidential elections is on the increase: in 1992: 69%; 1997: 65%; 2002: 57%; 2007: 69%; 2010 (referendum) 72%, but relative to the population of voting age, it is only 63%, and the percentage of invalid votes remains constant: in 1997 0.7%; 2002 1.9%; 2007 0.9% and 2013 0.88%.

5 The registration took less time than previously. Urgency marked the different times of this pre-election period.

6 Like "electoral behaviour building" of political practices and electoral culture in the long term.

7 *Sunday Nation*, February 3, 2013, "Sunday Review", p. 30.

8 With the "election coverage guidelines" of the MCK (Media Council of Kenya), the IEBC's "guidelines for media monitoring" and a high level of vigilance against hate speech in regional media and social media with an alert system (via SMS).

9 Compared to Jomo Kenyatta or Mwai Kibaki's electoral victories.

10 A dynamic or associative opinion as opposed to a static, inherited opinion characteristic of ethnic burdens.

11 In the Braudelian sense of the "longue durée" (long duration), "moyenne durée" (medium duration) and "courte durée" (short duration).

12 Opinion polls (Ipsos Synovate) show that Uhuru Kenyatta's electorate was more optimistic about their economic future than Raila Odinga's.

13 Unlike the central regions where registration is traditionally high, peripheral regions have the lowest rates for several reasons: short-term (duration, schedule, instability of the registration period), technical (the far distances and the number of registration centers), structural (mobility, drought) and cultural (low participation of women).

14 According to demographic-health survey data, DHS 2008: 43% of the population lives in conditions of extreme poverty and a majority is found in these areas.

15 There are many elders among families and relations such as councils of elders, of the wise often asked to handle some affairs.

16 The logo of the TNA party, the dove, also evokes the Holy Spirit.

17 Tribes, to use the English term, are ethnic groups that are distinguished by language, singular and sometimes common cultural traits, a territory, a memory and a collective identity without having a clear-cut institutional historywhich are characteristic of chiefdom or royalty. These identities have been manipulated by politicians, sometimes in ways that can be likened to nationalism, while an uneven regional development differentiated them socio-economically. National construction and modernization have superimposed "high culture", new identities and common languages (English and Swahili), but has not done away with the cultural attachment to this diversity, described as "moral ethnicity", between a "small country" attached to a territory and a "small nation" attached to a population or a diaspora.

18 The Jubilee coalition consisted of four parties: TNA, URP, RC, Narc, and small local parties; the CORD coalition consisted of the ODM, Wiper DP, Ford Kenya parties and allies; the third coalition, Amani, consisted of the UDF, New FORD-Kenya and KANU.

19 In 2009, the Kikuyu were 17%, the Luo 10%, the Luhya 14%, the Kalenjin 13%, the Kamba 11%, the Kisii 6%, the Mijikenda 5%, the Meru 4%, the Somali 2%, the Turkana 2%, the Maasai 1% and other ethnic groups 14% (national census).

20 The *matatu* is a public service vehicle, often overloaded, which along its journey carries many passengers to multiple destinations. Competition leads to dangerous driving. These images have been reflected by cartoonists.

21 207 complaints on the primaries were recorded by the IEBC.

22 IEBC data in Yash Pal Ghai's "Ethnicity, nationhood and pluralism", Katiba Institute, Nairobi, September 2013.

23 Statement based on a parallel calculation of votes. ELOG is a platform comprising Kenyan NGOs which deployed 7,000 observers and 1,000 observers involved in parallel computing.

24 These cases were identified by the Supreme Court in 22 counties.

25 According to exit polls (see AFRICOG and J.D. Long's data in "Choosing peace over democracy", *Journal of democracy*, XXIV, 3 July 2013, pp. 140-155) which only covered 2,983 and 6,258 people with high rates of non-responses; this cannot replace estimations by lack of a representative sample of reference stations.

26 See elections data online on the Mars Group website.

27 The record of election petitions is kept and maintained by the association of Kenyan lawyers.

28 These measures are available on the "election" site of the *Daily Nation* with significant variations depending on Facebook and Twitter.

29 The new legislation on campaign accounts was postponed and unexamined till the very end of the last Parliament.

30 From November 2012 to February 2013, according to opinion polls, the (positive) reputation of the ICC went from 66% to 56%, while the majority of Kenyans, including figures in the CORD alliance, was for the return of the ICC to the Kenyan courts.

31 The Amani coalition consists of the UDF of Musalia Mudavadi, New Ford Kenya and KANU, the former ruling party of President Moi.

32 The inability to weaken the Kikuyu bloc despite support from some Kikuyu businessmen and the absence of George Saitoti, who died in a helicopter crash, who represented a part of the Kikuyu and Maasai electorate, influenced this political game. In addition, a biography on Raila Odinga, which came out in two stages, in the summer of 2012 then in January 2013, by one of his former assistants, Miguna Miguna, weakened his respectable image. The "big men" represent notables who controlled regions in the Jomo Kenyatta and Moi era, a time now past; some of these iconic figures supported Raila Odinga.

33 The land conflict in the Rift Valley dates back from the colonial period with the displacement of people due to the allocation of land to settlers. Since then, the redistribution of land has fanned disputes, also fuelled by structural demographic and economic trends as the anthropological Kikuyu model pushes juniors to emigrate and clear out beyond their community space while the latifundary system limits small family property and creates a rural proletariat.

34 The welcome, as well as their departure, the day after their hearing was the object of popular protests and the starting point of the KKK alliance project, Kikuyu/Kalenjin/Kamba of Uhuru Kenyatta, William Ruto and Kalonzo Musyoka who later became a CORD running mate.

35 About the risk or the fear of a new alliance between GEMA and Kamatusa, a Kalenjin alliance, see B. Ogot (2012).

36 In each election, the managerial staff in ministries, agencies, diplomatic representations change to which are added new members of county teams.

37 In the words of a Kikuyu political leader, J.M. Kariuki, assassinated in 1975, "Kenya is a country of 10 millionaires and 10 million beggars". This remains, in part, true.

38 See the analysis of A. Awiti, "What does it take to transform Kenya?" *The Star*, April 4, 2013.

Bibliography

Bourmaud, D. *Histoire politique du Kenya*: *État et pouvoir local*. Paris: Karthala, 1988.

Branch, D. *Between Hope and Despair, Kenya 2003-2011*. New Haven, CT: Yale University Press, 2011.

Grignon, F. and G. Prunier (dir). *Le Kenya contemporain*. Paris: Karthala, 1998.

Hornsby, C. *Kenya, A History Since Independence*. London, New York: IB Tauris, 2011.

Kanyinga, K. and D. Okello. *Tensions and Reversals in Democratic Transitions: The Kenya 2007 General Election*. SID, 2010.

Lafargue, J. "Les élections générales de 2007 au Kenya", *Cahiers d'Afrique de l'Est* no. 37(2008).

Maupeu, H., M. Katumanga and W. Mitullah. *The Moi Succession: The 2002 elections in Kenya*. Nairobi: IFRA-Transafrica Press, 2005.

Ogot, B. *Kenyans, Who Are We?* Kisumu: Anyange Press 2012.

Rutten, M., A. Mazrui and F. Grignon (eds.), *Out for the Count: The 1997 general elections and prospects for democracy in Kenya*. Kampala: Fountain Publishers, 2001.

Throup, D. and C. Hornsby. *Multi-Party Politics in Kenya*: *The Kenyatta & Moi states & the triumph of the system in the 1992 election*. Oxford: James Currey, 1998.

Kenyan Elections: The ICC, God and the 2013 Kenyan General Elections

Hervé Maupeu [*]

The 2013 Kenya elections were post-crisis elections. They were held in an institutional framework closely linked to compromises reached to end the 2008 post-election violence that caused more than a thousand deaths and displaced several hundreds of thousands.[1]

In 2008, international actors negotiated with stakeholders a set of peace solutions very characteristic of the 2000s. The 'peacebuilding' industry has a long history but it has essentially been constituted in the context of the 1990s, marked by the changing practices of war (the multiplication of civil wars and the reduction of inter-state conflict) and a great wave of democratisation. As an end to the crisis, proponents of 'peacebuilding' proposed the promotion of democratic practices (political and economic liberalisation). However, it soon became apparent that the rash organisation of elections was accompanied by conditions of freedom. Since then, in the 2000s, new 'peacebuilding' strategies of "institutionalization before liberalization" have been imposed (Paris, 2004). They were designed to strengthen institutions before the holding elections. In the case of Kenya, a new constitution adopted in 2010 sought to balance the relationship between the various authorities and to ensure the independence of certain structures (particularly of the Electoral Commission) so as to guarantee free elections. In

* Lecturer in Political Science, Université de Pau et des Pays de l'Adour (UPPA); Director, Centre for Studies and Research on East African Countries (CREPAO), France. This article was originally published in French under the title "La CPI, Dieu et les élections kényanes de 2013 : De la pentecôtisation de la politique à une démocratie autoritaire" DOI: 10.3917/afco.247.0033 (*Afrique contemporaine*, n° 247, Élections Kenya, © De Boeck Supérieurs.a., 2013 1re édition, Fond Jean-Pâques 4, B-1348 Louvain-la-Neuve).

this reform package, a component was aimed at ending the culture of impunity of elites. Thus, the International Criminal Court (ICC) came in to indict several political leaders.

The ICC intervention led two leaders of opposing communities in 2008 to join forces in the 2013 elections. Uhuru Kenyatta and William Ruto formed a ticket and were respectively elected as President and Deputy President of Kenya. Certainly the ICC emerged as the statue of an omnipresent commander throughout the electoral process. How did these indictments, by an international court, become a major factor in this electoral campaign? Has the UhuRuto[2] election revealed some negative effects of 'peacebuilding?' Is the ICC only a statue of a paper commander?

Studying the ICC and the 2013 elections allows for the chronicling of the legalisation of the Kenyan political life at a crucial time when members of the top brass are for the first time threatened by credible prosecution. They are deploying strategies to escape this guillotine, which will have lasting effects on the credibility of the judiciary and more generally on the quality of democratisation currently underway.

To adapt the institutional framework, politicians engaged in intensified justification and legitimation, which led to change in the political culture. Thus, the leaders who won the electoral joust are those who had God on their side by creating what we will call the dynamic of "pentecostalisation of political life".

Impunity of elites and ethnicisation

'Peacebuilding' programmes designed to end a conflict consist of a series of more or less important measures. From the point of view of the Kenyan elite, the most critical component of the programme to end the 2008 crisis was the establishment of a national unity government enabling power sharing. Many political scientists have pointed out the dangers of these arrangements that give leeway to politicians involved in the tensions and whose ambitions are not genuinely democratic (Sriram and Zahar, 2009). In fact, these procedures tend to weaken if not to condemn the dynamics of transitional justice. At the least, these two formulas obey a contradictory logic: when the leaders of the various factions involved in the conflict participate in the same government, they agree to temporarily waive the prosecution of their colleagues. We then find ourselves in a situation where the political cost of the criminal charge of these leaders would be too high. In this type of government, the various factions protect each other. The attitude of the Kenyan political elite towards the ICC action illustrates this institutional logic. "The big fish will not fry themselves" as explained by Brown & Sriram (2012). These two political scientists trace the steps and the tactics of these leaders to escape criminal liability for their involvement in the 2008 post-election violence. They explain that Kenyan MPs repeatedly rejected the creation of a hybrid court to try their leaders. These parliamentary debates revealed very different views on the subject but all converging to the organisation of the impunity of their elite, all factions fearing being implicated in this process.

Because Kenyan politicians did not want a hybrid tribunal, the ICC took over. From then on, the Kibaki government engaged in intense diplomatic activity to ensure that the court at The Hague is divested. It tried to get a resolution of the African Union asking that the trial of Kenyans be entrusted to the African Court.[3] With the failure of this strategy, the Attorney General asked the

ICC to transfer these trials to the East African Court of Justice, even though this court has no jurisdiction to deal with these crimes.[4] At the same time, the Kenyan elite tried to empty the ICC proceedings of their substance by putting pressure on the witnesses (pressure on their families or assassinating key figures). The state itself forwarded the documents requested by the Court with delay if not reluctantly. Collaboration between these institutions was difficult. Following the failure of diplomatic tactics, the issue moved to the national level. And to protect themselves from prosecution, Kenyan leaders called on God for help.

At the end of 2010, when the ICC announced that Uhuru Kenyatta and William Ruto were among the leaders the Waki Report[5] advised to be judged, their political career seemed compromised. To regain control, these politicians appealed to public opinion. They played the power of the people against that of the judges. They relied on popular legitimacy to counter the legitimacy of the rule of law. In this way, they made the election of 4 March a referendum on the ICC. This winning electoral strategy was expressed in an effective populism that used and amplified the pentecostalisation of politics. This political camp managed to sell two unlikely ideas. It convinced many Kenyans (if not most) of the criminal irresponsibility of their leaders in the 2008 post-election violence and the need for an electoral agreement between the two main ethnic communities, the Kalenjin and the Kikuyu, which were violently opposed in the previous elections.

By cleverly using the ICC charge, Uhuru Kenyatta and William Ruto became heroes of their respective ethnic groups (but not that of their running mate) which helped unify their communities during the election time. The populism of UhuRuto was aimed at diverting attention from the actual causes of their charges and the root causes of the 2008 violence in order to focus on arguments that unified disparate electorates and to forget the old antagonisms that opposed them.

There is no Kalenjin electorate or a set of homogeneous Kikuyu voters 'naturally' available. These two identities are very divided. The Kalenjin thrive on an "overlapping identity" (Médard, 2008). The Kalenjin, like the Luhya, developed their identity mainly after World War II by uniting neighboring ethnicities which still remain strong today. Within the latter, divides and divisions operate according to clans and sometimes generational systems. Claire Médard shows that, depending on circumstances and needs, the Kalenjin wear or claim one or the other of their identities. Therefore, tensions between the different groups that make up the Kalenjin can be strong. It is equally difficult to unify the Kikuyu who are divided along region, gender (male/female tensions are stronger than among the Kalenjin), generations and especially social classes.

However, the Kalenjin like the Kikuyu have developed strong ethnic nationalisms that are constantly revised, which facilitates their mobilisation during elections, more so since each of these two communities, at each general election, possesses leaders who can reach the highest state level or can put pressure on the new head of state (if the Kalenjin have not proposed candidates in 2002, 2007 and 2013, they appear every time as kingmakers).

To gather together these electorates, those charged before the ICC employed the conspiracy theory which, we know, is one of the great classics of populism. Two social actors were presented for public prosecution: on the one hand, Raila Odinga and more generally the Luo, his original ethnic group and on the other hand, Westerners.

During the 2007 elections, the vast majority of Kalenjin voted for Raila and his popularity was undeniable. The divorce has been gradual. It first concerned the Kalenjin elite. In the 'Grand Coalition' government, Ruto got the Ministry he wanted, of agriculture. But in 2010, he campaigned against the constitutional text proposed for referendum while Raila called for a vote in favour of it. Since 2009 and especially in 2011, Kalenjin MPs opposed Raila on the management of the Mau Forest. This vast range is one of the main water towers of Kenya and deforestation continues, led by more or less legitimate occupants of the land, which threatens water supply for entire regions. Raila was accused of managing this case in favour of respect for the law and the environment at the expense of people, particularly the Kalenjin who live there. In fact, the Mau Forest has, for more than two decades, been one of the areas of recurring tensions in the Rift Valley. There we find major dynamics inherited from President Moi's era: ethnic cleansing, illegal distribution of public land under high-level state patronage (which leaves many Kalenjin frustrated), not to mention the tensions among Kalenjin sub-groups. In this context, Kalenjin MPs chose to unite against a foreign leader, in as much as Ruto, involved in a corruption case in areas related to his ministry, was forced to resign at the request of Raila… so they said. Gradually, most of the Kalenjin MPs rallied behind Ruto who appeared more than ever as the leader of the Rift Valley.

After the indictment of Ruto by the ICC, the Kalenjin elite took on the people and accused Raila of being behind this dirty trick. The speakers tugged at the heartstrings, of the feeling of persecution of the Kalenjin, crystallised since President Moi stepped down in 2002. According to Gabrielle Lynch (2011), the revival of Kalenjin nationalism was built on the deep sense of injustice that these people felt. In this context, the discourses are virulent and attacks against the Luo are hateful. In late July 2012, the ICC warned Uhuru Kenyatta and William Ruto that the court would verify that they do not engage in hate speech or that they do not incite violence.[6]

Westerners were also denounced as agents of the charge against the two leaders. They supported Raila's candidacy for the presidency and manipulated international justice so that their protégé was elected. The ICC was described as a neo-colonial justice that to date had only prosecuted African leaders and sought to ensure the domination of the North over the South. Thus, the ICC was an infringement on the country's sovereignty. It would be a serious threat to national security and would imply the resistance of all against this attack. This rhetoric also appeals to the past and a reinterpretation of the history of the Kalenjin and the Kikuyu. Thus, Ruto's fight echoes that of Koitalel Samoei, the Nandi leader who resisted against the British in the early twentieth century and Uhuru's struggle reminiscent of his father's, Jomo Kenyatta who was jailed after an infamous rigged trial (1952-1953). More than ever, the story of the history (histories) of Kenya is a critical political issue.

The figure of Koitalel Samoei remains very popular today because vernacular radio stations, particularly Kass FM, have produced many emissions on his history. The contemporary Kalenjin nationalism uses his heroism and resistance to colonialism as one of its main references. The state itself has, in recent years, emphasised his role by building a national mausoleum on the site of his imprisonment (Simatei, 2010: 427). Ruto particularly claims this legacy more so as his own father was called Daniel Cheruiyot Samoei and that Ruto himself is commonly called William Samoei Ruto.

Uhuru Kenyatta has no issue when he tugs on heartstrings with the Kapenguria trial that condemned his father on the basis of rigged testimonies. In fact, this trial saved Jomo Kenyatta's career which was greatly threatened by an elite even more radical than him. After his imprisonment in the north of the country in which time Uhuru was conceived, Jomo Kenyatta became the undisputed leader of the country and the father of the nation. Today, the British perfidy is more in the mind especially as the media reminds regularly the difficulties of former Mau Mau to get compensation, through legal means, for their suffering. But the reference to Jomo is actually quite discreet as the discourse mostly likens the fate of UhuRuto that of Dedan Kimathi, the Mau Mau leader who died tragically in the hands of the British. In fact, this figure speaks more to young people, primarily to appeal to them. Who would have thought that the heir, born with a silver spoon in his mouth would one day be considered the modern-day Kimathi? Kimathi, until then, was the symbol of the excluded, the underclass and especially the peasants demanding for land.[7]

Thus, victimisation accounts and the reference to a mythical past help build Uhuru and Ruto as heroes, figures rising from the legend and destined to guide their people. Through these heroes, people can dream of a collective prosperous and prestigious destiny in times of crisis and doubt. UhuRuto offer stories, different in each community, which connect a mythical past to an equally unlikely future, but of better days. They offer them a future of modernity: to become the "digital generation" as opposed to other communities which remain in the "analog generation", according to the analogy constantly hammered by William Ruto. This propaganda works especially during elections, ordinarily perceived as a time for change.

The victimisation trial and UhuRuto's glorification strategy derive their efficacy from the religious register that these politicians employ to articulate and mobilise.

The ICC and the pentecostalisation of the political life

In early 2011, these two politicians traversed the country and engaged in "prayer meetings". They were accompanied by prelates who led prayers and many parliamentarians who launched the most violent attacks and thus prepared the prospect of an Uhuru-Ruto ticket. Gradually, most parliamentarians of the ethnic groups of the two leaders began to attend these "prayer meeting-cum-rally" sessions. One could not be seen as pro-ICC if one wished to be re-elected. In addition, they were paid for their travel expenses.[8] Leaders of other ethnic groups participated actively when they opposed Raila. In 2011, these elected members came mainly from the KKK ethnic gathering (Kikuyu-Kalenjin-Kamba) and in 2012, with the G7 Alliance, the front opened notably to include Luhya through Eugene Wamalwa (Saboti MP) and Kisii through Omingo Magara (South Mugirango MP).

In 2012, the ceremonies launching the election campaign for Kenyatta and Ruto were also within a religious framework. The meeting of the Deputy Prime Minister, Uhuru Kenyatta in which he announced his candidacy took place in Limuru, at the NCCK premises (The National Council of Churches of Kenya, the main federation of Protestant churches). Two Bishops Emeritus,[9] Peter Njenga, an Anglican and Lawi Imathiu, a Methodist called for the unity of Gema people (Gikuyu, Embu, Meru) against the "false accusations of internal and external enemies". The meeting of William Ruto was at the Catholic Pastoral Centre and Bishop Korir welcomed the guests himself.[10] Many pastors spoke including Rev. Murupus who stated that the Kalenjin never premeditated the 2008 violence and that the responsibility of the conflict rested entirely on Raila Odinga who rejected the election results.[11]

This intertwining of politics and religion is seen by a columnist, Keguro Macharia, as "a re-consolidation of Christianity as a state religion".[12] In fact, the prayer meetings are part of a larger dynamic of the pentecostalisation of political and social life.

Throughout the twentieth century, and today more than ever, Christianity remains the cornerstone of the Kenyan national identity. In a context of strong ethnic polarisation, this Christian identity may occasionally exceed the other divisions. However, this takes place within narrow limits because the churches have consistently participated in the crystallisation of ethnic groups and for a decade, they have been tribalised in that their clergy frequently slip into communitarian positions (Droz and Maupeu, 2013). During the election campaign, UhuRuto employed a particular approach to Christianity. They endeavoured to pentecostalise the national Christian ideology. Kenya, like other African countries, experienced the Pentecostal wave, and today, nearly a third of Kenyans are Pentecostals (Barrett et al., 2001). But since the 30s, the Protestant movement has been influenced by the Pentecostal theology and rituals because of the extraordinary success of the East African Revival Fellowship (Peterson, 2012). UhuRuto especially employed this ideology and Pentecostal structures even though they are not from these churches.[13] In doing so politicians partner with real big men endowed with systems of patronage and consistent communication. In contrast, the historical churches have leaders but no big men. Power is often decentralised with a wide autonomy of parishes on a diocesan and national level; the churches' social services are bureaucratic and do not participate in patronage.

UhuRuto take most from Pentecostalism theology, which focuses on the action of the Holy Spirit, the privilege of being "saved", God's forgiveness when one repents and true justice is God's which esteems that all good comes from God.[14] Pentecostal rituals also involve prayer meetings in the form of confessions and of long testimonies. Emotion is always heightened and ideological messages become more persuasive. This simplistic approach to Christianity enables one to denounce before God those guilty of the misfortunes of Kenyans (Raila Odinga and Westerners) and to pray for peace in the country.

In fact, the communication policy of those accused at the ICC turned presidential candidates was in the skill of time management. During the fall of 2012, when the campaign officially began with different primary elections (governors, senators, Members of Parliament), Jubilee abandoned attacks, which helped to unify the Kikuyu and the Kalenjin. They then became the pilgrims of peace promising to end the tensions in the communities that had experienced post-election violence in 2008. This was to appeal beyond the Central Province and the Rift Valley. Meanwhile, Raila promised that if he were elected, he would repatriate the trial of those accused by the ICC. But his efforts made him appear a hypocrite if not a liar. As for the Westerners, they were clearly biased against the candidature of the accused and their actions seemed a confirmation of the plot denounced by Jubilee and were attacks on Kenyan sovereignty. Their warnings revived patriotism and validated the victim position of their leaders.

The prayer meetings also unified the Kalenjin who are very divided by the multiple ethnicities that make up this group. The Kikuyu also overcame the social divides that break them up and the underclass, particularly Mungiki, who find themselves politically voiceless. By being victims, the leaders temporarily buried the hatchet in their communities, but none of them has renounced the ideology of autochthony justifying violence in the Rift Valley in previous election cycles, and in particular in 2008 (Boas and Dunn, 2013).

With prayer meetings, UhuRuto invented a new political language that combined prophetism and redemption. The Kalenjin like the Kikuyu have cultures of prophetism (Anderson and Johnson, 1995). In times of uncertainty and insecurity, spiritual and other prophet figures, emerge to explain the new issues, rules and principles to observe in order to cope. These prophetisms can easily be expressed through the Pentecostal register (Droz, 1999). In this case, the political leaders tapped into the Pentecostal and evangelical stock references, the idea of "Born-Again" political redemption. This form of speech was attractive because by asking God to save the unjustly accused leaders, citizens are also saved, which answers to their material, social and moral insecurity. But as Ruth Marshall (2009: 10) points out, these "political spiritualities" correspond to a system of Pentecostal practices that focus on the work that the individual must do on himself. The Born-Again conversion implies an exemplary personal conduct, if not ascetic, which corresponds to a country or to individual morality (rather than public morality) and an increasingly demanding social control (especially on women). UhuRuto were able to explain that the country's success depends on the morality of individuals and therefore their ability to succeed economically. The state has no other function other than to provide a framework in which the will of God, and individuals acting in God's eyes, can be expressed. The Jubilee[15] electoral campaign appeared as prophetism or the redemption of leaders and their people that should lead to prosperity if not a golden age, which prosperity evangelists have repeatedly promised since the beginning of the great evangelical wave.

Politicians controlled these political spiritualities so well that churches did not have a clear message. The Catholic Church disseminated a statement in November 2012 calling for a vote against candidates lacking integrity. Some interpreted this message as aimed at Uhuru's candidature but at the local level, the Catholic clergy in Central Province clearly campaigned for Jubilee. The campaign elicited very different positions according to the religious leaders.[16] The clergy seemed more concerned about lobbying for the new Education Bill as opposed to the General Elections.[17] Indeed, it was devastated in the 2007 election campaign where religious actors had fueled the hatred that contributed to the post-election violence. During the 2010 constitutional referendum, the churches spearheaded opposition to this text that Kenyans adopted by a large majority.

Ironically, the 'historical'[18] churches were left outside an election campaign based on the Christian register. The message of the old mission churches was inaudible because the formulation of arguments was on a Pentecostal mode, which is not that of the 'historical'[19] churches. Even CORD used this mode of communication. Raila Odinga relied heavily upon Prophet David Owuor and his organisation. Thus, one of the highlights of the campaign was the large "national repentance" meeting at Uhuru Park, at the end of February 2013 led by this religious leader on behalf of CORD. On this occasion, all political leaders spoke of repentance in the country after the 2008 post-election violence. They announced that the elections would take place without recourse to force regardless of the outcome.[20]

So everyone repented and hoped that the March elections would enable the turning of the page. Does this mean that Kenyans renounce all forms of transitional justice?

An impossible transitional justice?

The election of the Kenyatta-Ruto ticket to the presidency weakens further the ongoing procedures of transitional justice.[21] Henceforth, the Kenyan state is fiercely opposed to the ICC, which is about to judge their leaders. As for reconciliation procedures, they do not seem to interest many anymore. In fact, the time for justice and commissions is not the same as for electoral democracy, causing malfunctions that politicians exploit skillfully.

As part of the 2008 peace negotiations, a Truth, Justice and Reconciliation Commission was established. It is in line with many commissions tasked with the study of episodes of political violence (such as the Akiwumi Commission and the Mutua Commission for example), which go unheeded. The TJRC was immediately marked by deep divisions among the commissioners, especially among those who wanted the resignation of their chairman Bethuel Kiplagat[22] and others. Its mandate was diluted because it investigated violations of human rights committed by the authorities from 1963 to 28 February 2008. Established in 2009, it was to deliver its report within two years, but following several reports, the work did not end until after the 2013 elections, making its interest rather limited: after elections, one must first address the frustrations caused by the campaign, by the organisation of the process and by the official results which did not satisfy all Kenyans. Consequently, all columnists raged against the commission. Even before knowing its findings, they all felt that it had not fulfilled its role. "In the spirit of moving on, the TJRC should just edit its report to two pages and send it to the Museum to give Kenyans a chance to embrace peace under the Jubilee government", said Kwamchetsi Makokha.[23] Even NGO human rights representatives, like L. Muthoni Wanyeki, thought "Dialogue? Reconciliation? Forget that stuff, move on".[24] The TJRC report was published in May. It accuses many leaders and in particular asks for charges to be pressed against more than thirty elected leaders. The media has relayed this information correctly but so far, the judiciary has not taken over and the politicians seem to have moved on. Other commissions have to continue this work of unmasking political violence and abuses. A commission on land was established at the end of 2013, but it is likely to suffer the same fate as previous reports on this subject (Ndung'u Report, Njonjo Land Report).

In fact, these commissions are now rejected by majority of the Kikuyu and Kalenjin political elite because they are intent on imposing their own understanding of the history of the country and in particular, the crisis of 2008. This revisionism is important when it comes to politically bringing closer people who have been opposed for decades. This exercise is dangerous because it is the same leaders who spoke yesterday of irreconcilable differences and yet today are competing for close collaboration. They must explain why the contentions of yesterday are no longer relevant in areas where blood has been shed several times. Thus, William Ruto argues that the Kiambaa massacre (January 2008) in which thirty people died in a fire at a church besieged by Kalenjin gangs is the result of an accident: "the cause of the incident was an accidental kitchen fire during preparations for lunch".[25] Therefore, the most famous 2008 post-election violence killing is not the work of young Kalenjin. As such, the ODM leaders boycotted the official funeral of the victims of Kiambaa in 2011 as well as the inauguration of the commemorative plaques. They refused a memorialisation that denounced Kalenjin abuses forgetting the massacres perpetrated by the other side, the Kikuyu. In the same vein, many Kalenjin leaders have refused to testify before the TJRC but they are justified in the media (often ethnic). Thus, Jackson Kibor, a businessman who, according to the Waki Report (2008) funded some armed groups, prefers to explain himself to journalists from Reuters and on the Kalenjin.net site rather than respond to the summons of the TJRC.[26]

The TJRC seems to have lost its social efficiency since it presented its work after the elections. Similarly, the ICC trial would have had a very different effect if it had occurred before the elections. Henceforth, the Kenyan government is working to remove the President and the Deputy President from the ICC trap. In April 2013, Kenya asked the UN Security Council for the repatriation of these trials to a Kenyan criminal court. The defendants' lawyers asked for the opportunity to attend the court sessions from Kenya through internet communications. William Ruto even wished to be tried in absentia. At the beginning of May 2013, Kenya informed the Security Council that it wished to end the trial of Uhuru Kenyatta, William Ruto and Joshua Sang because it threatens the stability of the entire region whereas voters had already decided on the situation.[27]

During the election campaign, UhuRuto gave good political communications addressing different messages depending on their audience: to Western governments, they promised that they would respect the ICC proceedings and to the people, they explained that the citizen is the true judge of the 2008 events, in the name of the principles of democracy and sovereignty that international actors cannot deny. Therefore, when the people elected UhuRuto, representatives of the international community found themselves destitute: "they took us by the balls" said a diplomat. In fact, peacekeeping sociologists had explained these dynamics well. If these procedures of structuring peace are considered as a process of ongoing negotiations between local elites and international actors, the latter are constantly losing their influence as time gradually passes after the crisis. The 'footprint' of the peace solution adapted to resolve the conflict gradually disappears and the conflicting interests of the 'engineers of peace' and local elites are increasingly apparent (Zürcher et al., 2013). In the case of Kenya, politicians are trying to uphold the democratic logic at the expense of the legal logic and their power play can succeed in a country where the rule of law is somewhat fragile.

Thus, political elites are trying hard to assert their interests at the expense of principles that an unsure international community tries to assert. This can cause tensions in the field of international relations.

Towards a postcolonial diplomacy?

The ICC proceedings are never 'simply' national affairs. They bring into play the international community and its responsibility, particularly in protecting persecuted people. In the case of Kenya, its intervention was in the engagement of representatives of the international community in the negotiations to end the 2008 crisis. Consequently, the UhuRuto trial becomes a highly international affair since these politicians were elected to head their state. And Kenyans are aware that solutions must be found on an international level.

To counter their indictment by an international court, UhuRuto or at least their supporters in the Kenyan state have used weapons of diplomacy since 2011 and they continue to do so after the 2013 elections, which can have far-reaching effects. First, the election of two politicians indicted by the ICC to head the state will lead to a shift in Kenya's relations with other actors in international relations. Some analysts predict the development of a post-colonial diplomacy consolidating ties between East African countries with a common distancing from Westerners to focus on relations with the emerging powers, mainly Asian, which better respect the sovereignty of African actors. On their part, Westerners find themselves entangled in the contradictions of the peacebuilding programme they sponsored during the 2008[28] crisis and after the 2013 elections they seem to have adopted a wait-and-see policy.

The international actors involved in the resolution of the 2008 crisis clearly expressed their opposition to the candidature of Uhuru Kenyatta and William Ruto in the presidential race. In October 2012, Kofi Annan, while passing through Nairobi to follow up on the crisis solution programme under the guidance of the Panel of Eminent African Personalities, said that the election of the two accused by the ICC would affect Kenya's relations with other countries.[29] In early February 2013, the U.S. Assistant Secretary of State Johnnie Carson reminds of the American position that the election to a country's presidency of one accused by the ICC could be received negatively by the United States.[30] Britain and France announced that in such an eventuality, their embassies would have "minimum contacts" with this leader.[31] Newspapers interviewed many academics who have written about the risks of diplomatic isolation, on Western aid, which could dry up, and the foreign trade that could suffer as a result of this.[32]

In this context, the Uhuru Kenyatta programme announced significant shifts in the Kenyan foreign policy that would rely less on relations with the West and would look further to the east ('shift East'), to emerging powers, the BRICS and especially India and China. It was not a break in the country's foreign policy since the regime of Mwai Kibaki had already implemented these principles. Since the adoption of Kenya Vision 2030, economic development relies on major projects and infrastructure construction, mostly in PPP (Public Private Partnerships), which usually lead to work with Asian companies. So far, this Asian tropism was justified by economic contingencies now, it also applies for ideological reasons, or at the least in the name of a conception of sovereignty.

After the election of Uhuru Kenyatta, Western countries praised the peaceful nature of the elections and they, for the most part, waited on the decision of the Supreme Court to hail the elected representatives. At first, Botswana announced that it would not receive Uhuru then relented.[33] Other African countries have hardly commented that the new elected officials are indicted by the ICC, with one notable exception, that of Museveni. During the inauguration ceremony of Uhuru Kenyatta, Yoweri Museveni, representing the countries of the East African Community, congratulated Kenyans on rejecting the "blackmail" of the ICC. In addition, he accused the Court of arrogance and ignorance. It does not solve the problems of the 2007-2008 post-election violence: "an external and legalistic process cannot address those events. Events of this nature first and foremost need an ideological solution by discerning why they happened".[34]

This position is a serious support to the new leadership team of Kenya. It surprised some analysts because Museveni has closer links to Raila Odinga.[35] Henceforth, he presents himself as a privileged partner, to help the newly elected leaders to lift the ICC obstacle. He in this way appears as the Godfather if not the leader of East Africa, which enables him to make up for the challenge he faces in Uganda, in his own camp. Kenyans, on their part, rely on the support of neighboring countries to avoid the diplomatic isolation that Western governments promised them. In fact, East African governments are relatively distrustful of the ICC system. We know that Rwandans exploited international justice and were sometimes opposed to the ICTR in Arusha (Guichaoua, 2011). Burundians have cleverly manipulated international peacebuilding plans and the policies of transitional justice (Curtis, 2012). Tanzanians voted for a repatriation of the ICC trial to East Africa (particularly to Arusha). And Ugandans see the ICC as a tool to fight against the LRA but certainly not as a court to try the rulers. In fact, Kenya might benefit from an informal front of distrust of the ICC from the Horn of Africa to the African Great Lakes via Sudan. All regional powers will support a Kenya which they appreciate is substantially weakened in the international field. No country in the region has an interest in Kenya being destabilised and ostracised by other nations. However, the East African leaders will not engage in a lively anti-Western offensive. These former guerrilla leaders are no longer in their ideological phase. They are before all pragmatic like Rwanda letting Bosco Ntagandago to The Hague (April 2013)[36] while in the Security Council supporting Kenya's initiatives against the ICC. During the month of May 2013, the East African states joined forces to use the ceremonies of the 50th anniversary of the African Union to get a nearly unanimous vote to condemn the ICC prosecution against the accused Kenyans and to ask for the repatriation of these trials to national courts.[37] The new Cabinet Secretary for Foreign Affairs of Kenya, Ms. Amina Mohamed is primarily responsible for renewing links with the West because foreign trade is first with these countries, much more than with Asia. This high-flying diplomat will mobilise her administration, still very able (but undermined by numerous cases of corruption), to reassure its partners. The task should not be insurmountable as Westerners know that the region needs a properly ruled Kenya. Thus, at the beginning of May 2013, Britain sought to normalise its relations with Kenya inviting Uhuru Kenyatta to London to attend a meeting on Somalia.[38] In the month of June 2013, Britain defused the situation further by asking for forgiveness for the crimes committed during the Mau Mau crisis.[39] In early July, the French invited President Kenyatta to go to Paris for the France-Africa summit in December.

Should we think like Peter Kagwanja[40] that the Kenyan foreign policy is currently experiencing a large-scale shift? It signals a more nationalistic diplomacy and one more involved in the construction of East Africa. It perceives a firm pan-African vision that would lead to a more just and equitable world order. In light of these principles, we must understand President Kenyatta's statement at his inauguration and that is probably referring to the ICC, "no one country or group of countries should have control or monopoly on international institutions or interpretation of treaties".[41] In fact, it is likely that saving the skin of the President and Deputy President has become the priority of Kenyan diplomacy and this sword of Damocles will weigh on other areas of the Ministry of Foreign Affairs. It is evident that the Kenyan government is an instrument in the service of an elite ruler: a power structure of neo-patrimonial type as political scientists like J.-F. Médard say. It is also a bureaucracy and an existing structure by its international recognition. Will its exploitation by UhuRuto change the diplomatic DNA of Kenya? Probably not because the West does not want a crisis with Kenya, even if it means swallowing a bitter pill to save appearances.

Conclusion

Transitional justice is usually studied by jurists or experts of international relations. They focus on the operation and interaction between institutions. In addition to these classic approaches, our study favoured a political sociology approach emphasising the importance of political culture and the play of identities to understand how Kenyans comprehend procedures of transitional justice. Thus, we showed that the two charged at the ICC, during the 2012-2013 electoral campaign, skillfully re-crystallised the identity of their respective communities by diffusing discourses of victimisation and formulating a re-reading of the history of their community making them heroes. This classic strategy worked particularly well as they used a religious register, of a neo-Pentecostal type, giving great strength to their message of repentance and self-justification. They created a new virginity and the impunity of Kenyan elites was thus renewed.[42] In doing so, they also deflected the political culture of the country by developing a true pentecostalisation of the political life.

The ICC charges of the two main leaders forced the political elite not to use violence during the electoral campaign. However, it does not mean that the next elections will be peaceful. Certainly, the institutional framework has changed and some factors of electoral violence are now dulled (without disappearing). With the new constitution of 2010, which establishes a high degree of decentralisation, the presidential election is less decisive. The famous rule of "winner takes all" taints less the political game since losers at the national level can control entire regions and thus can get access to the State. It is also necessary that decentralisationis properly implemented. The 2013 election brought to the top a duo consisting of a President who is rather hostile to the new constitution and a Deputy President who has always advocated for a strong decentralisation (of the *majimbo* type, according to the Kenyan political jargon). The fate of local government depends heavily on the quality of their competitive association.

Another institutional factor that contributed to peace during the 2013 elections: the existence of a Supreme Court, a judicial recourse accepted by the political class to resolve electoral disputes. However, its decision in 2013 that validated the presidential election was highly contested and undermined its legitimacy. The electoral commission worked reasonably well throughout the campaign but its work has been particularly criticised since the election. If this commission is not drastically reformed, the opposition will be convinced that it is impossible to truly win the presidential election owing to the manipulations of the incumbent.

More generally, the institutional system today seems particularly unstable. Since the elections, the various authorities are seeking to clarify their roles and relationships among themselves: the National Assembly is affirmed with respect to the Senate, Governors define their position in relation to the provincial administration and to the Members of Parliament, the judiciary consolidates with difficulty its newly acquired independence and the dual presidency is trying to impose its centrality. Thus, the institutional framework is fixed, which creates a situation of great political instability. To take the distinction of F.G. Bailey, at a time when the "normative rules" are not clear, the "pragmatic rules" are affirmed and seek to impose their interpretation of the norm.

Since the 2013 elections, the Kenyan state has gone to some trouble to ensure absolute impunity of its leaders. All institutions must comply with this categorical imperative. This creates the ideal conditions for establishing, in a lasting way, an authoritarian democracy.

Notes

1 I would like to thank Stephen Brown, Yvan Droz and Marie-Aude Fouéré for proofreading my article.

2 During the election campaign, journalists coined the term 'UhuRuto' to talk about this ticket in a well-oiled communication.

3 *The Standard*, July 17, 2012, Peter Opiyo, "Why Kenya-AU plot against ICC may stall".

4 *Daily Nation*, December 1, 2012, Bernard Namunane, "AG wants Uhuru, Muthaura cases moved to Arusha".

5 In the context of the end of the 2008 crisis, international actors sponsored several investigative reports of which the Waki Report was tasked in particular with specifying leaders' responsibilities in the post-election violence.

6 *Daily Nation*, July 27, 2012, Oliver Mathenge, "Uhuru and Ruto under ICC watch over rules", p.10.

7 This made journalists sarcastic: Otieno Otieno, "ICC case is turning Uhuru into the new Dedan Kimathi". *Sunday Nation*, February 17, 2013.

8 *Daily Nation*, April 7, 2012, "MPs milking the ICC cases dry"; "Amounts range from KShs. 20, 000 to KShs. 100, 000 depending on your seniority and influence".

9 'Emeritus' in the sense that they are no longer active.

10 The Catholic Church and its Justice and Peace Commission are very involved in the discussions aimed at regulating tensions between communities in Uasin Gishu and the arrival of Bishop Korir was very surprising.

11 *Daily Nation*, April 14, 2012, "Clerics on the spot over role in tribal groupings".

12 "The Kenya election and militarisation of 'peace'," *The East African*, March 9-15, 2013.

13 Uhuru Kenyatta is Catholic and William Ruto is a member of the Africa Inland Church, like President Moi. Their fling with Pentecostal structures and identity does not prevent them from featuring in and using their membership in these old churches of missionary origin.

14 The mother of William Ruto thinks her son's favorite verse is Jeremiah 33:3: "Call to me and I will answer you and tell you great and unsearchable things that you do not know". *The Standard*, April 10, 2013, Titus Too, "Ruto's mother attributes son's leadership fame to fear of God".

15 Jubilee is the electoral alliance that united Uhuru Kenyatta and William Ruto.

16 *Sunday Nation*, February 3, 2013, p.22, Emeka-Makaya Gekara, "Clergy differ on stand towards elections".

17 *Daily Nation*, November, 11, 2012, Lukoye Atwoli, "Involvement of religious groups in education";*Daily Nation*, January 1, 2013, "Don't assent to Education Bill, churches urge Kibaki". This new law would increase state control on Christian schools benefitting from public funds.

18 The 'historical' churches are former mission churches, which are neither Pentecostal nor Evangelical.

19 Ironically, the clergy was until the late 1990s heavily influenced by the Pentecostal theology and expression that it was often part of the East African Revival (Peterson, 2012). But the generation currently in operation in these churches is no longer involved in this movement.

20 *Daily Nation*, February 25, 2013, Dave Opiyo& Justus Wanga, "Kenyans pray for peaceful elections"; *Daily Nation*, February 26, 2013, Paul Ogemba, "Behind the scenes in run-up to prayers".

21 In transitional justice, the distinction is frequently made in criminal justice procedures (trials to prosecute those responsible for crimes related to the political crisis) from other non-judicial mechanisms aimed at addressing the violence in the time of crisis (Brown &Sriram, 2012: 246, n.3).

22 His name was mentioned in the organisation of the massacre of hundreds of Somali in Wagalla in 1984.

23 *Saturday Nation*, May 4, 2013, p.13, "Spare President the truth, it is too hard to handle".

24 *The East African*, May 4-10, 2013, p.16.

25 "Ruto Explains Kiambaa – Wikileaks", *The Star*, March 7, 2011; see also *The Standard*, January 8, 2013, "ICC gets new witnesses on Kiambaa killings".

26 Andrew Cawthorne, "Jackson Kibor denies masterminding violence", www.kalenjin.net

27 P. Mayoyo & D. Opiyo, "Kenya asks UN to end trial of Uhuru, Ruto", *Daily Nation*, May 9, 2013, p.1 & 6.

28 For a theorisationon the ambiguities of these programmes, see Roland Marchal (2003).

29 *Daily Nation*, October 12, 2012, Bernard Namunane, "Annan warns over ICC suspects' bids".

30 *Daily Nation*, February 8, 2013, "US restates stance on Uhuru and Ruto". The American position was weakened by statements by Republican leaders who are fundamentally opposed to the ICC system. Interventions by Jendayi Frazer (in charge of African affairs from 2005 to 2009) were widely re-run in the Kenyan media, e.g., J. Frazer, "ICC has fallen from high ideals of global justice, accountability", *Sunday Nation*, March 17, 2013.

31 *Saturday Nation*, February 9, 2013, "More embassies join push against Hague suspects".

32 See for example, Tim Wanyonyi & Patrick Mayoyo, "Kenya diplomatic isolation might lead to less financial aid and trade," *Daily Nation*, March 11, 2013, p.10.

33 *Daily Nation*, March 14, 2013, "Botswana minister in U-turn on Uhuru Ban", *Daily Nation*, March 11, 2013, "West yet to speak on election winners" ;*Sunday Nation*, March 10, 2013, "Bitter-sweet victory for Uhuru and Ruto".

34 *The Standard*, April 10, 2013, Ally Jamah, "Museveni hails Kenyans for rejecting ICC 'blackmail'".

35 He would have helped finance his electoral campaign, according to journalists of *The East African*("Uhuru banks on friends in East Africa for support", *The East African*, April 6-12, 2013).

36 For several years, he was within the scope of the ICC charges. There was a time when Rwanda was stripped of aid by several Western countries because of its involvement in the tensions in North Kivu.

37 *The East African*, May 25-31, 2013, "Kenya's quest to end cases at The Hague enters".

38 *Saturday Nation*, May 4, 2013, Isaac Ongiri, "British PM invites Uhuru for visit". *Daily Nation*, May 12, 2013, Peter Kagwanja, "Why UK ate humble pie after Uhuru win".

39 *Daily Nation*, June 7, 2013, "UK says sorry for Mau Mau crimes".

40 *Sunday Nation*, April 14, 2013, pp. 26-27, "Kenya's New assertive pan-African foreign policy";*The East African*, April 13-19, 2013, p .11, "Inside Kenyatta's emerging, assertive policy in East Africa",.

41 *The Standard*, April 10, 2013, "Uhuru Kenyatta – Inauguration: My pledge to Kenyans, International community", p.15.

42 According to polls conducted during the electoral campaign, only 40% of Kenyans believe that Kenyatta and Ruto must be prosecuted by the ICC (Long, Kanyinga, Ferree & Gibson, 2013: 147).

Bibliography

Anderson, D.M. and D.H. Johnson, eds. *Revealing Prophets*, London: James Currey,1995.

Barrett D, G.T. Kurian and T.M. Johnson. *World Christian Encyclopedia: A comparative survey of churches and religions in the Modern World*. New York: Oxford University Press, 2001.

Boas, M. and K. Dunn. *Politics of Origin in Africa: Autochthony, citizenship and conflict*. London: Zed Books, 2013.

Brown, S. and C.L. Sriram. "The Big Fish Won't Fry Themselves: Criminal accountability for post-election violence in Kenya". *African Affairs* 111, no. 443 (2012): 244-260.

Curtis, D. "The International Peacebuilding Paradox: Power sharing and post-conflict governance in Burundi". *African Affairs* 112, no. 446 (2013): 72-91.

Droz, Y. *Migrations Kikuyus: des pratiques sociales à l'imaginaire. Ethos, réalisation de soi et millénarisme*. Neuchâtel et Paris: Institut d'ethnologie et Maison des sciences de l'homme. 1999.

Droz, *Y. & H*. Maupeu. "Christianismes et démocratisation au Kenya". *Social Compass* 60, no. 1 (2013): 79-96.

Guichaoua, A. "L'instrumentalisation politique de la justice internationale en Afrique centrale."*Revue Tiers Monde* 205, no. 1 (2011): 65-84.

Long, James, et al. "Choosing Peace over Democracy". *Journal of Democracy* 24, no. 2 (2013): 140-155.

Lynch, G.*I Say to You: Ethnic politics and the Kalenjin in Kenya*. Chicago: University of Chicago Press, 2011.

Marchal, R. "Justice internationale et réconciliation nationale: Ambiguïtés et débats". *Politique africaine* 92, Décembre 2003: 5-17.

Marshall, R. *Political Spiritualities: The Pentecostal revolution in Nigeria*. Chicago: Chicago University Press, 2009.

Médard, C."Quelques clés pour démêler la crise kenyane. Spoliation, autochtonie et privatisation foncière". In J. Lafargue (dir.), *Les élections générales de 2007 au Kenya*, 75-88. Nairobi, Paris: IFRA, Karthala, 2008.

Paris, R. *At War's End: Building peace after civil conflict*. Cambridge: Cambridge University Press, 2004.

Peterson, D.R. *Ethnic Patriotism and the East African Revival: A history of dissent, C.1935-1972*. Cambridge: Cambridge University Press, 2012.

Simatei, P. "Kalenjin Popular Music and the Contestation of National Space in Kenya". *Journal of Eastern African Studies* 4, no. 3 (2010): 425-434.

Sriram, C.L. and M.-J. Zahar. "The Perils of Power-Sharing: Africa and beyond", *Africa Spectrum* 3(2009): 11-39.

Zürcher, C. et al. *Costly Democracy: Peacebuilding and democratization after war*. Stanford: Stanford University Press, 2013.

The 4 March 2013 General Elections in Kenya: From Latent Tension to Contained Violence

Mathieu Mérino [*]

Introduction

Kenya's general elections on 4 March 2013 appeared as a major test of the country's ability to move beyond election-related violence – particularly that of the 2007-2008 elections, which resulted in the death of 1,300 citizens and the displacement of more than 600,000.[1] The rather peaceful character of the 2013 elections might appear to vindicate the institutional reforms undertaken in Kenya since 2008, with the country firmly fixed on a path of pacified political competition. For the most part, politicians, political operatives and civil society have certainly understood the need to prevent electoral violence. This reflects a political transformation in Kenya: in the run-up to the 2013 elections, the main presidential candidates systematically and collectively appealed for peace and increased their calls for tolerance during the campaigns.[2] Several youth groups participated in violence-prevention campaigns, while the media worked with government institutions to broadcast messages of peace and to stifle inflammatory speeches, among other efforts. However, the ever-present fear of violence obscured discussion and debate about its causes, particularly those that have fuelled its increase since 1992.[3] Political debates largely avoided questions about land access rights, unequal natural resource distribution, and youth unemployment.[4]

[*]   . Political Scientist, researcher at IFRA, Nairobi. This article was originally published in French under the title "Les élections générales du 4 mars 2014 au Kenya: De tensions latentes en violences contenues" DOI: 10.3917/afco.247.0073 (*Afrique contemporaine*, n° 247, Élections Kenya, © De Boeck Supérieurs.a., 2013 1re édition, Fond Jean-Pâques 4, B-1348 Louvain-la-Neuve).

Unlike their public denunciations, some politicians still covertly favor the use of violence – concentrated in the run-up period that comprises voter registration, primaries, and so on – thus perpetuating a kind of structural electoral violence that has recurred in every election since 1992. The 2013 elections were no exception. Between 2012 and the beginning of 2013, clashes between communities in several regions of the country resulted in more than 500 dead and nearly 120,000 displaced (ICG, 2013a). Pre-election maneuvering fostered many of these incidents, as local politicians mobilized their supporters. During the second half of 2012, some of the most serious clashes occurred between the Pokomo and Orma in the Tana River Delta, resulting in the death of hundreds.[5]

Given these events, along with the filing of a formal complaint disputing the 2013 election outcomes, the current absence of a post-election crisis should not obscure the persistence of latent tensions and election-related violence, even if the latter has been contained. Despite calls for calm during the 2013 campaigns, the party primaries remain chaotic and disorganized, as does the administration of polling practices. The efforts that prevailed to maintain peace – before the vote, during the count, and following the Supreme Court arguments – must not obscure the deep tensions that still characterize this power-sharing exercise in Kenya.

Kenya: Violent outbreaks near the borders during the elections
Number killed and displaced by county (January 2012-June 2013)

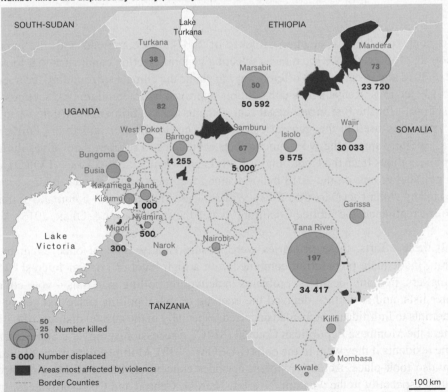

This map shows where violent outbreaks took place in Kenya from January 2012 to June 2013, using two indicators: the number of people killed and the number displaced. It combines two maps drawn by the United Nations Office for the Coordination of Humanitarian Affairs (OCHA) in Nairobi; the original maps cover two distinct periods, January 2012 to 2013, and January through June 2013. The maps use data gathered, aggregated and verified by Kenya's Red Cross, several nongovernmental organizations and observers in the field. This map shows that 665 people were killed and at least 168,200 displaced from their region of origin because of local and intercommunity conflicts between January 2012 and June 2013. The hardest hit regions are situated near the Kenyan border in the north and the east.
Source: OCHA maps (2013).

Édigraphie, 12/2013.

The shambolic candidate selection process

In accordance with the electoral reforms of 2010, and for the first time in the history of the country, six elections were slated for the same day (4 March 2013): for president and deputy-president, National Assembly,[6] women's representatives to the Parliament and the Senate,[7] local governors, and local legislators[8] in 47 newly created counties. In Kenya, political contests are fought, first and foremost, at the local level. Even before the introduction of multiple political parties in 1991, local election battles were intense; this was especially apparent during races between local chapters of the Kenya African National Union (KANU). KANU was the dominant party from Kenya's independence until 2002. The current multi-party era has not changed the situation: the local primaries that decide the general-election candidates remain hotly disputed. The dozen or so partial elections that took place at the end of 2011 proved no exception: in several electoral districts in Nyanza Province, for example, the main party primaries – particularly those of the Orange Democratic Movement (ODM), led by Prime Minister Raila Odinga – proved extremely competitive and sometimes lacked impartiality (Amina, 2012). During the ODM primaries, ten deaths among party members occurred in the electoral districts of Rongo, Nyatike, Kasipul and Kabondo in Nyanza Province (Nyasato and Ongwae, 2011; Ongwae and Otieno, 2011). Clashes between supporters of several candidates also took place in Likoni, Coast Province; as a result, one legislator, Suleiman Shahbal, filed a complaint for election process irregularities (Otieno, 2011).

Given this context – the post-election violence of 2007-2008 combined with the intensified competition that followed – the local races selecting general-election candidates that took place at the end of 2012 and in early 2013 offered ways to gauge the climate surrounding the upcoming 4 March2013 elections. Kenya's new constitution, approved by referendum on 28 August 2010, properly set out – for the first time – legal requirements for the primaries: Article 91 imposed the same principles used in the general election, "to be lawful, fair and free." Furthermore, the parties generally spread the word among their candidates to restrain themselves during the races. Representatives from the Coalition for Reform and Democracy Alliance (CORD), one of two main political groups on the 2013 ballot, warned that they would disqualify any candidate implicated in any violent act (Mosota, 2013). William Ruto, the second-in-command of the other leading political alliance, the Jubilee Coalition,[9] issued the same warning (Olick, 2013).

Despite all these efforts, these primaries were, unsurprisingly, marked once again by poor organization. Inadequate preparation combined with a high level of popular interest[10] did not facilitate matters. In many localities, problems in delivering polling materials – vote-collection boxes, voter lists, and so forth – delayed the opening of many polling places, angering many voters. Attempts to intimidate voters also occurred, especially in the coastal districts of Kilifi and Kwale where the Mombasa Republican Council (MRC), a secessionist movement, threatened to attack some residents if they went to the polls (EUEOM, 2013). Multiple allegations of fraud and corruption also took place. Actually, violent episodes concentrated around the announcement of the results, especially in the western, Nyanza, Nairobi, Central and Coast provinces. In fact, the races in the fiefdoms of the main political parties were often the most bitterly fought, as a certificate of investiture from one of the parties would normally all but guarantee election. Nyanza Province, the ODM stronghold, was especially affected, with clashes between youth and the police in Migori, Homa Bay, Kisumu and Siaya counties. Similarly, localized violence, such as roadblocks, stone-throwing, and attacks on candidates, occurred in Nairobi, Kisumu and Eldoret, the URP stronghold. Officially, the primaries resulted in two deaths, several dozen wounded and more than 40 arrests (P.A. Nyong'o, author interview on February 26, 2013 and Joel Mabonga, author interview on February 28, 2013).

Unlike the primaries, the nomination of presidential candidates took place at the end of January in an atmosphere of solemn calm – at least on the surface. Eight presidential candidates presented themselves in person: Martha Karua (NARC-K); Peter Kenneth (KNC),[11] James ole Kiyiapi (Restore and Build Kenya, or RBK), Musalia Mudavadi (UDF),[12] Uhuru Kenyatta (TNA),[13] Mohamed Abduba Dida (Alliance for Real Change), Raila Odinga (ODM)[14] and Paul Muite (Safina Party). The stage for this had been set several months earlier, at a cost of long negotiations to cement alliances and nominate frontrunners. In the wake of the 2007-2008 post-election violence, all candidates signed a new code of conduct that forbade violence and fraud, and solemnly swore, if defeated, to accept the verdict of the ballot box (Ngirachu, 2013). Nearly all candidates also took part in a large rally in Uhuru Park at the center of Nairobi, in support of peaceful elections (Opiyo, 2013).

Fundamentally, these appeals for peace were the significant feature of the 2013 elections, even before the campaign officially began. The calls seemed to be part of a larger movement that arose after the 2007-2008 post-election crisis. They aimed to prevent a repeat of the violence and to avoid irritating still-open wounds. In particular, Kenya sought to institutionalize violence-prevention and penalty mechanisms. These included the Truth, Justice and Reconciliation Commission (set up in 2008), and the National Cohesion and Integration Commission (NCIC); the latter had the mandate to detect and take legal action against acts of ethnic and racial discrimination (NCIC, 2008). Henceforth the law cracked down on hateful acts and speech "toward any group of people based on their color, race, nationality, ethnicity or origin", acts that had contributed widely to spreading violence after the 2007-2008 election (NCIC, 2008). For this reason, even as the NCIC came into being, it initiated charges against three Kikuyu musicians and six politicians, including two ministers; it also used the 2010 constitutional referendum to pursue two legislators. In September 2012, the NCIC demanded the arrest of the Nairobi assemblyman and deputy minister of water, Ferdinand Waititu, following media reports that during a visit to the Kayole area in Nairobi, he incited listeners to chase the Maasai out of the electoral district (BBC, 2012a).[15]

Even so, these calls for calm did not disguise underlying tensions; sparring between Raila Odinga and his main rival, Uhuru Kenyatta, had gone on for several months already, and the consequences of the 2007-2008 post-election crisis still haunted the media. Indeed, the 600,000 Kenyans displaced during the crisis had not been resettled, particularly those from the Rift Valley and Nyanza provinces, who were most affected at the time. Another grave concern weighed on the presidential elections, an unresolved question about the eligibility of one of the main candidates, Uhuru Kenyatta. Kenyatta has been charged with crimes against humanity, allegedly perpetrated during the 2007-2008 post-election violence, and will be tried before the International Criminal Court (ICC) in the Hague. Initial hearings were set for April 2013, a month after the first round of voting. The Jubilee coalition[16] sought to stifle all political debate about these charges, preferring instead to denounce "foreign intervention" and thus banking on a populist reaction in their favor.

An apparently calm campaign

The ever-present fear of violence prompted several preventative steps during the campaign, particularly affecting mobile telephone, radio, and social media network operators; these groups had spoken, written or relayed words that had contributed widely to violence after the 2007-2008 election. The National Communications Commission of Kenya targeted political messages sent via mobile phones, imposing an obligation on network operators to filter content that was likely to encourage violent behavior. The commission also insisted that political parties write their text messages (SMS) only in English or Swahili, thereby excluding many vernacular languages. In addition, the commission required all parties to submit their proposed messages to network operators 48 hours before broadcast time so that the content could be deleted, if necessary. The commission also required mobile network operators to keep a registry of names connected to all mobile phone SIM cards so that the operators could trace message senders and recipients; penalties for sending hate messages reached up to $56,000 (US) or three years in prison. Citizens were also encouraged to report any hateful message (BBC 2013) via a mobile-phone application set up by the National Police Service Commission (Ndonga, 2013). Targeting social network users, the Kenyan government announced that it would oversee the Internet and arrest anyone spreading hate speech aimed at other communities (Jackson, 2013; Ombati, 2013).

At the same time, public speeches encouraged support of peaceful elections; strong pressure also came from international sources.[17] Radio airwaves were full of calls for tolerance, local radio being the most important broadcast media in Kenya.[18] Some radio stations organized peace rallies, such as one in Mombasa in February 2013 set up by Ramogi FM, a Luo-language station. As Election Day neared, messages promoting tolerance multiplied. Popular stations generally played songs that praised national patriotism and intercommunity pacifism. One of the main Kikuyu-language radio stations, Kameme FM, broadcast a song appealing to God that Kenyans would not fight one another. A Kalenjin-language station, Kass FM, broadcast music that called for Kalenjin to love their neighbors and to forgive them if the love was not returned.

In the end, the general election campaigns remained relatively calm, and citizens generally respected candidates' freedom of movement and expression throughout the country. But that had also been the case in 2007. Some destruction of campaign materials was noted in Nyeri, Narok, and Nakuru counties in the Central and Rift Valley provinces. Elsewhere, violent incidents erupted, particularly in the Coast and North-Eastern provinces, as well as in the Rift Valley. The most serious incident occurred in Garissa, a suicide attack against a security forces building the day before the arrival of the NARC-K presidential candidate, Martha Karua. Serious disruptions also took place in Meru and Embu in Eastern Province in mid-February: TNA partisans of the Jubilee alliance interrupted two presidential rallies for the CORD duo, Raila and Musyoka, with both events ending in violence (Wanyoro, 2013). Furthermore, verbal violence between communities remained as intense as during the 2007 campaigns, despite the calls for restraint. While the media did not relay such speech (unlike in 2007), social networks became infested with it (Mukinda, 2013a), especially during the two weeks just before the vote (Omino, 2013). Attempts by the Committee on Media Monitoring to bring action against social networks achieved hardly any result (Mukinda, 2013b).

Voting outcomes cause localized violence

For the first time in Kenya's history, the Independent Electoral and Boundaries Commission (IEBC)[19] had to set up and coordinate six elections simultaneously.[20] By the end of 2012, the IEBC had fallen behind schedule for several key electoral steps, such as voter education,[21] election districting, and voter registration. It was also behind schedule in hiring the more than 160,000 Election Day workers and determining the number of polling places.[22] These delays eroded the commission's credibility. Notably, voter registration failed to achieve the intended targets. Although nearly 80% of the electoral administration's target was met,[23] people without identity cards – a significant share of young potential voters and citizens living in distant regions, particularly those on the border with Somalia – remained excluded from the voter registration lists,[24] as did a significant percentage of women.[25]

Even so, like the campaign, Election Day remained calm overall. Localized violence broke out in Nairobi and Kisumu, but was quickly contained. On the other hand, the Coast and North-Eastern provinces saw several violent incidents that killed more than 20, including members of the security forces and electoral administration agents (Smith, 2013). Although isolated, these incidents caused several delays in the opening of polling places in several districts, such as Mombasa, Kilifi and Kwale, which *a priori* favored the CORD coalition. Such incidents also decreased voter participation rates.

After the vote, the ballot-counting and compiling phase was marked by a lack of transparency and some inefficiency on the part of the IEBC. Electronic transmission of results failed due to incomplete training and cellular network coverage (Mark, 2013). Party agents were also evacuated from the national compilation center in Nairobi, ostensibly (and officially) to facilitate the manual counting of presidential votes following the electronic transmission failure (Joel Mabonga, author interview on March 6, 2013). All these events sharpened tensions between candidates and the electoral commission. Nonetheless, the main candidates called on their partisans and the whole nation to remain calm and peaceful during the five days of ballot counting.

Political party representation in the National Assembly and the Senate

Majority political coalitions represented in the National Assembly and Senate, by county

Coalitions and political parties represented in the National Assembly, by seat and percentage

Party and coalition

Seats (out of 337)

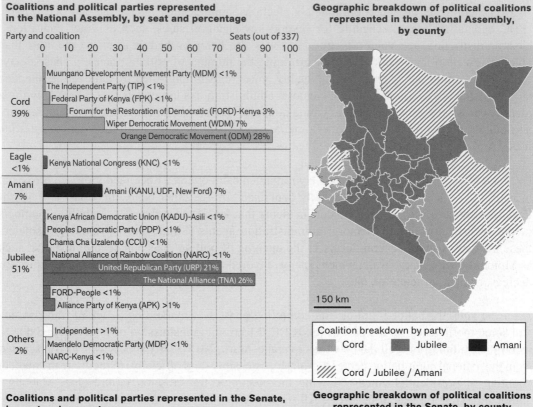

Cord 39%
- Muungano Development Movement Party (MDM) <1%
- The Independent Party (TIP) <1%
- Federal Party of Kenya (FPK) <1%
- Forum for the Restoration of Democratic (FORD)-Kenya 3%
- Wiper Democratic Movement (WDM) 7%
- Orange Democratic Movement (ODM) 28%

Eagle <1%
- Kenya National Congress (KNC) <1%

Amani 7%
- Amani (KANU, UDF, New Ford) 7%

Jubilee 51%
- Kenya African Democratic Union (KADU)-Asili <1%
- Peoples Democratic Party (PDP) <1%
- Chama Cha Uzalendo (CCU) <1%
- National Alliance of Rainbow Coalition (NARC) <1%
- United Republican Party (URP) 21%
- The National Alliance (TNA) 26%
- FORD-People <1%
- Alliance Party of Kenya (APK) >1%

Others 2%
- Independent >1%
- Maendelo Democratic Party (MDP) <1%
- NARC-Kenya <1%

Geographic breakdown of political coalitions represented in the National Assembly, by county

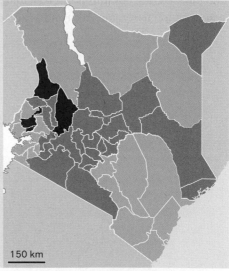

150 km

Coalition breakdown by party

- Cord
- Jubilee
- Amani
- Cord / Jubilee / Amani

Coalitions and political parties represented in the Senate, by seat and percentage

Coalition

Seats (out of 47)

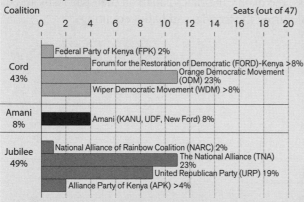

Cord 43%
- Federal Party of Kenya (FPK) 2%
- Forum for the Restoration of Democratic (FORD)-Kenya >8%
- Orange Democratic Movement (ODM) 23%
- Wiper Democratic Movement (WDM) >8%

Amani 8%
- Amani (KANU, UDF, New Ford) 8%

Jubilee 49%
- National Alliance of Rainbow Coalition (NARC) 2%
- The National Alliance (TNA) 23%
- United Republican Party (URP) 19%
- Alliance Party of Kenya (APK) >4%

This chart shows only the 47 elected Senators and does not include 16 women nominated by political parties, two youth representatives, two disabled-persons representatives or the Speaker of the Senate.

Geographic breakdown of political coalitions represented in the Senate, by county

150 km

Election results for representatives to the National Assembly and the Senate gave legislative leadership to the Jubilee Coalition with a definitive majority in both houses of Parliament. Cord, led by Raila Odinga, became the official opposition coalition in both houses.

Source: "Kenya after the elections." Africa Briefing N° 94. International Crisis Group (ICG). Nairobi/Brussels. 2013

Edigraphie, 12/2013.

The IEBC's announcement of the results on 9 March came as something of a surprise. While most observers expected a run-off between Odinga (CORD) and Kenyatta (Jubilee), the latter was declared the winner of the presidential election with 6,173,422 votes, or 50.07%. Odinga received only 5,340,546 votes, about 830,000 fewer. Above all, Kenyatta carried the first round of voting with a lead of 8,419 votes; this was a rather weak margin given the potential "errors" that may have occurred during the compilation of more than 12 million ballots.[26] Another surprise – given the high voter turnout (85.9%), the unprecedented complexity of the elections, and the requirement to vote for six positions – was that the rejected ballots represented only 0.8% of the vote, a very low percentage on the worldwide scale.[27]

Of course, the Jubilee camp perceived the presidential election results differently from the CORD camp. For the former, victory validated their risky strategy of an alliance between two leaders, Kenyatta and Ruto, and therefore between two communities, the Kalenjin and the Kikuyu, who had been opponents in 2007-2008. In effect, the logic of a *rapprochement* between communities ensured Jubilee a base of six million potential electors versus somewhat fewer than three million for CORD, supported by the Luo and the Kamba. Furthermore, the Kenyatta-Ruto ticket's efficient and expensive campaign swept aside the Orange camp, which had started too late, suffering from divisions that appeared during the early 2013 primaries (Anonymous, 2013b). CORD, for its part, very quickly filed a complaint about the results with the Supreme Court, on 17 March. In a non-anecdotal way, rather than asserting elector victory, the complaint focused on obtaining annulment of the results and rerun of the election. This suggests that CORD knew it could not demonstrate victory to the Court, given the large gap between Odinga's and Kenyatta's vote totals. To support its complaint, CORD argued that the number of votes that the IEBC compiled in some electoral districts differed from totals it announced nationally. On 25 March, the Supreme Court ordered a ballot recount for 22 polling places, calling these "tests." Although it acknowledged obvious material errors in 20 of the 22 polls, on March 30 the Court validated the results as announced by the IEBC.

The Supreme Court's decision provoked only isolated acts of violence, in Nyanza Province and in Nairobi, notably because of pacifying speeches made by Odinga and his political allies following the announcement of the Court's ruling. In this regard, it appears that the large margin of votes separating Kenyatta from Odinga played the crucial role in the CORD coalition's de facto if not formal acceptance; a theoretical second-round runoff could not possibly have reversed the trend. The coalition also faced internal and external pressure to avoid going back on the stump, pressures more decisive than those for making truly substantial improvements in electoral conduct. The climate in which the hypothetical runoff would have occurred remains an open but valid question, given the way that the administration had incompletely secured the electoral process.

Table 1: Results for Kenya's 4 March 2013 presidential election

Candidate	Number of votes	Percentage of votes
Uhuru Kenyatta	6,173,433	50.07%
Raila Odinga	5,340,546	43.31%
Musalia Mudavadi	483,981	3.93%
Peter Kenneth	72,786	0.59%
Mohamed Abduba Dida	52,848	0.43%
Martha Wangari Karua	43,881	0.36%
James Legilisho Kiyiapi	40,998	0.33%
Paul Kibugi Muite	12,580	0.10%
Rejected votes[28]	108,975	0.88%
TOTAL	12,330,028	100%

Source: IEBC, 2013.

Between 5 and 8 March, the electoral commission also announced the results for county governors, Assemblies, women's representatives to the National Assembly, and senators. As with the presidential results, these victory declarations did not cause any seriously violent incidents.

As of this writing, Kenyatta's Jubilee coalition controls 58% and 57% of the seats in the National Assembly and Senate, respectively. However, the new central power has to contend with the 47 local (county) governments that resulted from the 2010 constitutional reform. Decentralization remains in progress, and CORD controls 21 of the 47 counties. Tensions have already appeared between governors and the central government (Mosoku, 2013). The newly elected Governor Wycliffe Oparanya (ODM-Kakamega) and Deputy Governor Okoth Obado (UDF-Migori) have asserted that the constitution prescribes a clear separation of powers, making the counties "independent units"; the pair hold that the central government has no mandate to interfere with or regulate county governments. Additionally, Governor Alfred Mutua (WDM-Machakos) recently condemned Kenya's Treasury for not funding the counties in accordance with the constitution (Anonymous, 2013c). All of this inaugurates new ground for political competition between CORD and Jubilee, with a backdrop of competition between the central government and decentralized powers.

Notes

1   For more on the 2007 elections and the crisis that followed, see e.g. Lafargue and Katumanga (2013); Lafargue (2008); Anderson and Lochery (2008); and British Institute in Eastern Africa(2008).

2   For more on the links between religions and politics, especially during elections, see e.g. Lonsdale (2005) and Maupeu (2008).

3   For more about the history of electoral violence since the return of multiparty system, see especially Klopp (2001) and Basedau, Erdmann and Mehler (2007).

4   The land question is particularly sensitive in Kenya because of illegal land-grabbing practices, notably those highlighted by the Ndung'u Commission Report (2004). Property-related issues are one of the causes of the 2007-2008 post-election violence; for more see Médard (2008). Thus, during the 2013 election campaigns, high-level Kenyan officials, particularly those in the police force, stopped some candidates from speaking publicly on the subject, to avoid volatile questions and keep campaign appearances under control. For example, Police Chief Kimaiyo said, "the land issue at this point in time should not be used as a campaigntool by candidates; its effect has been seen before" (Sigei, 2013).

5   After these clashes, a deputy minister and two councilors were arrested and tried for their part in provoking violence (Anonymous, 2013a).

6   The National Assembly has 350 members, of which 290 are elected; 47 seats are reserved for elected women's representatives (one per county), and 12 seats for representatives appointed by political parties.

7   The Senate has 68 members; 47 are elected, each representing one county.

8   At the local level, 47 county governors are elected by direct vote, as are 1,450 members of local Assemblies.

9   Jubilee is mainly built on a coalition of the National Alliance (TNA) and the United Republican Party (URP), respectively managed by Uhuru Kenyatta, a Vice Prime Minister and a Kikuyu from Central Province, and William Ruto, a former agriculture minister and the leader of the Kalenjin community. The coalition between Kenyatta and Ruto thus turned on an electoral alliance between the Kalenjin and Kikuyu, even though the two communities are long time opponents and even clashed during the 2007-2008 post-election violence. Above all, the two communities were bound together by a pre-electoral agreement to share governmental functions equally between Kenyatta's partisans and Ruto's. In addition, to its main supporters, the alliance counted on Charity Ngilu – then minister for water and Chair of the National Rainbow Coalition (NARC), and Najib Balala of the Republican Congress (RC), from, respectively, Ukambani in Eastern Province, and Coast Province.

10   Nearly 3.4 million Kenyans are registered as members of a political party. According to the Electoral and Boundaries Commission (EBC), the four largest political parties are the National Alliance, with 290,730 members, the Orange Democratic Party with 278,217 members, the United Democratic Forum Party with 209,217 members, and the United Republican Party with 198,737 members.

11   Peter Kenneth, a politician with the KNC, and Raphael Tuju of the Party of Action (POA), joined forces to create the Eagle Alliance at the beginning of 2013 in preparation for parliamentary and local elections.

12   The Deputy Prime Minister Musalia Mudavadi, originally from the Luhya community in Western Province, was the leader of the Amani coalition that combined the UDF, KANU and the New Forum for the Restoration of Democracy Kenya (New FORD-Kenya).

13   For the Jubilee coalition.

14   For the CORD coalition.

15   Waititu's speech occurred after a childhaddied in Kayole area in Nairobi, However, Waititu was arrested for only a short time; after he apologized, the NCIC withdrew its complaint (Ahmed Yassin, author interview on October 4, 2012).

16   The Jubilee alliance was originally set up as a four-part coalition to support the Uhuru Kenyatta-William Ruto ticket for the presidential election. The founding members are the TNA, NARC, URP and RC.

17   Many nations called for Kenyan citizens to unite, especially the United States and European countries (Omondi 2013).

18   Radio is regularly listened to by 95% of Kenyans. The country counts 90 FM-radio stations, including 46 in Nairobi alone (Synovate 2011).

19   The IEBC, created in 2011 and directed by Ahmed Isaack Hassan, is the direct descendant of the Interim Independent Electoral Commission (IIEC). The latter was in charge of organizing the 2010 constitutional referendum, followed by 11 partial elections; its success led politicians to retain the same team of commissioners when the IEBC was created by the 2011 Independent Electoral and Boundaries Commission Bill. The IEBC is made up of nine commissioners selected by Parliament and appointed by the President.

20   Since the 2010 constitutional reform, Kenyan citizens have voted in six elections on the same day: presidential, legislative, senatorial, women's representatives to the National Assembly, governors, and local Assembly representatives. These six ballots account for 1,882 elected positions.

21   Despite Kenya's recent history of deep institutional reforms, and despite the complexity of producing six elections, the IEBC did not launch a voter education program until a month before Election Day.

22   Up until the final days before the election, the IEBC hesitated between setting up 33,000 or 40,000 polling places. This indecision affected the upstream organizational process of hiring polling-place workers and distributing ballots, ballot boxes, voting booths, and other materials.

23   Reaching a total of 14.34 million registered voters out of an estimated 18 million potential voters.

24   Observers regularly speak of three million potential voters that did not have identification (Anonymous civil-society representatives, February 20, 2013)

25   The persistent deficit of women registered to vote is clear from the final voter registration numbers that showed a minority of women in every age category under 50, except for 26-30 year olds, where women slightly outnumbered men.

26   According to Kenya's constitution, a candidate must receive 50% plus one vote of all votes cast and at least 25% of votes cast in at least half (24) of the country's 47 counties.

27   For a comparison, the percentage of ballots found to be invalid during the 2010 referendum was 1.7%, or more than twice as many than for the presidential contest, and for a far simpler election. A fine-grained analysis of the numbers tends to confirm the a priori anomalously low rate, since in similar contexts observers commonly see significant differences between urban or central regions and those on the border, to the logical detriment of the latter. In the case of Kenya's last elections, a county-by-county count shows no such tendency clearly. For example, counties as underserved as Garissa or Wajir saw invalidation rates of 0.56% and 0.54% respectively, lower than Nairobi's 0.86%. The simple fact that the capital city achieves the national average is in itself revealing, in as much as capitals generally finish in the lower range of invalidation rates; this phenomenon was observed, for example, during the last elections in Ghana and in Côte d'Ivoire.

28   Kenya's constitution allows for determining results on all votes, which is why the IEBC included rejected votes in its March 9, 2013 announcement about the candidates' totals and percentages.

Bibliography

Amina, P. "ODM party polls breached the new constitution". *The Star,* January 16, 2012. Retrieved from http://www.the-star.co.ke/news/article-34052/odm-party-polls-breached-new-constitution.

Anderson, D., and E. Lochery. "Violence and Exodus in Kenya's Rift Valley, 2008: Predictable and preventable". *Journal of Eastern African Studies* 2, no. 2, July 2008.

Anonymous (2013a). "Power struggles and conflict over use of land fans Tana Delta clashes". *Daily Nation*, February 9, 2013. Retrieved from http://www.nation.co.ke/News/Power+struggles+fan+Tana+Delta+clashes/-/1056/1487278/-/t7w6go/-/index.html.

Anonymous (2013b). "Nyanza leaders blame voters for Raila's election loss and trouble". *Daily Nation*, March 25, 2013. Retrieved from http://www.nation.co.ke/News/politics/Nyanza-leaders-blame-voters/-/1064/1729528/-/jg5wfpz/-/index.html.

Anonymous (2013c). "Talk of devolution without money to counties is a joke". *Daily Nation*, April 6, 2013. Retrieved from http://www.nation.co.ke/News/politics/Nyanza-leaders-blame-voters/-/1064/1729528/-/jg5wfpz/-/index.html.

Basedau, M., G. Erdmann and A. Mehler. *Votes, Money and Violence: Political parties and elections in sub-Saharan Africa.* Scottsville: KwaZulu-Natal Press, 2007.

British Broadcasting Corporation (BBC). Kenya MP Ferdinand Waititu accused of hate speech. *BBC News*, September 25, 2012. Retrieved from http://www.bbc.co.uk/news/world-africa-19713466.

_____. "Kenya cracks down on hate speech ahead of poll". *BBC News*, February 26, 2013. Retrieved from http://www.bbc.co.uk/news/world-africa-21538412.

British Institute in Eastern Africa. "Special Issue: Election Fever: Kenya's crisis". *Journal of Eastern African Studies* 2, no. 2 (2008).

European Union Electoral Observation Mission (EUEOM). *Final Report of the EU Election Observation Mission in Kenya.* Nairobi. March 6, 2013.

International Crisis Group (ICG). "Kenya after the election", Africa Briefing, 94. Brussels: ICG. May 15, 2013.

_____. "Kenya's 2013 elections", *Africa Report*, 197. Brussels: ICG. January 17, 2013.

IEBC (Independent Electoral and Boundaries Commission). "Kenya election results for March 4, 2013". Nairobi: IEBC. 2013.

Jackson, T. "Kenyan government warns social media users on hate speech". Humanipo.com, January 9, 2013. Retrieved from http://www.humanipo.com/news/3189/kenyan-government-warns-social-media-users-on-hate-speech/

Klopp, J. "'Ethnic clashes' and winning elections: The Kenyan case of electoral despotism". *Canadian Journal of African Studies* 35, no. 2 (2001): 473-517.

Lafargue, J. ed. *The General Elections in Kenya,* 2007. Dar es Salaam: Mkuki na Nyota Publishers, 2009.

Lafargue, J. and M. Katumanga. "Élections et violences au Kenya". *Politique Africaine* 109, no. 3 (2013): 107-121.

Lonsdale, J. "Religion and Politics in Kenya." The Henry Martyn Lectures. Cambridge: Cambridge University. 2005. Retrieved from http://henrymartyn.dns-systems.net/media/documents/HMC%20Lectures/2005%20Religion%20and%20Politics%20in%20Kenya.pdf.

Maupeu, H. "The Role of Religious Institutions". *Les Cahiers d'Afrique de l'Est* 38 (2008): 311-340.

Mark, O. "Polls officials ill-trained to use devices". *The Business Daily*. March 7, 2013. Retrieved from http://www.businessdailyafrica.com/Polls-officials-ill-trained-to-use-devices-/-/539546/1714216/-/fncv5q/-/index.html.

Médard, C. "Key issues in disentangling the Kenyan crisis: evictions, autochthony and land privatization". *Les Cahiers d'Afrique de l'Est,* 38 (2008): 375-390.

Mosota, M. "CORD to disqualify candidates who engage in violence". *The East African Standard*. January 7, 2013. Retrieved from http://www.standardmedia.co.ke/?articleID=2000074488&story_title=cord-to-disqualify-candidates-who-engage-in-violence.

Mosoku, G. "Raila: State officials out to kill devolution". *The East African Standard*. April 4, 2013. Retrieved from http://www.standardmedia.co.ke/?articleID=2000080782&story_title=Kenya-Raila:-State-officials-out-to-kill-devolution.

Mukinda, F. "Tool to track hate messages unveiled". *Daily Nation*, January 30, 2013a. Retrieved from http://elections.nation.co.ke/news/Tool-to-track-hate-messages-unveiled--/-/1631868/1680262/-/12a2cd3z/-/index.html.

_____. "Team urges Facebook to expose hate speech". *Daily Nation*, February 20, 2013b. Retrieved from http://elections.nation.co.ke/news/Team-urges-Facebook-to-expose-hate-speech-/-/1631868/1699694/-/egxersz/-/index.html.

National Cohesion and Integration Commission (NCIC). *National Cohesion and Integration Act*. Nairobi: NCIC, 2008.

Ndonga, W. "Public to report crimes, hate speech via SMS". *Capital News*, January 30, 2013. Retrieved from http://www.capitalfm.co.ke/news/2013/01/public-to-report-crimes-hate-speech-via-sms/.

Ndung'u Commission. *Report of the Commission of Inquiry into the Illegal/Irregular Allocation of Public Land.* Nairobi: Republic of Kenya, 2004.

Ngirachu, J. "Candidates warned to play by the rules". *Daily Nation*, January 30, 2013. Retrieved from http://elections.nation.co.ke/news/Candidates-warned-to-play-by-the-rules-/-/1631868/1680102/-/ks7p8p/-/index.html.

Nyasato, R., and R. Ongwae. "Four youth killed, scores injured after rival ODM supporters clash". *The East African Standard*, December 12, 2011. Retrieved from http://www.standardmedia. co.ke/?id=2000048263&cid=159&currentPage=3&articleID=2000048263.

OCHA (United Nations Office for the Coordination of Humanitarian Affairs).Kenya: 2012 Inter-communal conflict by district (Jan 2012 - Jan 2013). 2013a. Retrieved from http://reliefweb.int/ sites/reliefweb.int/files/resources/Kenya%202012%20Inter-communal%20conflict%20by%20 district%20%28Jan%202012%20-%20Jan%202013%29.pdf.

_____. Kenya: *Inter-communal conflict by district (January 2013 - June 2013). 2013b.* Retrieved from https://kenya.humanitarianresponse.info/sites/kenya.humanitarianresponse. info/files/KEN_Jan-Jun2013_Conflict_Tracking_10July2013.pdf.

Olick, F. "Ruto assures EU observers of peaceful polls". *The East African Standard*, January 23, 2013. Retrieved from http://www.standardmedia.co.ke/?articleID=2000075675&story_title=Kenya:%20Ruto%20assures%20EU%20observers%20of%20peaceful%20polls.

Ombati, C. "Team to monitor hate speech set up ahead of polls". *The East African Standard,* January 9, 2013. Retrieved from http://www.standardmedia.co.ke/?articleID=2000074588&story_title=team-to-monitor-hate-speech-set-up-ahead-of-polls.Omino, B. (2013). Media monitoring committee warns against hate speech. *The Star*, 13 March. Retrieved from http://www.the-star. co.ke/news/article-111925/media-monitoring-comittee-warns-against-hate-speech.

Omondi, G. "Obama calls on Kenyans to keep peace". *The Business Daily*, February 5, 2013. Retrieved from http://www.businessdailyafrica.com/Obama-calls-on-Kenyans-to-keep-peace/-/539546/1685538/-/n7b684z/-/index.html.

Ongwae, S. and K. Otieno. "Police probe politicians in killings of Migori youth". *The East African Standard*, December 13, 2011. Retrieved fromhttps://www.standardmedia. co.ke/?articleID=2000048305&story_title=police-probe-politicians-in-killings-of-migori-youth&pageNo=1.

Opiyo, D. "Joining hands for peace". *Daily Nation*, February 24, 2013. Retrieved from http:// elections.nation.co.ke/news/Joining-hands-for-peace-/-/1631868/1703522/-/158gqes/-/index. html.

Otieno, B. "Likoni election results still stand, ODM leaders insist". *The Star,* December 31, 2011. Retrieved from http://www.the-star.co.ke/news/article-35959/likoni-election-results-still-stand-odm-leaders-insist.

Sigei, J. "Land question divides experts and politicians right down the middle". *Daily Nation*, February 7, 2013. Retrieved from http://elections.nation.co.ke/news/Land-issue-divides-experts-and-politicians/-/1631868/1687056/-/124ey85/-/index.html.

Smith, D. "Kenyan elections marred by Mombasa violence". *The Guardian*, March 4, 2013. Retrieved from http://www.theguardian.com/world/2013/mar/04/kenyan-elections-marred-mombasa-violence.

Synovate. KARF Audience Research Establishment Survey Q1 2011. London: Synovate, Ltd. 2011. Retrieved from http://aitec.usp.net/Broadcast%20&%20Film%20Africa,%205-6%20 July%202011,%20Nairobi/JoeOtin_Synovate_Broadcast&FilmAfrica_6-7July2011,Nairobi. pdf

Wanyoro, C. "CORD braves bid to disrupt rally in Embu vote chase". *Daily Nation*, February 16, 2013. Retrieved from http://elections.nation.co.ke/news/cord-braves-bid-to-disrupt-rally-in-Embu-vote-chase/-/1631868/1695510/-/2r4fw7z/-/index.html.

Getting it 'Wrong' (Again)? Wahojiwa vs. Wapiga Kura in the 2013 Kenyan Election[1]

Thomas P. Wolf *

Introduction

Raila Odinga and Uhuru Kenyatta are locked in a neck and neck race heading into the last five days of Monday's General Election.
According to three opinion polls commissioned by the Nation Media Group, a runoff [sic] between Mr. Odinga of the Coalition for Reforms and Democracy (Cord) and Mr. Kenyatta (Jubilee) is inevitable.[2]
The polls show that Mr. Odinga would win during the second round of voting, largely benefitting from Musalia Mudavadi's supporters. Mr. Mudavadi of the Amani coalition is tipped to claim third position in the March 4 General Election (*Daily Nation*, 2013b).

A cruel hoax is being recklessly but gleefully played on innocent Kenyans. This hoax is the self-serving computer-generated numbers touted as opinion polls by pollsters.
These pollsters, if one blindly believes them, are showing that the two leading presidential candidates are tied and we should prepare for a second round of voting. Nothing could be further from the truth.
These polls are utter nonsense and I refuse to believe one single one. I am a religious believer in pollsters, but credible ones that use science and not fiction, black magic or fantasy [Abdullahi, 2013].

"How did the pollsters get it so wrong?!" Based upon the significant gap between the official results of the 4 March 2013 presidential election and the final set of survey results released less than two weeks earlier – together with the widely publicized assumption that a second round, run-off contest was inevitable – it was this question that reverberated most loudly in its aftermath. Indeed, as one Kenyan journalist put it shortly after the election: "The pollsters in Kenya have lost face. They were clueless as to what was happening on the ground" (Kabukuru, 2013a).[3]

* Dr. Wolf is a Research Analyst for Ipsos-Kenya (formerly Ipsos-Synovate, formerly Synovate, formerly The Steadman Group; (citations of these results use the operative company name at the time). Based on the author's access to the data as well as the company's leading profile among the public, through the media, this paper relies primarily on Ipsos' survey-results. The analysis and views expressed in this paper are his own.

Given the repeated claims by representatives of the survey firms of the 'scientific' nature of their work in the face of a widely skeptical political class, and a public for whom the 'toy' of random sample surveys remains relatively new, this remains an important question. And this is so even if, in contrast to the previous election, the country was spared any serious reactive-violence, attributed by some – at least in part – to the "false expectations" such polls had raised then, since none had shown incumbent President Mwai Kibaki as leading.[4] Moreover, and notwithstanding the Supreme Court's dismissal of the two petitions filed (by Odinga and Africog, a local governance NGO) to contest the official results as declared by the Independent Election and Boundaries Commission (IEBC), this chapter will show that even after the election, questions remain as to just how 'wrong' the pollsters were, and to the extent they may have been, what could account for this.

In addition, however, there are other (and perhaps less contentious) questions that are also addressed, including especially: (1) what did the polls show about the evolving field of candidates prior to the formation of running-mate coalitions, and what factors appear to have caused whatever major (and largely uncontentious) shifts in the survey figures that occurred during and after this period; (2) how much did these poll results change as a consequence of the completion of voter-registration that was conducted for a one-month period from 18 November 2012, and then after the official identification of presidential candidates with their deputy presidential running-mates the following month; and (3) how did the survey firms respond to their having 'gotten it wrong' after the results were officially declared?

Attempting to answer these questions first requires some appreciation of the context in which these elections occurred.

2013 Election background: Competitive uncertainty and the 'Certitude of Surveys'

In seeking to understand the role of pre-election polls in Kenya, of critical importance – beyond the imperative of possessing state power itself – are two related realities. The first is the tentative or 'quasi' nature of Kenya's democracy, in which elections cannot be assumed to conform to those in established liberal political systems, several aspects of which shall become evident in the description of events and discussion which follows.[5]

The second is the increasingly competitive nature of the country's electoral politics in recent years. Several factors account for this. One was the return to multi-party competition in 1992. Another was the insertion of presidential term-limits in that year (as part of President Daniel arap Moi's strategy to diffuse the challenge that such an 'opening' of political space represented), leading to the retirement of now, two presidents (Moi and Mwai Kibaki), making presidential succession more frequent and thus national leadership itself more uncertain. A third factor has been the nearly equal division in the country between those supporting continuity and change, at least as represented by the continuation in, or barring from, presidential power, the two ethnic communities that have 'monopolized' it since independence: the Kikuyu and the Kalenjin (whatever the tensions between these two groups).[6] Finally, and with specific relevance to the 2013 election, the fact of power-sharing under the Grand Coalition Government during 2008-2012 fostered what "some have termed [the country's] most liberal period since independence"

(Holmquist, 2014), an interlude that could not be assumed to continue once the 'winner-take-all' presidential system embodied in the new constitution took effect.

In such an environment, public affairs surveys in general and voter-intention polls in particular have both reflected this freer atmosphere and contributed to it – while receiving considerable public approval – by riveting attention on government performance and the broader competition for power.[7] In large part, this was a consequence of the 'marketing-magnet' such surveys had become, with most media outlets eager to energetically trumpet (if less frequently prepared to pay for) them, especially after their generally impressive track-record in the previous two elections (2002, 2007) and the two constitutional referenda (2005, 2010[8]); indeed, Kenya appears to lead across Africa in terms of the frequency and breadth of subject matter of such surveys, and their coverage by the media (Wolf, 2009: 281-82).[9] As such, it had become more difficult to dismiss their results as 'fake' by those inclined to do so, while bolstering – perhaps too uncritically – the confidence of those shown to be initially enjoying significant leads, and later, poised for victory, in actual election campaigns.

Beyond just encouraging confidence or despondency, however, in the extended 'pre-election' period, these voter-intention surveys played a number of significant roles, especially but not limited to the presidential contest. These include: indicating the size and cross-ethnic distribution of support with regard to assessing candidates' viability and thus subsequently, party nominations, including potential deputy president running-mate selection; mobilizing important symbolic-rhetorical and material-financial campaign support both domestically and internationally; attracting and holding media (and diplomatic) attention; and guiding campaign strategy once the ballot-choices were set, especially in terms of the contrast between (a) seeking to win over 'undecided' voters and (b) maximizing turnout in areas where support was already considered strong.[10] While all such factors likewise applied to the 2007 contest, the overall 2013 electoral environment was different in a number of important respects, beyond the absence of an incumbent seeking re-election.[11]

Two contrasts were a function of the new constitution: first, that an outright majority is henceforth required for a first round victory, failing which a second round, run-off contest between the top two candidates is to be held; and second, that each presidential candidate must formally name a deputy-presidential running mate at the time of submitting one's own nomination to the IEBC, rather than selecting a vice-president once in office as was previously the case.[12]

Away from the constitution, another contrast relates to the 'menu' of the main presidential candidates.[13] Prior to the 2007 contest there was never any doubt that Kibaki would seek re-election, whereas only in August of that year did the constellation of his opponents become clear: that it would comprise two major factions/parties: Odinga's Orange Democratic Movement (ODM), and Kalonzo's ODM-Kenya, notwithstanding the fact that these two leaders had been united within the Liberal Democratic Party (LDP) in the 2002 contest (in support of Kibaki) and during the first (2005) constitutional referendum when they had successfully fought against the draft's ratification (which Kibaki supported).

With regard to this 2013 election, however, Odinga was early on identified as the only serious challenger against whomever the 'Kibaki' side would front, though it was unclear whether he would have only one credible opponent. Most prominent initially was William Ruto, MP for

Eldoret North and initially Minister for Agriculture representing the Odinga/ODM side of the power-sharing Grand Coalition Government. Almost immediately after breaking with Odinga by the end of 2009,[14] he sought to 'market' himself as a presidential candidate in his own right, though few took such ambition for the top 'prize' seriously. Among various factors contributing to this view were: the modest size of his quite disparate Kalenjin community (14% of Kenya's population), his association with some of the negative aspects of Moi's 24-year reign (including several highly visible on-going 'corruption' cases in the courts), his vigorous opposition to the widely popular new constitution leading up to the 2010 referendum, and his relatively modest personal wealth (given what is required for such a campaign).[15] As such, most observers saw his efforts as aimed at establishing himself as the most valuable running-mate with a substantial ethnic bloc-vote in tow wherever he went.

Kenyatta, from the country's 'First Family', was in a different category altogether. This was so not just because his own Kikuyu and other 'Mt. Kenya people' constitute nearly one-third of the electorate, and his family's almost limitless wealth, but also because of his previous (however unimpressive) presidential attempt in 2002.[16] Yet several factors militated against a Kenyatta candidacy, at least at this time.

Above all was the matter of his case before the International Criminal Court, having become, along with Ruto and four others, a defendant at The Hague from January 2012 when the charges against them (first unveiled in December 2010) were confirmed, stemming from the violence that followed the 2007 election. At a minimum, there were four aspects to this fact.[17] First, some expected, or at least hoped, that the leadership-integrity provisions of the new constitution (in Chapter Six) would prevent them both from contesting (*Saturday Nation*, 2011). Second, even if they were not barred from doing so, it was considered even less likely, at least until mid-2012,[18] that either would be able to effectively campaign due to the expected commencement of their cases well before the election.[19] Third, whatever Kenyatta's and Ruto's common (anti-ICC) cause, many likewise assumed that due to the enmity between sizable proportions of their respective communities extending back much earlier than the 2008 post-election violence, a Kikuyu-Kalenjin alliance was an electoral non-starter (Lynch, 2011: 182-200; 211-12).[20]

A final factor militating against a Kenyatta candidacy was the profound anxiety among a small but highly influential group of political and business leaders associated with the Kibaki/Party of National Unity (PNU) side of the Grand Coalition Government. Two issues were involved here. One was an assumption (or at least concern) that even if Kenyatta could overcome the obstacles noted above, after a decade of 'Kikuyu rule' (under Kibaki, and notwithstanding the previous five years of 'power-sharing' with Odinga), the level of the nation's 'Kikuyu fatigue' was too high for him (or anyone else from this community) to mount a viable campaign.[21]

The other was economic anxiety over the ICC issue: that whatever the ultimate outcome of these cases, electing a president with such an 'albatross' around his neck (let alone having a running-mate with the same burden) would likely trigger inestimable damage to their own considerable business interests – acquired or at least considerably augmented since Moi's departure just a decade earlier – in the form of punitive measures imposed by Kenya's most important trading and development 'partners.[22] As such, a Kenyatta candidacy was simply not a risk worth taking. But if 'not (yet) Uhuru', then who?

Initially, the most likely alternative seemed to be Musyoka, given the vital role he had played in first, shoring up the legitimacy of Kibaki's dubious December 2007 election by accepting Kibaki's offer of the vice-presidency, and later, when he was not attending the massive 'peace' and 'prayer' rallies headlined by Kenyatta and Ruto, undertaking numerous 'shuttle-diplomacy' visits in an ultimately futile attempt at the international level to ward off the ICC threat (*The Standard*, 2011a).[23] Indeed, as of March 2011, a Synovate poll found that among those who supported Kenyatta as their future presidential choice, Musyoka had a significant, if modest, lead over Ruto in terms of his preferred running-mate (35% vs. 29%; Synovate, 2011), however hypothetical these options still were, evidently reflecting a combination of his own anti-ICC efforts and Ruto's recent ICC indictment (along with other factors mentioned above).

From mid-2011, however, Musyoka suffered increasing isolation by the rest of the 'G-7', the set of leaders of Kenya's larger ethnic groups (aside from the Luo) united by an anti-Odinga agenda. At least in part, this was due to the, stark shift in the stance on the ICC issue by (fellow-Kamba) Musyoka-associate and Minister for Justice, Constitutional Affairs, and National Cohesion, Mutula Kilonzo, who suddenly began to trumpet support for it (*Daily Nation*, 2012a; *The Standard*, 2012d).Such exclusion, eventually reflected in Kilonzo's replacement by Eugene Wamalwa, younger brother of the late Vice-President Kijana Wamalwa (while he suffered de facto demotion to the Education ministry),[24] suggested (to some, including Wamalwa himself) that the latter was subsequently being considered for this role. And this 'demotion' was effected even if it was the vice-president himself – responsible for Kilonzo's appointment to the cabinet in the first place – who formally made this recommendation to President Kibaki.[25]

However, in the absence of any other viable 'Mt. Kenya' candidate following the death of Internal Security minister (and former vice-president) George Saitoti in a mysterious helicopter crash in June 2012 (KTN, 2013), and later with the quick-collapse of the 'agreement' with Musalia Mudavadi in December that he stand in Kenyatta's stead (Capital-FM, 2012),[26] the 'Kenyatta option' to an Odinga presidency was the only credible one left.

Altogether, such uncertainties on the anti-Odinga side of the political divide thus made the poll numbers during 2011-2012 even more important to key actors than they had been hitherto. For example, according to a March 2011 survey, while Odinga enjoyed a clear lead with 38%, Kenyatta and Ruto were far 'behind', with 18% and 8%, respectively (with another 8% either "undecided" or unwilling to reveal their presidential preferences; Synovate, 2011).[27] Moreover, as late as one month to the deadline of the filing of binding coalition agreements (4 December 2012), uncertainties remained as to just which leaders, with their (in several cases, new) political parties in tow, would be aligned with whom (i.e., deputy presidential running-mates, preferred Speakers in the two houses of parliament, and so on; *Sunday Nation*, 2012).[28]

Aside from the aborted effort to have Kenyatta withdraw for Mudavadi (cited above), the most striking example of such uncertainty was the eventual Odinga-Musyoka partnership, not cemented until the first week of December (*Daily Nation*, 2012c).[29] Earlier, in August 2012, the latter claimed that he and Ruto had agreed on a joint ticket (presumably, with himself the presidential candidate; *Sunday Standard*, 2012). And just a week before the Kenyatta-Ruto announcement, Odinga had attempted to strike a similar deal with the latter (*Daily Nation*, 2012c),[30] while barely a week before he joined Odinga as his running-mate, Musyoka claimed that Kenyatta and Ruto had earlier agreed to support his candidacy but had subsequently 'betrayed' him (*The Star*, 2012).[31]

The above discussion suggests the general point that responses to the pollsters' main question – "If the next presidential election were held now, whom would you vote for if that person is a candidate?" – from surveys conducted in advance of the forging of key alliances and the official identification of candidates, are less indications of actual voting intentions as opposed to more general measures of individuals' popularity;[32] moreover, most (though not all) Kenyans appear to eschew voting for candidates lacking any conceivable chance of winning – which the polls themselves help to provide – however much they might admire or identify with them.[33] In the context of the 2013 election, therefore, it was only from mid-January (when the relevant question was changed to ask: "Which pair of candidates for president and deputy president do you intend to vote for in the forthcoming election?") that the polls began to approximate the election's voting patterns.[34]

At the same time, whereas survey results are based on 'private' interviews in which respondents appear generally confident that their identities will not be revealed, the same cannot always be said for their choices at polling stations. Indeed, pre-election intimidation in favor of certain parties/candidates is apparently quite widespread, which could also cause voters to 'change their minds' as they cast real ballots (Ferree et al, 2014: 16). However significant such considerations, the basic question remains: how true a reflection of voters' intentions are such 'late-hour' polls, at least at the time they are conducted?

Crunching – or 'massaging' – the numbers?: The Pollsters vs. the IEBC

When a politician complains about an independent opinion poll, it could mean the polling was conducted without undue influence from vested political interests. This is a good thing given our recent history when the country moved close to a civil war over disputed presidential results.
At the time, at least one pollster was accused of having been influenced to swing the results of its research one way, and although no evidence was ever provided to prove this, the huge gap between the pollster's results and others was puzzling [*The Standard*, 2011].[35]

For years, Odinga's campaign relied heavily on pollsters, who continuously painted him as leading in the polls. This costly mistake made Odinga lethargic and made him live in a "make-believe-bubble" based on the assumption that victory was already assured [Kabukuru, 2013a].

The final outcome had local analysts scratching their heads. The difference [between the polls and the official results] was surprising and way outside the margin of error of what most local pollsters had predicted…
The mystery of how the polls were at variance with the final official IEBC results confound many to date [*The Standard*, 2014].

With the above context in mind, the record of Ipsos' presidential voter-intention polls over nearly a four-year period leading up to the March 2013 election may be considered (Fig. 1).

Figure 1*: Support for potential/actual (main) presidential candidates: 2009-2013[36]

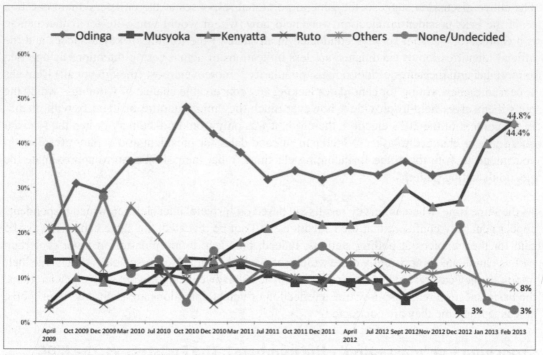

*For reasons of visual clarity, percentages are shown for only the top two candidates, their (eventual) deputy president running-mates, all others combined, and those who preferred no one/were still undecided.

Several points may be derived from these trend-figures. First, in the initial aftermath of the formation of the Grand Coalition Government in 2008, many of Odinga's supporters assumed that the position of prime minister would become permanent following its incorporation into a new constitution (the specification of which was well underway by the middle of 2009). Consequently, at the start of 2009, relatively few (about 20%) respondents identified him as their presidential choice for the next election. However, towards the end of that year, and especially after January 2010, when both sides of that government abruptly agreed on a presidential system (Wolf, 2010), an increasing number of these supporters (among others) expressed their intention to vote for him as president, with his overall level of support peaking just after its August 2010 promulgation at nearly 50%.

Second, immediately thereafter (January 2011), Kenyatta's rating rose markedly, following first, his 'anointing' as the undisputed future leader of the Kikuyu by cabinet minister John Michuki (*The Star*, 19 October 2010), and subsequently, his identification as one of six "main suspects" in the cases opened by the ICC's Chief Prosecutor, Luis Moreno-Ocampo, in December 2010.

Third, from mid-2011 through 2012, and with support for all other candidates largely depressed to between 10% and 20%, the gap between Odinga and Kenyatta was relatively constant, with the former's support nearly unchanging at about one-third of all respondents. Once their deputy president running-mates were known, however, support for both jumped significantly (by more than 10%) in January 2013, with a concomitant decline in support for all others, and dramatically so in terms of the proportion of those still undecided, which had swung upwards in December when a brief moment of major uncertainty occurred on both sides of the main political divide (as noted above): whether Kenyatta would be replaced by Mudavadi, and who would be Odinga's running-mate. Most significant, however, Odinga still enjoyed a clear lead (of 6%), and one that was statistically unchanged since September 2012 (when both were 10% lower (36% vs. 30%).[37]

Finally, the last surveys in mid-late February by four firms revealed that this gap had been closed, putting the two main pairs of candidates in a statistical tie, though neither within 5% of a first round win, as the balance needed to achieve this remained with a combination of support for all the 'minor' candidates combined (about 8%, most of this for Mudavadi) and those still undecided and/or who declined to reveal their preferences (about 3%), as shown in Table 1:

Table 1: Final pre-election survey results of four Kenyan firms[38]

Survey Firm	Sample Size	Completion Date	Kenyatta-Ruto	Odinga-Musyoka	Mudavadi-Kioni	Others/Undecided-RTA*
Ipsos-Synovate	5,971	19 Feb.	44.8%	44.4%	5.2%	2.7%/2.9%
Strategic PR	2,500	26 Feb.	43.8%	45.7%	5.7%	4.7%/2.0%
Infotrak-Harris[39]	3,444	26 Feb.	45.0%	46.0%	5.0%	2.6%/2.0%
Consumer Insight	2,500	26 Feb.	44.3%	46.8%	4.2%	4.7%

*No breakdown is available for "others" /"undecided" or those who refused to answer (RTA) in the Consumer Insight poll.

Such figures, collectively having far less variance than was the case in 2007 (Wolf, 2009: 288), underscored the fact that the contest between the top two candidates was so close that (aside from any irregularities) voter turnout would likely determine which of the two would win most votes, as well as whether either could attain a first round victory.[40] When the IEBC declared the official results, this is just what Jubilee managed to (barely) achieve, obtaining 50.07% of all votes cast.[41] So where did this leave the survey firms, and Ipsos-Synovate in particular?

The post-election poll debate: Proof or posture?

In the wake of the IEBC's declaration, the survey firms found themselves in a quandary: remain silent and thus imply admission of a modest but widely-noted professional error, or alternatively, defend their polls and thereby add their voice to those questioning the IEBC's figures, even if far less directly than had CORD and Africog in filing their petitions with the Supreme Court.

In the event, only Ipsos-Synovate chose to publicly revisit its final survey results, which it did within a week of the IEBC's declaration of results. In seeking to straddle this divide, it undertook an analysis aimed at defending its credibility while avoiding the then-ongoing controversy about the integrity of the official results. In its media release of 15 March, therefore,[42] it based its analysis on the official, IEBC figures (since no alternative ones existed), and (among other calculations) compared the reported turnout rate in the two sets of fifteen counties where Kenyatta and Odinga won most votes,[43] which revealed a 6% advantage for the former (Ipsos-Synovate, 2013c). Given how populous these 30 counties are, this gap explained most (but not quite all) of Jubilee's winning margin, and total votes. Aside from this 'anomaly' for the Kenyatta figure, however, the release underscored the fact that all of the official results for the seven remaining candidates were within its survey's margin-of-error (as shown in Table 2):[44]

Table 2: Ipsos-Synovate vs. the IEBC (Media Release)

Presidential Candidate	Ipsos-Synovate February, 2013 Results	IEBC March 4 Results	Variance	Error-Margin
Uhuru Kenyatta	44.82%	50.07%	5.25%	Higher than error margin
Raila Odinga	44.36%	43.31%	-1.05%	Within error margin
Musalia Mudavadi	5.18%	3.93%	-1.25%	Within error margin
Peter Kenneth	1.61%	0.59%	-1.02%	Within error margin
Martha Karua	0.84%	0.36%	-0.48%	Within error margin
Mohamed Dida	0.20%	0.43%	0.23%	Within error margin
James ole Kiyiapi	0.05%	0.33%	0.28%	Within error margin
Paul Muite	0.00%	0.10%	0.10%	Within error margin
Rejected Votes (IEBC)	0.00%	0.88%	0.88%	N/A
Undecided (Polls)	2.95%	0.00%	-2.95%	N/A

Notes:
- The total positive variance amounts to +6.74%
- The total negative variance amounts to -6.75%

An additional factor emphasized in the Media Release was the 'evaporation' of 2.14% from the six minor candidates (combined), most of which appears to have gone to Kenyatta, a critical gain considering his miniscule margin above the 50% hurdle.[45] Whether such attrition stemmed from a desire of their supporters to avoid the high cost of a possible second round contest (which had received considerable media attention),[46] and/or to avoid casting ballots for candidates – however admired during the campaign – who anyone with the least knowledge of the polls knew had no chance of winning, is unclear, and was left to speculation.[47]

Beyond the figures presented in the Media Release, it later emerged that this firm had slightly weakened its own case by failing to remove from its calculation the 188 respondents (i.e., 2.95%) who declined to reveal their vote-intentions. Had this been done, the numbers for all the candidates would have been higher, but especially those of the leading two pairs: Kenyatta-Ruto to 46.4%, and Odinga-Musyoka to 45.4%, putting Jubilee's total within a range of 45.1%-47.7% (based on an error-margin of about +/- 1.3%).

Beyond such re-calculations, however, the firm's analysts called attention to Jubilee's gain of 6% since its January survey – a trend, it was argued, that most likely continued over the last two weeks of the campaign.[48] It was suggested, therefore, that the question to be asked was not why its poll results were 'wrong', but rather, how close to the IEBC's figures would they have been had an additional survey been conducted the day before the election?[49]

Given the drama surrounding the nationally-televised Supreme Court proceedings of the several presidential election petitions, overall reaction to the company's analysis was muted. Yet, while Jubilee supporters remained silent, several complaints were received (via SMSs and social media) from those associated with CORD on the grounds that since the IEBC figures themselves were 'incorrect' (a claim impossible to refute), Ipsos-Synovate, whether by design of default, was simply lending legitimacy to a 'stolen' election. And subsequently, the fact that much of the evidence amassed in support of the two petitions was disallowed on technical grounds (and thus never examined by the Court) eliminated a potential opportunity to at least partially 'rescue' the pollsters.[50]

Once the drama associated with these petitions had subsided, intermittent criticisms of the pollsters (and especially of Ipsos-Synovate), presumably due to its higher credibility, or at least profile) were forthcoming from both sides. For example, a senior CORD politician complained to the author that "you misled us", referring to their apparent assumption – as noted above, based on the polls – that a run-off election was inevitable (Personal Interview, Nairobi, 19 August 2013). For their part, and against the backdrop of Jubilee's robust pre-election prediction of an outright first round victory[51] – and their extremely narrow win (in terms of reaching the 50%+1 threshold) – when this subject arose, the most common response by its officials and supporters was a repeat of pre-election accusations that the survey firms were either incompetent, pro-CORD, or both. For example, interviewed for a story looking back at the election one year later, TNA Secretary-General Onyango Oloo 'revealed' that the Jubilee campaign had made use of a foreign survey firm (which he declined to identify),[52] on the grounds that "we didn't trust the local ones, since they failed to take into account the ethnic factor" (*The Standard*, 2014).[53]

At the very least, such a criticism is misplaced, however, since random sampling (among registered voters) should accurately capture the electorate's ethnic profile (among other demographic factors),[54] even if (as noted above) local firms decline to release results with such ethnic correlations.[55] What could have added value, however, are some finely-tuned voter turnout scenario-estimates based on such factors (and using past experience), which none of the local firms offered,[56] a task that might have been performed by either local or foreign analysts using existing data. Indeed, the Jubilee campaign strategy document described by one local journalist appears to have served exactly this purpose (Kabukuru, 2013b).[57] Yet this story made no reference to the use of any foreign survey firm; it said only that a team of Jubilee experts had "crunched the numbers" before declaring that 'UhuRuto' would win on the first round with more than 6 million votes. As such, it seems doubtful that any such 'foreign firm' was used, at least for the actual data-gathering, thus raising the question as to why impulse to denigrate local firms in the first place?[58]

Conclusion: Pollsters' past, pollsters' future?

As was the case in the previous election (Kanyinga et al, 2010; USAID, 2008; Throup, 2008; KPTJ, 2008), controversy will remain as to the credibility of the official presidential election results.[59] A key difference, however, is that whereas in 2007 the dispute was over which candidate obtained the most votes, in 2013 the issue was whether Jubilee actually achieved a first round victory (despite an initial claim by Odinga that he actually won the most votes (NTV, 2013). Given that the message from all the pollsters, as noted above, was the likelihood (if not certainty) of a second round, run-off contest, it was the failure of this to materialize that constituted the main challenge to their credibility. In other words, if Jubilee had obtained even a single vote less than the outright majority it needed for a first round win, the widespread conclusion would have been that 'the pollsters were right', even if the statistical distance between 'right' and 'wrong' in this case is infinitesimal.

The failure of the second round contest to materialize, therefore, invited a number of quite scathing criticisms, such as this one from a U.S.-based Kenya doctoral student:

> The results were nowhere near what the polls had predicted a week to the election. Most opinion polls showed the race as close, with Mr. Odinga leading by two percentage points. My own pre-election analysis several weeks before the election warned against belief in the national polls as they were over-estimating Mr. Odinga's support. The outcome of the election showed that even I had underestimated the extent to which the national polls had over-estimated Mr. Odinga's popularity. The polls' biggest error was to base their results on interviews of registered voters, as opposed to likely voters.[60]

> In reality Mr. Kenyatta won the election long before voting day. His strongholds, relatively wealthier and more urban, had higher voter registration rates than Mr. Odinga's (85.4% vs. 69.7%).[61] This coupled by [sic] a higher turnout rates [sic] on polling day (88.6% vs. 84%) pretty much assured Mr. Kenyatta's election as Kenya's 4th president [Opalo, 2013].[62]

While making no specific reference to this assertion, however, it was subsequently contradicted in the analysis of the election-day exit poll conducted by a team of Western academics. They asked the question: "Do the exit poll results confirm the IEBC counts?", and found that they did not. Specifically, they estimated that after removing from their sample those who had refused to be interviewed, but taking into account the dominant voting patterns in the areas where they voted, "Overall, Odinga took around 45.3% of the vote and Kenyatta 45.6%, a statistical tie", results that "are consistent with the final Ipsos pre-election tracking poll implemented ten days before the election." They were therefore behooved to ask:

> Could last minute swings in the share of votes for the third through sixth place finishers to Kenyatta have pushed him over the 50% threshold? It is extremely unlikely: the sum of all the presidential candidates besides Odinga who lost votes moving from the Ipsos poll to the IEBC tally only produces 2.8%. This implies that about half of the 5.27 percentage point increase Kenyatta received when moving from the Ipsos poll to the IEBC count would have had to have come from Odinga supporters – the most unlikely group to switch their votes. Moreover, because the exit poll interviews people directly after they voted, it should capture all last minute swings in support. In sum, registration, turnout, and shifts in candidate preference do not seem to explain the difference between the exit poll and the IEBC results [Ferree et al, 2014: 12-15].[63]

What, then, is one to make of this discrepancy? Until and unless further (and conclusive) evidence regarding the conduct of the election emerges, we are bound to suffer the uncertainties posed by this author some two weeks before the actual event:

> While restoring credibility – and thus legitimacy – to the electoral process after the debacle of 2007-8 is a far more important goal than is any research objective related to pre-election polls, voting behavior, or the study of politics more broadly, being able to pursue any of the latter depends absolutely on the achievement of the former [Wolf, 2013].[64]

As suggested above, looking through a broader, 'governance' lens, the main contrast between the last two elections and their aftermaths was the fact of the 'institutionalization of grievance', in that the 'loser' (again, Odinga) agreed to take his dispute to the new Supreme Court, and abide by its ruling against him;[65] the question of the 'true' results as suggested (if not 'proven') by either pre-election or exit polls thus became moot in practical terms.

Whatever the case, given this 'slice' of history as related to the 2013 election, the fact of Jubilee's post-election near-monopolization of power at the national level – in stark contrast to the de facto or de jure power-sharing arrangements over most of the previous decade[66] – leaves the future 'space' available to civil society voices, including survey firms and the media through whom they convey their findings, open to serious question.[67] In this regard, their fate in terms of further, more restrictive legislative fetters, cannot be ruled out. As such, how the media, the public, leading political figures and especially the government respond to and/or treat the pollsters is likely to be a more precise 'barometer' of the country's governance environment over the near future than are the survey results they obtain from, and share with, the Kenyan public.

Notes

1   In English, "survey respondents" vs. "voters"…

2   Each of these two alliances was a combination of several political parties. For CORD, these were Odinga's Orange Democratic Movement (ODM) and Kalonzo Musyoka's Wiper Democratic Movement, and for Jubilee, William Ruto's United Republican Party (URP, registered in January, 2012) and Kenyatta's National Alliance (TNA, registered five months later).

3   The writer is here quoting P. Githae of *The People Daily*.

4   This is true notwithstanding significant variations between Kenya's four leading survey firms' final polls: an Odinga advantage between 2% and 10% (Wolf, 2009: 288); an election-day exit poll gave Odinga a 6% margin (Gibson and Long, 2009). Such an accusation-attribution was subsequently repeated often, such as by several Kibaki-aligned MPs in their (eventually successful) effort to enact the Publication of Electoral Opinion Polls Act in 2012 (*The Star*, 2011a).

5   Cotrell and Ghai (2013) provide a review of the 2013 election's democratic/constitutional shortcomings. For an earlier conceptual critique of 'liberal'/'Western' elections with reference to Kenya, see, Chweya (2002), and for Africa more generally, see, Basedau et al (2007).

6   Together, they represent just over one-third of Kenya's population. Relevant here is the fact that a Kalenjin (Moi) served as deputy to Kenya's first president (Jomo Kenyatta) during most of the latter's fifteen years in power, and that for all of his twenty-four year incumbency (excepting the final three months), the country's second president (Moi) partnered with Kikuyu vice-presidents (that could be selected at will, according to the previous constitution, from among elected Members of the National Assembly).

7   Some relevant background is provided by Wolf, who noted that as of early 2008, some 55% of Kenyans believed that such vote-intentions surveys "strengthen democracy", whereas only 12% felt that they "weaken" it, the remainder being uncertain about this issue, or having no opinion (2009: 293). In a mid-2014 survey, 72% expressed either "a lot" or "some confidence" in survey firms, as opposed to 22% with "only a little" or "no confidence" in them (the latter figure being just 8%; Ipsos, 2014b).

8   Removing those who were still "undecided" from those interviewed, the three main survey firms produced the following results in their final polls: Synovate – 73%; Infotrak – 72%; Strategic Public Relations – 77%, as compared with the official result of 72% (Daily Nation, 2010).

9   Regionally, the few additional published assessments of such (decidedly less frequent) surveys related to elections range from the scathingly negative by Makulilo (2012) for Tanzania's 2010 exercise, to the more positive in connection with Uganda's 2011 election by de Torrente (2013). For an early pan-African treatment of the increasing profile of more general (non-election related) survey research, see Bratton et al (2005).

10   This claim, based on a number of interviews and casual conversations, is made even if it simultaneously invites more systematic research.

11   The term is used only in its most formal sense. Odinga, as prime minister, had been 'sharing power' with Kibaki, according to the terms of the National Accord, while Kenyatta, who was serving as one of two deputy prime ministers (representing the Kibaki/PNU side of the government), had 'incumbent-like' status as a function of this very fact. As such, neither of these candidates could easily re-invent himself as an 'outsider'.

12   For its part, the new (2009) Political Parties Act required the formal registration of any party coalitions with the Registrar of Political Parties.

13   The total number of such candidates was similar: nine in 2007 and eight in 2013.

14   He did so without ever formally resigning from ODM which would have necessitated defending his parliamentary seat in a by-election. Earlier in that year, Odinga had suspended Ruto from the Cabinet in connection with allegations of a maize-importation scandal.

15   There were widespread rumors that most if not all of the costs of such 'early' campaign efforts were covered by 'benefactors'.

16   Kibaki defeated him by nearly a 2-to-1 margin. While many observers have suggested 'common-sense' reasons why Moi imposed him as the Kenya African National Union's (KANU) candidate, this subject – including Kenyatta's own initial receptivity to Moi's wish – remains to be thoroughly researched.

17   Though Ruto had returned to Cabinet as minister for Higher Education, he was relieved of this position in August 2011 due to corruption charges he was facing in the Kenyan courts – not because of his ICC indictment. The explains why Kenyatta continued to serve as Deputy PM (an appointment which Kibaki pointedly declined to revoke), even though he resigned his cabinet position (as Minister of Finance, as did fellow ICC-indictee Francis Muthaura as Secretary to the Cabinet and Head of the Civil Service) shortly after the confirmation of charges against him (*The Standard*, 2012a; The Standard, 2012b). Kenyatta also relinquished the chairmanship of KANU, whose National Executive had generated their own pressure on him over the ICC issue (*Daily Nation*, 2012b).

18   On 11 June the Office of the Chief Prosecutor announced that it was "not opposed in principle" to having the trials commence after March 2013.

19   Whereas a December election would have marked a full five years since the previous one, and the new constitution sets the election in August, in January 2012 the High Court ruled that it should be held five years after the sitting parliament had been sworn in – thus the 4 March 2013 date. Barring constitutional amendment, however, the next election shall be held on the second Tuesday in August 2017.

20   For a more general discussion on the impact of the ICC cases on the election, see Wolf (2013b).

21   As one local 'alternative' publication put it some two years before the election: "Both the Kikuyu and Kalenjin factors in the Kenyan presidency are…about to be retired for a while with the 2012 election, which will almost certainly take the top office to a region away from Rift Valley and Central (*Weekly Citizen*, 2011). Recall here that by this time, the country's 50 years of independent rule had been evenly divided between these two communities at the presidential level.

22   These two factors raised the importance of the United Democratic Front (UDF) as a potential vehicle for an alternative candidate in case Kenyatta was not able to contest. Such possible use was ironic, however, given that it had initially been registered in mid-2011 on Kenyatta's behalf by a number of key figures around Kibaki reportedly including his Personal Secretary Dr. N. Wanjohi, Intelligence chief M. Gichangi, Ndaragwa MP J. Kioni, and businessman J. Wanjui, among others when it became clear that he would have to abandon KANU but could not take over Kibaki's 2007 election vehicle, PNU, that was now in the hands of G. Saitoti (Personal Interview, Nairobi, 28 September, 2014; Kenya Stockholm Blog, 2011).

23   The elusive goal was either having the cases returned to some judicial process in Kenya, or dropped altogether.

24   Earlier, the Musyoka-led Wiper Democratic Movement party (having been re-named from 'ODM-Kenya') had threatened to take "disciplinary action" against the Justice Minister if he continued to make such "insensitive" remarks. These included his statement shortly after the confirmation-of-charges that it was "immoral" for anyone to be associated with the accused, which many observers subsequently concluded had triggered this 'demotion' (The Standard, 2012c); at the same time, naming his two pet cheetahs 'Mutula' and 'Ocampo', and their cage 'The Hague' in his rural home (*Daily Nation*, 2011) may not have helped, either.

25   As one observer was reported to have commented in response to the several changes made on both sides of the power-sharing divide, "The biggest target was Justice Minister Mutula Kilonzo", whose removal from that position "is a big boost" to Kenyatta and Ruto (Voice of America, 2012).

26   According to several accounts, Ruto would have remained as his running-mate (for example, Weekly Citizen, 2012). In the event, Mudavadi pursued his own lack-lustre presidential campaign, its appeal evidently seriously 'wounded' by this humiliation.

27   Significantly, however (aside from the final pre-election survey when he was paired with Musyoka), only during the latter part of 2010 did Odinga's rating exceed 40% (as shown below) – a fact that must have been worrisome for his supporters, and presumably for him as well.

28   Such fluidity – if not simply self-serving opportunism – among the political elite with regard to the previous election is discussed by Wolf (2009: 290-91).

29   Note, however, that as early as September, 2009 an alternative publication had reported meetings between Odinga and Musyoka operatives with a view towards crafting such an alliance, given Musyoka's fears "that he might fall out of favour with those who call the shots in Central Province" (*Weekly Citizen*, 2009); such negotiations were reported again some two years later (*The Star*, 2011).

30 Two factors reportedly thwarted Odinga's 'advances': his inability to provide convincing ICC-protection 'guarantees', as well as to offer anything approaching what the Kenyatta side could in financial terms, such funds considered vital for him to build his URP (Personal Interview, Nairobi, 23 March 2013).

31 He further claimed that he, Kenyatta and Saitoti had "signed a pact" that only one of the three of them would contest the presidency.

32 Such a summary-point also ignores the actual unfolding of events following the official designation of candidates that can shift voter-appeal, including especially campaign strategy as the election approaches, at least for those voters whose support is not a function of 'automatic' patronage-reward or ethnic loyalty.

33 In this regard, the criticism that conducting presidential voter-intention polls without pairing candidates with deputy presidential running-mates is misleading, given the new constitution's requirements, must be accepted (Ndegwa, 2012). Yet, as indicated above, the field was so fluid until nearly the deadline for the presentation of nomination papers that it would have been quite speculative to gauge the popularity of all such potential pairings.

34 For example, Ipsos-Synovate's January, 2013 poll found that 11% of Kalenjin (among those who claimed to have made up their minds) expressed an intention to vote for Odinga (Ipsos-Synovate, 2013a), a figure which dropped to 9% in its final, February, poll (Ipsos-Synovate, 2013b). In the election, Jubilee obtained over 90% of the vote in 20 out of 41 of Kalenjin-dominant constituencies (Lynch, 2014: 100).

35 In the final set of poll results prior to the 2007 election, two firms gave Odinga a 2% lead and two others gave him a 10% lead (Wolf, 2009: 288). It is unclear, therefore, which particular "pollster" this article was referring to.

36 The results were compiled from SPEC (Social, Political, Economic and Cultural) Barometers April 2009-February 2013. The verbatim question, through the end of 2012, was: 'If the next election were held now, aside from President Kibaki, who would you vote for, if that person was a candidate?' As noted above, for the last two (2013) polls, the question was: 'Which pair of candidates for president and deputy-president do you intend to vote for?'

37 Note again here that this was first survey conducted after completion of the voter registration exercise. For it, and the subsequent, February, survey, only those (randomly-selected) who could produce proof of having registered were interviewed.

38 The Table is adapted from Wikipedia (2013). Sample sizes for Strategic PR and Consumer Insight were obtained from their managements as they do not appear in the Wikipedia entry.

39 One month earlier, Infotrak released results showing Odinga with 51%, Kenyatta with 39%, 7% for the remaining six candidates, and 3% undecided (Infotrak, 2013).

40 For example, and whatever the accuracy of the official results, turnout at the Coast was just 70% in a region where Odinga received 75% of the vote (and where the level of voter registration was also below its share of the national population), which underscores the fact that even a slightly higher turnout there could have forced a run-off, other things begin equal (Saturday Nation, 2014).

41 After the Supreme Court controversially ruled that 'rejected' votes should be excluded in calculating these results, the figures for all candidates increased slightly, especially Kenyatta's (to 50.5%) and Odinga's (to 43.7%).

42 This was two weeks before the Supreme Court issued its judgments on 30 March.

43 These excluded the five counties which were among both of their 'most-votes' totals, due to their high populations, starting with Nairobi.

44 Its county-level survey figures were also largely correct. These included especially those for the seven largest counties, for which three positions had been polled – governor, senator, and women's representative – with the survey obtaining correct results for all, aside from two (close) women's representative contests (in Kakamega and Nakuru).

45 As compared with 5.74% of the vote these candidates collectively obtained, the four pollsters' estimates for all of them (combined) ranged from 7.6% to 10.4%.

46 This included a statement one month before the election from the Finance Minister, Njeru Githae, who told Kenyans to "make up your minds" on the first round since Treasury did not have the additional Ksh. 5b a run-off would cost (Daily Nation, 2013a), and another one by Kenyatta a week before the election who promised to use this money for a new youth fund if Jubilee secured a first round victory (The Star, 2013).

47 In addition, while none of these 'minor' candidates filed an election petition, several of them were said to have (quietly) accused the IEBC of malpractice.

48 Recall here that this survey's fieldwork dates were 15-19 February. Here also note that while the Publication of Electoral Opinion Polls Act (2012) prohibits the publication of such results within five days of an election, it imposes no restriction on the conduct of research during this period.

49 At the same time, not one of the other three survey firms – all of which completed their final pre-election surveys nearly a week after that of Ipsos (on 26 February, as shown in Table 1) – placed Jubilee (even barely) ahead of CORD, as did Ipsos-Synovate.

50 Two lawyers involved, one with each petition, separately estimated that such excluded evidence amounted to "about 80% of what had been amassed for the case" (Personal Interview, Nairobi, 23 April 2014; Personal Interview, Nairobi, 4 September 2014). For critical appraisals of the Court's decisions, see, for example, Kegoro (2013), Maina (2013), and Ongoya (2013).

51 Repeated claims were made at campaign rallies and media appearances of getting 55%, such as by Mukurwe-ini MP, Kabando wa Kabando during a television news-discussion over a month prior to the election (K-24, 2013), and by Mvita MP, Najib Balala, at Jubilee's final rally at Uhuru Park, Nairobi (KTN, 2013a).

52 He similarly declined to reveal in which country the firm is based.

53 For its part, several months after the election The African Report offered a number of 'straw-men' arguments to convince readers that the pre-election results the pollsters had served up were "corrupt" (Njagi, 2013).

54 Thatiah (2014) displays similar ignorance of national random-sampling in his claim that whereas the last set of polls had Kenyatta and Odinga in a virtual tie, when Jubilee strategists "factored in population density", Kenyatta was actually ahead by 7%.

55 Note, however, there is no legal prohibition against doing so, and all raw data that is not client-privileged are always available for purchase, as least from Ipsos.

56 This is just what was called for by a local columnist (Warigi, 2013), echoing (in more detail) a similar suggestion by the author (Wolf, 2013).

57 The report cited is entitled, "A Report on the Analysis of the Registered Voters and the Predictions Thereof."

58 Specifically, the several senior Jubilee officials consulted for his story reportedly told the journalist in question that they were alerted to the 'weakness' of Ipsos-Synovate's results by its published findings for Nakuru County in its January 2013 survey, which they asserted had "greatly underestimated" 'UhuRuto's' assumed popularity there (Personal Interview, Nairobi, 18 August 2014). This assertion is curious, to say the least. Ipsos-Synovate's media release of its January survey included no county-level results, since error-margins at this level (for most counties) would have been too high: +/-5.9% for Nakuru (based on 278 respondents). Moreover, if Jubilee had, nevertheless, been able to obtain the results for this county, they would have found that Jubilee enjoyed a 78%-19% advantage over CORD– in statistical terms almost identical with the official election results nearly two months later – 82.4% to 17.6% – (especially taking into account the associated margin-of-error), surely no cause for "hiring a foreign pollster." Ipsos-Synovate did release results for all key races in Nakuru one month later (based on mobile phone surveys for this and several other counties), but these were published by the media-client who had hired Ipsos-Synovate for the purpose less than two weeks before the election (The Standard, 2013), far too short a period for any firm – local or foreign – to plan, undertake, usefully analyze, and make strategic use of the resultant data. Based on 750 respondents (and thus yielding an error-margin of +/- 3.6%), it showed Jubilee with a 74%-17% advantage over CORD in the presidential race.

59 For more general assessments of the IEBC's performance that raise questions about the official presidential results, see, Africa Confidential (2013), Africog (2013), Carter Center (2013), MARS Group (2013), and KTN (2014). More recent revelations about the 'rot' within the IEBC have only added to doubts about its integrity (Nairobi Law Monthly, 2014).

60   Issenberg (2012) provides numerous examples of this distinction, and methods to exploit it, in the U.S. where the relevant data are far more reliable; just how it could have been applied in the Kenya context is unclear.

61   While helping to explain Jubilee's win, this factor is irrelevant to the pollsters' collective 'failure', since (as noted above) their sampling frames were adjusted on this basis after the voter registration figures were released (early in January 2013).

62   Curiously, Opalo failed to even acknowledge that both Odinga and Africog had immediately announced their intentions to contest the results.

63   This finding was at a slight yet significant variance from the domestic 'civil society' observer parallel vote count exercise. Based on reported results at 7% (952) of all 31,977 polling stations, it estimated Jubilee's vote at 49.7%, with a 2.7% margin-of-error, yielding a possible range of 47.0%-52.4% (Election Observer Group, 2013: 63). At the same time, if the 'true' turnout at all the polling stations where the exit poll was conducted cannot be verified, how were the results at each one weighted to reflect it?

64   A full year after the election, an Ipsos survey found that only 39% of all respondents were "certain" that Jubilee had obtained an outright majority (with a 70%-9% split on this issue between Jubilee and CORD supporters), while 29% were "certain" that they had not (again, with an 8%-54% split between these two sub-sets of the sample; Ipsos, 2014a).

65   A post-election survey found that only 13% backed the proposition that "a true election result is more important than maintaining peace", with 85% of the contrary opinion (Long et al, 2013: 151).

66   The period could be extended further backwards into the later Moi years, if the 'cooperation arrangement' with Odinga's NDP from 1998 and then its absorption into KANU in March, 2002 are taken into account.

67   Again, see Holmquist (2014). A case in point is the recent enactment of a raft of security amendments, several of which are viewed as violating critical constitutional rights (The East African, 2014b). Earlier, the government proposed legislation aimed at 'reigning-in' especially governance/human rights NGOs (part of a clear regional trend; The East African, 2014a). These follow what have been described as potentially "draconian" restrictions on the media embodied in legislation enacted the previous year (BBC, 2013).

Bibliography

Abdullahi, A. 'Opinion polls are a hoax: don't believe them', *Sunday Nation*, 2013. http://elections. nation.co.ke/Blogs/Opinion-polls-are-a-hoax-dont-believe-them/-/1632026/1702594/-/ x98u9iz/-/index.html.

Africa Confidential. 'The Long, Long Vote Count', 54, no. 13, 21 June 2013.

Africog/KPTJ. Election Series: 'Election Day 2013 and its Aftermath', 2013. www.africog.org/ sites/default/files/Election-Day-2013-and-its-Aftermath.pdf.

Alshahid. 'Kenya's referendum: latest opinion Polls show Kenyans support draft law', July 23, 2010; English.alshahid.net/archives/9964.

Basedau, M., G. Erdmann and A. Mehler., eds. *Votes, Money and Violence: Political parties and elections in Sub-Saharan Africa*. Uppsala: NordikAfrikaInstitut, 2007.

BBC News Africa. 'Kenya media: President Kenyatta signs 'draconian' bill, December 17, 2014; www.bbc.com/news/world-africa-25418234.

Bratton, M., R. Mattes and E. Gyimah-Boadi. *Public Opinion, Democracy and Market Reform in Africa*. Cambridge: Cambridge University Press, 2005.

Capital-FM. "Dark forces' arm-twisted me – Uhuru', December 18, 2012; http://www.capitalfm. co.ke/news/2012/12/dark-forces-arm-twisted-me-uhuru/2/.

Carter Center."Observing Kenya's March 2013 National Elections: Final Report". November, 2013.

Cottrell, J. and Y. P. Ghai. "Ethnicity, Nationhood and Pluralism and 2013 Elections". In eds. Y. P. Ghai and J. C. Ghai, *Ethnicity, Nationhood and Pluralism: Kenyan Perspectives,* 107-135. Nairobi: Colorprint, 2013.

Chweya, L."Western Modernity, African Indigene, and Political Order: Interrogating the Liberal Democratic Orthodoxy". In ed. L. Chweya. *Electoral Politics in Kenya*. Nairobi: Claripress, 2002: 1-27.

The East African. 'East African govts to crack down on civil societies, NGOs', November1-7, 2014a.

The East African, 'Kenyatta signs controversial security law', November 20-26, 2014b.

Election Observer Group (ELOG). 'The Historic Vote: Elections 2013', Nairobi; http://www. gndem.org/ELOG_Report_2013.

Ferree, K. E., C. C. Gibson and J. D. Long. "Voting behavior and electoral irregularities in Kenya's 2013 Election". *Journal of Eastern African Studies* 8, no. 1, 2014:153-172.

Gallup. 'The Grand Coalition Government', Public Presentation, Serena Hotel, Nairobi, September; http://www.gallup.com/poll/111634/kenyans-speak-about-their-postelection-crisis. aspx, 2008.

Gibson, C. C., and J. Long."The presidential and parliamentary elections in Kenya, December 2007".

Electoral Studies 28, no 3 (September), 2009: 497-502.

Holmquist, F. 'Kenya: On Edge, Rights at Risk', 2014;http://www.jadaliyya.com/pages/ index/18734/kenya_on-edge-rights-at-risk.

Infotrak Research and Consulting. 'Infotrak Poll on the Race to State House January', 2013; www.nation.co.ke/blob/view/-/1663206/data/447361/-/k4phgf/-/poll/pdf.

Infotrak-Harris. 'An Infotrak Harris Poll on Kenyans' Voting Intentions for the August 4, 2010 Referendum on the Proposed New Constitution'.

Inter Press Service News Agency. 'Kenya's Electoral Opinion Polling Marred by Suspicion', February 27, 2013; http://www.ipsnews.net/2013/02/kenyas-electoral-opinion-polling-marred-by-suspicion/.

Ipsos. SPEC Barometer (Unreleased Data), May 2014a.

Ipsos. SPEC Barometer (Media Release), September 19, 2014b.

Ipsos-Synovate. Political Barometer Survey (Media Release), January 25, 2013a.

Ipsos-Synovate. Political Barometer Survey (Media Release), February 22, 2013b.

Ipsos-Synovate. '4th March IEBC Election Results vis a vis IPSOS February SPEC Poll: Voter Turnout Explains (nearly all) the Difference' (Media Release); March 15, 2013c.

Issenberg, S. *The Victory Lab: The secret science of sinning campaigns*. New York: Crown Publishers, 2012.

K-24 News. 'Kabando: Jubilee will win on first round', January 23, 2013; www.news24.co.ke/ MyNews24/Kabando-Jubilee-will-win-in-first-round-20130129

Kabukuru, W.'The 10 mistakes that Odinga made', New African, April 4, 2013a; http:// newafricanmagazine.com/the-10-mistakes-that-odinga-made/.

———. 'The return of President Kenyatta', New African, April 4, 2013b; http:// newafricanmagazine.com/the-return-of-president-kenyatta/.

Kanyinga, K., J. Long and D. Ndii. 'Was it Rigged?: A Forensic Analysis of Vote Returns in Kenya's 2007 Elections'. In *Tensions and Reversals in Democratic Transitions: The Kenya 2007 General Elections*, eds. K. Kanyinga et al, Nairobi: Society for International Development/ Institute for Development Studies, University of Nairobi, 2010:373-411.

Kegoro, G. 'A Review of the Supreme Court Judgment', Saturday Nation, April 20, 2013.

Kenya Stockholm Blog. 'New Uhuru Party in Secret Recruitment', August 26, 2011; http:// kenyastockholm.com/2011/06/23/uhuru-sneaked-1-2-billion-in-budget-to-pay-fake-company/

KPTJ. 'Unwelcome Evidence', Truth and Justice Digest, Issue 3, September 15, 2008; http:// www.africog.org/category/kptj?page=3

KTN (Kenya Television Network).Inside Story: 'The 2013 Elections', 2014.http://www. nairobiexposed.com/2014/04/22/jicho-pevu-inside-story-2013 elections-part-1-part-2-video/.

KTN (Kenya Television Network). Inside Story: 'Death in Ten Minutes', 2013; http://mail. ktnkenya.com/ktn/video/watch/2000064888/-the-inside-story-mystery-of-saitoti-s-death

Lynch, G. 'Electing the 'alliance of the accused': the success of the Jubilee Alliance in Kenya's Rift Valley'. *Journal of Eastern African Studies* 8, no. 1 2014: 93-114.

————. *I Say to You: Ethnic Politics and the Kalenjin in Kenya*. Chicago: University of Chicago Press, 2011.

Maina, W. 'Five key reasons Kenya's Supreme Court failed crucial election petition test', *The East African*, April 20-26, 2013.

Makulilo, A. 'Where have all researchers gone?' Use and abuse of polls for the 2010 elections in Tanzania". *International Journal of Peace and Development Studies* 3, no. 32012: 33-56.

Mars Group. 'Kenya Audit Report on 2013 Kenyan Presidential Election Results',2013.http:// www.marsgroupkenya.org/blog/2013/09/03/mars-group-kenya-report-audit-report-on-2013-kenyan-presidential-election-results/

Nairobi Law Monthly. 'Secrets of Election 2013', 5, no. 12 (December), 2014: 20-29.

Daily Nation. 'Election to cost Sh25 billion', January 4, 2013a; http://www.nation.co.ke/News/ politics/Election-to-cost-Sh25-billion-/-/1064/1657848/-/7k1nf2z/-/index.html

Daily Nation. 'Second round inevitable, Raila will win in run-off', February 26, 2013b; elections. nation.co.ke/news/Raila-and-Uhuru-in-tight-race-poll-shows/-/1631868/1705518/-/8e5956z/-/ index.html.

Daily Nation. 'Kalonzo left out of Uhuru-Ruto political alliance', February 16, 2012a.

Daily Nation. 'Hunt for Uhuru vehicle stepped up', April 3, 2012b.

Daily Nation. 'Raila and Kalonzo finally sign deal', December 4, 2012c; http://www.nation.co.ke/News/politics/Raila-and-Kalonzo-finally-sign-deal/-/1064/1635856/-/a3xmex/-/index.html

Daily Nation. 'Mutula king of the jungle' January 1, 2011; http://allafrica.com/stories/201101030165.html

Daily Nation. 'Opinion polls correctly predicted public mood' August 5, 2010;http://www.nation.co.ke/Kenya-Referendum/Opinion-polls-correctly-predicted-public-mood-/-/926046/971884/-/7fvmis/-/index.html.

Saturday Nation. 'Low turnout at Coast may have been Cord's undoing', April 19, 2014;http://mobile.nation.co.ke/news/Coast-2013-General-Election-Cord-Turnout/-/1950946/2286164/-/format/xhtml/-/12uc3wlz/-/index.html

Saturday Nation. 'Secrets of Raila meeting with ex-ODM ally', October 13, 2012; kenyauptodate.blogspot.com/2012//what-raila-offered-ruto.html.

Saturday Nation. 'Hague cases set to change the 2012 election game plan', April 9, 2011.

Sunday Nation. 'Presidential aspirants race against time', November 4, 2012.

Ndegwa, C. 'Opinion polls misleading Kenyans',October 5, 2012; http://safariafricaradio.com/index.php/kenya-elections/102-elections-2012/1897-opinion-polls-misleading-kenyans

Njagi, D. 'What if Kenya's election violence points to corrupt pollsters?', The Africa Report, July 22, 2013; http://www.theafricareport.com/News-Analysis/what-if-kenyas-election-violence-points-to-corrupt-pollsters.html.

NTV. 'Raila claims he won elections', March 18, 2013; http://ntv.nation.co.ke/news2/topheadlines/raila-claims-he-won-elections/

Ongoya, E. 'Supreme Court too casual in 'Raila Vs IEBC & Others'; http://www.thepeoplescourt.co.ke/opinions/173-supreme-court-too-casual-in-raila-vs-iebc-others, 2013.

Opalo, K. 'Post Election Report: Kenyan Elections 2013',by Joshua Tucker on March 11, 2013 themonkeycage.org/2013/03/11/post-election-report-kenyan-elections-2013/

Republic of Kenya. *Report of the Independent Review Commission* (IREC), Nairobi, Government Printer, 2008.

The Standard. 'Uhuru: I will not quit, only MPs can push me out of post', January 26, 2012a.

The Standard. 'Kanu plans Uhuru ouster over The Hague trial', January 28, 2012b.

The Standard. 'Wiper castigates defiant Mutula over ICC remarks', January 31, 2012c.

The Standard. 'Storms gather in G7 as Kalonzo ally pays price for utterances', February 17, 2012d.

Sunday Standard. 'Opinion polls controversy and why Jubilee hired a foreign pollster', March 11, 2014.

Sunday Standard. 'Leaders defend Uhuru, Ruto leadership skills', January 13, 2013; http://www.standardmedia.co.ke/?articleID=2000074887&story_title=leaders-defend-uhuru-ruto-leadership-skills.

Sunday Standard. 'Kalonzo, Ruto to form coalition for easy win', August 19, 2012; http://www.standardmedia.co.ke/article/2000064347/kalonzo-ruto-to-form-coalition-for-easy-win

The Star. 'Jubilee takes its pitch to Mt Kenya', February 28, 2013; http://www.the-star.co.ke/news/article-109772/jubilee-takes-its-pitch-mt-kenya

The Star. 'TNA, URP betrayed me – VP', December 3, 2012.

The Star. 'Ban Opinion Polls – PNU', May 13, 2011a; http://www.the-star.co.ke/news/article-63793/ban-opinion-polls-pnu

The Star. 'Kalonzo Emissaries Approach Raila', August 31, 2011b; www.the-star.co.ke/news/article-51207/kalonzo-emissaries-approach-raila

The Star. 'Michuki remarks can incite chaos', October 19, 2010; http://www.the-star.co.ke/news/article-81768/michuki-remarks-can-incite-chaos.

Synovate. 'SPEC Barometer Media Release', April 15, 2011.

Synovate. 'Referendum Baseline Public Opinion Poll' (Media Release), July 23, 2010.

Thatiah, I. 'When Uhuru Kenyatta pulled fast move in TV debate to surge ahead of the pack' *Sunday Nation,* November 23, 2014.

Throup, D. 'The Count'. *Journal of Eastern African Studies* 2, no. 2 (July), 2008: 29-304.

de Torrente, N. 'Understanding the 2011 Ugandan elections: the contribution of public opinion surveys'. *Journal of Eastern African Studies* 7, no. 3 (August), 2013: 530-548.

USAID. 'Kenya's President Lost Disputed Election, Poll Shows', *Frontlines*, August 2008.

Voice of America. 'Kenya Cabinet Reshuffle Changes Presidential Race', March 26, 2012; http://www.voanews.com/articleprintview/179765.html

Warigi, G. 'Pollsters should focus on voter turnout as that will determine next president', *Sunday Nation*, February 9, 2013.

Weekly Citizen. 'Secret plot to isolate Uhuru begins', 15, no. 47, November 19-25, 2012.

Weekly Citizen. 'Will a Kikuyu succeed Kibaki?', 14, no. 18, May 9-15, 2011.

Weekly Citizen. 'Kibaki humiliates Kalonzo on phone', 12, no. 38, September 21-27, 2009.

Wikipedia, 'Kenya presidential election, 2013'; http://en.wikipedia.org/wiki/Kenyan_presidential_election, 2013.

Wolf, T. 'Opinion Polls: Factors that might influence outcome', *Sunday Nation*, February 24, 2013.

———. 'International Justice vs. Public Opinion? The ICC and ethnic polarisation in the 2013 Kenya Election'. *Journal of African Elections* 12, no. 1 (June), 2013: 143-177.

———. 'Kenya's New Constitution: Triumph in hand, testing times ahead?', in *Judiciary Watch Report*: '*Constitutional Change, Democratic Transition, and the Role of the Judiciary in Government Reform: Questions and Lessons for Kenya'*, Vol. 8, 2010: 23-94, International Commission of Jurists-Kenya.

———. 'Poll Poison'?: Politicians and polling in the 2007 Kenya Election'. *Journal of Contemporary African Studies* 27, no. 3 2009: 279-304.

Political Integration of Minority Communities: The Ogiek of Eastern Mau Forest in the 2013 Elections

Lisa Fuchs *

Introduction

All over the world, minorities have been neglected in public and political affairs. In the last two decades, however, research has documented an increased political will at the international and national level, whether in 'old' or 'new' democracies, not only to recognise the importance of identity diversity in national set-ups but also to promote active inclusion of minorities into public life, including political participation.[1] Throughout the world "democratic elites are less likely to rely on strategies of assimilation and repression, [and] more likely to follow policies of recognition, pluralism, and group autonomy" (Gurr, 2000). The slowly changing attitudes on societal pluralism allow observing a trend that indicates a decline in intrastate violent conflict with a shift from violence towards negotiation (Ibid:xiii).

The Kenyan experience seems to support this broad pattern. Historically marginalised and sometimes even reneged in their very existence, minorities have succeeded in bringing their fate on the political agenda and achieved important steps towards greater inclusion into public and political affairs – and thereby in the (making of) the country as such. However, these advances are mainly visible on paper, particularly in the Constitution, while the implementation of these prerogatives remains rudimentary. According to accredited social commentators, inclusion of all citizens in public life "is a significant governance challenge facing Kenya" (Cottrel-Ghai et

* PhD student, Institute for Social and Cultural Anthropology, University of Cologne, and IFRA-Nairobi.

al., 2013: 1) – even more so when it concerns individuals and groups of minority communities. Political participation can be understood as a tool of such integration, ultimately presenting a chance to reverse marginalisation – or to put it differently, to foster democratic dispensation (Nassali, 2011: 3).

The present paper discusses marginalisation of minority groups and political participation in relation to a specific group of Kenyan citizens inhabiting the Eastern Mau Forest. This area can be described as remote despite its location in the central Rift Valley and its physical proximity to Nakuru, one of Kenya's major cities. It is traditionally inhabited by members of the Ogiek community, formerly hunters and gatherers who are considered as belonging to the wider Kalenjin community. The Ogiek are historically one of Kenya's most marginalised peoples whose members sometimes represent themselves as second class citizens.[2] Having become the object of political discourse through campaigns by Rift Valley MPs' against former Prime Minister Raila Odinga's Mau Forest rehabilitation and restoration program since the late 2000s, the political identity of forest dwellers has received increasing attention. Against the backdrop of a deeply rooted mistrust and apprehension towards members of other Kalenjin sub-groups, the effects of the politicisation of the Ogiek's fate on their participation in the 2013 elections and the outcome of their engagements are questioned. Beyond the insights into political participation in this micro-setting, the present case study seeks to draw conclusion in terms of integration of indigenous minority communities in national politics. The reflection on the political participation of the Ogiek can be understood as a wider questioning of the inclusion of Kenya's minorities in the use and shaping of democratic spaces.

Given that participation of minorities, including the possibility "to [have] a voice of their own, to articulate their distinct concerns and seek redress" (Ghai, 2003: 5), has been recognised as crucial for democratic political systems, the Mau Ogiek case can be associated with the wider discussion on democratisation processes in African states. The present study arrives timely as analyses of political participation of the Ogiek are few[3] and solely concentrate on participation in everyday life activities intended to influence the political sphere. No single study analyses the Mau Ogiek's electoral practices. The present research seeks to fill this gap and give a status report on Kenya's ability to include all segments of her society in national decision-making processes, by elaborating on the experience of the Ogiek indigenous minority.

In association with discussions related to clientelism and patronage in African politics, it is common in Kenya to explain voting patterns by invoking ethnicity.[4,5] In that context, the present study questions whether the Ogiek vote can be captured within such explanatory schemes. Beyond that, the very integration of the Ogiek in the public and political affairs of the country is called into question.

The main argument of this article is that Ogiek political participation eludes common classifications in terms of ethnically oriented voting. Whereas the decision-making process for higher elective posts can be understood as being based on an ethnic rationale, closer scrutiny reveals a more complex pattern pointing towards a phenomenon that is here defined as 'electoral indifference'. This concept of electoral indifference will be explained throughout the text and reflected upon in the conclusion. In the elections for the local representative, however, the outcome of the 2013 election disclose as clientelistic logic transcending the ethnic rationale. Yet, the integrative capacity of this apparent affinity seems limited, encouraging the Mariashoni Ogiek to seek redress through other means.

Departing from a definition of the Ogiek as marginalised indigenous community, the present study analyses whether and in which ways the Ogiek affiliation with the wider Kalenjin community impacts their voting behaviour. In the light of those first results, alternative understandings to the popularly advanced 'ethnic' argument are proposed before expanding briefly on alternative attempts of achieving political inclusion administered by members of the Ogiek community themselves.

The Ogiek: Apolitically marginalised indigenous community

The claims for the recognition of minority and indigenous community rights became more pronounced with the timid opening up of a democratic space in Kenya in the early 1990s. These events influenced the Ogiek community in their formulation of an own identity and informed their subsequent fight for recognition.

Recognition and political inclusion of minorities in Kenya

Before discussing the events leading to greater minority rights, we ought to define what we mean by indigenous and minority. There are no globally recognised definitions for either of these two terms (Nassali, 2011:4). Following similar advances of the international scale, the African Commission, in 2005, stipulated four criteria for defining indigenous peoples. First, the occupation and use of a specific territory; second, voluntary perpetuation of cultural distinctiveness such as language, religion, spiritual values, modes of production, laws and institutions; third, self-identification as well as recognition by other groups as a collectivity; and fourth, an experience of subjugation, marginalisation, dispossession, exclusion and discrimination.[6] Nassali emphasises appropriately that indigeneity within Africa goes beyond the question of 'who came first' but centres around exclusion, negative appraisal of alternative cultures and ways of life, as well as threats to the very survival of a specific group. Three aspects in the definition of indigenous peoples can therefore be extrapolated: existence of a distinct culture intrinsically linked with a specific territory; self-identification as being part of that distinct culture; and (perceived) negative projection of that culture with regards to mainstream (developmental) paradigms (Ibid: 5).

According to Alfredson, the term 'minority' also contains the idea of self-identification as belonging to a certain group, as well as the fact of having stayed within a given territory for a long period of time. The most crucial criteria however is numbers: the concerned group has to constitute less than half of a given population to be in a non-dominant position within that population (Alfredson, 2005 in Nassali, 1993: 4).[7] The Minority Rights Group defines minorities in Kenya as numerically inferior to the rest of the population of a state; in a non-dominant position; residing in the state, being either nationals or a group with close long-standing ties to the state; possessing ethnic, religious or linguistic characteristics that differ from those of the rest of the population, and show, if only implicitly, a sense of solidarity directed towards preserving their distinctive collective identity (Henrard, 2001 in Cottrel-Ghai et al., 2013: 2). Three groups of minorities are most commonly recognised: ethnic, religious and linguistic minorities. In the Kenyan context, indigenous peoples can be defined as a fourth category of minorities (Makoloo, 2005: 9). This classification obviously is not exclusive and a given group can fall into several categories.

The boundaries between indigenous and minority rights are not clearly defined either. The main difference between minority rights and indigenous peoples' rights is that the first are individual rights whereas the latter are collective rights (Nassali, 2011: 6-7). In this context, it is important to note that indigenous groups can be minorities but that not all minorities are indigenous; at the same time, the minority title does not automatically convey marginalisation.

In Kenya, the origin of the perception of minority groups as a separate entity can be dated back to the European colonial powers' land management policies. As prime land was forcefully acquisitioned for agricultural production, those who formerly occupied were forced into economic, social and eventually cultural marginalisation if they were not able or willing to adapt. With the introduction of private property dimensions in land tenure, previous social structures disappeared or lost validity. The colonial land use and property changes thereby led to circumstances under which certain communities were forced to identify as minorities or indigenous people, amongst other reasons to fight for their land rights (Ibid: 162). The minority status in Kenya is thereby not necessarily conveyed by numbers but by socio-economic marginalisation.[8] Marginalisation in politics, the economy and the civil service continued in post-independent Kenya. Minority rights were far off the agenda, as in most African countries at the time, because minority rights were represented as fostering negative ethnicity and tribal division, ultimately endangering national unity. Kenya, like most African states, manifested a desire to de-culturalise and assimilate minorities into dominant cultures alongside stigmatisations of their cultures as primitive and calls for a 'need' of civilisation (Ibid: 35-36).

Before the establishment of the Centre for Minority Rights Development in the year 2000, there was no evidence of any federated group lobbying the Kenyan government on minority rights at the national level.[9] Minority rights had received considerable attention on the international and continental scale. Whereas neither the UN Charter, the African Charter on Human and People's Rights (ACHPR) nor the African Union Charter explicitly refer to minorities, the representation of minorities needing special protection is not new: the now defunct UN Sub-Commission on the Prevention of Discrimination of Minorities was created as early as 1947 and later, in 1982, established a Working Group on Indigenous Populations. Furthermore, the Permanent Forum on Indigenous Issues under the Economic and Social Council (ECOSOC) was inaugurated in 2000 and a special Rapporteur nominated. Within those forums, a number of international agreements relevant for minority rights protection were adopted. Most importantly the 1992 UN Declaration of the Rights of Persons belonging to Ethnic, Religious and Linguistic Minorities. Others are ILO Convention No. 169 of 1989 or the UN Declaration on the Rights of Indigenous Peoples in 2007. At the continental level, a similar advance was made in 2001 with the adoption of the Resolution for the Rights of Indigenous Groups by the African Commission. Kenya is state party to a number of those international and continental agreements. Yet, difficulties in their enforcement, as well as in the monitoring of compliance by state parties, have bestowed only moderate successes upon those treaties (Ohenjo, 2011: 13-14).

In the absence of specific consideration and/or legislation, automatic representation is unrealistic for members of minority groups. Lobby groups have therefore petitioned the state to enforce special legislation to guarantee the full participation of members of minorities as citizens of the democratic state. This is because ethnic networks have the potential to convey a sense of belonging and security to minority groups which are difficult for the state to attain (Cottrel-Ghai et al., 2013: 1). The inclusion of minorities is thereby to engender a sense of national belonging amongst the members of the groups. Since the democratic regime change in Kenya in 2002, minorities have been accorded gradual recognition on the national scale, starting with the inclusion of minority representatives in the constitutional review process in the same year. Borrowing from the initial 'Bomas' Draft for a new constitution, Kenya's 2010 Constitution explicitly recognises and protects the rights of minorities for the first time in Kenyan history. Hunter-gatherers are therein defined as marginalised by virtue of their livelihood, without having to prove actual discrimination (Ibid: 2).With regards to political participation, Article 56 (a) specifies that the State shall ensure that minorities and marginalised groups "participate and are represented in governance and other spheres of life". The constitutional review process was furthermore of importance as minority representatives decided to present their claims together as indigenous peoples' voice instead of pursuing their interests as separate groups.[10]

Minority representatives also took part in the development of the new National Land Policy. To their satisfaction, the resulting policy, which was adopted in 2009, addresses historic land injustices, community rights to land and strives to protect minority rights. The land policy also notes clearly that "minority communities (...) have lost access to land and land-based resources (...) that is key to their livelihood"; that "these groups (...) deserve [sic] special protection from the State with regards to their land rights and ability to manage their natural resources in a sustainable manner"; that they "have not been represented adequately in governmental decision making at all levels",[11] while naming colonial assimilation policies and capitalism as main drivers of the marginalisation of minorities. There are further provisions allowing for the participation of minorities in local decision-making processes contained in the 2005 Forest Act and the 2003 Constituency Development Fund Act; yet their influence has so far remained limited.

In legal terms, a precedent was set when the High Court in 2008 decided that the Ilchamus hunter-gatherer group, a culturally distinct minority group, "had a right to influence the formulation and implementation of public policy, and to be represented by people belonging to the same socio-cultural and economic context as themselves" and, consequently, should be represented by a nominated Ilchamus Member of Parliament. However, most of these advances are only on paper and it remains to be seen whether they are more than paper elephants borne out of political expediency.

Historiography of the Eastern Mau Ogiek' self-representation as politically marginalised community

The wider Kalenjin community has received little academic attention despite its prominence in the history of Kenya and in current political debates. The few available studies mainly focus on specific Kalenjin sub-groups (Lynch, 2011: 5). Several localised micro-studies on the Ogiek have been undertaken since the beginning of the 20th century. Most outstanding are the works of G.W.B. Huntingford since the 1920s, as well as R. Blackburn and C. Kratz both since the 1970s. Apart from Blackburn's studies, the Kalenjin-speaking Ogiek of Mau Forest, whose political participation is analysed in this article, have not figured in any major linguistic or historical studies (Distefano, 2011: 51). Furthermore, beyond these classical anthropological studies, little has been written about the more recent evolutions and transformations of contemporary Ogiek societies.

The Ogiek are considered as forest-based hunters and gatherers who have traditionally lived in different forest areas in western Kenya and northern Tanzania. They are arguably the largest remaining hunter-gatherer group in Kenya (Ohenjo, 2003: 1). The wider Ogiek community is composed of 12 different sub-groups, out of which three are represented in Eastern Mau. Those three sub-tribes are further subdivided into 21 clans (Muchemi and Ehrensperger, 2011). The mother tongue of the Ogiek (singular Ogiot[12]), also called Ogiek, is a Kalenjin language of the Southern Nilotic group (Kratz, 1999: 220-224). Due to the language-based definition of the Kalenjin, uniting all Nandi speakers, the Ogiek are understood as part of that community; their association with the Kalenjin has however been subjected to contestation by other Kalenjin and academics alike (Lynch, 2011: 5). The Ogiek are more commonly referred to as Dorobo, a derogatory term derived from the Maasai term 'Il Torobbo' designing people without cattle – who are thus understood as poor (Blackburn, 1974: 139). Images of the Ogiek have mostly been conceived from the outside through a process of differentiation. The Ogiek are constructed antithetically as the 'others' following a contrasting to the self-representation of their neighbouring community (Kratz, 1993: 37). Due to their particular lifestyle of hunting and gathering, the Ogiek have been represented as backward people "at the end of the evolutionary scale", or even "social outcasts" (Distefano, 1990: 43). Those and other connotations associated with the term Dorobo have led the 'true' Ogiek to refute that name as it is considered to be cruel – and insist on using the term 'Ogiek' which supposedly signifies 'caretaker of all animals and plants' (Towett, 2004). As a result of a number of factors such as long contact with other communities and environmental stress leading to further sedentarisation and adoption of small-scale farming, it is nowadays almost impossible to differentiate the Ogiek lifestyle from that of other communities. Nevertheless, other communities have continued to distinguish the Ogiek on the basis of their traditional economic activities associated with life in the forest – a characteristic that also remains crucial in the Ogiek self-representation (Kratz, 1993: 37, 47).

The "othering" of the Ogiek (Lynch, 2011: 52) was actively pursued by the colonial government that attempted to assimilate the Ogiek and recommended their relocation in the native reserves of bigger tribes, insisting they "should become members of and [be] absorbed into the tribes with which they have most affinity".[13] Confronted with the Ogiek opposition to assimilation, various arms of the government have made numerous attempts to dispossess and relocate the Ogiek or frustrate them by imposing veterinary controls, as well as hunting and grazing bans in what the Ogiek themselves understand as an attempt "to exterminate, assimilate and impoverish them through constant evictions and disruptions of their traditional lifestyle" (Towett, 2004). Up to date, all Ogiek land is controlled by government land, forests and wildlife Acts (Ohenjo, 2003:1). Historically, agricultural expansion, the introduction of exotic plants, large-scale logging and the settlement of 'in-migrants'[14] contributed to the loss of their ancestral land. As land use and access were crucial to the Ogiek lifestyle, these changes became key features of their economic and political marginalisation. Furthermore, this marginalisation has had negative impacts on Ogiek housing, health and food security.[15]

This social and economic marginalisation was facilitated by the fact that the Ogiek have continuously held a minority status in the national set-up. Due to their dispersion in different areas and their statistical inclusion into the wider Kalenjin and sometimes Maasai categories, there are no clear records on the evolution of their population numbers. Until the last census, there were no available statistics on hunter-gatherers in general as the government continued to pursue non-recognition policies. For instance, the Dorobo category of 1989 includes other groups apart from the Ogiek, while the 1999 census was released without reference to ethnic affiliations. Estimates on the total Ogiek population range from 20,000 to 37,000 (Ohenjo, 2003:

182-183) and even 78,691 for Nakuru County alone.[16] After their population census results were cancelled in the 2009 count, a government project linked to the Mau Forest Restoration Initiative proposed to compose an alternative Ogiek register. A number of difficulties, especially differences among the members of the government initiated Ogiek Council of Elders tasked with the supervision of the project on who should be included in the register and who should not, have hindered a timely publication of the report. Unofficial sources however indicate the register comprises around 11,000 adult Ogiek[17] – a figure disputed and reduced by a connoisseur of the Ogiek who estimates the Ogiek by lineage could be as few as 5000 only.[18]

In terms of direct political representation, the Ogiek have been largely locked out of active decision-making: In Nakuru County alone, only two Ogiek councillors were in office during the last legislative period despite their presence in 52 county wards distributed over six constituencies (Cottrel-Ghai et al., 2013: 3). At the same time, there has never been an Ogiek in any superior elective position.

A sense of belonging? Following the lead of the wider Kalenjin community

Despite the difficulties in their affiliation with the wider Kalenjin community, a general tendency can be observed in the voting behaviours of the Mariashoni Ogiek: alignment with the political lead of the Kalenjin big men.

Electoral choices in past elections and referendums

Apart from oral records on election results from Mariashoni, there are few other sources that allow deeper insights into electoral practices in the past elections. As population censuses within the forest area have not been conclusive, and population figures for the Ogiek even disputed and withdrawn for the 2009 census, it becomes difficult to match the little information available with solid figures. It is thus not possible to indicate percentages of voters' registration and election participation. The little information available relates mainly to the outcome of different elections conducted since the reintroduction of multi-party democracy in December 1991. Five general elections, including the 2013 elections, have since been conducted.

The presidential elections' results demonstrate a trend of voting for the candidate supported by the wider Kalenjin community. In 1992[19] and 1997, incumbent Daniel arap Moi was confirmed in office by voters in Mariashoni. During the elections of 2002 that trend resulted in a majority of voters giving their vote to Uhuru Kenyatta, the KANU candidate and designated successor to former President Moi's 'throne'. In 2007, the Mariashoni voters largely opted for Raila Odinga's ODM thereby expressing their alignment to the political line of the most important Kalenjin politicians.[20] In 2002 and 2007, the Mariashoni voters thus supported the losing candidate.

The same pattern of voting along wider community lines can also be observed with regard to the elections for Member of Parliament: after voting for the FORD-Asili candidate John Njenga Mungai in 1992 and confirming the incumbent in office in 1997, the candidate of the party supported by the wider Kalenjin community at that time got most votes in Mariashoni thereafter: Peter Kipng'etich Sang, aspirant for KANU in 2002 and for ODM in 2007.[21]

During the constitutional referendum in 2010, a majority of voters followed the ODM course and voted 'Yes', whereas they had voted 'No' in 2005, as advised by community leaders.

All three instances – presidential elections, MP elections and constitutional referendums – indicate the same trend: Mariashoni voters vote along the lines of the wider Kalenjin community.[22] They were equally drawn into the post-election violence dynamic, attacking the homestead of the only Kikuyu remaining in the area by destroying his livestock and harvest and supposedly trying to kill him.[23]

However, it is questionable whether the 'ethnic' pattern is circumstantial or substantial. Furthermore, the 2013 elections have presented a new 'challenge' to Mariashoni voters: as mentioned, the Ogiek had never been part of any direct political discussions or campaigns before the 2013 elections. After a section of former ODM MPs fell out with Raila Odinga over the Mau Restoration issue in the late 2000s, the Ogiek's fate was pushed in the limelight and thereby received unprecedented attention. Being shoved into one of the centres of political attention, the Ogiek were presented with an opportunity to politicise their voting behaviour – pro or contra forest restoration and therefore pro Raila or pro Uhuru.[24] The following analysis will consider the possibility of issue-based electoral choices all the while examining whether the 2013 electoral experience lends credence to an interpretation of the Eastern Mau Ogiek's electoral behaviour in ethnic terms.

Political participation in the 2013 general elections

The 4 March 2013 general elections in Mariashoni were held in a tense atmosphere due to an outbreak of pre-election violence after what was commonly understood as flawed Jubilee party nominations. The exercise had not only been ill planned and executed; it also led to the exclusion of a majority of Mariashoni voters (only 1,130 out of 4,265 registered voters cast their vote, representing 26.5%).This exclusion was most pronounced for the Ogiek voters who represent a minority within the ward anyway (less than 20% of all those who had registered within the 'Ogiek strongholds'[25] were able to vote, whereas the 'in-migrant' areas[26] recorded averages of around 30%). After a premature conclusion of the primaries, a group of Ogiek manifested their dissatisfaction with the proceeding, and particularly with the difficulty that most Ogiek inhabitants faced in participating in the exercise. Even more so, because Agnes Salimu was nominated as Jubilee candidate for the seat of Member of County Assembly (MCA) against the backdrop of the most promising Ogiek candidate's win in Mariashoni Primary School polling station. Salimu challenges a number of taboos in the area, first by being a woman, second by being an ethnic Nandi (despite having been married to an Ogiek husband for many years, she is still not considered an Ogiek by the local community) and third, and perhaps most importantly, by being the wife of the controversial area chief. Following the declaration of her nomination, the chief's office in Mariashoni trading centre was destroyed in a nightly attack, a number of non-Ogiek were verbally and physically assaulted, and others threatened. Despite heightened police presence, no arrests were made. Thus, the nomination debacle left a stain on the local peoples' confidence with regards to the upcoming elections. Many residents of the area, Ogiek and others alike, expressed fears of widespread commotion in case Salimu was confirmed as MCA.

Voter turnout

After achieving a registration rate of almost three quarters (4,265 persons representing 73.46%) of the targeted 5,806 adults[27] in Mariashoni Ward, an impressive 83.9% (3,578 persons) turned out to cast their vote during the general elections according to official records.[28] This figure is congruent in all nine polling stations that consistently recorded a voter turnout of above 80%. Translated back to the targets defined by the IEBC, a good majority of almost two thirds (61.6%) of the 5,806 targeted voters cast their vote.

A vast majority (97.9%) of those who turned up to vote also cast their vote in a valid manner: only 3 votes were spoilt (0.1%) and 78 rejected (2.2%). The rate of rejected votes is nevertheless higher than in the wider Molo Constituency (1.0%). In sum, 60.3% out of the targets 5,806 adults in Mariashoni expressed a valid vote during the 2013 general elections.

The presidential election

The election results for the presidential election in Mariashoni Ward indicate a clear win for Jubilee coalition's flag bearer Uhuru Kenyatta and his deputy William Ruto. They won with an overall average of almost 80% of votes cast and won in seven out of the nine polling centres within Mariashoni. The final results per presidential candidate and polling stations are as follows (Table 1).

Table 1: Presidential election results in different polling stations within Mariashoni Ward

	1	2	3*	4	5	6	7	8	9	Total	%
Dida	2	0	4	1	1	2	0	0	0	10	0.3%
Karua	7	3	0	1	0	1	1	1	0	14	0.4%
PK	3	2	0	0	2	0	3	0	1	11	0.3%
UK	502	235	16	389	416	153	510	25	518	2,764	78.9%
Kiyapi	7	3	0	1	3	4	6	1	3	28	0.8%
MM	2	3	2	4	2	2	3	1	1	20	0.6%
Muite	0	1	0	0	0	0	2	0	0	3	0.1%
RAO	97	97	19	12	139	149	90	35	15	653	18.6%
	620	344	41	408	563	311	615	63	538	3,503	100%

* As the results are based on the Mars Group Audit, the adjusted number of 41 votes cast is used instead of the 38 indicated in IEBC's Form 34 for Tertit polling station.

Note: Kenya Mars Group website for Mariashoni Ward; individual accounts for each stream within each polling station of IEBC Forms 34 and 36, equated with independent Mars Group Audit figures.

These results confirm the historic pattern of following the lead of acclaimed leaders within the wider Kalenjin community when casting their vote. Thus, a vast majority of more than two-thirds (78.9%) voted for the Jubilee Coalition and thereby helped electing Uhuru Kenyatta as fourth president of the Republic. That result echoes the trends of the wider Molo constituency, where Uhuru Kenyatta officially won 85% of all valid votes – leaving Raila Odinga to be a distant second with 14.4%.

Looking at the areas where 'in-migrants' are in majority, Uhuru Kenyatta won clearly in all polling stations (with percentages of between 73.9% and 96.3%). The overall win for Uhuru Kenyatta in those four polling stations was therefore also clearer (84.1%) than in the entire ward (78.9%). The allegiance of members of other Kalenjin communities to the Uhuru-Ruto alliance thus seems unambiguous.

A closer look at the results in the so-called 'Ogiek-strongholds' allows for interesting insights: Whereas Uhuru Kenyatta won with a large majority (over 80%) in the two biggest out of the 6 polling stations in 'Ogiek territory', the two smaller ones located further inside the forest were won by Raila Odinga (two out of only three in the entire Molo Constituency) and the middle-sized one had an almost even distribution of votes between the two strongest candidates with a slight advantage of 4 votes for Uhuru Kenyatta. The overall win for Uhuru Kenyatta in those five polling stations is still considerable (73.1%) but less pronounced than in the entire ward (78.9%) and 10% below the 'in-migrant' stronghold average.

Other elective posts

All other posts in Mariashoni were equally won by candidates of the Jubilee coalition. After conflicts emerged in the party primaries, separate candidates were listed for the parties forming the alliances, namely TNA and URP. It is worth mentioning another event at the local level: Salimu's main opponent Tiemosi, whose loss against her in the TNA party primaries led to limited pre-election violence in the vicinity, changed parties and participated in the election as UDF candidate. Table 2 below indicates the results for all other posts within Mariashoni Ward and compares them with election outcomes.

Table 2: Election results for other elective posts in Nakuru County

Position	Candidates	Winner in Mariashoni	Elected candidate
President	Uhuru Kenyatta (Jubilee) Raila Odinga (CORD) Musalia Mudavadi (Amani) + 5 others	Uhuru Kenyatta (Jubilee)	Uhuru Kenyatta (Jubilee)
Governor	Kinuthia Mbugua (TNA) Francis Peter Kiranga (UDF) Lawrence Kiprop Bomett (ODM)	Kinuthia Mbugua (TNA)	Kinuthia Mbugua (TNA)
Senator	Job Kimitei Siror (URP) Samwel Omondi Ogada (ODM) James Kiarie Mungai (TNA) + 10 others	James Kiarie Mungai (TNA)	James Kiarie Mungai (TNA)

Member of Parliament	Samwel Mong'are Gesare (ODM)	Jacob Waweru Macharia (TNA)	Jacob Waweru Macharia (TNA)
	Abdulmalik Maina Thuo (URP)		
	Jane Wangechi Kigotho (Agano)		
	Jacob Waweru Macharia (TNA)		
	John Muriu Mbitu (GNU)		
Women Rep.	Mary Njoki G. Mbugua (TNA)	Mary Njoki G. Mbugua (TNA)	Mary Njoki G. Mbugua (TNA)
	Murumbwa B. Nyabonyi (Safina)		
	Rose Nyakiba (ODM)		
	Grace Wambui Kibuku (CCM)		
Member of County Assembly	Agnes Jerotich Salimu (URP)	Agnes Jerotich Salimu (URP)	Agnes Jerotich Salimu (URP)
	Solomon Kibet Tiemosi (UDF)		
	Nahashon Kibet Kiptoo (ODM)		
	Pharis Kiptoo Ngiria (KANU)		
	Jonathan Kipkemoi Ronoh (TNA)		
	Kibet Kigen (Agano)		

In comparison to the previous elections, Mariashoni's residents, for the first time since the end of Moi's presidency, largely voted for the winning candidates. It was also the first time that Kikuyu candidates were elected to secondary positions by the mostly Kalenjin electorate of Mariashoni. It was also for the first time since 2002 that the major Kalenjin leaders sided with the party to which a majority of Kikuyu leaders pledged allegiance. Furthermore, the controversial party primaries and their chaotic aftermath did not deter voters from electing Salimu. Despite widespread fears, Mariashoni remained calm after her confirmation. This might have been due to the chief's capacity to swiftly set up tight security in the area, which most probably helped avoiding any further escalation. Salimu was however also elected by a vast majority of voters, rendering a challenge of the vote more improbable. We present the frameworks for interpretations of these results in the following section.

Beyond ethnic arithmetic: Alternative explanations for electoral choices

This section addresses several points to explain the possible motivations for the Eastern Mau Ogiek's electoral behaviour. The apparent ethnically motivated vote is closely analysed. The particularity of the election for the local representative is also highlighted in this section. Common alternative explanation models are subsequently examined. In the end, the overall importance of the party primaries is observed and problematised.

The 'ethnic' vote

The overall voting behaviour of the Mariashoni Ogiek seems to confirm the commonly held assumption that most Kenyans vote along ethnic lines. It can therefore be argued that the quasi six-piece vote for the Jubilee Coalition is ethnically oriented, because it arguably reflects an allegiance to the 'general' political choices of the Kalenjin elites. However, the Ogiek ethnic association with the wider Kalenjin community is no *direct* predictor for electoral choices and there is no clearly ethnically motivated vote.

The first election result in question is the gubernatorial election result. In this election, the TNA Kikuyu candidate Kinuthia Mbugua got more votes than the ODM Kalenjin candidate Laurence Kiprop Bomett. While this might legitimately be understood as allegiance to the 'ethnically backed coalition', the senatorial election evades such an understanding. In the race for senator, a majority of Mariashoni voters cast their vote in favour of the TNA Kikuyu candidate James 'Jemo' Mungai despite the presence of the Kalenjin URP candidate Siror Job Kimitei.[29] Both candidates were part of the same coalition supported by the wider Kalenjin community – and yet Mariashoni voters elected 'Jemo', a man who had never visited the area and was therefore personally unknown to a vast majority of the residents – but had won in the party primaries.[30] The simple fact that a majority of Mariashoni voters elected a Kikuyu candidate – in the presence of a Kalenjin ODM candidate in the race for governor and even a Kalenjin URP candidate in the race for senator – points towards the need for understanding voters' motivations beyond a mere ethnic arithmetic.

The election of the Member of County Assembly (MCA) challenges an 'ethnic' understanding on yet another level: despite the fact that a slight majority of votes cast within Mariashoni Ward were cast by 'in-migrants', Agnes Salimu was supported and her victory was also brought about by Ogiek.[31] A number of Ogiek supported Salimu openly; the supporters of former councillor Johnson Meopi for instance rallied behind her candidacy after his lack of success in the party nominations.[32] The Ogiek thus did not vote in majority for an Ogiek candidate in the elections for local representative. One possible explanation for the Ogiek' failure to elect an Ogiek MCA may draw on the fact that the most promising Ogiek candidate, Solomon Tiemosi, was not able to gather a majority of Ogiek votes; amidst rumours that he is radical, non-inclusive and preached negative ethnicity. As the minority candidate attracted controversy, his election to office was unlikely. Many voters seem to have perceived Salimu as only the veritable alternative to Tiemosi. Another relevant factor is that the Ogiek, as any other group of people, are not a monolithic block but a community subjected to internal fraction, particularly between those who are part of the chief's entourage and those who are not.[33] Additionally, opposing the chief has not always proved easy for Mariashoni residents. Thus, many of them might have feared opposing him (or his wife) or supporting the candidate that the chief clearly disapproved of (Tiemosi).[34] Therefore, Salimu's election into office can be understood as an expression of a clientelistic relationship by extension, with the voters banking on an inclusion into the chief's entourage and thereby benefitting from his influence in the local political economy. This supposed patronage system on the micro-level casts doubts on the inclusion of the Mariashoni Ogiek's integration into the wider national political context.

Alternative patterns of explanation

Whether any of the political decisions taken by Mariashoni voters was issue-based, a second approach to explaining electoral behaviour in Kenya is questionable. According to popular belief, the Uhuru-Ruto (or 'Uhuruto') alliance guarantees an end of the Mau restoration program; or at least of evictions of forest-dwellers. Whether the fact that a majority of Mariashoni voters elected Uhuru Kenyatta as President was in any way linked to his perceived stand on forest policy or not is difficult to determine. In the light of the decisions taken for other elective posts, a general allegiance to the wider Jubilee Coalition is more likely than a conscious decision due to his supposed stand on forest policy. The relatively higher support for Raila Odinga in the 'Ogiek strongholds' in general and his victory in the most 'pure' Ogiek polling stations in Kiptunga and Tertit might however be based on issues. At the same time, these results might also stem from electoral continuity or be influenced by the fact that Joseph Towett, the renowned Ogiek leader, was an open supporter of ODM and Raila Odinga in the 2013 elections. As there is little issue-based political talk in Mariashoni, an issue-based approach to politics is in general rather unlikely.

With regard to the elective posts transcending the regional sphere of influence, beyond the fact that all of them were won by the Jubilee candidates, party allegiance has no wide-ranging explanatory power as such: a majority of Mariashoni residents are neither party members nor generally voting for a particular political party. In 2002 a majority of Mariashoni voters voted for the KANU candidate, for the ODM candidate in 2007 and for the Jubilee candidate in 2013. The candidate for Member of Parliament of the respective party gathered a majority of votes each election year meaning that party allegiance can therefore be understood as circumstantial and not permanent.

While personal relations and familiarity clearly played out in the Jubilee primaries, the final results in the 2013 elections, confirming all those candidates who had been nominated in the party primaries,[35] suggest that the party primaries might indeed be of central importance. It can be presumed that candidates emerging as winners in the party primaries were able to distinguish themselves as potential winners in the voters' perceptions. Moreover, the candidates who figured in the Jubilee primaries became more 'familiar' to the electorate in Mariashoni after the nomination exercise. Understood within the context of Mariashoni, a remote area without electricity or general access to newspapers, where the phone, radio and personal interactions are the only means of communication, the party primaries might have served as extraordinary campaign event. As a majority of those Ogiek living deeper in the forest, especially in Tertit and Kiptunga areas where Raila Odinga won a majority of votes, were excluded of the party primaries, their less fervent support of all Jubilee candidates in general and Uhuru's presidency in particular, might be understood in that light as well.

The party primaries might even be the single most relevant determinant of the election outcomes for higher level positions. Their prominence calls for problematisation of their implementation in an almost rule-free space.[36]

Conclusion

Mariashoni is an area clearly marked by its marginality and the Ogiek can thus be described as a community that lacks trust in the political machine which, in turn, hardly allows them to understand political participation as a means of alleviating their situation. Due to its remoteness, Mariashoni is a kind of law-free zone, where citizens' rights are hardly granted.

In this context, the election for president is mainly interesting because of the publicity his office attracts; not because the residents believe the election outcome would make a difference to their lives in the forest. The Mariashoni residents are all too aware of their lack of attractiveness for wider political calculations and of their lack of stake in national politics. The same is true for all other elective posts: none of them are of particular importance to a majority of voters in Mariashoni. Nevertheless, voters are not apathetic towards elections and participate willingly; they are however largely indifferent as to the results of those elections.

The only electoral position relevant to a majority of voters in Mariashoni is the one for local representative. Mariashoni voters have displayed a clear understanding of electoral proceedings and their possibility of bringing about change through their vote: none of the local representatives has even been re-elected after their first term. Voters have however also experienced that the expression of their will, even at the lowest level of representation, has had little potential to influence their daily lives: marginalisation has not been overcome through participation in elections, not even on the local level. At the same time, despite general misinformation, most people are aware of the limited power and competencies of their local representative in the national or even regional set-up. Thus, the only relevant political space is the locality, shaped by the chief's arbitrary decisions. In this context, it is difficult to determine whether the election of his wife as MCA is an expression of a passive fear of falling in the chief's disgrace or based on an active relationship of clientelistic exchange. Yet, her election might be understood as a deepening and further institutionalisation of a clientelistic logic applied to elections by vesting the chief's influence in an elective mandate and hence 'officialising' it, thereby transcending his previous administrative function. This evolution however does not necessarily point to democratic alienation among Mariashoni voters: by adapting to institutional changes (after all the chief's position is to cede in the current administrative and institutional re-shuffling to a devolved system of governance), his influence might in a first step be cemented, while opening a window of opportunity for voting him or his 'legitimised' power out in a second step in case his wife is not re-elected as MCA in 2017-2018.

In light of continuous marginalisation, and the inability to bring about substantial change though elections, members of the Ogiek elites have taken to other means of political participation in the last two decades: seeking legal redress in courts. Since the mid-1990s, a group of Ogiek have been fighting the evictions from their land by taking the government to court.[37] Despite significant setbacks, the Ogiek elites were able to enforce several decisions relevant to their inclusion in public and political affairs – also with regard to the 2013 elections.

A first important step was achieved in the run-up to the elections by bringing about a decision by the High Court in July 2012 that compels the IEBC to consider the rights of minority and marginalised groups and to adjust the ward boundaries so as to bring the Ogiek together, basically agreeing to the idea that the Ogiek should be able to have one of their own representing them politically (Cottrel-Ghai et al., 2013:5).This was an important albeit partial victory after the IEBC had previously announced it would not create tribal zones in the North Rift by giving specific wards to specific communities,[38] a decision nullified by the courts. Yet, the boundaries were not adapted before the 2013 elections.

In the aftermath of the elections, faced with the fact that neither in Mariashoni nor anywhere else a 'real Ogiek' was elected or nominated to the national or any county assembly, members of the community filed petition No. 177/2013 pointing out that the state had failed to assure the representation of members of the Ogiek community as provided for by Article 56 of the Constitution. The case was first mentioned on 3 May 2013.[39] The following day, the IEBC published an updated list indicating that they had made changes in the four persons representing special interests to be nominated to the Nakuru County Assembly. After the initial list contained three representatives of the disabled and one of the youth, the IEBC corrected its list and included a representative of the 'marginalised': Joseph Miangari, an Ogiek activist from Nessuit in Eastern Mau.[40] Despite this important decision obtained by IEBC, the Ogiek case is still in court and Ogiek leaders are trying to rally members of other indigenous minorities behind their case so as to present a common case[41] – an important lesson learnt. This evolution manifests that devolution is used as a welcome vehicle to insist on minority interests; all the while knowing that one single Ogiek in Nakuru County Assembly will not be able to exert any real influence on decision-making processes. At the same time, the establishment and confirmation of the Ogiek identity in terms of indigenous minority group has limited impact on the peoples' lives on the ground.

In sum, the Mariashoni Ogiek are trapped between two distinct dynamics – seeking protection and representation on the national scale through court orders on the one hand, and responding to push and pull factors on the local scale on the other hand. These general conclusions on the sense that elections convey in Mariashoni cast doubts on the politicisation of Mariashoni residents in terms of integration in and identification with the national political and social fabric. The Mariashoni case study illustrates that voters are not apathetic towards elections and participate willingly. At the same time, it also shows that they are largely indifferent as to the outcomes of those elections, hence lending credence to the notion of electoral indifference. The case study thereby allows portraying the democratisation of rural Kenya as problematic.

Acknowledgements

This article draws extensively on research conducted in the context of my doctoral studies, as well as for the Kenya 2013 Elections project of the French Institute for Research in Africa (IFRA). This research was funded by DAAD, IFRA and the BIEA to whom I am grateful. Special thanks go to Marie-Aude Fouéré, IFRA's deputy director, for her dedication, patience and good advice.

Notes

1   Political participation is employed in its strict confines in the present study, focusing on activities related to the electoral process. Political participation, electoral behaviour and voting behaviour are used synonymously.

2   Field notes collected between December 2011 and March 2013.

3   Mainly carried out by the different authors belonging to the Kenyan section of Minority Rights Group International.

4   This paper does not discuss the complex and contentious debate about the (im)possibilities of defining ethnicity or ethnic groups statically. An ethnic group is here simply understood as a group of people who share certain characteristics such as language, religion, common history and culture that recognises itself as a somewhat distinct community.

5   For African politics in general, see Bayart (1993); or Chabal and Daloz (1999); for Kenya specifically see Branch, Cheeseman and Gardner, (2010) or Throup and Hornsby (1998); for specific case studies set in rural areas in African states and beyond see Bertrand, Briquet and Pels (2007).

6   United Nations Sub-Commission on the Prevention of Discrimination and Protection of Minorities in Resolution 2 (XXXIV) of September 8, 1981, cited in Nassali (2011: 5).

7   Alfredsson, G., 'Minorities, indigenous and tribal peoples, and peoples: Definitions of terms as a matter of international law', in Ghanea, N. and A. Xanthaki (eds.), *Minorities, peoples and self-determination: Essays in honour of Patrick Thornberry*, 2005, p. 166, in Nassali, M. 'Movement Towards Political Inclusion', 2011, p. 6.

8   Ohenjo's article is guiding in terms of minority recognition in Kenya. The whole paragraph is sources from his article, particularly from Ohenjo (2011), pp. 157-158; 173; 207-2012; 215-217. Additions are marked separately.

9   All three quotations from Republic of Kenya, *Draft Land Policy*, 2009, pp.69-71, in Ohenjo (2011: 211).

10 As is the general use, the term 'Ogiek' is used in this paper to refer to members of the community in singular and plural.

11 Ag. Chief Native Commissioner Mr. A. de Wade of the Carter Land Commission in 1933, in: Sang, J. 'The Ogiek in Mau Forest', 2003, p. 118.

12 The expression of 'in-migrants' is derived from the fact that the Ogiek refer to non-Ogiek as 'foreigners' in English and 'wageni' (guests) in Swahili. That term designates persons who have settled in the forest since the mid-1990s and mainly belong to the wider Kalenjin community, including Kipsigis, Tugen, Nandi and sometimes also Kamba and Kisii. Due to the somewhat derogatory connotation of the term, it is used in quotation marks.

13 Report of the UN Special Rapporteur on adequate housing, Miloon Kothari, E/CN.4/2005/48/Add.2, para. 61, cited by Anaya, J., 'Alleged Eviction of the Ogiek', 2010.

14 Number cited as representing the figures indicated in the 2009 census in Cottrel-Ghaiet al. (2013: 3).

15 Information given by a contact person at the ICS, the Interim Coordinating Secretariat responsible for the coordination of Mau restoration activities, who does not want to be cited in person.

16 Information disclosed by a senior professional in an interview with a colleague in February 2013.

17 Mariashoni was not yet an independent location in 1992 and belonged to Elburgon Location until 1997.

18 Interview with Chief Samson Salimu, Mariashoni Centre, 27/02/2013.

19 Interview with Chief Samson Salimu, Mariashoni Centre, 27/02/2013; completed by ECK, *Official Results*, 29/01/2008.

20 It should be noted that the Mariashoni voters, and particularly the Ogiek, might have based their decisions on the constitutional drafts on actual issues: Among other things, Article 43 recognising the rights of minorities and indigenous peoples of the previous 'Bomas draft' had been deleted in the altered 'Wako draft' presented for referendum in 2005 - whereas the clause found its way back into the 2010 Constitution (see Ohenjo, 2003: 196-197).

21 He was warned by Ogiek friends and ushered out of the area at night. Today he is operating a small restaurant in Mariashoni trading centre located in a shelter provided by the Rudi Nyumbani Initiative of the Ministry for Special Programmes (Interview with middle-aged Kikuyu man who has lived in Mariashoni all his life, Mariashoni centre, December 2, 2013).

22 The representation of Uhuru Kenyatta as being opposed to the forest restoration is mainly informed by his association with William Ruto who had been an outspoken opponent of evictions in the Mau Forest. Kenyatta never took a clear stand on matters involving forest conservation.

23 The 'Ogiek-strongholds' are polling station number 1 (Mariashoni Primary School), number 3 (Tertit Nursery School), number 6 (Kapcholola Nursery School), number 7 (Kaprop Nursery School) and number 8 (Kiptunga Nursery School).

24 The so-called 'in-migrant-strongholds' are polling stations number 2 (Ndoswa Primary School), number 4 (Rombei Primary School), number 5 (Oinobtich Primary School) and number 9 (Lawina Primary School).

25 Figure obtained in an interview with Joseph Mele, Constituency Elections Coordinator for Molo Constituency, Molo, December 19, 2012.

26 This figure invites for speculations as to its accuracy – as no evidence is available, there is however no legitimate basis for claiming fraud.

27 In their first confrontation for the joint Jubilee seat, Job had only obtained 30 out of the 385 valid votes cast in Mariashoni Primary (including the four other stations mentioned).

28 As many voters did not know who to vote for, the agents 'advised' them and sometimes even marked the voters' ballot papers. The agents followed a pattern and advised the voters in turns. As only three out of the ten aspirants for senator had sent agents, these three aspirants gathered most votes in Mariashoni accounting together for 277 out of 385 valid votes (71.9%) with James Kiarie Mungai ('Jemo') emerging as winner (Interview with a group of party agents in Mariashoni Centre on January 21, 2013).

29 It is also interesting to note that she is one out of only eight female MCAs elected within the 55 wards of Nakuru County (Obiria, Moraa, "Nakuru county assembly to get 16 more women", *The Star*, March 22, 2013).

30 Interview with middle-aged male resident, Mariashoni centre, February 25, 2013.

31 Interview with acknowledged male Ogiek elder in his late forties, Mariashoni, January 21, 2013.

32 Voiced again in an interview with a young male professional in his mid-twenties, Mariashoni centre, January 25, 2013.

33 All TNA candidates who had won the Jubilee primaries were elected by a large majority of Mariashoni voters in the general elections; even those who had not gathered a majority of their votes in the primaries.

34 In line with national proceeding, party nominations were carried out within Mariashoni location on Thursday 18 January2013; with the Jubilee coalition being the only one to carry out primaries. Confusion accompanied the primaries in Mariashoni though as five out of the nine polling stations were assembled together in Mariashoni Primary School polling station the very day of the exercise: Those who had registered as voters in registration centres deeper in the forest – namely Kiptunga, Kapcholola, Kaprop and Tertit– were therefore compelled to attend party primaries in Mariashoni Primary School – at a distance of up to 30 km from their original polling centres. Due to a lack of capacity and planning, a majority of voters were locked out of the exercise: only 413 out of the 1,992 listed voters in those 'Ogiek-strongholds' were able to cast a vote. In total, 1,130 out of the 4,265 registered voters within Mariashoni Ward cast a vote – out of which almost two thirds (717 persons representing 63.5%) in 'in-migrant' strongholds. This imbalance is a clear testimony to the Ogiek's restricted possibility to fully participate in the nomination exercise. Unconfirmed cases of rigging and cheating were also reported in different polling centres within Mariashoni Ward. Whereas the course of action in Mariashoni might have been influenced by the chief in order to favour his wife for the MCA position, the Mariashoni voters had little influence on the nomination of candidates for higher offices. Sporadic observations in other polling stations within Nakuru County however indicate similar difficulties in the implementation of the party primaries

(field observation; interview with a group of party agents in Mariashoni Centre on 21 January2013.

35   For a detailed account of strategies employed to fight the dispossession of the Ogiek see Sang (2003), and Towett (2004).

36   Too, Titus, "IEBC refuses to create tribal zones", *The Standard*, January 27, 2012.

37   SMS from Joseph K. Towett on April 29, 2013.

38   IEBC Dispute Resolution Committee, *Amended Allocation of Nominees to County Assembly Special Seats*, 4 May 2013 and accompanying document entitled *Amendments made to the nomination list following the complaints and the decision of the IEBC committee*, May 4, 2013.

39   SMS from Joseph K. Towett on May 3, 2013.

Bibliography

Anaya, J. "Kenya: Alleged Eviction of the Ogiek Indigenous Peoples from the Mau Forest Complex". *Report of the United Nations Special Rapporteur on the Rights of Indigenous Peoples,* A/HRC/15/37/Add.1, September 15, 2010.

Bayart, J.F. *The State in Africa: The politics of the belly.* London: Longman, 1993.

Bertrand, R., Briquet, J.L. and Pels, P. (eds.), *Cultures of Voting. The hidden history of the secret ballot.* London: Hurst & Company, 2007.

Blackburn, R. "The Ogiek and Their History". *Azania* 9 (1974).

Branch, D., N. Cheeseman and L. Gardner, *Our Turn to Eat: Politics in Kenya since 1950.* Berlin: Lit Verlag, 2010.

Chabal, P., and J.-P. Daloz. *Africa Works: Disorder as political instrument.* Oxford: James Currey, 1999.

Cottrel-Ghai, J., Y. Ghai, K. Sing'oei and W. Wanyoike. *Taking Diversity Seriously: Minorities and political participation in Kenya.* MRG international briefing, January 2013.

Distefano, J.A. "Hunters or Hunted? Towards a History of the Okiek of Kenya". *History in Africa* 17(1990): 41-57.

ECK, *Official Results,* 29/01/2008.

Ghai, Y. *Public Participation and Minorities,* MRG international Report, 2003, 32 p.

Gurr, T.R. ed. *People versus States. Minorities at risk in the new century.* Washington: US Institute of Peace Press, 2000.

IEBC Dispute Resolution Committee. *Amended Allocation of Nominees to County Assembly Special Seats.* 4 May 2013

IEBC Dispute Resolution Committee. *Amendments Made to the Nomination List Following the Complaints and the Decision of the IEBC committee.* 4 May 2013.

Kenya Mars Group website for Mariashoni Ward, *http://election.marsgroupkenya.org/2013/places/wards/0826/mariashoni/,* (accessed 11/04/2013).

Kratz, C.A. " 'We've Always Done It like This... except for a few details': 'Tradition' and 'Innovation' in Okiek Ceremonies". *Comparative Studies in Society and History,* 35 no. 1 (1993): 30-65.

Kratz, C.A. "The Okiek of Kenya". In *Foraging Peoples: An encyclopaedia of contemporary hunter-gatherers*, eds. Richard Lee and Richard Daly, 220-224. Cambridge: Cambridge University Press, 1999.

Lynch, G. *I Say to You. Ethnic politics and the Kalenjin in Kenya*. Chicago and London: University of Chicago Press, 2011.

Muchemi, J. and A.Ehrensperger. *Ogiek Peoples Ancestral Territories Atlas. Safeguarding territories, cultures and natural resources of Ogiek indigenous people in the Eastern Mau Forest, Kenya.* ERMIS Africa and CDE, 2011.

Nassali, M. "Conceptual Framework. Ethnic and racial minorities and movement towards political inclusion in East Africa: Cases of Kenya, Uganda and Tanzania". In *Towards a Rights-Sensitive East African Community. The case of ethnic and racial minorities*, ed. Hamudi Majamba, 1-65. Kampala: Fountain Publishers, 2011.

Ohenjo, N. *Kenya's Castaways: The Ogiek and national development processes*. London. MRG Micro Study, Minority Rights Group, 2003.

Republic of Kenya. *The Constitution of Kenya*. Nairobi: Government Press, 27/10/2010.

Sang, J.K. "Case Study 3: Kenya - The Ogiek in Mau Forest. April 2001". In *Indigenous Peoples and Protected Areas in Africa: From Principles to Practice*, eds. John Nelson and Lindsay Hossack, 111-138. 2003.

Throup, D., and C. Hornsby. *Multi-Party Politics in Kenya: The Kenyatta & Moi states & the triumph of the system in the 1992 election*. London: James Currey, 1998.

Towett, J. *Ogiek Land Cases and Historical Injustices 1902-2004*. Nakuru: Ogiek Welfare Council, Vol. 1, 2004.

Bishop Margaret Wanjiru and the 2013 Kenyan Elections: Between Politics of the Spirit and Expanding Entrepreneurship

Yonatan Gez * and Tanya Alvis *

"Politics is about governance, politics is about leadership. Church is about governance, church is about leadership. […] So for me, it's about leadership, it's not about religion." (*Bishop Margaret Wanjiru on Capital FM, February 8, 2013*)

Introduction

In November 2012, after a period of speculations over her political future, Bishop Margaret Wanjiru, standing at the pulpit of her Jesus Is Alive Ministries (JIAM) church in Nairobi, announced her intentions to run for the position of the governor of Nairobi in the upcoming 2013 elections on an Orange Democratic Movement (ODM) ticket. She was to be the first woman to vie for this position, created as part of the extensive structural changes resulting from the new 2010 constitution (*Citizen TV*, November 18, 2012). By then, Wanjiru's political career had been nothing short of remarkable. As early as 2003 she had begun to expand her operations outside the church and its immediate business ventures (Parsitau, 2011: 135). In 2007, Wanjiru was elected MP on an ODM ticket for Starehe Constituency, an area in the North Eastern part of Nairobi. In 2008, Wanjiru was appointed Assistant Minister for Housing, and in 2010 she successfully reclaimed her Starehe seat after bi-elections were called following a petition filed in the courts by her 2007 rival, Maina Kamanda. Throughout these proceedings, Wanjiru maintained her leadership role in the church. Her political rise seemed all the more impressive considering

*   The Graduate Institute of International and Development Studies, Geneva.

her unorthodox starting point, to which she herself often alludes: a poor background, a self-made woman in a men's world, a single mother, and the founder and leader of one of Nairobi's leading Pentecostal congregations. On top of these all, in light of ethnic rivalries that culminated in the post-elections violence of early 2008, the association of the Kikuyu bishop with ODM, a dominantly Luo party, has been an unlikely choice.

In recent years, scholars have noted that Kenyan clergymen, and above all Pentecostal leaders, have been increasingly hankering after political positions (Cheeseman, 2008; Kavulla, 2008; Gifford, 2009; Droz and Maupeu, 2013). In that regard, the success of the Christian lobby in rallying support for blocking the 2005 constitutional referendum was a sign of encouragement for religious leaders seeking to engage in national affairs (Gifford, 2009; Droz and Maupeu, 2013). At the same time however, such involvement might be traced further back in time, to the churches' involvement in the fight for democratization in the 1990s (Sabar, 2002; Knighton, 2009). Kenya's 2007 elections have thus seen a new phenomenon of church leaders running for political office. This included most notably the candidacy of Wanjiru herself, as well as that of fellow Pentecostal, Pastor Pius Muiru of Maximum Miracles Centre, who ran for presidency and performed dismally.[1] The 2013 elections saw an additional rise in the number of candidates drawn from the ranks of clergy.[2]

In this chapter we raise the question as to how we should understand the growing trend of Kenyan church leaders, and Pentecostals above all, doubling as politicians. We appeal to the case of Bishop Wanjiru, which has already attracted some scholarly attention (Parsitau, 2011; Kalu, 2008: 150-152; Kavulla, 2008; Gifford, 2009; Gathogo, 2011; Mwaura, 2002). Using Wanjiru's 2013 campaign as a case study, we isolate two 'strands' inherent in neo-Pentecostalism as well as in Wanjiru's own discourse and conduct, either of which can offer possible explanations for expanding one's operation beyond the church and into the political arena. The first strand is made of spiritual ideals grounded in the idea of being an agent of a 'Godly plan' and a member of a 'righteous class', whereas the second strand is associated with a pragmatic entrepreneurial spirit. Through examination of the two strands, and recognizing their inherent tension, we offer a reading of Wanjiru's 2013 campaign and her eventual failure, both at the polls and in the eyes of the public. More broadly, we use this case study to articulate a general argument concerning the neo-Pentecostal movement, whose claims to be a vehicle of untarnished divine authority, often conflicts with its embrace of 'worldly' and pragmatic modes of operation.

Pentecostalism and politics: identifying two strands

In his book on Pentecostalism and politics, Amos Yong (2010) suggests that Pentecostalism's political engagement speaks in 'many tongues' and shows how Pentecostals through the years have been taking political, apolitical, and counter-political stands. The grain of counter-political Pentecostalism is found in devotees' embrace of a global identity that challenges the dominance of ethnic, national and other social constructs in identity politics (Alexander, 2005). And yet, despite Pentecostalism's by and large apolitical approach during its formative stages in the early 20th century, in recent years, politics and other public affairs have increasingly become incorporated into Pentecostal theology and considerations, especially with what is regarded as "third wave" Pentecostalism or neo-Pentecostalism (Freston, 1995, 2004; Cartledge, 2010). Thus, in their study of Pentecostalism as a socially engaged movement, Donald E. Miller and Tetsunao Yamamori distinguish between a Pentecostalism which has "often been otherworldly, emphasizing personal salvation to the exclusion of any attempt to transform social reality," and what they term "Progressive Pentecostalism," which "also believes that Christians are called to be good neighbors, addressing the social needs of people in their community" (Miller and Yamamori, 2007: 2). Pentecostal thinkers such as Eldin Villafañe evoke such terms as "politics of the Spirit," arguing that the Holy Spirit's agenda for God's creation can unfold within existing political structures (Villafañe, 1996; Steigenga, 2001). We should keep in mind that the vast majority of Pentecostals today live in the Global South where inadequate state provisions urge churches to take a proactive role in providing alternative services (Meagher, 2009; Piot, 2010).

In Kenya, neo-Pentecostalism has been enormously successful in penetrating the religious landscape at least since the 1980s (Parsitau and Mwaura, 2010; *Daily Nation,* DN2, February 13, 2013: 2-3). As elsewhere in Africa, where religion and politics are closely interlinked (Mary, 2008), Kenya has also seen Pentecostalism increasingly establishing itself in the public sphere (Parsitau, 2008; Droz and Maupeu, 2013). An approach founded on "political culture" (White, 1984; Patterson, 2004), which recognizes that political and social outcomes are determined in large part by the shared beliefs and values of people and subgroups, might predict a successful rise in Pentecostal politics in Kenya, aligned with the movement's spread and the growth of its social visibility. Such a view is supported by Partisau's (2008) argument that Kenya's 'Pentecostal Constituency' has grown exponentially both numerically and institutionally and as such has become a force to be reckoned with in national politics, forming a "critical election mass that can be easily mobilised by its influential leaders" (Partisau, 2008: 15).

In examining Pentecostalism and neo-Pentecostalism's political operation, we identify two strands justifying such an alleged cross-over. One such strand aligns Pentecostals' political program with the notion of "politics of the spirit" (Villafañe, 1996; Steigenga, 2001). According to this approach, engaging in politics can pose a spiritual and moral alternative to the corrupt, secular political system, while at the same time promoting a particular religious agenda. Proponents of this view believe that religious ideals are able to rise above earthly ills as they are driven by noble spiritual concerns, bringing into politics higher moral standing, firmly grounded in religious teachings. Such qualities could form a bulwark against rampant sleaze and corruption, and pose an alternative to the clientelism and tribalism-related nepotism common in Kenya's neo-patrimonial state (Gifford, 2009; Wariboko, 2012). In that sense, such crossover can be seen as part of the "pentecostalisation of the public sphere" (Parsitau, 2008: 22), prompted by a desire "to sanitize Kenyan politics" and to "bring some morals back to political life" (Parsitau, 2008: 26).

Yet a second strand for understanding the involvement of religious leaders in politics would see this move as an extension of one's frame of leadership. Here we follow scholarly observations that contend that neo-Pentecostals are "among the most enterprising entrepreneurs of the religious world" (Anderson, 2004:280). As Paul Gifford argues, referring to Wanjiru among others, the Pentecostal entrepreneurial spirit often revolves around a charismatic leader, who represents "an entire new class of religious professional, the church founder-owner-leader" (Gifford, 2009: 154). Such an approach is distinct from the former, for here we speak less of a crossover between spheres and more of a collapse of boundaries between social, political and religious leaderships. The danger of this strand, as we will show, is that, by collapsing the differences between spheres, we are left wondering whether religion remains distinct and uncontaminated enough, as it were, to serve as a moral alternative to the corruption associated with Kenyan politics. Such a view is supported by a large number of Kenyans, who argue with dismay that religion has become "just like a business", that is to say, an entrepreneurial venture whose true motives are self-serving.

It might be argued that these two strands are in fact complementary, since both subscribe to some of the basic tenets of the neo-Pentecostal movement, which emphasize the notion of a struggle between good and evil made concrete in the world as well as the encouragement of entrepreneurial spirit (Anderson, 2004: 144-165). However, as we intend to show, the two are not without tension. It is with these two strands in mind that we now turn to our case study, starting with a description of Wanjiru's 2013 campaign.

Bishop Wanjiru and the 2013 elections

Kenya's 2013 elections stood in the shadow of the 2008 post-election violence that had swept the nation and left up to 1,500 dead. Some of the responsibility for the violence was placed on the doorstep of religious institutions and leaders who, before the 2007 elections, came out supporting particular candidates, thus fueling tensions between communities. It has further been suggested that the churches have failed to work as a unifying power and as a bulwark against ethnic violence. Following these horrific events, the churches went into a period of reflection. The run-up to the 2013 elections was thus marked by various programs in plea for national unity, some of them operating from within churches. For instance, Nairobi Chapel ran a pre-elections program in which episodes from the history of the Israelites were evoked to shed light on Kenya's inter-tribal rivalries.[3] In addition, many churches initiated prayer sessions and even fasting in plea for peace. The Nairobi Baptist Church had a fixed pre-elections program in which every week, during the main service, a different county was being prayed for.[4] Multiple initiatives and prayers for peace also ran throughout the country using public media. As Bishop David Oginde of Nairobi Pentecostal Church (NPC) observed during a televised interreligious forum, referring in particular to the practice of politicians using churches as a podium for promoting their own candidacy:

> If you are keen in observing, you will notice that this has greatly reduced. It is not eliminated but it is greatly reduced. If you compare this year with the 2007 for example, you hardly notice any church group or any church leader that are praying for, endorsing any particular candidates. This is because the church took a definite, made a definite decision, not to do that. We had a meeting and we agreed –we pray generally for the elections to be peaceful, we pray for our members who are campaigning that God may go before them, but that is general prayer. So the kind of thing that we saw in 2007 where there were prophecies, there were direct endorsements, there were direct callings on God to say this is your chosen servant, that kind of thing, you will notice that this time around, that is not (*Citizen TV*, February 16, 2013).

Despite such non-partisan rhetoric, on the ground, questions were raised as to how strictly the promises of impartiality were actually kept, throwing into question religious leaders' commitment to help steering the country off on a new course.[5] As for politicians themselves, while they may have been more careful this time around, many were still using religious platforms to promote their own candidacy even as they were talking of unity. As one member of JIAM aptly put it, politicians try "to win votes from the congregation, because all of the sudden you can see all these politicians are going from church to church, all over the country". Another member of JIAM remarked that "their interest is not to build the church; their interest is we build them. We choose them, we elect them, they need your votes, that's all".

At JIAM, already during the 2007 campaign, Wanjiru mobilized much of her supporters from the church. If her claim that 20,000 members of her church were also eligible Starehe voters is even remotely true, then it gave a significant boost to her election (*The Standard*, November 5, 2006). This mobilization of church supporters continued during the 2013 campaign, for instance when a senior leader at the church, Reverend Danson, openly endorsed Wanjiru from the podium, and encouraged the congregation to vote for her as ODM's nominated candidate for the Nairobi gubernatorial seat (JIAM morning service, December 30, 2012).Wanjiru herself spoke along similar lines, proposing to her congregation that "if you do not know who to vote for, call the numbers on the screen and we will tell you who to vote for" (JIAM morning service, January 13, 2013). JIAM has also had publicized visits from politicians, including most prominently from Raila Odinga, William Ruto, and Wanjiru's former rival Evans Kidero, who was later rumored to have cast a spell on Wanjiru whilst receiving prayers from her (informal discussion following JIAM morning service, January 20, 2013). But even when politics was not the order of the day at JIAM, Wanjiru's political struggle was brought in implicitly. Thus, once Wanjiru lost her chance to vie for the position of governor and was instead nominated for the senator's position, the theme for the corresponding JIAM service, presented by the visiting Ugandan Apostle Richard Mayanja, explored the idea whereby whenever one door closes another one opens (JIAM morning service, February 3, 2013).

Of the many church leaders running for office in 2013, it is safe to say that the one that attracted most attention was Wanjiru. Despite the fact that Wanjiru "often tells her life story during her sermons" (Kalu, 2008: 150), that "most news articles about her feature a retelling of her biography" (Kavulla, 2008: 258) and that "her personal history figures prominently on her half-hour Sunday broadcast on *Family TV*" (Kavulla, 2008: 258), there is a limit to how much can be said with certainty about her biography. As Kavulla suggests in an article devoted to exploring Wanjiru's figure, "[t]here is a gap between who Wanjiru once was and who she has now become, and in between her story becomes murky" (Kavulla, 2008: 257). Margaret Wanjiru Kariuki is said to have been born in 1961 and brought up in a lower class Kikuyu family in the outskirts of Nairobi. The first half of her life was a struggle, a period during which she kept odd jobs including cleaning, had three children out of wedlock, and – according to her own admission – became a skillful user of witchcraft. Having ended up working for a marketing firm, Wanjiru gave her life to Christ in 1990 during a crusade led by Nigerian self-confessed former Satanist Emmanuel Eni (Gifford, 2009: 116), and started preaching along Aga Khan Walk on Harambee Street in downtown Nairobi. She soon gathered a group of supporters and laid the foundation for what would eventually become JIAM. In the church, Wanjiru is delivering an energetic, down-to-earth brand of prosperity gospel. For Wanjiru, her biography is a telling source both of her divine favors and of her extraordinary determination and entrepreneurial skills.[6] In 1997, Wanjiru was ordained pastor and in 2002 was ordained bishop by Bishop Arthur Gitonga of Redeemed Gospel. Setting aside the problem of authority associated with Pentecostal ordinations, Wanjiru is said to have been the first Kenyan woman to be ordained a Pentecostal bishop (Parsitau, 2011: 134).

From her position today, Wanjiru commands an impressive range of activities. In 1998, she had moved JIAM to its current location at the central Haile Selassie Avenue in downtown Nairobi, in a hall that can host thousands. That same year, she started her televised show, "The Glory Is Here," a term which also became her catchphrase (The Star, September 16, 2011). Today, JIAM "runs a branch of the Good Samaritan Project, a Bible school, Faith Digest magazine, a cafeteria, Glory Development Fund, and a fleet of buses" (Parsitau, 2011: 134). The church, which claims branches in many countries, including Uganda, South Africa, the United Kingdom, the United States, Tanzania and Malawi, boasts around 20,000 members locally and internationally (Parsitau, 2011: 134; Gathogo, 2011:10), and runs fifteen to twenty services throughout the week.[7] It is clear therefore that "[b]esides being a televangelist, Wanjiru is also a shrewd businesswoman" (Parsitau, 2011: 134). More recently, Wanjiru announced the ambitious 'Glory Twin Towers' project, that would consist of two modern towers – 12 floors each, connected by a flyover – that will replace JIAM's current dilapidated building. In the spirit of Wanjiru's entrepreneurship, the towers are aimed to be more than a church, and to include, alongside a "main church auditorium, college and children's church" a "five star hotel with dedicated health facilities e.g. Swimming pool, Sauna and Gym; Banking Halls, Supermarket, Conference facilities; Office Space; Basement Parking".[8] Looking at the project's design, the towers resemble office blocks more than anything else, and certainly more than a church.[9]

Despite her success, Wanjiru is no stranger to controversies, scandals and rumors. While the bishop lives as a single woman and mother, a certain Mr. James Kamangu Ndimu caused a stir in 2007 as he surfaced and publically claimed, to Wanjiru's dismay, to be her common-law husband and father of her children. This saga unfolded "like a soap-opera" (Gifford 2009: 164) in the Kenyan media, and made a splash nationally.[10] But even after the matter has been silenced, Wanjiru remained in the headlines. In 2011 she was banned from conducting marriages by the Senior Deputy Registrar of Marriages FSM Ng'ang'a. When asked about the issue, Wanjiru claimed that the ban was due to her still being registered as a pastor at Redeemed Gospel, and that she simply needed to go through the bureaucratic procedure of cancelling her previous license. However, questions over this explanation have been raised (*The Star*, September 16, 2011). In 2012, Wanjiru, in her capacity as the Assistant Minister for Housing, was suspected of illegally grabbing houses, two under her own name and one in the name of JIAM (*Daily Nation*, March 18, 2012). Although she was officially cleared, our interviews with JIAM members showed that some questions remained unanswered.

The murkiness of Wanjiru's biography was to get her into trouble once again upon her decision to run for the governorship of Nairobi. According to the Kenyan constitution, anyone vying for the position of governor must be in possession of a university degree from an institution recognized by the Independent Electoral and Boundaries Commission (IEBC). Furthermore, the constitution stipulates that any party found to be contravening this law is committing a criminal offence. It is in light of such serious repercussions that several ODM members petitioned the chairman of the party's electoral board and the party secretary, Franklin Bett and Anyang Nyong'o respectively, to investigate allegations against Wanjiru. Commonly referred to as the "Honorable Bishop Doctor," Wanjiru alleges to have studied at the United Graduate College and Seminary International and at the Harvester Bible College in the United States, where she had obtained, in 2003, a doctorate in Divinity. However, both these institutes have not been recognized by the Board of Higher Education as certified institutes of higher learning. Wanjiru herself argued that she has been "crucified" by her opponents, who feared her popularity, and that the American institutes where she purportedly had gone to school have not been recognized because of discrimination against theological institutions (*CitizenTV*, January 29, 2013). She further argued that, in fact, she has five degrees–two taught degrees and three honorary ones–but was unable to convince the board, that went as far as questioning Wanjiru's high school diploma (*The Standard*, January 6, 2013). Neither did she enjoy the support of the general public, who was skeptical on how she could have been sitting through classes for years in the United States whilst preaching in Nairobi and managing JIAM. Even Wanjiru's supporters found this hard to believe. One of our interviewees, whom we will call George, a senior member of JIAM who has been involved in the church for nearly fifteen years, told us that, in his view, Wanjiru was "too overambitious" for running to the governorship position. George went on to explain his view on the university certificate question:

> The certificate business [...] For me, my conscious tells me that there was no witch-hunting certificate [sic]. Bishop doesn't have the certificates, I can tell you for sure she doesn't [have] them, I have been in JIAM. For her to produce transcripts that she has been to school, I have never heard about the school. If she's been in church from January to December, even if she's learning through correspondence, she's in church [...] She's at every month for a conference, every Tuesday she's there for a miracle service, every Sunday she's been preaching three services. If she's been a student, when does she have time to study?

On 17 January 2013, party nominations were held and Wanjiru was not on the ballot paper. Several days later, on 22 January 2013, ODM announced that, in lieu of her gubernatorial nomination, Wanjiru will be given direct nomination for the senatorial race for the Nairobi constituency. Accepting this party nomination, Wanjiru was pushing aside Mheshimiwa Elizabeth Ongoro, a female candidate who was already officially designated for the position. Once again, commentators were furious. Ms. Ongoro herself, who has claimed to be campaigning for the senate position for years using her own funds, said she was not consulted by the party before her place was given to Wanjiru. As she said to reporters in response to the news, "[i]t is unfortunate that the Senate, which is the highest level of legislation, has become a dumping ground for dwarfs. If Bishop Wanjiru did not qualify for the gubernatorial position on the ground of academic qualifications, what makes it right for her to vie for any other top position?" (*The Standard*, January 25, 2013). In the papers and on the social networks, Wanjiru was vehemently attacked for her behavior. In their comments, some suggested that even if such behavior has come to be expected from politicians, Wanjiru's religious position should have committed her to higher moral standing. One commentator thus wrote on Wanjiru's Facebook page (January 30, 2013, 09:06): "You have been acting to be a bishop but you have finally proven that it is all about business and duping people as many other bishops today. What you did to Mheshimiwa Ongoro will forever haunt you!!!!!!!!!!!!!!"

On the day of the elections, not even the direct nomination over Ongoro helped Wanjiru. With 526,437 votes, she came a distant second after her main rival, TNA's Gideon Kioko Mike Mbuvi, popularly known as Sonko, who won 814,184 votes. Wanjiru thus came out of the race as a definite loser. And as if her own loss at the polls had not been bad enough, Wanjiru's son, Steven Kariuki, who was running for the Mathare parliamentary seat, was erroneously declared winner, receiving a certificate only to have it taken away shortly after (*Daily Nation*, March 9, 2013). Perhaps worst of all, Wanjiru's public image suffered a blow. Following the public realization that her claim for academic certificate is hardly defendable, one columnist sardonically wondered: "How shall I address Margaret Wanjiru if ever I am so fortunate to meet her? I could try 'Bishop', but I am not sure if her Jesus Is Alive Ministry qualifies as a diocese. I could call her 'Doctor', but it turns out that the ODM nominations board may disagree with my assessment. I could always call her Honorable MP." (*Daily Nation*, DN2, January 28, 2013). Considering Wanjiru's operations being centered on her charismatic, and supposedly moral, leadership, such a blow to her personal prestige may have far-reaching implications, some of which are yet to be seen.

We now turn to focus on the two strands discussed at the start of the article: (1) Wanjiru as a member of a 'righteous class' and an agent of a 'Godly plan', and (2) Wanjiru as representing entrepreneurial spirit.

Strand A: "When the righteous are in authority" – but who are the righteous?

From a Pentecostal perspective, the question of leadership is set within a dualistic framework of spiritual warfare. As Amos Yong argues, Pentecostals have a tendency to expand this dualistic struggle from the personal-spiritual to the socio-political, which he calls the "polis" (Yong, 2010). In the context of elections, good leaders are believed to draw their electioneering appeal from God, whereas bad leaders are suspected of drawing their appeal from evil powers. Two committed Pentecostals, interviewed together some months before the 2013 elections, illustrate this perspective. As the interviewees suggested, on the side of evil, the devil and his followers would use witchcraft and even human sacrifices to boost their political influence. By contrast, for those on God's side, elections are a time for being on guard, attending church and praying regularly in order to counter such malevolence:

> *Interviewee A*: Going to church, praying, it's really for fighting those evil spirits or whatever. Even us, we are told every time we pray about our country. We have to pray for those elections which are coming so that God can give us the right leaders.

> *Interviewee B*: what we are actually trying to do for Kenya at the moment, it's only praying. You know, like now, all these politicians they've already given now, as in, they've done their rituals, like, they are so optimistic, like, "I'm going to win," you see, like, you are told to do a certain thing like maybe you are told, "give us ten people for a sacrifice." What do they do? So nowadays there are so many accidents in Kenya, and they are all claiming people's lives. […] So how do we know that these are not the sacrifices that these people are giving out? So we need to pray more, and if they are giving us for sacrifices then those, yeah the chains need to be broken for us to be set free.

> *Interviewee A*: That one is through praying and through going to church. We should not cease going to church even if he's there, even if those [evil] people are there. We have to fight with them, and fighting with them we don't use our hands, we fight with them through praying and going to church and communicating to our God.

The two interviewees presented a straightforward dualistic perspective which aligns good political leadership with religious righteousness and bad leadership with wrongful spiritual manipulations, including witchcraft and human sacrifices. However, noting interviewee A's final remark, it is often hard to make out which is which, since even the supposedly evil might nonetheless pose as active church members.

By and large, a key advantage that religion can help sustain is a feeling of trust, a rare commodity in light of Kenyans' cynical approach towards leaders' integrity. Kenyan churches have the potential of stepping in to fill the void left by politicians, because churches, much more than politics, command certain moral ground. Supporting this view, a study by the Pew Research Center (2006) highlighted the concern of 88% of its Kenyan respondents, who argued that "corrupt political leaders" pose a "very big problem". Similarly, two Afrobarometer nationwide studies showed the majority arguing that officials who commit crimes go unpunished most or all the time (64% in 2011, 70% in 2008), while only about a fifth of the respondents (20% in 2011, 18% in 2008) believe that ordinary citizens who break the law face similar chances of evading justice. More recently, in a study conducted by Transparency International, 70% of Kenyans admitted to have paid bribe to a public body over the last year, findings which unflatteringly place Kenya fourth among the 95 countries under study (Transparency International, 2013).[11] By contrast, one of the questions in the 2011 Afrobarometer survey had to do with trust in religious leaders, where a significant minority of 28% of the overall respondents answered that they trust religious leaders "a lot". Similarly, the Pew Research Centre study (2006) had 36% of Kenyan respondents answering that they have "a lot" of trust in "people at your church or place of worship". Religion, it seems, provides a haven of relative institutional trust.

However, if such religious trust seems moderate, there are signs that it is eroding even further. As we have argued elsewhere (Gez and Droz, forthcoming), the social image associated with Born Again Christianity has been wearing down in recent years, accompanied by a growing sense of mistrust and even suspicion towards those designating themselves as such. Church-related scandals and what many regard as a cynical abuse of prosperity teachings leads believers to doubt the nobleness of church leaders' intentions. Politically, Kenya's elite has given countless examples of religion being employed in the service of impunity (Gifford, 2009). In recent years, the post-elections violence provided an unforgettable warning that religiosity is not a guarantee for peaceful, moral conduct. As one interviewee told us, "after the last [2007] election, a country of 80% Christian people fought. Are we Christian? [...] people were willing to wipe us up all of the sudden because of stolen elections. That is not right for people who are spiritually saved." Thus, while most Kenyans would agree that, in principle, religious leaders are more likely to have good moral standing, they are also familiar with examples of religious offices and rhetoric being misused. While accepting that God must have a 'plan' for Kenya, the average Christian nonetheless shows growing doubts in people claiming to speak on His behalf.

Upon announcing her political candidacy for 2007, which came to her "from God" through the encouragement of American Prophetess Brenda Todd (Kavulla, 2008), Wanjiru quoted Proverbs 29:2–"when the righteous are in authority, the people rejoice"–as she was turning to her congregation for support (Parsitau, 2011:135). This verse has been taken to convey the belief that members of a "righteous class," as we may call them, chosen by God, would serve as ideal political leaders. In our interviews with JIAM members in the run-up to the 2013 elections, several of them evoked this verse in justifying their support of Wanjiru's candidacy. Here are two examples, taken from two separate interviews:[12]

> *Interviewee C*: Me, I think I felt good [with Wanjiru running for politics], because this Kenya of ours, we have nowadays, there is a lot of corruption around. There is somewhere in bible [that] says, I can't remember the verse, "when good people, or righteous people, are in power – people rejoice" [...]. You see, so if these people, the righteous people, could have been in power, you know they fear God, and when you fear God you do not want to do any wrong, you see, so to me I would like to see many of Bishop Margaret [get elected].

> *Interviewee D*: I'm very comfortable with it [with Wanjiru running for politics]. So many people argue out that she's not supposed to be one [running], but then you see, even in the bible, [it] says "when the righteous rule the people are happy." You know, so if you have someone who is born again, someone [...] who is reliable, I know she's a good manager, so really I don't think there is any problem her being an MP.

From this perspective, Wanjiru, as a Born Again religious leader, could be thought of as a suitable political leader. Inherent here is the idea, commonly evoked by Kenyan Pentecostals, that God is the answer to all of life's misfortunes afflicting body, soul and society. This idea is presented clearly in popular gospel artist Esther Wahome's song Kuna Dawa ("there is a cure"), which presents Christian salvation as a panacea. In the video clip, we see Wahome bringing the Word to people in various settings, including children in school, Maasai in tribal clothes, slum dwellers, and the sick in a hospital ward. Although not overtly political, the song contrasts between divine blessings and the tribulations of daily existence, and can thus be used to convey the idea that "clerics can bring Christian values to politics, which in Kenya is widely seen as 'dirty'" (*Daily Nation*, February 21, 2013). Interestingly, the song was employed by Wanjiru in her 2013 campaign, in which she claimed that the ODM and herself can provide the much needed cures to the ills faced by Nairobians and by the country as a whole.[13] One of our interviewees, a member of JIAM, elaborated on this analogy: "church is like a hospital. I have never seen a hospital take someone who has had an accident as maybe someone who is healthy […]. Whether you are healthy or you're sick, the church should admit you, and know where your problem is and treat you. That is why church is like a hospital."

But while making such uses of her religious appeal, Wanjiru found it hard to convincingly sustain the required untarnished image. From the beginning of the campaigning season it seemed that, despite her religious credentials, Wanjiru would probably not be bringing in an added moral value. Note the discourse by George, whom we have already quoted, as he combines his faith in Christian leadership to overcome corruption with his disillusionment with Wanjiru's own political ethics:

> If really this country is full of corruption, if we got somebody who is a Christian, things are likely to be different. Bishop [Wanjiru], she may also have her own weaknesses, and I just want to admit here, and God forgive, we are not supposed to talk about the men of God, [but] during the [2007] elections, because I was almost completely involved, I saw things happen, I saw even money exchanged, even from her side I saw money exchanged *laughing* […]. I could see them do things that were not right, I could see them involved in rigging, those things happened. You can't say it's the other party; they happened across the board.

Indeed, Wanjiru's decision to enter politics risked compromising her religious image. Already upon joining politics in 2007, Wanjiru's decision received mixed reactions among her religious followers, many of whom have left the church as a result. In addition to general opposition to combining religion with politics, some were unhappy with Wanjiru's decision to join the ODM despite her Kikuyu ethnicity. Moreover, by claiming that her candidacy was ordained by God, Wanjiru was taking a high risk. Although not in direct opposition to Pastor Muiru of Maximum Miracles Centre, who ambitiously ran for presidency, many saw the potential for frictions over those claiming divine endorsement as a sign of disingenuousness, for the true spirit of God is believed to be a bringer of harmony. Commentators voiced their reservations against the Pentecostal entrance into politics, emphasizing in particular both pastors' controversial emphasis on the prosperity gospel (Gathogo, 2011: 14-16). One interviewee, himself a staunch Born Again, told us how back in 2007, the political aspirations of the two leaders have led him to question their authenticity: "You come and tell me that the spirit of the Lord has spoken to you, that I should take this seat. Then I come to you and I tell you that the spirit of the Lord has spoken to me and I will take this seat. I mean, we claim to have the same God. Who is speaking the truth? You are saying that one is lying, or none is telling the truth. Less chances that one is telling the truth."

A much more direct clash was to occur in 2013. While in 2007, Muiru and Wanjiru were each running for a different position, in 2013, once Wanjiru was forced to quit the gubernatorial race and to enter the senatorial race instead, she found herself running against another well-established religious leader, namely Bishop Dr. Adoyo of NPC, a popular church also known as Christ is the Answer Ministries (CITAM).[14] An obvious comparison can be drawn between Adoyo and Wanjiru, two bishops and leaders of large Pentecostal congregations in Nairobi. Even as Adoyo's low-key campaign, that got him merely 10,527 votes, never posed a significant challenge to Wanjiru, it does shed light on her candidacy. Thus for instance, while Wanjiru was determined to maintain her role as head of JIAM throughout her campaign, Adoyo claimed to have resigned his position at the NPC in order to join politics (*Daily Nation*, February 21, 2013). At the same time however, and much like Wanjiru, Adoyo mobilized support from within the church, using church volunteers as campaigners (*Family TV*, February 12, 2013).

Explaining how two men of God could be vying for the same position, Adoyo argued that he has been preparing to run for the senatorial position long before Wanjiru, who, having "failed to get the governor seat", fell back on the senatorial race. According to Adoyo, Wanjiru had asked him to switch with her and to run for governor, supposedly in order to avoid this conflict between men of God. In a response that engages the two strands – divine plan and personal entrepreneurship – Adoyo claims to have responded to Wanjiru that "this is not my calling. My calling is to set up a vision formulation, structures and systems, laws and by-laws and policies. That [is what] I have done in my church and left it going, that is my strength" (*Family TV*, February 12, 2013). While avoiding arguing that his candidacy was mandated by God, Adoyo's race against Wanjiru nonetheless raised theological questions.

Adoyo further claimed that, for the purposes of running for office, he had resigned from all his positions at the church. "You cannot serve two masters. I had to leave being an active bishop to join politics," he said (*Daily Nation*, February 21, 2013). On this backdrop, Wanjiru's commitment to remain an active church leader came under attack.[15] Wanjiru admitted that "even some of the clergy themselves, the older generation" – here implying perhaps Adoyo's indirect accusation – "they say: if you want to go to politics – resign, then you go to politics. My argument is 'I am too young to resign. I am energetic. You want me to resign and go where? I mean, I have three kids, four grandchildren, let me serve the people'" (*Capital FM*, February 8, 2013). Although Wanjiru's refusal to step down as a church leader while running for the 2013 elections was not different from her actions in 2007, it still drew debates and critiques. In the senatorial race, Wanjiru's main rival was Sonko, the flamboyant, youthful TNA candidate, who vehemently criticized Wanjiru's dual vocations, saying "I am a Christian and I do not like anyone misusing the name of God. Imagine she announced her bid for governorship in her church. That really pissed me off" (*Daily Nation*, March 17, 2013).[16] Between the two candidates developed an indirect exchange, citing biblical verses back and forth concerning the legitimacy of religious leaders pursuing political careers (*Citizen TV*, January 23, 2013; *Citizen TV*, January 29, 2013). This exchange also drew attention to the generational gap between the two, which both acknowledged to their advantage.[17] Such attacks, although delivered of course by Wanjiru's rivals, nonetheless highlight a popular sentiment that sees Wanjiru's political career as an expansion not of religious commitment but of her personal ambitions towards amassing power and titles.

Strand B: "BMW": Wanjiru as an entrepreneur

As said, the race for the Nairobi senatorial position saw the unusual contestation of two Pentecostal bishops. Although Adoyo was clearly the underdog, the comparison between the two was unavoidable. Adoyo's formal agenda was primarily geared towards matters of good governance, saying for instance that he will "confront corruption without fear or intimidation as 'the Bible says do not fear those who can destroy the body but the spirit'" (*Daily Nation*, February 21, 2013). By contrast, Wanjiru had put the subject of "wealth creation" on top of her list, promising to set in place laws which would favor small businesses, helping for instance to regulate the work of street hawkers and transport workers. Here are two brief excerpts from interviews she gave, both in response to a question concerning her agenda for the city:

> Number one on the list – wealth creation [...]. Our manifesto [is]: jobs, jobs, jobs. So, wealth creation is top of the list. We must create jobs for our people. To do that we must have the right laws in place, to implement what we want to do. That is my number one job (*Citizen TV*, January 29, 2013).

> Number one, I would like to start with wealth creation. My number one agenda is wealth creation. We have such a wide gap between the rich and the poor, it's miserable. I mean, when you see the poor people, even the laws that we have are not friendly to the poor, but they are very friendly to the rich people. [...] So my number one assignment is to make sure that the small businesses are well taken care of, accommodated, have trading areas, and got friendly trading laws (*Capital FM*, February 8, 2013).

The two bishops' different political agendas are telling of the "many tongues" (Yong, 2010) of Pentecostal political engagements. More than that, these differences might be a reflection of the two's different religious leanings. Notwithstanding his conservative stand on some matters,[18] Adoyo – as his church – is widely held as a lenient, respectable, mainstream Pentecostal.[19] In one of his books he explains his theological stand by suggesting that "we believers [can] be gracious and liberal when it comes to issues on which the Bible is silent, but uncompromising and dogmatic where God's Word is specific" (Adoyo, 2009: 108). Wanjiru, on her side, is one of Kenya's leading proponents of the prosperity gospel (Gathogo, 2011). Among her multiple nicknames and titles is the telling acronym BMW – standing for Bishop Margaret Wanjiru– which is sometimes used by her supporters. This appellation plays on the common association of luxury cars not only with economic power but also as a mark of membership at the privileged club of political upper class. Thus for instance, the Swahili term "wabenzi" is sometimes used to allude to Kenya's ruling elite, referring of course to its members' affection for luxury vehicles including Mercedes Benz (Wrong, 2009: 79-80, 338). The identification of Wanjiru as BMW points at her religious teachings, which openly and unapologetically invoke material abundance, but also insinuates Wanjiru's acceptance into Kenya's ruling class, an affiliation affirmed despite her humble origin. But such acceptance into the ranks of the powerful risks distancing Wanjiru from the principles of justice associated with her religious leadership. Michela Wrong, for instance, cites a survey by the Kenya National Commission on Human Rights (KNCHR) which showed that, during the year following Kibaki's first election, government officials spent an inflated amount of at least \$12m on luxury cars (Wrong, 2009: 79-80). By embracing the symbolic nickname BMW, Wanjiru has been lending herself to compromising her prospects for passing as a divinely mandated alternative to the corrupt system.[20] The following except, taken from her preaching at JIAM, is reminiscent of the entrepreneurial spirit which Wanjiru sought to bring to her position as senator:

> We simply don't have to be poor. We can be rich, and have wealth, and not apologize for it. Don't apologize for your shamba, for your farm. Why are you trying to explain to people how you got it? You were praying for it. Go and plant the flowers and then export them. Don't apologize for your good car. Drive it like you own it, not like you borrowed it.[21]

One last example can illustrate the place of Wanjiru's religious success in the service of her political ambitions. During her 2013 campaign, Wanjiru participated in a morning radio show, where she presented her agenda as a senatorial candidate. Throughout the thirty minutes interview, Wanjiru made little appeal to her religious capacity. In the following excerpt, however, her religious position is evoked in a peculiar fashion, as an example that supports her image as a successful entrepreneur and leader. Note as well the religious language used ("rise from your ashes"), the notion of "transformation" and in particular the idea of "transforming the mind" away from poverty, which strike a deep cord with Wanjiru's church teachings:

> Nairobi needs a role model. Nairobi needs a leader who is very transformative. You need to transform the communities. I always say: poverty is not a state of the pocket; it is a state of the mind. If you can transform the minds then you are able to transform the pocket. If you are not able to transform the mind, it doesn't matter [what is] the state of the pocket, that person cannot change. So my number one assignment is – create the opportunities. Then transform the mindset of our people that you do not have to be poor. Whether you got good education or not, you do not have to be poor. You can rise up from your ashes. Look at me; look at the church that I run today. It's an international organization. But that's not where I started. I started on the streets; I was a preacher on the streets (*Capital FM*, February 8, 2013).

Conclusion

Through examining the two strands which ran throughout Wanjiru's 2013 campaign, we conclude that, of the two, it is the latter one, which portrays Wanjiru as a strong female entrepreneur, which had by and large prevailed. It might further be that this indicates of a change from 2007, when Wanjiru's campaign was more clearly dressed in religious terms (Kavulla, 2008). This does not mean, however, that the first strand has been lost altogether in the 2013 campaign. Indeed, we note that the first strand, which identifies Wanjiru with the 'righteous class' and as part of a 'Godly plan' for Kenya, was also present in 2013, if less pronounced. To some extent, appeal to either of the two strands seems to depend on context. We have noted that in church contexts, Wanjiru more easily promotes herself, using the first strand, as an agent of a 'Godly plan' (Kavulla, 2008), while outside the church– e.g. in formal interviews– she puts more emphasis on the second, entrepreneurial strand. Such selective self-presentation would present Wanjiru as engaging in a "strategy of action" which, depending on circumstances, highlights any of a number of justifications that may reinforce her claims (Swidler, 1986).

Shortly before the elections, in a televised interview with Wanjiru's rival Bishop Adoyo, a Presbyterian pastor made a comment to the effect that "Christians who get into political positions – somehow there is something about politics that eats into the Christianity of these people, and they never get to stand. They get to be diluted, they are watered down." (*Family TV*, February 12, 2013). Wanjiru's failure in the 2013 elections can be read in such a light, as the result of her inability to convincingly balance between her political capacity and the moral and spiritual standings expected of a Born Again Christian and church leader. From doubts over her legitimacy for carrying out her duties as a Bishop while in political office, through corruption scandals at the Ministry of Housing, controversial academic documents that have led to her losing her chance at the Nairobi gubernatorial race, and her taking the ODM's senatorial nomination seat from Elizabeth Ongoro who was nominated democratically – these contentious issues played against Wanjiru's possibility of promoting herself as a vehicle for 'Godly' politics. By passionately navigating herself towards the strand of 'worldly' affairs, promoting herself above all else as a self-made strong woman, Wanjiru's religious reputation was compromised, making her appear disingenuous in the eyes of the electorate.

Indeed, we suggest that, by the time of the 2013 elections, Wanjiru was almost forced out of the 'righteous class' strand by the scandals that surrounded her, and which were related to her non-religious, morally questionable pursuits of business, power and influence. In other words, while the two strands can similarly find grounding in neo-Pentecostal teachings, they are not always easy to bring together. We thus reach the claim that, even as the two strands are not contradictory per se, there is, nonetheless, tension between them. Having established herself, through discourse and action, as an entrepreneur above all else, Wanjiru has been drifting away from reliably establishing herself as a true agent of "politics of the spirit" out to sanitize the Kenyan political sphere. Instead, by looking at Wanjiru's compromised reputation, tarnished in large part by the extension of her affairs outside the church, it can be argued that her strong entrepreneurial ambitions are partially to blame for her loss. Deemed by the public as too much like secular leaders through her preoccupations and implications in scandals, Wanjiru had lost the privilege of convincingly branding herself as the herald of clean, Godly politics.

Building up on this case study, we touch on what we believe is a fundamental tension for scholars and an ongoing challenge for neo-Pentecostals: if we recognize that Born Again identity implies certain moral and spiritual values, and if we also recognize that neo-Pentecostalism tends to invoke the integration of the believer into the wider public spheres of social, economic and political engagements, how can the two be kept in harmony, and how may such 'worldly' Pentecostalism provide a moral high ground, uncontaminated, as it were, by rampant social ills? This constant tension has been recognized, in different ways, by our Pentecostal informants, and it is affirmed by many Kenyan Christians working as civil servants.22One way of resolving this tension is by allowing one strand to overcome the other. Already Paul Gifford argued that, among Kenyan proponents of the prosperity gospel, the "success motif" "effectively substitutes" the more "foundational Christian doctrines and ideas" (Gifford 2009: 124). The difficulty of negotiating a Pentecostal identity that is active in the world while also grounded in uncompromising moral principles that rise above immoral norms of conduct appears to be widespread in contemporary Kenya. As one informant uttered with concern, "Christianity has become a very big challenge."

Acknowledgements

Our thanks go to Samuel Owiwa for his help during fieldwork. We further thank Yvan Droz and Hervé Maupeu for their enlightening comments on the draft manuscript.

Notes

1 Other religious candidates in 2007 have included Kamlesh Pattni, the architect of the Goldenberg scandal, who, having become Born Again, set up the now defunct Kenya National Democratic Alliance (Kenda) party, many of whose candidates were drawn from the ranks of Evangelical and Pentecostal clergy. Other religious candidates included Rev. Moses ole Sakuda, who ran on the ODM ticket in Kajiado North and lost; Pentecostal minister Mike Brawan who ran on the ODM ticket for the Nakuru Town constituency and lost, and Rev. Mutava Musyimi, former secretary-general of the National Council of Churches of Kenya and pastor at Nairobi Baptist Church (currently an Anglican), who ran on the Party of National Unity (PNU) ticket and won the Gachoka seat.

2 In addition to Wanjiru, the 2013 elections saw a wide array of Christian leaders from across the country wanting to fill gubernatorial and senatorial seats. Anglican Reverend Lawrence Bomet from Nakuru, which was one of the areas worst hit by violence and ethnically motivated attacks in early 2008, was vying to be the first senator of Nakuru on an ODM ticket. In West Pokot, Reverend Julius Murgor of the African Inland Church also sought a senatorial position. In Mbeere South Constituency, former secretary general of the National Council of Churches of Kenya and Gachoka Member of Parliament, Anglican Reverend Mutava Musyimi, was defending his parliamentary seat on a The National Alliance (TNA) ticket. Bishop Jackson Kipkemboi Kosgey of Baringo County, a Reverend at the Full Gospel of Kenya Church, backed William Ruto's United Republican Party (URP) and sought a senatorial seat. Lastly, Bishop Bonifes Adoyo of Nairobi Pentecostal Church (NPC), whose candidacy will be discussed briefly in this paper, ran against Wanjiru and Sonko for the senatorial race.

3 Visit to the church, February 5, 2012.

4 Visit to the church, April 8, 2012. This example is also telling of the ambiguity of such initiatives. Having visited the church on the week in which it was praying for Kilifi County, we noted that the prayer did not limit itself to the aim of peaceful elections alone, but also included the aspiration for bringing the work of God to the county's "indigenous people." Considering the county's Muslim dominance, such a declaration of intentions risks fueling tensions between communities rather than quelling them.

5 The endorsement of candidates by religious organizations was evident in the case of Muslim leadership, where Raila Odinga was the presidential candidate of choice by the Muslim Leaders Forum, whilst the Association of Muslim Organizations backed the now President of Kenya, Uhuru Kenyatta (*Citizen TV*, February 16, 2013).

6 See Wanjiru's brief biography on JIAM's website, http://www1.jiam.org/index.php/about-jiam/bishops-profile.html. Considering Wanjiru's self-branding and tendency towards the prosperity gospel, we may muse over the possible influence that her marketing background could have had on her ministry.

7 See JIAM's homepage at: http://www1.jiam.org.

8 See JIAM's homepage at: http://www1.jiam.org.

9 Following complaints by our interviewees at JIAM about lack of transparency concerning the allocation of their church contributions, we may question the timing of the project, and wonder whether its announcement could not have been planned in such a way as to provide additional revenues to support Wanjiru's 2013 electioneering.

10 Kamangu died in October 2008, while his court case against Wanjiru was still pending. Due to the timing of his death, concern was raised that Kamangu may have actually been murdered, leading the family to call for a post-mortem examination(*Capital FM*, November 17, 2008; Citizen TV, October 10, 2008). While such accusations have never been formally substantiated, rumours continued to abound implicating Wanjiru

in Kamangu's death. Such accusations were supported by Wanjiru's open hostility towards Kamangu, whom she threatened on a number of occasions, calling him to "hang on a tree and we will have a funeral" (Kavulla, 2008: 258).

11 On top of the list were Sierra Leone (84%), Liberia (75%) and Yemen (74%).

12 The two interviewees are family related, and are also related to the interviewee whom we have called George.

13 For instance, watch http://www.youtube.com/watch?v=VG0AnFuNEW8.

14 Bishop Adoyo's long career covered a number of distinguished leadership roles, including chancellor for the Pan Africa Christian University, chairman of the Pentecostal Assemblies of Africa, and moderator of the Interreligious Council of Kenya. During Moi's last years in office, Adoyo was a member of the Commission of Inquiry into the Cult of Devil Worship (Adoyo, 2009).

15 Already when running in 2007, there had been strong opposition from Wanjiru's milieu to her keeping both positions. Among the objectors, according to the aforementioned interviewee George, was even Bishop Gitonga of Redeemed Gospel Church, the man who ordained Wanjiru as bishop.

16 Sonko himself converted to Christianity at Kamlesh Pattni'sHope International Ministries in 2010. During the 2007 and the 2010 campaigns, both Sonko and Wanjiru enjoyed the support of former Mungiki leader Maina Njenga, who is currently the bishop at Amazing Grace International Church in Nairobi (Maupeu, 2014; Daily Nation, November 7, 2010).

17 This exchange was carried out through subtle insinuations veiled as generational respect. Thus, Sonko referred to Wanjiru as "my mother," hinting at her irrelevance by adding that "she is the same age my mother was when she died" (Citizen TV, January 23, 2013). Wanjiru, on her side, referred to Sonko as "one of my many, many, many sons," implying her seniority by arguing that "I have nothing against Sonko, Sonko is a young man that just needs to be guided, a young man who needs to be mentored" (*Citizen TV*, January 29, 2013).

18 Adoyo has taken a leading part in the "hide the bones" campaign, in which Kenyan Christians were mobilized to boycott the National Museum of Kenya, which housed the "Turkana boy" fossils and demanded that it should be removed from display. The debate was captured in Richard Dawkins' TV series "The Genius of Charles Darwin" (Part 2: The Fifth Ape, 2008), where Adoyo is interviewed by Dawkins.

19 Interestingly, a study ordered by Odoyo's CITAM has shown that its congregants are divided as to whether their church indeed counts as Pentecostal or not. The survey, conducted among members of the church's Buruburu branch, had 55.3% of the respondents arguing that their congregation is not in fact Pentecostal (Chelule, 2012). This confusion may have to do with CITAM's orderliness and the moderate engagement with the Holy Spirit, which contrast the church with what one of our interviewees termed "churches that are SO Pentecostal."

20 Also note that, unlike many devout Christians who wear a cross necklace, Wanjiru tends to wear a necklace featuring a stylized "M" – presumably standing for Margaret. This might offer another manifestation of Wanjiru's privileging of personal success and entrepreneurship.

21 http://www.youtube.com/watch?v=sCZ16eAam_Y (Published on October 14, 2012). This sermon was given on the occasion of Raila Odinga's visit to her church.

22 Such clash of values has been recognized in the case of Kenyan Born Again policemen, many of whom end up either leaving the force or forsaking their faith (Muturi, 2001:35).

Bibliography

Interviews

George, interviewed by Tanya Alvis in Nairobi, February 6, 2013

Interviewees A-B, interviewed by Yonatan N. Gez in Nairobi, July 12, 2012

Interviewee C, interviewed by Tanya Alvis in Nairobi, February 5, 2013

Interviewee D, interviewed by Tanya Alvis in Nairobi, January 11, 2013

Media and Electronic Resources

Barasa, L. "Nairobi Bishops Have to Beat Sonko, Livondo (UDF) and Omtatah to Win Mixing Pulpit with Politics to Serve the People." *Daily Nation*, February 21, 2013: 18-19.

Capital FM. "Capital Breakfast Hosts Bishop Margaret Wanjiru (Part 1)." February 8, 2013. http://www.youtube.com/watch?v=Ld89BfkAWUM (accessed July 28, 2013).

Capital FM. "Kamangu Death Probe Launched" November 17, 2008. http://www.capitalfm. co.ke/news/2008/11/kamangu-death-probe-launched (accessed September 17, 2014).

Citizen TV. "Poisoning Not Cause of Kamangu's Death." October 10, 2008. https://www. youtube.com/watch?v=m6-1MYaCrvY (accessed September 14, 2014).

Citizen TV. "Margaret Wanjiru Enters Nairobi Governorship Race." November 18, 2012. http:// www.youtube.com/watch?v=uDUkMlBYu1o (accessed July 28, 2013).

Citizen TV, "LilianMuli Interviews Church Leaders on Religion and Politics." February 16, 2013. http://www.youtube.com/watch?v=66zaDjoEMHM (accessed July 28, 2013).

Citizen TV. "Bishop Margaret Wanjiru Live Studio Interview." January 29, 2013. http://www. youtube.com/watch?v=DQqcahVyQ7c (accessed July 28, 2013).

Citizen TV. "Mike Sonko Live Studio Interview." January 23, 2013. http://www.youtube.com/ watch?v=rDw5jznna_0 (accessed July 28, 2013).

Dawkins, R. *The Genius of Charles Darwin*. Part 2: The Fifth Ape. UK. 2008.

Family TV. "Crosstalk: Nairobi Senatorial Race, Bishop Adoyo (Part 1)." February 12, 2013. http://www.youtube.com/watch?v=SSjaZ6Om4S8 (accessed July 28, 2013).

Kareithi, A. "Bishop Wanjiru Hopes to Be President." *The Standard,* November 5, 2006. http:// allafrica.com/stories/200611060988.html (accessed July 28, 2013).

Kimatu, S. "Sonko Now 'Turns to the Lord'". *Daily Nation*, November 7, 2010.

Mayoyo, P. and O. Mathenge. "Wanjiru Was Allocated Two NHC Houses, Audit Shows."

Daily Nation March 18, 2012. http://www.nation.co.ke/News/Minister+was+allocated+NHC+houses+/-/1056/1368992/-/15q6yi5z/-/index.html (accessed 28 July 2013).

Muiruri, B. "The Rise and Rise of Servant Sonko in Politics of the City." *Daily Nation*, March 17, 2013:20.

Nation Reporters. "Wanjiru Son Loses Win after 'Error'." *Daily Nation*, March 9, 2013:5

Ng'etich, J. "Questions Raised over Wanjiru's Papers." *The Standard*, January 6, 2013:9.

Odongo, W. "The Glory of Separation of Church and State is Coming." *Daily Nation*, DN2, January 28, 2013:4.

Oduor, P. "The Kenyan Church and the Gospel of Prosperity." *Daily Nation*, DN2, February 13, 2013: 2-3.

Olick, F. "Ongoro Rejects Direct ODM Ticket for Ruaraka Seat, Vows to Fight on." *The Standard*, January 25, 2013:15.

The Star Reporters. "Bishop Wanjiru Banned from Doing Weddings." September 16, 2011. http://www.the-star.co.ke/news/article-49131/bishop-wanjiru-banned-doing-weddings (accessed July 28, 2013).

Academic Material, Books, and Reports

Adoyo, B. *The Weaving Hand: Lessons from my life and ministry.* Nairobi: Evangel Publishing House, 2009.

Afrobarometer. *"Round 4 Afrobarometer: Survey in Kenya."* Institute for Development Studies (IDS), University of Nairobi & Michigan State University (MSU), 2008.

———. *"Round 5 Afrobarometer: Survey in Kenya."* Institute for Development Studies (IDS), University of Nairobi & Michigan State University (MSU), 2011.

Alexander, P. "Historical and Contemporary Pentecostal Critiques of Nationalism". In *The 34th Annual Meeting of the SPS*. Regent University, Virginia Beach, VA, 2005.

Anderson, A. *An Introduction to Pentecostalism: Global charismatic Christianity.* Cambridge: Cambridge University Press, 2004.

Cartledge, M.J. "Practical Theology". In *Studying Global Pentecostalism: Theories and methods*. Eds. M. Bergunder, A. Anderson, and A. F. Droogers, 268-85. Berkeley, Los Angeles and London: University of California Press, 2010.

Cheeseman, N. "The Kenyan Elections of 2007: An introduction". *Journal of Eastern African Studies* 2, no.2 (2008): 166-184.

Chelule, E. "Pentecostalism and Being Born-Again: A case study of Nairobi Pentecostal Church (NPC) / Christ Is The Answer Ministries (CITAM) Buruburu, Nairobi". In *Mobilité Religieuse en Afrique de l'Est / Religious Mobility in Eastern Africa*. CUEA, Nairobi, 2012.

Droz, Y. and H. Maupeu. "Christianismes et démocratisation au Kenya". *Social Compass* 60, no.1 (2013): 79-96.

Freston, P. *Evangelicals and Politics in Asia, Africa and Latin America*. Cambridge: Cambridge University Press. 2004.

———. "Pentecostalism in Brazil: A brief history". *Religion* 25 (1995): 119-133.

Gathogo, J. "The Challenge of Money and Wealth in Some East African Pentecostal Churches". *Studia Historiae Ecclesiasticae* 37, no. 2 (2011): 133-51.

Gez, Y.N. and Y. Droz. "Disrupted Born Again Gains: Negotiation and erosion of Pentecostal prestige in Nairobi". *Nova Religio* (forthcoming).

Gifford, P. *Christianity, Politics and Public Life in Kenya*. New York: Columbia University Press, 2009.

Hardoon, D. and F. Heinrich. "Global Corruption Barometer." *Transparency International*, 2013.

Kalu, O. *African Pentecostalism: An introduction*. Oxford & New York: Oxford University Press, 2008.

Kavulla, T.R. "'Our Enemies Are God's Enemies': The religion and politics of Bishop Margaret Wanjiru, MP". *Journal of Eastern African Studies* 2, no.2 (2008): 254-63.

Knighton, B. (ed.) *Religion and Politics in Kenya: Essays in honor of a meddlesome priest*. New York: Palgrave Macmillan, 2009.

Meagher, K. "Trading on Faith: Religious movements and informal economic governance in Nigeria". *Journal of Modern African Studies* 47, no. 3 (2009): 397-423.

Mary, A. "Actualité du paganism et contemporanéité des prophétismes". *L'Homme*, 185-186 (2008): 365-86.

Maupeu, H. "La politique du butinage religieuxet le butinage religieux en politique: le cas de Mungiki (Kenya)". In *Retours croisés des Afriques aux Amériques : de la mobilité religieuse*, eds. Y. Droz, P. Chanson, Yonatan N. GezetEdioSoares, 2014.

Miller, D.E. and T. Yamamori. *Global Pentecostalism: The newface of Christian social engagement.* Berkeley, CA: University of California Press, 2007.

Mwaura, P. "'A Burning Stick Plucked out of the Fire' – the Story of Rev Margaret Wanjiru of Jesus Is Alive Ministries". In *Her Stories: Hidden histories of women of faith in Africa*, eds. Govinden, D.B., S. Nadar and P. A. Isabel, 202-24. Pietermaritzburg: Cluster Publications, 2002.

Parsitau, D.S. "'Arise, Oh Ye Daughters of Faith': Women, Pentecostalism, and public culture in Kenya". In *Christianity and Public Culture in Africa*, ed. Harri E., 131-48. Athens, OH: Ohio University Press, 2011.

———. "From the Fringes to the Centre: Rethinking the role of religion in the public sphere in Kenya". In *CODESRIA 12th General Assembly, Governing the African Public Sphere*, 1-35. Yaoundé, Cameroun, 2008.

Parsitau, D.S. and Mwaura, P.N. "God in the City: Pentecostalism as an urban phenomenon in Kenya". *Studia Historiae Ecclesiasticae* 36, no. 2 (2010): 95-112.

Patterson, E. "Different Religions, Different Politics? Religion and political attitudes in Argentina and Chile". *Journal for the Scientific Study of Religion* 43, no. 3 (2004): 345–62.

Pew Research Center. "Spirit and Power: A 10-country survey of Pentecostals." Washington, DC: The Pew Forum on Religion & Public Life, 2006.

Piot, C. *Nostalgia for the Future: West Africa after the Cold War.* Chicago, IL: University of Chicago Press, 2010.

Steigenga, T.J. Politics of the Spirit: *The political implications of Pentecostalized religion in Costa Rica and Guatemala.* Lanham, MD: Lexington Books, 2001.

Sabar, G. *Church, State and Society in Kenya: From mediation to opposition, 1963-1993.* London: Frank Cass, 2002.

Swidler, A. "Culture in Action: Symbols and strategies". *American Sociological Review* 51, no. 2 (1986): 273-86.

Villafañe, E. "The Politics of the Spirit: Reflections on a theology of social transformation for the twenty-first century". *Pneuma: The Journal of the Society for Pentecostal Studies* 18, (fall 1986): 161-70.

Wa Muturi, K. *La police chrétienne.* Nairobi: Centurion Publishing, 2001.

Wariboko, N. "Pentecostal Paradigms of National Economic Prosperity in Africa". In *Pentecostalism and Prosperity: The socioeconomics of the global charismatic movement*, eds. Katherine, A. and A. Yong, 35-58. New York, NY: Palgrave Macmillan, 2012.

White, S. "Political Culture in Communist States: Some problems of theory and method". *Comparative Politics* 16, no. 3(1984): 201-18.

Wrong, M. *It's Our Turn to Eat: The story of a Kenyan whistle-blower.* New York: HarperCollins, 2009.

Yong, A. *In the Days of Caesar: Pentecostalism and political theology.* Grand Rapids, MI: Eerdmans, 2010.

Role of Election Observers: Diplomatic Bias and the Findings of The Kenyan 2013 Election

Mwongela Kamencu *

Introduction

The electoral environment for Kenya's 2013 elections was greatly influenced by the tumultuous 2007 elections and its aftermath that saw hundreds killed, thousands displaced from their homes and property destroyed.Dispute over fraudulent 2007 election results, given credence by observer reports and statements, was thought to be the trigger of such violence. Proof of the election fraud became evident with release of various statements such as the European Union Elections Observation Mission Preliminary statement dated 1 January 2008 (Lafargue, 2008: 23). The political impasse between Mwai Kibaki of the Party of National Unity (PNU) and Raila Odinga of the Orange Democratic Movement (ODM) was later on resolved through a combination of international and local initiatives under the auspices of the African Union Panel of Eminent African Personalities led by the former UN Secretary General, Koffi Annan. These initiatives were able to finesse a power sharing deal by creating a grand-coalition government after the signing of the National Peace Accord which committed Kenya to an ambitious reform program. This deal, brokered with the help of Western donors and the African Union, set aside rather than settling the question of who had rightfully won the presidential elections (Brown and Raddatz, 2014: 7).

* Masters in History and part-time Lecturer at Machakos University College.

One of the main terms of reference of the Grand Coalition Government was to work toward political, social and institutions reforms that would contribute to national reconciliation and provide the appropriate framework for future elections. In line with this, Kenya made efforts to establish the necessary political and legal context within which the 4 March 2013 elections were expected to take place. The election was therefore guided by the 2010 Constitution of Kenya, the Electoral Act 2011, the Electoral Code of Conduct, and the Political Parties Act 2011, among others.[1] Guided by this new institutional framework, the average Kenyan voter was able to vote for candidates in six elective positions, a departure from the usual three positions, in the 2013 elections. This institutional framework compounded with the collective memory of the tumultuous 2007 election set the scene for Kenya's 2013 electoral environment (Shihanya and Okello, 2010: 690-698).

Out of the eight Presidential candidates in the general election, party leaders and presidential aspirants for the CORD and Jubilee coalitions emerged as the frontrunners. The CORD coalition was led by Raila Odinga whose running mate was Kalonzo Musyoka while the Jubilee Coalition was led by Uhuru Kenyatta whose running mate, on the other hand, was William Ruto. Campaigns by both camps were dominated by various themes which ultimately influenced the political environment.

Uhuru Kenyatta and William Ruto were facing charges for crimes against humanity at the International Criminal Court (ICC) understood to have been committed in the course of the post-electoral violence (PEV) of 2007 and 2008. These candidates, it was argued, used their charges as a rallying cry for their communities' electoral support by reframing their charges as a conspiracy by the west to impose its preferred leaders on Kenyans (Perry, 2013). This stance was amplified by assertions made by diplomats from Western donor countries that seemed to coerce Kenyan voters not to vote for Uhuru Kenyatta and William Ruto. The US Assistant Secretary of State Johnnie Carson had intimated in a media telephone briefing that although the United States was not backing a specific candidate, "choices have consequences". Similarly dire pronouncements were made by numerous other donors after Johnnie Carson's statement (Brown and Raddatz, 2014: 10-11).

Raila Odinga, on the other hand, made land and historical injustices a dominant theme in his campaigns promising to solve the injustices once elected. He further made political capital out of the land issue by alluding to land grabbing charges facing William Ruto and the ownership of extensive tracts of land by Kenyatta's family. Kenya's Inspector General of police and the Chairman of The National Cohesion and Integration Commission sought to gag the debate on land by politicians on the strength of its potential to trigger violence because of its emotive quality.[2]

The need for peace in view of the collective memory of the 2007-2008 election related violence and rising political temperatures underlined the need for violence mitigation by election stakeholders. A concerted effort was therefore made to maintain peace and prevent violence during the election period. ELOG, the Elections observation group, a consortium of civil society organizations, was among the national actors involved in violence prevention through reporting of any incidences or potential threats to peace during the election period. Their mandate, however, was not limited to violence mitigation but the observation of the whole electoral process. The National Cohesion and Integration Commission (NCIC), one of the commissions that drew its existence from the National Accord, was an active actor in the peace campaigns. In line with its mandate to promote national integration, the commission recruited peace and cohesion monitors who were to monitor hate speech and promote harmony during the election period. The NCIC also called upon the Kenyan public to maintain peace during the elections, the IEBC to "strictly enforce the law to sustain the confidence of Kenyans" and politicians to desist from making inflammatory statements that could incite citizens to violence during campaigns.[3]

Goodwill ambassadors, appointed in July 2012, complimented the Commission's work in promoting peace during the elections. These Ambassadors were known to have considerable influence in Kenya's public sphere. Other platforms such as Uchaguzi (Elections) Kenya 2013 also monitored the elections and were to receive reports of any incidences from the public through text messages, emails and online messages. The information, depending on its nature, would be relayed to agencies responsible for them to act on it. The Kenya Red Cross would be notified of Emergencies, for instance, while information Electoral issues would be relayed to the Independent Electoral Boundaries Commission. The Uchaguzi platform, however, had a limited media outreach as they did not have the resources to effectively compete for media space with politicians.[4] Numerous international partners, ranging from the United Nations to the Electoral Institute for Sustainable Democracy in Africa, supported Kenya's peace efforts. For instance, from the United States alone, the State Department's Conflict and Stabilization Operations bureau and the U.S. Institute of Peace deployed teams to high-risk areas to assess conflict mitigation efforts. The U.S. Agency for International Development funded a large effort that mobilized youth against violence (Lord and Wilson, 2013).

The media also participated in peace campaigns by giving coverage to peace messages. Michela Wrong's article, "To be Prudent is to be Partial" implied that the media preached peace to a fault and compromised its coverage during the election. This was especially the case as results began streaming in. Stories that may have whipped up ethnic tensions – such as anomalies and irregularities – were overlooked. She argues: "But self-censorship comes at a price: political impartiality. The decision not to inflame ethnic passions meant that media coverage shifted in favour of whoever took an early lead, in this case Uhuru Kenyatta".[5] Domestic and International Observer groups may not have compromised their impartiality in a similar fashion but their reporting of the election, influenced by the electoral environment, could have been compromised to filter out information. This information potentially would have undermined the Kenyan public's confidence in the Presidential Election results released by the IEBC that were later challenged by the CORD presidential candidate Raila Odinga, the African Centre for Open Governance and other petitioners.

The article will focus on the findings and the reporting of the Observer missions to build up the argument that a diplomatic bias influenced the observer groups' reporting of the election. Discrepancies in the reports and statements of observer groups will be analysed to give credence to this argument. The paper will also use some insights from other secondary sources such as journal articles that will build its main argument. Newspapers and statements will mainly be used to cite specific events while interviews from a number of election observers and stakeholders will give first-hand insights on election observation.

Judith Kelly's article "D-minus Elections: The Politics and Norms of International Election Observations" argues that election observers at times endorse elections to protect their member states' or donors' interests or to "accommodate other compelling but tangential or organizational norm" (Kelly, 2009: 766). The article's argument may not be entirely pertinent to this study as it primarily focuses on international Election Observation missions; the study will also include national observation missions. It does however bring out the biases observer groups may have that may compel them to endorse flawed elections.

The question of a "technological bias" as opposed to "diplomatic bias" in election observation has been brought out by Dirk Kohnert's article "Election Observation in Nigeria and Madagascar: Diplomatic vs. Technocratic". Based on the observation of transitional elections in Nigeria and Madagascar, his article argues that professionalism of observers as understood by experts does not necessarily improve the outcome of an election observation. He argues that it in fact could lead to a technocratic bias by reporting based on the observer group's ideals while disregarding factors such as indigenous socio-cultural settings and level of social and cultural development of the host country (Kohnert, 2004: 87-88). The article argues that the degree of damage caused by the technocratic bias could be as high as that caused by diplomatic bias. On diplomatic bias, the article explains that "there exists a considerable margin of error and of wrong judgments concerning electoral processes in politically sensitive situations" (Ibid: 84). The article cites conflict prevention and interests of the member states as some of the reasons for the existence of diplomatic bias responsible for compromising observer aims. Kohnert gives two aims of election observation – backing good governance by recognizing legitimate elections and governments and assisting in the process of democratization and the development of a human rights culture. The insights offered on the article set a framework for which the article will be looked through.

KHRC: Election monitoring by human rights networks

The Kenyan Human Rights Commission, a Kenyan Non-Governmental organization, set up an observer team comprising short-term observers and long-term observers. The team was drawn from 25 members of staff from the organisation as well as 57 monitors from Human Rights Networks strategically placed in the counties that the organisation had previously worked with.[6] It covered 15 of Kenya's 47 counties considered as potential hotspots for violence as a result of the counties' cosmopolitan demographics as well as the individual histories of these areas. The commission released statements at times they considered critical such as after the party nominations, before and after the Election Day. On the Election Day process, some of the commission's monitors witnessed irregularities such as issuance of more than two ballots per person, double voting and bribery. These irregularities were raised at a press conference but were not released to the public due to certain considerations: "We gave a brief statement but we did not release it to the media or the public as we did not want to be seen to interfere with the Presidential Petition being heard at the Supreme Court… we had some disagreements with the media because they tended to believe that we were partial and yet all we were saying was that there were irregularities that may or may have not favoured either of the Presidential candidates".[7]

One of the aims of Election Observation by Dick Kohnert is backing good governance by "recognizing legitimate elections and governments". By failing to share information with the public as a result of their perceived partiality, the KHRC as a domestic observer fell short of the aim of good governance. Incidentally, one of the national values that anchor the principle of governance in the Constitution of Kenya is public participation.[8] The Commission therefore, by failing to release its statement to the public, compromised its reporting as a result of influence from the electoral environment – particularly because of the ongoing Presidential petition in the Supreme Court and the impression sections of the public had of the commission.

AGLI and FCPT: Grassroots election observers

The African Great Lakes Initiative and the Friends Church Peace Teams were some of the grassroots organizations accredited to observe Kenya's 2013 elections. These organizations worked jointly and used a grassroots approach. Save for 3 foreign volunteers, all volunteers were Kenyan nationals living in areas the organisations earmarked for observation. The organisations trained election observers in western areas of Kenya and assigned 112 of them to polling stations in their local communities. Out of the 112 observers, 104 completed and submitted observation forms which were used to come up with a report. AGLI's observers observed the elections in 83 polling stations. Out of the 83, no problems were reported in 19 of them, 23% of the polling stations observed. IEBC irregularities, however, were reported in 34 of the polling stations which accounts for 41% of the polling stations observed. Inappropriate agent behavior was observed in 11 polling stations while overt bribery was witnessed in 6 polling stations: these accounted for 13% and 7% of the polling stations observed respectively.[9] In 4 polling stations the observers witnessed the issuance of multiple ballots for the Presidential race with one of these stations having 23% more presidential votes than in the other 5 races. According to the AGLI and FCPT report, their observers believed that all the disputed votes were included in the national totals. Bearing in mind that there were "pervasive problems with IEBC manual and automated procedures" the organisations' report concluded that there was a likelihood that fraud took place on a wide scale during the elections and "most likely did".[10] The report recommended a thorough audit of the election process. AGLI did not report on the tallying at the national tallying Centre as its observers were posted in polling stations in western areas of Kenya.

Besides the irregularities of the KHRC observation team, the content of an internal European Union Election Observation Mission (EUEOM) report corroborates some of electoral irregularities of the AGLI/FCPT's report. In the internal report, EU Observers noted that various complaints had been made to the IEBC including: returning officers leaving the tallying centre with materials including computers (Nairobi, Nakuru); manipulation of results (Kakamega, Nyeri, Nakuru); ballot stuffing by a presiding officer (Kakamega), issuing more than one ballot paper per voter (Eldoret); bribing of voters (Nakuru, Kisumu); not sealing the ballot boxes (Embu); and damaging a TNA billboard (Nyeri).[11] Perhaps the grassroots approach used by the AGLI/FCPT kept its diplomatic bias to a bare minimum. The fact that the organization had a low national profile and may have not been at the centre of peace campaigns may have also been responsible for its reporting which mentioned more anomalies than any of the observer groups mentioned in this study.

ELOG, civil society observers: Election watchman or watchman of peace?

The Election Observation Group, ELOG, a consortium of civil society and faith based organizations, had more observers on the ground than any other accredited observer group in the 2013 election. The group had 7000 observers in all of Kenya's 290 constituencies and in addition, deployed 580 constituency supervisors.[12] Out of those observers deployed in the constituencies,

976 were deployed as Parallel Vote Tabulation (PVT) observers in sampled polling stations "to enable ELOG to confidently comment on electoral processes and also provide an independent verification of results announced by the Independent Electoral Boundaries Commission (IEBC)".[13] The rest of the observers were posted as general observers who were to provide an observer presence on the ground whose findings would complement the data generated by the Parallel Vote Tabulation technology.

ELOG released interim statements on the polling day that gave statistical breakdowns on how the voting process was conducted. It had an opening polls statement that put the percentage of polling stations that opened on time at 59.7%, that of polling stations not missing strategic equipment at 99.4% and polling stations lacking electronic poll books or had malfunctioning poll books at 8%.[14] The observer group added in its opening statement that some of their observers were denied entry to polling stations as they lacked stamped IEBC letters while in some cases, presiding officers asked for oaths of secrecy. The second interim statement also focused on statistical projections. It put the percentage of Kenyan voters who had voted by 4pm at 68.5% and the percentage of polling streams in which "many voters were assisted" at 54%. ELOG's most critical message in the statement was the percentage it gave for "polling streams where ballot secrecy was violated not including assisted voting" which it put at 17.6%. An appeal to maintain peace was also included in the statement.[15]

ELOG issued another statement on 7 March 2013 concerning the tallying of the election results where they argued that the opening and closing processes of the election went well besides "some challenges – late opening of polling streams and malfunctioning of the electric poll books".[16] The statement did not mention the violation of the secrecy of ballot as one of the challenges of the election process despite its statistical prominence in ELOG's previous statement. In the first statement, the percentage of polling stations with malfunctioning poll books was put at 8% while the second statement "put the polling streams where ballot secrecy was violated not including assisted voting" was put at 17.6%. The challenges mentioned in the third statement, however, gave prominence to malfunctioning electronic pollbooks as a challenge but used the phrase "among others" to include cases of violation of ballot secrecy as one of its challenges despite its statistical significance. This oversight of violation of ballot secrecy as a challenge whose statistical significance was bigger than that of malfunctioning poll books points to a diplomatic bias that saw ELOG downplay an electoral challenge while putting a premium on a challenge that was arguably beyond the polling clerks' control – malfunctioning of electronic poll books. In addition, the statement added that the abandonment of the electronic tallying process and the usage of manual tallies did not invalidate the credibility of the process.[17] The statement appealed to Kenyans to maintain calm and urged the IEBC to open the manual tallying process to thorough scrutiny in order to retain the transparency which ought to have been enhanced by the electronic tallying system. This may have been a thinly veiled reference to the exclusion of Party agents and Observers from observing the tallying process.

ELOG's fourth statement issued on 9 March 2013 verified that IEBC's results fell within their projected range for all the eight presidential candidates based on the Parallel Vote Tabulation. ELOG's assertion in the statement that the PVT projections could confidently verify the accuracy of votes for each Presidential candidate disregarded the margin of error given for its projections. The figures released by IEBC only fell within ELOG's projected range but the confidence in the results vouched by ELOG is invalidated by the projected margin of error. One of the ELOG observers indicated: "Our PVT can tell us that Uhuru Kenyatta was ahead of Raila Odinga… What our PVT cannot tell you is that Uhuru won the first round… Our data cannot tell us that Uhuru passed the 50%+1 threshold".[18] The statement further urged the IEBC to"immediately make public any information relevant and material to the results as announced". The Observer group emphasized the need for IEBC to "make public the individual results (form 34) from all polling streams".[19]

ELOG and other reports: The question of rejected votes

Discrepancies between ELOG's statements and AGLI/FCPT's report are glaring given the higher number of observers ELOG dispatched to the 290 constituencies – higher by more than five thousand. ELOG's three statements and indeed the fourth, had no mention of the anomalies raised in the AGLI's report which included: inappropriate agent behavior, overt bribery in polling stations, issuance of multiple ballots for the presidential race, polling stations having a significantly higher (23% in one) number of presidential votes than in the other five races. ELOG's statements did not also mention several anomalies which the Internal EUEOM report raised such as mathematical inconsistencies thought to have a significant impact and the unsigned results "at lower levels". In some cases, ELOG's statement glossed over the anomalies the Internal EUEOM report raised. The statements for instance did not mention the barring of Party agents and observers from the observing the Tallying process by IEBC officials at the National Tallying Centre at the Bomas of Kenya but instead appealed to the IEBC to "open the manual tallying process to thorough scrutiny in order to retain the transparency".[20] However in their final report, ELOG mentioned that Presidential party agents were excluded from the verification of presidential election forms transmitted to the National Tallying Centre by the constituency returning officers.[21] The number of ELOG's observers – approximately 7,580 – exceeded the EUEOM observers who were approximately 65 in number.

ELOG's projection of rejected votes, whose range IEBC's figures fell in – 0.9% for ELOG with a margin of error of 0.1% and 0.88% for the IEBC – also contrasted the findings of the Carter Centre and the African Union Election Observation Mission (AUEOM). In a congratulatory message to Kenyans for a peaceful election, the Carter Center "observed a high number of rejected votes and appealed to the IEBC and other stakeholders to address this in the short term". The Mission deployed 14 long-term observers and 38 short-term observers who collectively visited 265 polling stations in 34 counties.[22] The AUEOM, on the other hand, in its report of the Kenyan 2013 Elections noted with concern "the high number of rejected ballots at the polling stations".[23] Observations of a high number of rejected votes made by observer groups such as the AUEOM and the Carter Centre Observation Mission were not, however, anchored on a national sample as ELOG's PVT projections.[24] The initial high figures for rejected votes given by the IEBC's electronically transmitted results did not tally with ELOG's figures. The abandonment of the electronic transmission of results, however, saw a significant drop in the number of rejected ballots which fell within ELOG's range.[25]

IEBC's statistics and ELOG's projection on rejected ballots warrants further interrogation, however. Results of Kenya's 2010 Constitutional referendum – in which voters were to cast their ballots for Yes or No options – saw the rejected ballots surpass a 3% mark.[26] With the world average of rejected votes being 3%,[27] IEBC's percentage and ELOG's projection on rejected votes in the March 2013 Elections not only fell below this average, but also below the percentage of rejected votes in the 2010 referendum, in an election that saw Kenyan voters vote for candidates in six elective positions. ELOG's ranges for the rejected votes in the Kenya 2013 elections, in which IEBC's 0.88% lies, were 0.8% for the lower limit and 0.9% for the upper limit. ELOG, which had covered the 2010 referendum did not analyse the percentage of spoilt votes that the IEBC had reported. An observer with ELOG noted: "We did not go far as to analyse the rejected votes… Looking at the rejected ballots vis-à-vis the poorly conducted voter education and yet that high number of rejected votes… we did not make an analysis on the rejected votes".[28]

ELOG, an observer group whose mantra is "credible, peaceful, free and fair elections", could have compromised its findings for the sake of peace – not reporting electoral anomalies that may whip up tension among Kenyans. The entity itself was comprised of peace lobby groups such as Ecumenical Centre for Justice and Peace as well as the Catholic Justice and Peace Commission that may have had a significant effect on the findings of the observer group. As argued by Dirk Kohnert, Diplomatic bias could stem from conflict prevention hence deviating "from the declared aims of election observation" (Kohnert, 2004: 84).

AU, EAC, IGAD and COMESA: Regional observers

Kenya's 2013 elections were also observed by regional observers which included a coalition of regional bodies – East African Community (EAC), Intergovernmental Authority for Development (IGAD) and the Common Market for Eastern and Southern Africa (COMESA). The African Union also had an Observation Mission in the country.

The EAC-IGAD-COMESA observation mission adopted a "short-term methodology" and deployed a pre-election assessment mission and later twenty-one teams in 40 out of Kenya's 47 counties.[29] The coalition released a preliminary statement which stated it would prepare a comprehensive report upon the conclusion of the election process. Its preliminary statement – released a day after the elections – argued that the election had met "regional, continental and international standards for credible and transparent elections".[30] The statement was an endorsement of the election process during and perhaps before the Election Day and contrasted with the findings of AGLI/FCPT's report which mentioned irregularities and anomalies that took place during and after the voting process.

The African Union Election Observation (AUEOM) mission had a total 74 observers in 26 of Kenya's 47 counties on the Election Day who visited 482 polling stations covering 130 constituencies.[31] The report did not give a blanket description of Kenya's 2013 election but zeroed in on several themes such as Security, Closing and counting procedures and party agents and observers. Under the theme 'Closing and counting procedures', the AUEOM reported that it had noted with concern the high number of rejected ballots at the Polling stations. Initially, IEBC's electronically transmitted results showed a correspondingly high number of rejected votes. After abandoning the electronic transmission of results and relying on manual tallies, the number of rejected votes decreased dramatically. The Chairman of the IEBC attributed the reduction to a "bug in the commission's database that multiplied the rejected votes by a factor of eight".[32] Under the theme 'Post-Election Issues' the AUEOM did not revisit the issue of rejected votes, a high number of which had been observed by their observers in the polling stations. In comparison to the AGLI's report and the EUEOM internal report whose contents appeared in the

Nairobi Star, aforementioned anomalies did not appear in the AUEOM final report.

Critics of observer missions representing regional groupings have argued against their objectivity. They argue that the missions are intergovernmental bodies whose governments share geopolitical interests and therefore are careful not to offend the incumbent government in their reporting of their observations. Kenya's country Director for the Electoral Institute of Sustainable Democracy in Africa argued: "Observer missions from the AU, SADC (Southern African Development Community), EAC, ECOWAS (Economic Community West African States)…because they are intergovernmental bodies, there is the 'you rub my back, I'll rub yours' approach to certifying elections… In other words they were not very critical in an effort not to offend the current government".[33]

Occidental observers: EU Election Observation Mission

The European Union Election Observation Mission, EUEOM, deployed 65 observers to assess the whole electoral process. The Mission observers issued a statement two days after the election which stated that the overall conduct of operations in all of the "polling station was good and that the recorded results reflected the will of voters".[34] This statement later on contradicted an internal report of the same Mission that was reported in one of the Kenyan dailies. The Star, a Kenyan daily, reported on some contents of the internal report that stated that "the processing of official election results, based on tallying the results on polling station forms lacked transparency at every stage". The report further said that party agents and observers were not allowed to see how tallying was carried out, including in the National Tallying Centre at the Bomas of Kenya. It raised reservations on the transparency of the process and credibility of the results: "Neither election observers nor party agents had adequate access to the processes in the constituency, county and national tallying centres. Small but numerous mathematical inconsistencies could have had significant impact, given the small number of votes by which Kenyatta passed the 50% threshold".[35]

The Mission's final report however, glossed over the contents of the internal report which were reported by the Kenyan daily, The Star. Mathematical inconsistencies thought to have been possible to have had a significant impact in the internal report were written off in the final report as "widespread minor discrepancies in tallies and between numbers of votes cast for presidential and other races". The report added that the differences "were almost all less than 1%" attributing the discrepancies to tallying errors and downplaying the likelihood of a rigged result.[36] There was therefore an implication that the mathematical inconsistencies, earlier reported as significant, were negligible and could not have had any significant effect on the election.

According to the EUEOM final report, EU observers found that the IEBC and its staff "succeeded in overcoming the technical and operational difficulties that arose on the Election Day to ensure that the integrity of the vote was protected".[37] The report also states that the secrecy of the vote was not sufficiently protected and that tallied results at lower levels were often not signed by party agents. The latter was mentioned in the internal report alongside noted mathematical inconsistencies by observers. Unsigned tallied results, some of which had mathematical inconsistencies vitiate the integrity of vote considering there was no mention in the EUEOM report of a rectification of the inconsistencies. In this respect, the report contradicts itself. The EUEOM could have compromised its reporting of the election so as to sanitise its image to the elected Jubilee government. A lawsuit intending to ban "Western" observer groups on the strength of "open bias" – EU and US Election observer groups – had been filed in Court by a Nairobi lawyer, Harrison Kinyanjui on 13 February 2013.[38] The petitioner argued that the EUEOM had displayed open hostility to the election of Uhuru Kenyatta and William Ruto in the March 4, 2013 Elections. The Observation Mission also came under fire from the Jubilee coalition for "unprofessional and Partisan Involvement in Kenya's Political and Internal affairs". The coalition alleged that the EUEOM was helping CORD in its Election Petition.[39] In a statement the Jubilee Coalition also lumped up the Observer Mission with the European Union, which was accused of covertly funding CORD's main partner, Orange Democratic Movement, through a Non-governmental Organisation. Considering that most observer groups had given the election a clean bill of health, the EUEOM were probably unlikely to have a radically different report especially in the face of an accusation of bias during the election period.

Occidental observers: The Carter Center International Observation Mission

The Carter Center International Election Observation Mission to Kenya deployed 52 observers to observe the Kenyan election. The Observation Mission issued a statement 2 days after the polling day. It congratulated Kenyans Voters on peaceful elections, observed a high number of rejected votes just as the African Union Election Observer Mission did and appealed to political parties and candidates to exercise patience as the result process continued.[40] A more comprehensive statement was issued on 4 April 2013, after results had been released, challenged in court and upheld. The statement found that the Kenya Election results, based on the manual tallying, reflected the will of Kenyan voters. The Centre believed that the manual tallying presented enough "guarantee to preserve the expression of the will of Kenyan voters" in spite of serious shortcomings in the Independent Electoral and Boundaries Commission's management of technology and tabulation of final results.[41] The statement however, decried a lack of transparency in the tallying process as well as an unwillingness to publish results by polling station.[42] With regard to transparency, the Carter Center took exception to the IEBC decision to confine party agents and observers to the gallery of the national tally center, making effective observation impossible. The lack of transparency calls into question whether the process presented enough "guarantee to preserve the expression of the will of Kenyan voters" especially for the Presidential election which saw 8,418 votes prevent a run-off.[43] Indeed, the observation of the results may or may not have had a significant impact on the results – a victory for Uhuru Kenyatta in the first round or a run-off – but the fact that there was no observation of the tallying process by agents and Observers at the tallying center, raises reservations on the credibility of the result.

Like the EUEOM, the Carter Centre Election Observation Mission was accused of being partial while observing the 2013 election. An official of the mission revealed: "We were targeted by a petition that was trying to stop the accreditation of observers – American Observers. We were also targeted by a coalition that put the ICC and the west in one block – including the observer missions. In case the results were in favour of their rivals, they would say that they had influenced the outcome of the elections".[44]

Conclusion

The paper has shown how international and domestic observer missions, influenced by a politically sensitive environment, could compromise the reporting of their election Observation findings. In the case of KHRC, EUEOM, and the Carter Center Election Observation Mission,

Election Observation was carried out amidst accusations of partisanship of these observer groups. This may have ultimately influenced their reporting. Missions such as the AUEOM and the EAC-IGAD-COMESA observation missions, it has been argued, may have been forged from intergovernmental bodies and could also have been diplomatic in reporting their observations to maintain the reciprocal relationship between the host state – Kenya – and other member states. Subsequent elections in other member states would oblige such like Election Observation Missions to endorse the electoral processes and results as credible, transparent and reflecting the will of the people. In ELOG's case which employed citizen participation, the need for calm is likely to have influenced their reporting which did not query IEBC's results nor raise any irregularities that were raised by the CORD Presidential Candidate and the Non-governmental organisation AFRICOG in the Presidential Election Petition. Kenya's electoral environment was characterised by calls for peace and an adjustment to a new constitutional dispensation. This ultimately set the scene for messages whose content was measured from stakeholders in the election. A high premium was put on peace and this could have compromised the reporting of election observers. The endorsing of the election process by various observers could have set the scene for other observers to moderate their reporting. This would take place even if the endorsement was not a true picture of the nature of the actual process and validity of election results.

Notes

1   African Union Commission, Report of African Union Election observation Mission to the March 4th 2013 General Elections in Kenya, p.8.

2   Walter Menya, "Raila Ignores Police Warning," *The Star*, February 6, 2013, http://www.the-star.co.ke/news/article-106017/raila-ignores-police-warning.

3   National Cohesion and Integration Commission, "A Call to Peaceful elections," January 27, 2013.

4   Interview with Daudi Were, Uchaguzi Project Leader, June 20, 2013, Valley Arcade, Nairobi.

5   Michela Wrong, "To Be Prudent is to be Partial", *IHT Global Opinion*, March 14, 2013, http://latitude.blogs.nytimes.com/2013/03/14/erring-on-the-side-of-caution-kenyas-media-undercovered-the-election/.

6   Interview with Eva Kaloki, Programme Associate, Kenyan Human Rights Commission, August 1, 2013, Kenyan Human Rights Commission, Nairobi.

7   Ibid.

8   Article 10, Constitution of Kenya, 2010.

9   African Great Lakes Initiative, Report on Observation of March 2013 Kenyan National Elections, April 6, 2013.

10   Ibid.

11   Star Reporter, "Election Not Transparent – EU Observers". *The Star*, March 20, 2013: 3.

12   Elections Observation Group, "The Official results are consistent with Elections Observation Group's Parallel Vote Tabulation (PVT)," March 9, 2013.

13   Ibid.

14   Elections Observation Group, "Opening of Polls Statement," March 4, 2013.

15   Ibid.

16   Elections Observation Group, "Press statement on Ongoing Tallying of Presidential Results," March 7, 2013.

17   Ibid.

18   Interview with Mercy Njoroge, National Coordinator, July 31, 2013, ELOG, Nairobi.

19   Elections Observation Group, Press Statement, "The Official results are Consistent with Election Observation Group's Parallel Vote tabulation," March 9, 2013.

20   Elections Observation Group, "Press statement on Ongoing Tallying of Presidential Results," March 7, 2013.

21   Election Observation Group, The Historic Vote: Report of The Elections Observation Group On the 2013 General Elections.

22   The Carter center, "Carter Center Congratulates Kenyan voters on Peaceful Election," March 6, 2013.

23   African Union Commission, Report of African Union Election Observation Mission to the March 4, 2013 General Elections in Kenya, p.17, undated report.

24   Interview with Mercy Njoroge, National Coordinator, July 31, 2013, ELOG, Nairobi.

25   Ibid.

26   Ibid.

27   Interview with Stephen Mondon, Field Office Director, Carter Center Election Observation Mission, April 12, 2013, Upper Hill, Nairobi.

28   Interview with Mercy Njoroge, National Coordinator, July 31, 2013, ELOG, Nairobi.

29   The Joint COMESA-EAC-IGAD Election Observer Mission, Preliminary Statement, March 5, 2013, p.2.

30   Ibid., p.6.

31   Ibid., pp.3-4.

32   Alphonse Shihundu, "IEBC Blames Database bug for rejected votes error, "*Daily Nation*, March 7, 2013, http://www.nation.co.ke/News/politics/-/1064/1714132/-/ayghod/-/index.html.

33   Mienke Mari Stertler, "Kenya's elections: Observing the observers," Good Governance Africa, http://gga.org/analysis/kenyas-elections-observing-the-observers/?utm_source=OpenNetworksCRM&utm_medium=Email&utm_campaign=OpenNetworksCRM.

34   European Union Election Observation Mission, "Preliminary statement: Kenyans demonstrate Strong Commitment to Democratic Elections," March 6, 2013, p.7.

35   Star Reporter, "Election Not Transparent – EU Observers", p.1.

36   European Union Election Observation Mission, General Elections March 2013 Final Report, p.31.

37   Ibid, p.1.

38   Sam Kiplagat and Carol Maina, "Lawyers want US, EU Observer groups Kicked Out," *The Star*, February 14, 2013, p.2.

39   Jubilee Coalition Press Statement, "Unprofessional Involvement by EU Observers in Kenya's Political Scene and Internal Affairs," March 2013.

40   The Carter Center, Carter center Congratulates Kenyan Voters on Peaceful Election, March 6, 2013.

41   The Carter Centre, "The Carter Center Finds Kenya Election Results reflect Will of Voters," April 4, 2013.

42   Ibid, pp.1-5.

43   Ibid, p.7.

44   Interview with Stephen Mondon, Field Office Director, Carter Center Election Observation Mission, April 12, 2013, Upper Hill, Nairobi.

Bibliography

African Great Lakes Initiative, *Report on Observation of March 2013 Kenyan National Elections,* April 6, 2013.

African Union Commission, *Report of African Union Election Observation Mission to the March 4, 2013 general Elections in Kenya.*

Brown, S. and R. Raddatz. "Dire Consequences or Empty Threats? Western pressure for peace, justice and democracy in Kenya". *Journal of Eastern African Studies,* 8 no. 1 (2014): 1-20.

Carter Centre International Election Observation Mission, Press Statement,"Carter center Congratulates Kenyan Voters on Peaceful Election", March 6, 2013.

Carter Centre International Election Observation Mission, Press Statement,"The Carter Center Finds Kenya Election Results reflect Will of Voters", April 4, 2013.

Elections Observation Group, "Press statement on Ongoing Tallying of Presidential Results", March 7, 2013.

Elections Observation Group, Press Statement,"The Official results are consistent with Elections Observation Group's Parallel Vote Tabulation (PVT)", March 9, 2013.

European Union Election Observation Mission, *General Elections March 2013 Final Report.*

European Union Election Observation Mission, Preliminary statement,"Kenyans demonstrate Strong Commitment to Democratic Elections", March 6, 2013.

Jubilee Coalition Press Statement, "Unprofessional Involvement by EU Observers in Kenya's Political Scene and Internal Affairs", March 2013.

Kelly, J. "D-Minus Elections: the Politics and Norms of International Election Observation". *International Organisation* 63, no. 4 (2009): 765-787.

Kohnert, D. "Election Observation in Nigeria and Madagascar: Diplomatic vs. Technocratic". *Review of African Political Economy* 31, no. 99 (2004):83-101.

Kiplagat, S. and C. Maina. "Lawyers want US, EU Observer Groups Kicked Out", *The Star,* February 14, 2013.

Kristin L. and J. Wilson, "Lessons Learned from Kenya's Election", *Foreign Policy,* http://www.foreignpolicy.com/articles/2013/03/19/lessons_learned_from_kenya_s_election?page=0,0retrieved March 19, 2013.

Lafargue, J. ed. *The General Elections in Kenya, 2007.* Dar es Salaam: Mkuki na Nyota, 2008.

Menya, W. "Raila Ignores Police Warning", *The Star,* February 6, 2013, http://www.the-star.co.ke/news/article-106017/raila-ignores-police-warning.

Michela, W. "To Be Prudent is to be Partial", *IHT Global Opinion*, March 14, 2013, http://latitude.blogs.nytimes.com/2013/03/14/erring-on-the-side-of-caution-kenyas-media-undercovered-the-election/.

National Cohesion and Integration Commission, Press Statement,"A Call to Peaceful Elections", January 27, 2013.

Perry, A. "Kenya's Election: What Uhuru Kenyatta's victory means for Africa", *TIME World*, March 9, 2013, http://world.time.com/2013/03/09/kenyas-election-what-uhuru-kenyattas-victory-means-for-africa/.

Shihundu, A. "IEBC Blames Database bug for rejected votes error", *Daily Nation*, March 7, 2013http://www.nation.co.ke/News/politics/-/1064/1714132/-/ayghod/-/index.html.

Sihanya, B. and D. Okello. "Mediating Kenya's Post Election Crises: The politics and limits of power sharing agreement". In *Tensions and Reversals in Democratic Transitions,* eds. K. Kanyinga and D. Okello. Nairobi: University of Nairobi.

Star Reporter, "Election Not Transparent – EU Observers," *The Star,* March 20, 2013.

Stertler, M.M. "Kenya's elections: Observing the observers," Good governance Africa, http://gga.org/analysis/kenyas-elections-observing-the-observers/?utm_source=OpenNetworksCRM&utm_medium=Email&utm_campaign=OpenNetworksCRM.

The Joint COMESA-EAC-IGAD Election Observer Mission, *Preliminary Statement,* March 5, 2013.

Interviews

Eva Kaloki, Programme Associate Electoral Governance Programme, KHRC, August 1, 2013, KHRC Headquarters, Nairobi.

David Were Project Leader, Uchaguzi, June 20, 2013. Valley Arcade, Nairobi.

Mercy Njoroge, National Coordinator, ELOG, July 31, 2013, ELOG Headquarters Nairobi.

Stephen, Mondon. Carter Center Election Observation Mission, April 12, 2013, Upper Hill, Nairobi.

Negotiating History for Negotiated Democracy: The Case of Kisii County in 2013 Kenya Elections

Eric Rosana Masese [*]

Introduction

Kenya went to the 2013 national General Elections with lingering bad memories of the 2007/2008 post-election violence that engulfed many parts of the country. While this violence differed from place to place, it generally stemmed from competition for national resources that were packaged in form of historical injustices, identity and power (Waki, 2008; Wong, 2009; Veit et al, 2011).

Consequently, to avoid the recurrence of this violence, the country took broad steps to address its root causes. Among these steps was the enactment of the new constitution in August 2010. The new constitution drastically altered the government structure by coming up with devolved units (counties) that have a sole purpose of decentralizing resources from the national government.

The management of decentralized resources at the county level is, however, to be done through popular participation. This means that local people will elect their representatives through popular suffrage (Westminster democracy) to represent them in decision making and more specific to manage the decentralized resources.

In Westminster democracy, political parties or individuals compete for government offices. Each political party or individual with significant majority becomes the sole custodian of government

*   Lecturer, Department of Sociology and Psychology, Moi University, Kenya.

offices that are tasked with everyday decision-making and management of resources. Consequently, the minority have no opportunity to take part in everyday decision-making and management of resources other than playing the role of the watchdog.

Arising from the principle governing Westminster democracy, the majority will always have their way in both decision-making and resource management. However, in reality the new devolved government units are characterized by majority and minority dichotomy based on individual identity. Identity[1] in this case refers to belonging to one social group based on ethnic, cultural, social and historical background. Thus in most devolved government units there is competition for leadership positions based on ethnicity and clanism.

This leadership competition, however, raises fears of marginalization among social groups that perceive themselves as minorities. This perception of marginalization is argued as a possible fertile ground for conflict and violence (Kimutai, 2012; Psirmoi, 2012). To avoid this, and ensure inclusiveness in decision-making and resource management, most stakeholders inmost devolved units advocate for negotiated democracy. Negotiated democracy in this context refers to a process where various interests of social groups come up with a negotiated formula of sharing out leadership positions.

Consequently, there were concerted efforts in most devolved units among various social groups to come up with a formula on how to share various leadership positions in 2013 election. For example, the Kuria community (minority) living in Migori county was allowed to have the "Senate" seat without having to undergo a contest with their Luo (majority) counterparts (Oluoch, 2012). Similarly, in Wajir County, elders and stakeholders came up with a power sharing formula that ensured all clans, irrespective of their numerical strength, got a share in leadership positions (Kimutai, 2012).

Proponents of negotiated democracy argue that this strategy ensures inclusiveness in decision-making and management of decentralized resources among various social groups. To them, this acts as an antidote to conflict and violence. However, opponents of negotiated democracy see it as an infringement on people's universal rights to elect their leaders irrespective of their social identity.

Whereas as the two arguments on negotiated democracy are valid, it is important to note, however, that this process was mostly driven by political leaders or community opinion leaders with the justification that it would foster unity and equal sharing of resources among all clans. Consequently, in Kisii County, opinion and political leaders from various clans came up with different formulas on how to share the various leadership positions (Miruka, 2013). For example, the opinion and political leaders affiliated to Orange Democratic Movement (ODM) agreed that the seat of the county governor was to be contested by the Kitutu clan, Senator was given to Bobasi, Women representative to Bonchari, Deputy Governor to Bomachoge, Speaker to Nyaribari and county executive to South Mugirango. This arrangement was also put in practice by opinion and political leaders affiliated to the Jubilee Coalition with the governor position given to Bobasi, Senator to Nyaribari and Deputy Governor to South Mugirango.

As evidenced from the sharing of leadership positions, it is clear that each political party had its own formula that informed the sharing of leadership positions among various clans. This is given credence by the fact that each political party in Kisii County allocated different positions to different clans. This means that other than equal sharing of county resources among all clans, other factors played a role in determining the sharing of such positions. This study sought to understand the "taken for granted" factors that informed the sharing of leadership positions (negotiated democracy) in Kisii County during the 4 March national election.

Methodology

This study was done in Kisii County from November 2012 to May 2013. Kisii County is located in Nyanza province and constitutes nine constituencies namely; Bonchari, South Mugirango, Bomachoge Chache, Bomachoge Borabu, Nyaribari Masaba, Nyaribari Chache, Kitutu Chache South, Kitutu Chache North and Bobasi. The county has four districts comprising Kisii central, Kisii South, Gucha, Gucha South and Masaba.

Kisii County was selected purposively for this study because it is inhabited by one ethnic group "the Abagusii" but with strong clan affiliations. In the current county structure, the people of this county "see" these "clans" in terms of constituencies. These clans have been characterised by long-term political, economic and social rivalry especially in the competition of leadership and national resources (Ombongi, 1997; Akama, 2006). Hence, political mobilization has in most cases revolved around clan interests (Moraa, 2013; Ocharo, 2005). As a consequence the community has never approached the general elections as a block save for 2002 when they overwhelmingly voted for Simeon Nyachae (Ocharo, 2005).[2] This study site was therefore found to be ideal for understanding internal factors that informed negotiated democracy among members of the same community in the 2013 Kenyan national elections.

This study was concerned with the taken for granted factors that informed negotiated democracy in Kisii County. In this regard it was concerned with translating everyday discourses (Burr, 2003; Parker, 1992; Foucault, 1980) that informed everyday action by teasing their meanings and implications on political decisions from the perspective of the Abagusii. As a consequence the study adopted ethnographic research approach because it provided an ideal opportunity to study the Abagusii political decision making processes, by directly getting involved with them and their culture over an extended period of time (Geetz, 1973).

This study used snowball sampling and direct approach techniques to select research participants. In snowballing, the researcher made an initial contact with one old man –opinion leader –who was for many years involved in making political decisions for the community. Upon gaining his consent and interviewing him, the old man helped the researcher identify other participants who in turn led the researcher even more participants. For a period of four months a total of 20 participants were selected and interviewed through this sampling technique.

The direct approach method was utilised to procure interviews from political decision makers within the community after briefing them about the purposes and objectives of the research. This approach produced mixed results because not all would be respondents in this category consented to the request because some feared that the information they would give could later one used by their political competitors to their disadvantage. As such the researcher only managed to interview 8 participants through this technique.

The research data was collected through qualitative methods – comprising in-depth conversational interviews, key informant interviews and participant observation– because it gave room for the researcher to delve on the participant's experience, social processes and discourses (Mason, 2002; Gillham, 2000).

This study sought to understand the factors that informed negotiated democracy in Kisii County. As such data from in-depth conversational interviews formed the corpus of data analysis. Information from in-depth conversational interviews was taken as discourses that not only transferred information but also indicated what cultures accomplish through language in political decision-making processes. The data obtained from the exercise was merged into various themes which are discussed here under.

Understanding the Abagusii voting pattern

For a long time the Abagusii voting pattern has been attributed to clanism other than political party affiliations (Ombongi, 1997; Ocharo, 2005; Moraa, 2013). As a result majority electoral candidates are usually cautious on how to handle the clan factor. Miruka (2013), for example, observes that clanism was a major factor in the choice of running mates for Kisii county governor and the electoral seats sharing arrangement that was agreed by the two major political parties namely Orange Democratic Movement (ODM) of the Coalition of Reform and Democracy (CORD) and The National Alliance Party (TNA) of the Jubilee coalition during the 2013 elections. In ODM, gubernatorial contestant James Ongwae (from Kitutu clan) picked his running mate from Bomachoge clan. Similarly, TNA's Patrick Lumumba (from Bobasi clan) picked his running mate from South Mugirango clan.

The above observation however raises two questions: why do the Abagusii vote along clan lines? And what informs the creation of voting coalitions among various clans? This study attempts to answer these two questions as no past study has ever done so.

But before answering these questions it is important to understand what drives the Abagusii people in their day-to-day actions. Indeed, the need to solve this mystery has over the years generated a huge debate across various disciplines. Many scholars who have participated in the discourse have used a range of paradigms starting from essentialism to post-structuralism in order to answer these two questions. Post-structuralism, also known as postmodernism" rejects the idea that the world can be understood in terms of grand theories and meta-narratives, and instead emphasizes the coexistence of multiplicity and variety of situation-dependent ways of life" (Burr, 2003: 12). Social constructionism is believed to have developed out of the works of 20th century scholars in the field of sociology of knowledge, who were interested in understanding how socio-cultural forces influenced the construction of knowledge (Burr, 2003).

In 1966, Berger and Luckmann published The Social Construction of Reality: A Treatise in the Sociology of Knowledge where they argued that whatever members of the public perceived as a social reality was, instead, a construction to which each member contributed through knowledge accumulated from "the reality of everyday life" (Berger & Luckmann, 1967). According to Berger and Luckmann, meaning is inter-subjective, which means that the meanings of different individuals in a society relate to, and are to some extent dependent upon, the meanings of others. Berger and Luckmann's theory drew heavily on Mead's (1934) concept of symbolic interactionism, in which individuals are conceived as constructing their own and each other's identities through daily encounters with each other in social interactions (Burr, 2003).

Accordingly to social constructionists (Berger and Luckmann, 1967; Garfinkel, 1967), everyday action is driven by how people make sense of social phenomena/discourses. This means that for the Abagusii people to make political decisions on how to vote they must first synthesize various political discourses into common shared knowledge as it exists in their social institutions, everyday language, shared meanings and understandings. This common shared knowledge then determines their action and is constructed through socialization as a result of social interaction, negotiation and power.

Logically therefore, people will construct their own realities about various political discourses. These constructed realities may or may not be accurate translations of what each political discourse espouses, though it will guide their action. Of critical importance, however, is the fact that these constructed realities are influenced by both cultural and historical factors (Burr, 2003). This in essence means that people's political action will not only be determined by specific cultural factors but also the prevailing social and economic context.

This study therefore examined various narratives as highlighted by various research participants to understand why the Abagusii vote in terms of clans. The narratives in this context were not conceived as participants' personal perceptions, but as "manifestations of discourses, of representations of events upon the terrain of social life (which) have their origin not in the personal private experience, but in discursive culture that they inhabit" (Burr, 2003). These narratives are thus seen in this study to constitute the discourses that represent the way the Abagusii people make sense of various political discourses and explain their political actions.

Two research participants namely Mr. Keroka (80 years) and Okioma (76 years)explained that the Abagusii people vote along clan lines because of a curse that befall on members of community as contained in Gusii myths. Myths in general relate us to events supposed to have happened "Once upon a time", "Long ago", and "At the beginning of time", and account for the present order of things at the most comprehensive level, providing "an authoritative foundation for the continual construction, maintenance, and reproduction of an ongoing social order" (Paul, 1996: 10). The primary element in mythical narrative is the plot that, by bringing together goals, causes, and chance within the temporal unity of a whole and complete action, creates their meaning-effect and links individual desire to inter-subjectivity.

But unlike the Christian myth that traces the origin of divisions among people to the Tower of Babel (see Genesis) the Gusii narrative attributes it to a curse. According to Gusii mythology as narrated by Mr. Keroka and Okioma, when the Gusii arrived in Kisumu from Mount Elgon, they were faced with calamities like un-conducive environmental conditions that led to mass crop failure and demise of livestock. There was also outbreak of human diseases, which supposedly affected the Abagusii mother called Nyankomogendi, making her extremely weak. The myth goes on to say that due to her condition, her siblings abandoned her and moved to Kano plains where conditions were favourable for their sustenance.

At Kisumu, Nyankomogendi felt abandoned by her own children and died. But before she died she cursed them that "Mosarare nko mokwaniranerie emegongo"which literary translates to "you will multiply but you will never be united as a people." According to these two research participants, this curse is up to this day responsible for high population growth and disunity among Gusii clans.

Coincidentally, Akama (2006) also note that it is at Kano plains that the Abagusii's seven contiguous, but politically autonomous groups/clans emerged. These groups/clans are Abagirango (North and South Mugirango), Abagetutu, Abanyaribari, Abanchari, Ababasi and Abamachoge. All these Gusii clans identify themselves with four totems. The Abagirango relate to Engo(Leopard), Abasweta who consist of Abagetutu, Abanyaribari and Abamachoge relate to Engoge (Baboon), Ababasi relate to Enchage (Zebra) and lastly Abanchari relate to Engubo (Hippotamus). In all clans these totems are perceived as a sign of veneration and respect to their ancestors, community and spiritual well being. The totems are thus perceived as harbingers of good omen and prosperity.

To the Abagusii people the totems represent the beliefs, attitudes, values, language and behaviors, which in turn determine how each clan makes meaning of various political scenarios. These meanings are influenced by the desire of each clan to maintain power and identity over other clans. Therefore it's the power and identity discourses that tend to normalize certain voting patterns while constructing others as a preserve for each clan. This normalisation of voting patterns is mostly fortified by the stereotypes that each clan owes the other. This is given credence by the following interview with Mr. Onyoni aged 60:

Researcher: In the senate position whom did you vote for?
Onyoni: Definitely our son from this area (meaning the candidate from his clan)
Researcher: Why vote for him and not the other candidates who hail from other places?
Onyoni: You see our neighbour (referring to a certain clan) here sees our clan as inferior and that is why I voted for our son to show them we are equally superior and we can rule them.

Mr. Onyoni's reason of voting for the candidate who hails from his clan is also evidenced when one examines the votes gained by three top senate candidates in 2013 national election in their respective constituencies. As shown in Table 1each of the top candidates triumphed extremely well in his home constituency/clan. These candidates are: Hon. Christopher M. Obure (Bobasi), Hon. Prof Sam K. Ongeri (Nyaribari Masaba) and Hon. James O. Magara.

Table 1: Top three Senate candidates votes from the constituencies they hail from

	Bobasi	Nyaribari Masaba	South Mugirango
Christopher M. Obure	37673	5642	5163
Sam K. Ongeri	14182	28701	3194
James O. Magara	3096	1808	32578

Source: IEBC Form 36 Senate Kisii County, 2013
Key: Bold indicates the constituency where the candidate hails from

According to 67-year-old Mr. Ongau, clan based voting can also be attributed to the exogamy and patrilocal principles governing marriage. According to the Abagusii marriage system clan members were only allowed to marry from different clans and the bride relocates to live with the family of the groom. Due to this, the intermarrying clans viewed each other as enemies as recognized in the Gusii proverb "Those we marry from are those whom we fight".

This hostility among clans has its genesis from cultural practices where members of a particular clan would raid other clans for women. This forced the raided clan to defend itself as a way of self –preservation and respect (Masese, 2011). Henceforth, it is this antagonistic tendency as reflected in marriages, argued Mr. Ongau, which makes a particular clan to vote in a certain way to demonstrate its supremacy over other clans. Thus in an election contest supremacy is interpreted in terms of clans competing over a "woman". In this case the clan that wins over the others regards itself as superior and therefore assumes that it has power to control them. Control in this context is equated to the kind of control a man exercises over his wife.

This study also found that some clans voted on the basis of clan as a strategy of fighting social exclusion. Social exclusion according to Duff (1995) is the inability to participate effectively in the economic, social, political and cultural life, alienation and distance from the mainstream society. In this case some clans such as the South Mugirango, Bonchari and Bomachoge voted in large numbers for Hon James Magara who hailed from one of these clans as shown in Table 2. These three clans mostly feel socially excluded from other Gusii clans. This voting pattern by these clans was also evidenced during the first multiparty elections in 1992 (Ombongi, 1997). In this election these clans were the only ones that voted for opposition candidates in the then Kisii district.

Table 2: Voting in self perceived social excluded constituencies

	South Mugirango	Bonchari	Bomachoge Chache	Bomachoge Borabu
James O. Magara	32578	14084	10545	11578
Christopher M. Obure	5163	11373	11017	8066
Sam K. Ongeri	3194	5029	4175	10854

Source: IEBC Form 36 Senate Kisii County, 2013

According to 78-year-old Mr. Ombasa, the Abanchari and South Mugirango for instance feel that they are socially excluded from other Gusii clans because of their historical background and dialect. The area they inhabit is the least developed. Their voting for a candidate who hails from these socially excluded clans was an expression of liberation and affirming their status to be equal to that of other Abagusii clans.

Among the Abagusii, the Abanchari are socially excluded because the founder of the clan was a woman3 and thus they are regarded as the children of a woman (Monchari). Oral literature has it that Monchari married Omache- Rachuonyo (a Luo) because at the time of marriage she had already two sons out of wedlock and therefore wouldn't find a man from any Gusii clans to marry her. According to Gusii customs, it is a shame for a woman to conceive out of wedlock and any man who marries such woman is despised. Further, the community equally despises a woman who fails to get married. To lessen her shame of not being married and to help her sons get land, Monchari was forced to get married to a man of another tribe – a Luo even though such marriage was not encouraged by the community. The Abanchari are thus not perceived as pure Gusii clan.

On the other hand also, the South Mugirango clan is socially excluded because of their dialect. According to Mbori (1994) there are two main regional dialects of Ekegusii that can be distinguished as the Rogoro (Northern) dialect and the Maate (Southern) dialect. The Maate dialect is spoken by Gusii clans that border the Luo and the Maasai ethnic communities, including the Abamachoge and South Mugirango. The Rogoro dialect is spoken in the rest of Gusiiland. The existing differences between the two Ekegusii dialects are, mainly, lexical and/or phonetic in nature. However, because the Rogoro dialect is spoken by majority of the Gusii clans, it is taken as the standard dialect. Therefore those who speak the Maate dialect are socially excluded.

The issue of social exclusion was also found as a major campaign theme among some candidates vying for county seats in 2013 election. According to Moraa (2013), Magara campaigned on the ground that Obure and Ongeri had failed to unite the community through politics of inclusion. Magara campaigned on this platform because he comes from one of the marginalized clans and therefore he wanted to take advantage of the votes from these areas.

Sharing of leadership positions[4]

This study found that the sharing of political leadership positions in the 2013 Kisii County Elections among various clans was guided by political parties' affiliation but based on clanism. In this case the two major political parties namely ODM and TNA came up with a power sharing formula that saw each clan assured of some leadership position in the county. For example, in ODM, the seat for the governor was allocated to Kitutu clan, Deputy Governor, Bomachoge, Women representative, Bonchari, county speaker, Nyaribari and county executive, South Mugirango.

However, further investigations revealed that this sharing of leadership positions was motivated more by historical happenings that have defined the relationship between various clans dating back to pre-colonial period. In ODM, for example, the choice of a governor from the Kitutu clan was motivated by the fact that during pre-colonial and much of colonial period the Gusii overall leadership position was held by members of Kitutu clan as alluded by a 50 year civil servant, Mr Onserio. According to him, the last known Kisii prophet was from the Kitutu clan. Therefore given the fact that the governor is the overall leader of the county, it was felt that governorship should be given to the clan that has historically held similar leadership positions.

Onserio's sentiments are also captured by Akama (2006) who observes that leaders or chiefs from the Kitutu clan governed the Abagusii clans during the colonial period. These chiefs/leaders presided over cases involving various clans and made some decrees that were binding to all clans. For example, in 1906 when bride wealth had gone so high beyond the means of young men, Ogeto the leader of the Kitutu clan summoned all leaders from other Gusii clans and decreed that bride wealth should be reduced from six cows to three cows, that is; one bull and not more than four goats. To enforce this ruling that came to be known as "the Ogeto ruling" all clan elders performed magic-religious rituals binding everyone to abide by it. Accordingly, most clans adhered to "Ogeto ruling" for a long time.

However, the rate of bride wealth had by 1920 increased substantially to over eight cows. This again prompted Inchwari, a leader of Abagetutu clan to summon other Gusii clan elders for a meeting. In this meeting, it was agreed by all clan elders that bride wealth should be brought down to three cows and one bull. This ruling was commonly referred to as "the Inchwari ruling."

The other factor that motivated the sharing of leadership positions was the relationship that existed between clans over a long period. This relationship mostly focused on whether a particular clan was domineering in determining the social, economic and political issues affecting the whole community. Thus the clan that was perceived to be most domineering was isolated from assuming powerful leadership positions according to 56-year-old Mr Ongori.

In this study, the fear of domineering was borne from the perceived role members of a particular clan had hitherto played on issues affecting the whole community. These issues centred mostly on the delimitation of constituencies and the creation of new administrative units such as districts. On this basis the Nyaribari clan was isolated from assuming leadership positions that were perceived as powerful such governorship and the senate.

According to Mr. Ongori, some of the happenings which worked against the Nyaribari clan were: the allegation by members of Bonchari that in1986, influential individuals from Nyaribari had proposed to the Kenya electoral chairman, the late James Nyamweya[5] to extend the borders of Nyaribari to Bokeira, the heartland of Bonchari. This move that was opposed by Hon. Dr Zachary Onyoka (MP Kitutu Chache) and Bonchari MP Hon. Mark Bosire was to have the only airstrip in Kisii under Nyaribari. Another allegation was that in2012 powerful individuals from Nyaribari conspired to have Bonchari constituency phased out. This was to be done through amalgamating its boundaries with Nyaribari Chache by taking the large electoral areas of Kisii municipality under the political jurisdiction of Bonchari.

Another cited allegation was the controversy that arose after president Moi in 1996 created a new district out of Kisii district. The new district was to include: South Mugirango, Bomachoge and Bobasi constituencies. In this saga it was alleged that Hon. Simeon Nyachae, the influential Nyaribari Chache MP wanted the new district headquarters to be located in Kenyenya where he had his relatives and the district to be called Irianyi.[6] This was contrary to the wishes of local members of the constituencies that made up the new district. The locals wanted the district headquarters be at Ogembo and its name be Gucha because of the significance of River Gucha that transverses through the three constituencies.

Other research participants such as 54-year-old Mr. Manoti and 60-year-old Mr. Onchomba alluded that the sharing of leadership positions was also influenced by earlier experiences some clans had among themselves in terms of leadership. In this case clans that had experienced antagonistic leadership earlier on were keen to avoid such situations from reoccurring. Members of these clans achieved this aim by pushing for some leadership positions that gave them the perceived advantage over the other.

According to Manoti, for example, the Kitutu who share the jurisdiction of Kisii County headquarters with Nyaribari were very keen on the governorship position. Their keenness was motivated by the desire of reclaiming back the leadership position that they felt was taken from them unfairly by the Nyaribari in 1930. The case in reference here is that of Musa Nyandusi

(Nyaribari) who easily outshined Onsongo (Kitutu) to become the chief of both Nyaribari and Kitutu.

The antagonistic leadership relationship between the Nyaribari and Kitutu can also be traced to 19th century. According to Mr. Onchomba when the Sweta leader Oisera died around 1830, Onyangore, half-brother to Nyakundi, staked claim to inherit the Sweta leadership by virtue of being the eldest son of Oisera. However, most of the Abasweta elders felt that Nyakundi had better leadership qualities than his half-brother who was accused of being arrogant and aloof. Consequently, the Sweta elders decided to anoint Nyakundi as the new Sweta leader. Feeling let down, Onyangore, with most of his supporters, mainly from the Nyaribari subclan, revolted against the leadership of Nyakundi. In the open hostility and feud that ensued, Onyangore with his followers broke away from the rest of the Kitutu clan and moved away to form the Abanyaribari clan. This leadership feud is still evident even today between the two clans though covertly.

To demonstrate further how perceived leadership antagonism between clans influenced the sharing of leadership positions, Mr. Onchomba used the symbolism of four major mountains in Kisii County namely: Sameta (Bobasi), Manga (Kitutu), Gesere (Nyaribari) and Iberia (Nyaribari). According to Onchomba, Gesere and Iberia mountains are in Nyaribari and they directly face each other in close proximity. Because of this, the Abagusii believe that the two mountains are always in competition over whichone of them is taller than the other as expressed in the metaphor "Iberia yachencha Gesere" (literally translated as 'Iberia criticises Gesere').

This metaphor is commonly used among the Abagusii to make reference to people who are closely related but are always in constant conflict over power and recognition. In this context Onchomba argued that since the two mountains are in the same clan (Nyaribari) and close to each other but in constant conflict, symbolises the antagonistic nature of the clan members.[7] Consequently, in the sharing of leadership positions, Onchomba argued that there was a strong urge among many clans to avoid leadership squabbles in the county, as it would retard development. Therefore it was important for key County positions namely, the governor and Senate, be given to the clans that were perceived less antagonistic. According to Onchomba, this is the reason why the seats of the governor and senate were allocated to the Kitutu and Bobasi respectively.

When this study asked Onchomba to demonstrate the truism of his symbolism, he responded:

> You see when President Kenyatta differed with his vice president Hon. Oginga Odinga; he wanted to give the seat to one of Omogusii sons. Therefore he called James Nyamweya and Lawrence Sagini, both from Nyaribari, the senior most political leaders of Abagusii at that time to state house. He told them that he wanted to appoint one of them to the position of the vice president. Therefore he asked them to agree who among them should be appointed. Instead of agreeing they started undermining each other both privately and in public forums. This made Kenyatta to bypass them and appoint someone else as his vice president. So the Abagusii lost a chance of leadership due to this sibling rivalry. Similarly, when Simeon Nyachae was seeking the country's presidency in 2002, it was Prof. Sam Ongeri who was leading the campaign against him at Gusiiland. Even before this, most members from the Nyaribari clan who occupied senior government positions are known to have undermined each other. So you see the risk of having a member from this clan in a senior position of our county!

In furtherance of his symbolism, Mr. Onchomba observed that in Gusii oral literature it was common for storytellers to start their story with " Once upon a time" and end it with the saying "Nkinenkinendeng'ane Emanga ne Sameta" (literally translates as 'May I grow and grow as big as Manga and Sameta mountains'). This ending of stories was seen as significant in two ways: one, it demonstrated the desire of the storyteller and his/her audience to prosper in future by upholding the moral lesson of the story. Two, it symbolised the importance of harmonious co-existence of various people despite their geographical area.

In relating this symbolism to the sharing of leadership positions in Kisii County, Mr. Onchomba narrated:

> The fact that every Gusii oral narrative ended by making a reference to Sameta and Manga mountains in a harmonious manner is indicative of the accommodative nature of the two clans and where they are situated. This means that leaders from the two clans can work together without conflict and can easily accommodate other clans. Actually as a people of this county, that is what we want so as to prosper. Even in my lifetime I have never witnessed any conflict involving leaders from these two clans or any of them with other clans. Therefore the choice of the Kitutu and Bobasi to take the governor and senate seat respectively was a predetermined fact even before the start of county government in Kenya.

Summary and Conclusion

As noted from narratives from various research participants, it can be concluded that sharing of leadership positions in devolved units was not only motivated by the desire of inclusivity of various groups in the management of devolved resources. Instead it was based on historical happenings that have defined relationships among various clans. These historical happenings were the social, economic and political experiences among various clans and were mostly expressed in form of myths.

As noted in this study, myths were used to justify the social exclusion and inclusion of some clans in the sharing of some leadership positions in the county. In this study clans that were perceived as domineering were excluded from taking powerful leadership positions. This exclusion though informed by historical happenings or facts that have shaped social relationship among various clans, was justified through myths. Myths in this context were used as a means of creating group solidarity among various clans by imparting certain values that justified the exclusion of certain clans from perceived powerful leadership positions. For example, myths that depicted members of Nyaribari clan as antagonistic were used to justify their exclusion. Also, myths that depicted the Kitutu and Bobasi clans as accommodating and less antagonistic were used to justify their consideration for key county positions namely governorship and senate respectively.

In this study also, myths were used to create the need of solidarity among clans that had agreed on the sharing of leadership positions. This was made possible by using myths that appealed to feelings and emotions especially those which created a sense of uncertainty. This sense of uncertainty was important as it encouraged conformity and commitment to the agreed leadership sharing formula. For example, in this study the clans that missed out in getting perceived powerful leadership positions were forced to give up their own interests for the good of the group they belonged to partly because of fear of domination by some clans. In this case the myths were used as means of social and political persuasions.

Lastly, this study found that clanism not only played a key role in sharing of leadership positions but also influenced the voting pattern. As noted each clan tended to vote for her own members when they were competing with members of other clans. This voting pattern was motivated by the desire of each clan to maintain her own social identity and power over other clans.

Acknowledgements

Research on which this paper is based was made possible through the kind support of the French Institute for Research in Africa (IFRA). I also acknowledge all my research participants for their patience and time during the course of this study, and all those who gave me valuable comments on this paper. However, I admit that I am solely responsible for all the opinions expressed in this paper.

Notes

1 Identity in most social groups is perceived to be synonymous to resource accessibility. In this case any social group that has their own in leadership perceive themselves as more accessible to resources.

2 In 2002 Simeon Nyachae contested for presidency under FORD-People party. Majority of the Abagusii felt it was important to support their own as other communities do in national leadership.

3 The Gusii lineage system followed patrilineal principles.

4 This study relied mostly on the leadership sharing formula by ODM. The rationale for this is that it was the most popular leadership sharing formula during 2013 elections.

5 Hailed from Nyaribari clan.

6 Irianyi in Gusii dialect means south. However, in this context it was alleged that Nyachae wanted the new district named so because there was some local administrative unit in his constituency called Irianyi. Therefore the local people took that by calling the new district Irianyi, Nyachae wanted to have control over it just like he did in the local administrative unit in his constituency.

7 The Kikuyu also believe that some mountains found within their community are reflective of the behaviour of the inhabitants where they are located. See for example Thiong'o's Grain of Wheat (1967).

Bibliography

Akama, J."Historical Evolution of the Gusii". In *The Vanishing Cultural Heritage and Ethnography of An African Community: The Gusii of Western Kenya*, eds. Akama, J.S. and R. Maxon. New York: Edwin Mellen Press, 2006.

_____. "Surviving Against All Odds: Gusii movement into their current homeland". *The Vanishing cultural Heritage and Ethnography of An African Community: The Gusii of Western Kenya*, eds. Akama, J.S. and R. Maxon. New York: Edwin Mellen Press, 2006.

Berger, P. and T. Luckmann. *The Social Construction of Reality*. New York: Anchor Books, 1967.

Burr, V. *Social Construction*. London: Routledge, 2003.

Duffy, K. *Social Exclusion and Human Dignity in Europe*. Strasbourg: Council of Europe, 1995.

Foucault, M. *Power-knowledge*. London: Harvester Wheatsheaf, 1980.

Garfinkel, H. *Studies in Ethnomethodology*. Eaglewood Cliffs, N.J.: Prentice-Hall, 1967.

Geetz, C. "Thick description: Towards interpretive theory of culture". *Interpretation of Culture,* ed. Geetz, C., 3-30. New York: Basic Books, 1973.

Gillham, B. *Case Study Research Methods*. London: Continuum, 2002.

Kimutai, V."Negotiated democracy takes centre-stage in county politics". Nairobi: *The Standard* Wednesday, December 12, 2012.

Masese, E."The social construction of HIV/AIDS prevention strategies among Abagusii youth-Kenya". Unpublished PhD thesis in anthropology/ ethnology, UPPA- France, 2011.

Mason, J. *Qualitative Researching*. London: Sage, 2002 (2rd ed).

Mbori, B. "A Study of the Noun Phrase Errors among Ekegusii Speaking Standard Seven Pupils in Kisii District". Unpublished M. Phil. Thesis, Eldoret: Moi University, 1994.

Miruka, K."Clanism rules search for Kisii governor". Nairobi: *The Standard* February 6, 2013.

Moraa, J."Coalitions jostle for a piece of Kisii vote". Nairobi: *Daily Nation* February 8, 2013.

Ocharo, R. "The Gusii Block Vote". In The Moi succession: *The 2002 election in Kenya*, eds. Maupeu, H., M. Katumanga and W. Mitullah,275-298. Nairobi: Transafrica Press, 2005.

Oluoch, N."Will ODM brokered power-sharing deal in Migori county stand"? Nairobi: *The Standard* December 12, 2012.

Ombongi, K."Gusii Politics: An analysis of 1997 elections". In *Out for the Court: The 1997 general elections and prospects for democracy in Kenya*, eds. Rutten, M., A. Mazrui and F. Grignon,471-494. Fountain Mountain, 1997.

Parker, I. *Discourse Dynamics: Critical analysis for social and individual psychology*. London: Routledge, 1992.

Paul, R. *Moses and Civilization: The meaning behind Freud's myth*. New Haven: Yale University Press, 1996.

Psirmoi, D. "Bungoma County: Nightmare over 'negotiated democracy'". Nairobi: *The Standard* October 11, 2012.

Veit, A. and S. Vanessa. "Violence and Violence Research in Africa South of the Sahara". *International Journal of Conflict and Violence* 5, no.1 (2011): 13-31.

Waki, P. *Final Report: The Commission of Inquiry into Post-Election Violence (CIPEV)*. Nairobi: Government Printer, 2008.

Wong, M. *It is Our Turn to Eat. The story of a Kenyan whistleblower.* London: Forth estate, 2009.

Twitting Votes: The Middle Class and the 2013 Elections in Kenya

Patrick Mbataru [*]

Introduction

The 2013 general elections in Kenya were in canvas of a mixed background of high expectation and a lingering aftertaste of the 2008 chaos. The high expectation was that this time round the elections would exorcise the ghosts of the 2008 post election violence and the voters would vouch for economic performance, social welfare improvement, banish tribalism and further consolidate the voting process. These hopes were largely placed on the shoulders of the growing middle class which was seen as having no time for old style politics (Barkan, 2011). The 2013 vote was thought as the tipping point (Ong'ayo, 2012); either we backtrack into chaos or forge ahead into a more pervasive nationalism.

Riding on the middle class-led civil movement that thrived in the 1980s, expectations in Kenya were that the level of civic consciousness especially among the youth would lead to a new political dispensation by pulling the lower classes to a level where voting would be decided on issues affecting the country. This paper asks and discusses if the efforts of the civil societies succeeded in aggregating political organization and mobilization at the national level and if it helped to consolidate concessional political values in the country.

[*]   Lecturer at the School of Agriculture and Enterprise Development, Kenyatta University.

The 2013 election was largely an ethnic derived contest and despite the animated debate in social sites that created a veneer of issue based voting above ethnic considerations, the middle class to a great extent voted along ethnic lines. It is however emerging that creating ethnic blocks is giving way to much broader mobilization along regions. This paper analyses the question of the expanding middle class and its role in the electoral politics in Kenya. Specifically, the paper unpacks the commonly held image of the middle class before the 2013 elections in Kenya.

Middle class debate and Kenya expanding economy

Public expectations in the 2013 general elections in Kenya would be 'a middle class' decision was largely based on the social media that so boisterously proclaimed that, 'an issue based' middle class cutting across ethnic lines was finally here to vote against ethnic identities (Ng'ethe, 2000). This was premised on the notion that there has finally emerged in Kenya a generation 'speaking across politics...about issues and ideas' (Smith, 2013). However, the elections revealed several things about the expanding Kenyan middle class. First, it is too fluid and amorphous to draw clear contours and inferences. Secondly, and most important is that lively, intellectual debates about issues like 'equity', 'services' and justice and framing twittered intentions masks the Kenya political intransitivity from ethnicisation and status quo.

The expectation that the middleclass would make a difference in the outcome of election by channelling debate away from ethnic parameters attempted to create a false and polarised dichotomy between the so-called 'issue based politics' and enforcing one's identity (Wolf, author interview, April 18, 2013), precisely because categories of public and private spaces are always juxtaposing if not conjoined. The subjects of development, equity, security, dignity, poverty, justice are mutually interacting and constantly so. There in, in these categories are embedded issues of negotiation, context (local or international?), constancy (are the issues immutable or flowing?). This does not deny though, the dualistic nature of Kenyan voting character; where the local vote is modern and the national vote traditional (Christian Thibon,author interview, April 17, 2013). The tensions of this polarity keep the Kenyan state at an edge.

The 2013 World Bank report indicates that that between 1995 and 2005, the African middle class expanded from 18% to 28% (Mumo, 2013).The role of the middle class in popular NGO definitions is defined in economic terms (Melber, 2013). The indicators of this consumerism in Nairobi is the rapid expansion of high end consumer item shops like Truworth, Identity, 4u2, Mr Price, Angel and KFC. The Kenya middle class hippy image is reported US$ 715 million yearly on clothes alone.

While the middle class growth indicates the general economic growth, this social stratum has been viewed by analysts as being risk averse and politically aloof (Viongozi, 2013). This prognosis is based on the premises that economic groups have little interest in change. In Africa, the middle class is therefore interested in the status quo because its very existence is symbiotic with that of the state. Change of guard is therefore resisted, to safeguard jobs and enterprise operated by the middle class hence the undercurrent that other than the ICC cases, a important and plausible push fact behind the election of Uhuru is the perennial fear by the central Kenya voter of losing economically, a fear that is borne out of the pedestrian belief that Moi used much state power to dismantle Kikuyu industry, a fear that Kasala rubbishes in her seminal work on political patronage and taxation, arguing that to the contrary, Moi and hegemonic incumbents benefit 'enemy turf' more than their ethnic bases precisely because enemies should be kept much closer (Kasala, 2004) than friends.

There has emerged a new population of urban middle class conceptually hedging in the spreading information and communication technology, creating a new layer of activists of cosmetic nature (Manrique, 2011). The internet is simply a rapidly expanding frontier of urban space which is both socially differentiated and functionally interrelated beyond physical contiguity but which can also be seen as trendy escapism. The high expectation on the middle class overlooked the fact that convergence of experience in same space through computer mediated communication blurs the institutional separation of domains of activity and confuses codes of behaviour and the symbolic meaning, location of functions and the social appropriation of space in rapidly urbanizing countries (Castells, 1996). It confuses value and action.

The middle class has always attracted interest as a subject of social-economic and political analysis. The contribution of the middle class to political process in Kenya especially in nudging down the drain of Moi clientelist state cannot be gainsaid. However what is controversial is if through the civil society, the middle class lead to an aggregation of political organization and consolidated concessional political values. This is important because in industrializing societies, the middle classes are expected to be protagonists of the civil society, in articulating and transiting 'universal' values while building broad, multiclass political coalitions (Braton, 2002). But this has not been the case as we see further below. The spirit of the civil society seems to have petered out after Moi. Braton (2002) also points out that 'the emergence of a bourgeoisie prompts new forms of resistance from working people, women and the dispossessed."The election primaries in January 2013 confirmed a sobering reality that these economically disadvantaged groups can always use the vote to protest against the rising consumerism in the background biting poverty, though the concreteness of this remains in the future. Currently, their vote goes to the one who confirms their existential alienation from the mainstream social and economic exercises.

Debates referring to the 'middle class' invariably begs the question of definition. Even as it enters economic discourse of African studies, its definition remains inflationary and one that needs clarification otherwise "...it covers almost everything...thereby signifying little or nothing" (Melber, 2013). The resultant obtuseness of such a definition is obfuscated further by the relativity of geography, culture, and history. The behaviour of the American middle class is different from that of Singapore for example. Weberian middle class is different from the Kenyan middle class at the onset of the 21st century, yet in general, the contours of a real Weberian continuation of classes and status differences and status group conflicts. The conflict seen during the elections manifest such social stratification (Turner, 1998). This differentiation in time and space, lends the parameters characterizing this stratum controversial and difficult to pin debate upon. The middle class in Europe is not economically the same as that of Africa. We can look at some overarching parameters. Who exactly is characterised to be in the middle class? In economic terms, the definition of the 'middle class' often follows the parameters defined by the World Bank, where only social-economic, and by induction, political participation is averred. It is country specific and the defining constraints are mostly money-metric. In Kenya, the World Bank and consumer analysis put in this class people with a daily per capita expenditure of about three dollars.

Historically, from the middleclass originated the modern economies of production. In economic theory, the middle class is behind the concreteness of basic notions like "comparative advantage' and 'opportunity cost'. Since this class supplies and scouts the means of modern production, it purveys the doctrine of private enterprise, the core of which is profit.

In the early days of economic development, if the emerging positivistic values of middleclass, nudging the society away from the status quo, were antithetical to those of the crumbling feudal fallibility, in modern times, the positivistic ideals now fuse with the entrenching values of the status quo in emerging democracies and economies. Unlike the bourgeoisie bohemian view of politico-economic life, the Kenyan middle class exists in unashamed symbiosis with the sinews of the status quo. But the economic evolution is such that in the modern economic reality, social classes are so intrinsically intertwined with the owners of the means of production in the Marxian sense. These include also middle class members like politicians, priests, policemen, academicians, making the labour sector too fluid for class analysis.

This delicate balance is punctuated in modern history by grand and not so grand revolutions. The ritual of democracy and suffrage is to vary the different scales of this balance, depending on the prevailing interest, or in case of Bourdieu's political market view, the current demand and supply situation. In the case of Kenya, as in other African countries, the fears and perception of power with its possible instrumentalisation make the demand curve for political goods very steep.

The social classes are in a large sense jumbled: there are the small and big factory owners who employ middle class and proletariats. There are the multinationals whose CEOs are equivalent of middle age landlords, supporting platforms with their own class strata. In Bourdieu's market view of political process, class differences relate differently to diverse forms of capital because they are not linearly placed and neither do they lay in a single axis (Sayer, 2005). Currently, the middle class in Kenya is strong in economic capital but weak in other capitals. This however does not exclude the reality that the rise of elitism also leads to resistance from the low classes and the marginalized. The 2007 election violence was in many ways the expression of this. There is a real danger that this lack of uniformity could subvert democracy (Okuku, 2002).

Indeed what is real in Kenya is not so much class struggle but status clamour. The social contract is broken, leading to a high degree of interpersonal and inter group conflict and competition as people struggle to master and control the economic resources uninhibited by cultural or other restraints. Turner (1998) says that in social, cultural and political terms, economic class is declining in importance as the primary or leading driver in social political life. Status rather than class is therefore the crucial axis of contemporary politics. The Kenyan middle class is in this sense not a defining class but a loose vehicle of achieving status. Those who aptly capture the aspirations of the majority low classes and are able to exploit old social crevises invariably retain power.

It is modern symbiosis between the middle-income earners and the sinews of the status quo that characterises the middle class today as a gadget owning class. The personal automobile, the bungalow, the personal insurance, the mall shopping defines the outlines of this class. It is this seemingly union of consumer purpose that leads Smith (2013) to conclude that in the 2013 general elections, ethnic identity would be a lot less important and that this 'educated middleclass cuts across ethnic lines... (boosted)... by migration and urbanisation,' (Ng'ethe, 2000). However, the interviews for this report confirm that the national bourgeoisie in Kenya has an inconsistent stance toward political progress (Kinyatti, 2008).Kenya's expanding middle class has not homogenized in political thought to a level where it plays an important role in social life. Its main limitation is this lack of national agenda (Wolf, author interview, April, 18, 2013) and the crucial connexion with grassroots activism. This will probably change when the majority in the country are members of the middle class. Only then the blatant inequalities between the classes will reduce and become less important in defining the voting (Ossowski, 1963).

This dualism posits the vacuity of consciousness of political-economic change. So long as the adult toys are easily sourced, the middle class votes for the status quo (Ong'ayo, 2012). These toys support a material lifestyle, spawning in itself various sub-cultures and economies thriving in bars, beauty parlours, car washing centres, which space in Kenya socialization, is informed by shallow political analysis framed upon ethnic beams. In the west the middle class was important in the democratic progress (Widner, 1993) and counteracts state excesses since itself is a natural outcome of democratisation and economic development, culture (Chol, 2013) which further permits associational life, an important ingredient of the middle class (Braton, 2002). In Africa, the political state is often trussed by the middleclass, who often owe their lifestyles to continue the existence of the bureaucrats, knowing very well what it means to lose power to their minnows in a zero-game situation. In this, both the state and the middle class led civil societies are predatory, each seeking gain from the other. This is because the very existence of the middle class is based on the same bases that give legitimacy to the modern state, the protection of private property. Capitalism led to an economic middle class which preyed on the state systems for further accumulation (ISS 2006). These predator elites easily hide in the amorphous and fluid cyber space.

The middle class members can individually abstract themselves from the existential problems arising from the weakening of the social contract. This is done by outsourcing civic responsibility to 'quick fix' non-governmental and private organisations that provide alternative social services. Private schools and hospitals, water services and transport are the preserves of the middle class. They are substitute to poor services by the state and subsidize state failure (Swingvote2013, 2013). By outsourcing civic responsibility to private providers, the middle class has become irrelevant to political decisions making in Kenya and eventually given up its power to initiate change.

This is neither a Kenyatta mark 1, nor a Moi era characterization. It is bequeathed from the colonial era. Kenyatta mark 2 and his predecessor Mwai Kibaki would only entrench this trend. Colonial policy on agriculture created a class based on access to land, where three classes emerged: European settler farmers, the middle class African farmer and the landless Africans (Muhula, 2009). The progeny of these forms the content and ingredients of the political incendiary in Kenya and informs that currency of 'historical injustices'. The middle class in the 2000s Kenya is a replica of the settlers' self-interest and profound sense of entitlement girded by shared aristocratic pedigree (Elkins, 2005). Only the expression of it differs. Virulent racist ideology becomes tribal ideology, while the elitist function of it is employed to mobilise the unemployed youth in competing and guarding the market dynamics of power. Colonial legacy and post independence bourgeoisies jostle for power and control of the state fuels present inequalities and tension.

Middle Class apathy as an expression of civil movement atrophy

Circumstantial evidence suggests that participation of middle class members in the political process is lower than that of higher and lower classes. Both of these have the time. The former has also the money to induce participation of the later in political activities for pay. Among the middle class, the attitude is that political participation is for the idle, the poor (Ong'ayo, 2012) or the very rich. Being the key drivers of economic generation, the middle class member do not have the time for political participation, leaving it to the less economically endowed, malleable and less educated members of the society, which gives credence to the view that the primaries before the elections is where elections are won or lost and that this is decided by the poor youth majority from the slums.

One of the reported hallmarks of the Kibaki administration is the expansion of the middle class. According to the World Bank, the country middle increased from 18 % to 32% in the 10 year span of his rulemaking it one of the highest increments in Africa.

In self-praise and objective analysis, economic change in Kenya is cited in superlative terms. Whether this has perceptibly changed the way the middle class will vote, that on account of what the Kibaki administration has 'done for them' was debatable before the election. Alarm bells begun to ring with the chaotic primaries in January 2013. As the epitomic battle for a break with the past, the middle class–if those participating in the cyberspace din is any indication of it-had campaigned for more urban and 'mannered fellow' (Gigo, 2013) for the Nairobi gubernatorial and senatorial contests. However, the voters chose those 'who connected with them and their needs' (Mugo, 2012). Immediately after the widely discredited primaries in early 2013, critiques stridently described the astute aloofness of the 'so-called' middle class. Online reviews observed that the chattering middle class were too busy on Twitter and Facebook to vote in the primaries (Kiberenge, 2013).

The animated debate in the social media on how and who should lead Kenya did not translate into votes. Kiberenge gives one of the reasons for this non-commitment of the middle- class. Since the parties are based on the ethnic chieftaincy, anyone out of favour with the party chief would be disbarred as the party's flag bearer. Since the middle class did not want to get mired in open tribal politics, they opted not to participate in the primaries, many viewing active political participation as the work of the politicians, NGOs and 'the man on the streets' (Swingvote2013, 2013).

Theoretically and in economic perspectives, the opportunity cost of participating in the primaries is somehow lost to the middle class, hence the entrenchment of the trend where the whole exercise is left to non-middleclass actors and debate is delegated to the lumpen-proletariat and the upper-class boardroom deciders (Viongozi, 2013). The lower income groups, mostly unemployed youth from the poor areas, move out in large numbers, a situation plainly described by Kiberenge.

The poor will also endure extreme weather conditions to nominate their preferred candidate. Often, the bait is a few hundred Kenyan shillings (up to £3.80; $5.80), which would not excite the middle class. Those in the middle class will often give up after a few minutes and then tweet their frustrations from the comfort of their living rooms or offices.

Unlike the general election, the nomination day is not a public holiday. It would seem absurd to seek a day off to participate in party primaries. This is not the case with the poor, most of them unemployed. To be fair, though, most in the middle class are registered voters and will take part in the general election.

On the practical side, being behind the service sector (teachers, lecturers, doctors and lawyers) the voters from the middle classes are likely to be on duty during the primaries. The fact that the elective culture of primaries is not deeply rooted in Kenya and the chaos occasioned by party financial constraints and indiscipline discourages many middle class voters from participating in the activity, leaving the electoral activity largely controlled by those who captures the imagination of the aspiration of the low class voters, a category gaining currency as 'ma-hustler and 'ma-sufferers' both slung for the unemployed youth in the slums, who demographically, as we see down in this article used their vote in favour of the presumed champions of their suffering and hustling. In the 2013 campaigns, these 'champions' were epitomized by the candidatures of Ferdinand Waititu and Michael Mbuvi aka Sonko, who successfully used the 'youth- takeover-leadership' campaign call. Both Sonko and Waititu,[1] the two bete noire of Nairobi city politics, were notoriously anti elitist in behaviour[2] and campaigns. They successfully used the traditional perceptions of class crevices between the 'ma-sufferers/hustlers' and the middle class. This age-old age conflict is part of Kenyan history (Braton, 2002).

Although the political process and the expression of it has been shifting, composing and recomposing since independence and before then, depending on the internal and external forces impacting on the state entity, the social-economic class crevices have remained. The apathy of the middle class in the primaries conceals not only the class differences but the atrophy of the civil society movement in Kenya. Much of the constitutional and civil rights changes in Kenya were consolidated by the civil society in the 1990s.Encouraged by the inherent weaknesses of Moi's clientelist machine, and the epochal dismantling of the Soviet Union, the middle-class dominated civil societies steadily pressured Moi to allow political space expression. It appears that after the achievement made by the civil liberties and rights, (as well as associational politics), the civil societies lost the steam. Once Moi was out of the way, they lost the raison d'etre (Kihoro, 2012). Those left in the movement against old vice like corruption, tribalism and economic disparity were largely seen as discordant voices hence the general hostility against Maina Kiai, John Githongo and others even by their former colleagues then serving in Kibaki's government.

At best, there was muted silence by the middle class on pertinent issues that still kept the crevices between classes deep. Again this characterizes much of the Kenya post-independence history; as if the code of silence exists lest old ghouls of unresolved contested claims of the struggle over land come out (Anderson, 2003).The grassroots societies are gradually taking over the space previously occupied by the civil society.

What we see are the same colonial crevices cast in the same harsh and polarised economic mould, in which capital has dual character; on one hand political protection and exclusion and on the other, having a global circulation that disregards localized privileges, (Lonsdale, 1985). This has obtained since when the Swynnerton Plan, in dying embers of British physical colonisation created a landed yeomanry on the one hand and a landless proletariat on the other (Maloba, 1996) especially in Central Kenya where propertied capital was designed for the repossession of productive assets from workers rather than by allocating resources to dependents (Lonsdale, 1985).It is this status quo that the middle class civil society would want to unravel or so the movement casted itself. Being creatures of pleasure, once Moi ceded the essential rights, the middle class had no other reason to continue the fight. Moi managed to retain power longer since the basic social economic architecture was not interfered with while the middle class enjoyed their associational rights. Kibaki's state actually granted the middle class their dream land situation, where everything else continued well outside the political arena and where the private sector continues to function in the absence of political leadership (Mcconnell, 2010) or interference.

The outcome of the elections

Subsumed in the electoral process in Kenya is the question or the rapidly expanding middle class. This study sought to find out the factors influencing political exercise of the middle class in the 2013 elections. By looking at the motivations behind participation or non participation of the middle class in the electoral process, the study hopes to lay bare the class contours that informed the outcome of the elections. With all its ambiguity, there was a general expectation that the Kenyan middle had come of age and coalesced politically in common consciousness hard enough to influence the outcome of the March 2013 general elections. I interviewed members of welfare associations patronised by the middle class in Nairobi. Some of the questions were based on the broad themes of economic performance, ethnicity and corruption.

What emerged from the 2013 elections was that the middle class campaigned vigorously in the social media. There have emerged twitting intellectuals, analysts and activists for all types of Kenyan social, economic ills. This virtual activism, while posing as progressive, hardly impacted on the outcomes of the elections. If anything, the middle class loosened the old order by considerable mobilization of their material and intellectual power; it singularly failed to make a difference in the voting patterns in the 2013. There are several reasons for this.

Firstly, demographically, the middle class in Kenya is still a minority class. It is estimated that this class makes only 25-28 percent of the Kenya population. It is therefore notable that its vote should be eclipsed by that of non-middleclass electors. The observation in this study is that this group votes, contrary to (self) accusation, but the 'tyranny of numbers,' is wielded by non-middle classes, notably the lower income groups, or the non-twitting class, hence the observation by one interviewee that 'those who come out to vote don't have Facebook account... they tweet with their votes' (Muhuhu, author interview, March 8, 2013).

Secondly, the middle class has failed to pull the lower classes to a level where voting is decided on issues affecting the country. While middle class dominated civil society played a major role in challenging Moi's monopoly of state power, it did not lead to an aggregation of political organisation and mobilization at national level which would have hopefully led to concessional political values. What has happened is that other political mobilisation axes have emerged, easily coalescing new forms of resistance and shrewdly manipulating expectations of non-middle classes, hence Gideon Mbuvi 'Sonko' ability to mobilise the youth vote, despite his notoriously cantankerous composure, to win the Nairobi senatorial sit. The same can be said of Ferdinand Waititu. Of the same political hew as Sonko, Mr. Waititu came second to Evans Kidero, the most middle class friendly candidate in the gubernatorial race. Those interviewed saw Waititu and

Sonko as the best representatives of 'poor people and their problems... identifying with common problems," (Kimamo, author interview, March 7, 2013). Indeed, Waititu-Kidero's contest brings us to the third reason.

Thirdly, the 2013 election was still much an ethnic derived contest although it is emerging that creating ethnic blocks is giving way to much broader mobilisation along regions. Though it can be argued that Evans Kidero was a middle class creation, the volatile Nairobi vote was decided by the arithmetic of the parties and boardroom shenanigans. In the face of it The National Alliance (TNA) had two strong candidates in Waititu and Jimnah Mbaru, but the later had little grassroots support. In the supposed 'issued based politics,' it was expected that Mbaru would win the primaries. Being a very successful businessman and well known champion of private accumulation through the stock market, he was seen as a natural choice for the non-Luo or non-CORD supporters. He performed poorly in the primaries, nonetheless. Waititu won for the TNA ticket. Ironically most middle class members interviewed portrayed Mbaru as 'too aloof... detached and out of touch with the common man' (Kanyoro, author interview, March 7, 2013). CORD on the other hand had only one strong candidate in Mr Kidero, who in the 'issue based' thinking would appeal across the board, to the middle class and the low classes. He won the gubernatorial contest for the city by a mere 50, 000 votes over Mr Waititu, spawning claims that the votes were rigged in his favour.

Fourthly, the Kenya middle class is composed of professionals in different fields. The fledgling electoral process is not yet ingrained in the collective behaviour, especially the concept of primaries, which most middle class members did not think was important to participate in. Professional obligation comes first and this is much the same for both the employer and the employee, hence the common refrain by those interviewed that "I had to go to work", "I could not get permission...even if I wanted to…" (Wachira, author interview, March 7, 2013).

Conclusion

The view that the middle class will play the political gadfly in the 2013 general elections in Kenya was spurious. There was a pervasive believe by analyst, fuelled by the animated debate in the internet that Kenyan politics had somehow come of age. However, the suffrage countermanded the presumption that the elections would be decided around issues, an overarching reference to the expansion of the middle class in Kenya. Although the majority of the parliamentarians elected in 2013 are new, only time will tell if the crop of leaders the middle class campaigned for in the social sites were elected.

The middle class hardly participated in the primaries, an electoral culture that is not entrenched in the Kenya politics. Most members of the middle class saw the primaries as of little importance, leaving the exercise to the lower and upper classes. The election outcomes is decided in the boardrooms by the upper classes and operationalised through bribery and manipulation of the lower classes. Several reasons can be adduced to explain middle class lack of impact on the electoral process. Furthermore, other political mobilization axes have emerged, easily coalescing new forms of resistance and shrewdly manipulating expectations of non-middle classes

Demographically, the middle class in Kenya is still a minority class, making only 25-28 percent of the Kenya population. This vote is overshadowed by that of non-middleclass electors.

Although the middle class votes, the 'tyranny of numbers,' is wielded by non-middle classes, notably the lower income groups, the majority of whom participate in the elections largely as an exercise hoping to get some money or for lack of anything else to do.

In addition, the Kenyan middle class is composed of professionals in different fields. The non participation of the middle class in the primaries and therefore the general minimal impact on political direction specifically in the 2013 general elections could be due to genuine reasons. Though the fledgling electoral process, is not yet ingrained in the collective electoral behaviour, most members of the middle class are busy professionals and job obligation comes first which is much the same for both the employer and the employee. Theoretically and in economic perspectives, the opportunity cost of participating in the primaries is somehow not lost to the middle class.

In all, although the political process and the expression of it has been shifting, composing and recomposing even before independence, depending on the internal and external forces impacting on the state entity, the social–economic class crevices have remained. The animated debate in the social media on how and who should lead Kenya did not translate into votes. Kenya's expanding middle class has not homogenized in political thought to a level where it plays an important role in social life. Its main limitation is this lack of national agenda and the crucial connexion with grassroots activism. This will probably change when the majority in the country are members of the middle class. Only then will the blatant inequalities between the classes reduce and become less important in defining voting.

Notes

1   Mr. Waititu lost the Nairobi gubernatorial contest to Evans Kidero, a middle class darling

2   Both have been caught on camera as mobsters, with Waititu throwing stones to policemen and Sonko hack- sawing away a city council car cramp from his car, which was double parked in the city.

Bibliography

Anderson, D. "The Battle of Dandora Swamp". In *Mau Mau and Nationhood,* by John Lonsdale E.S Atieno Odhiambo, 155-175. Oxford: James Currey, 2003.

Barkan, J. *A Report of the CISIS African Program; Kenya, asssing risks to stabilty.* London: Centre for Strategic and Internation Studies , 2011.

Braton, M. *Civil Society and Political Transition in Africa.* London: IDR reports, 2002, 18.

Castells, M. *The Rise of the Network Society.* Oxford: Blackwell Publishers , 1996.

Chol, J.D. "Kenyan Experience:Lessons Southern Sudan can learn". *Sudan*, January 23, 2013: 1-3.

Elkins, *C. Britain's Gulag:The brutal end of Empire Kenya.* London: Jonathan Cape, 2005.

GGigo. *tellem.* February 20, 2013. tellembrog.com (accessed March 1, 2013).

ISS. *Leadership, Civil Society and Democratisition in Africa.* London: ISS, 2006.

Kasala, K. "State Politics and Taxation". *African Political Economy* (2004): 20-48.

Kiberenge, K. "BBC news." BBC. Feburuary 3, 2013. http://www.bbc.co.uk (accessed April 3, 2013).

Kihoro, W. *The Price of Freedom: The story of political resistance in Kenya.* Nairobi: MvuliAfrica, 2012.

Kinyatti, M. *Classes and Class Struggle in Kenya.* Nairobi: Mau Mau Research Centre, 2008.

Lonsdale, J. "The Conguest State,1965-1980". In *A Modern History of Kenya,1895-1980*, by W.R. Ochieng, 6-34. Nairobi: Evans Brothers Limited, 1985.

Maloba, W.A. "Decolonization: A theoretical Perspective". In *Decolonization and Independence in Kenya, 1940-1993,* by W.R.Ochieng B.A Ogot, 25-47. London: James Curry, 1996.

Manrique, M. Supporting *Africa's New Civil Society: the case of Kenya.* Helsink: Fride , 2011.

Mcconnell, T. "News Global Post." *Global Post Web site.* May 8, 2010. http://www.glonslpost.com (accessed April 16, 2013).

Melber, H. *Africa and the Middle Class(es).* New York: UNDP, 2013.

Mugo, W. *Waweru Mugo wall.* February 4, 2012. wawerumugo.facebook.com (accessed February 6, 2013).

Muhula, R. "Horizontal inequalities and ethno-regional politics in Kenya". *Kenya Studies Review* (KESSA), 2009: 85-105.

Mumo, M. "Firms target Africa's fast-growing middle class with fresh products." *Daily Nation.* Nairobi, Nairobi: Nation Media Group, April 16, 2013.

Ng'ethe, O.J, S. Nasongo, D. Bethamand S. Bracking. *Democracy Reportfor Jamhuri ya Kenya.* Leeds: IDEA-SAREAT, 2000.

Okuku, J. "Civil Society and Democratisation Processes in Kenya and Uganda. A comparative analysis of the contribution of the Church and NGOs". *Africa Journal of Political Science* (2002): 26-39.

Ong'ayo, A. "Afra-Euro.org." *Afra-Euro.org magazine.* April 14, 2012. www.afro-euro.org (accessed April 14 , 2013).

Ossowski, S. *Class Structure in the Social Consciousness.* London: Routledge and Kegan Paul LTD, 1963.

Sayer, A. *The Moral Significance of Class*. Cambridge: Cambridge University Press, 2005.

Smith, D. Guardian News. March 8, 2013 (accessed April 18, 2013).

Swingvote2013. "Swingvote2013." *Swingvote Web site*. February 6, 2013. www.swingvote2013. org (accessed May 6, 2013).

Turner, B. *Status and Politics*. Edited by Milton Keynes. London: London University press, 1998.

Viongozi, Tujenge. *Tujenge Viongozi project*. February 13, 2013. tujengeviongoziblogpot.com (accessed April 18, 2013).

Widner, J. *The Rise of a Party State in Kenya: From Harambee to Nyayo*. Berkeley : Berkeley Univeristy Press, 1993.

The Quest for New Political Leadership in the South Rift, Kenya

Joseph Misati Akuma *

Introduction

In any country, the authority of the government can only derive from the will of the people as expressed in genuine, free and fair elections, held at regular intervals on the basis of the universal, equal and secret suffrage (Gill, 2006). In Kenya, the electoral campaigns that preceded the March 2013 general elections were expected to enable the citizens to objectively vote for personalities who would access political power.[1] The new Kenyan constitution empowers the citizens to control and stop the manipulation of electoral process by political aspirants to fraudulently gain political power. Indeed, this election was for the first time different in various aspects. Firstly, the leading presidential contenders participated in two presidential debates in which they were asked to articulate their policy proposals with regard to important themes, like governance, national unity, corruption and wealth creation, thus putting political, institutional and development issues at the center of the electoral stage rather than ethnicity or political competition. Secondly, the vote was held under a supposedly transparent and accountable Elections body, the Independent Electoral and Boundaries Commission (IEBC) and a newly instituted independent judiciary, the Supreme Court had been instituted. It was expected that these institutions could impact positively on the conduct of the campaign process at the grassroots and prompt a focus on programs and ideas. However, the outcome of the vote compared to the opinion poll results released two months before Election Day demonstrate that, contrary to expectations, Kenya's

*   Lecturer, School of Arts & Social Sciences, Maasai Mara University.

2010 constitution has neither proved able to enhance the legitimacy and stability of the political system, nor its capacity to foster democratic elections, as demonstrated by sites on debates and discussions about the present and the desired future for Kenyan society. In this regard, this chapter attempts to answer two questions: Firstly, how did the political opinion at the national level impact on the voting behavior at the level of the local political arena? Secondly, did the call for rallying for a new crop of leadership popularly referred to as "digital generation" made at the national level play a key role in the choice of the local leadership? The discussion is based upon the case study of Narok County in southwestern Kenya.

Narok voting patterns in competitive politics, 1992-2012

Narok County is situated in South-West Kenya. It borders Nakuru, Bomet, Nyamira and Kisii to the North West, Kajiado to the East and Migori to the West and also shares a border to the South with Tanzania. Prior to 1992 first multi-party elections, Narok County (then comprising of Narok North, Narok South and Trans-Mara Constituencies) voted solidly for KANU (Kenya African National Union) as was the case in most areas in the South Rift. Upon the introduction of multi-party politics in the country in the 1992 general elections, and despite protracted attempts mounted by local opposition politicians, former president Daniel arap Moi garnered an absolute majority of the votes in Maasailand, scoring as high as 97% of the presidential vote in Narok South Constituency. In the 1997 general elections, the ethnicity factor gained importance as a result of the opening up of the region and the influx of non-Maasai[2] voters who were seen as a threat to the existing political leadership.[3] William Ole Ntimama stood on a KANU ticket and was elected unopposed. In the presidential vote, Moi's KANU scored 81.2 % against Mwai Kibaki's Democratic Party of Kenya's 15.4%. From then on, William Ole Ntimama used the simmering land issue to his advantage, persistently making the minority communities of Narok county –whom he often referred to as "alien trouble makers" – responsible for deprivation of Maasai rights. By cleverly overlaying and ethicizing the problem of land in the area, he built himself as the undisputed leader surrounded and supported by a cohesive local constituency. In Kilgoris, a KANU zone, William Sunkuli (KANU) won the parliamentary seat with 63.89 % of the votes against Gideon Konchela's (Democratic Party of Kenya) 35.77 %.[4]

In the general election of 2002, which represented a true consolidation of democracy in Kenya, the Maasai voted in favour of Mwai Kibaki and NARC, with the opposition coalition winning four out of the six seats held by Maasai politicians with the exception of Narok South and Kajiado Central. In the Kenyan constitution referendum held on November 21, 2005, the people of Narok voted overwhelmingly against theWako draft.[5] In the subsequent 2007 general elections, the Maasai of Narok stood solidly behind the ODM party.

The 2013 election campaign in Narok County

In the 2013 general election campaigns, clan politics, party politics– majorly pitting ODM and URP political parties revolved around the 'sticky land issue' stood dominant. Also issues on the state of infrastructure, mainly the road network, which has remained pathetic for a long time, and the lack of basic health care facilities, that has often caused local residents to die of curable diseases were at the core of political debates in the county. The state of poverty, which has been attributed to the poor leadership in the past and the deeply entrenched suspicion between the "host" (Maasai) and the "migrant communities", was also a major issue in the local elections.

Other major concerns raised by the electorate were the need to address corruption and gender concerns, and to "break with the past" so that a "new generation leadership" is put in place.

One of the most important determinants of the outcome of the 2013 vote in the country at the national level was the desire to pass over the mantle to a "youthful leadership". This resonated well with the thinking and aspirations at the local level. The idea that the "old guard" ought to give way for the "young blood" in order to steer the county's political leadership to greater heights was widely articulate dearly during the electoral campaigns in the county.[6] The residents equated this to mean that they shunthe old crop of politicians like William Ole Ntimama, who had hitherto been considered as the Maasai community's spokesman. Determination for change was openly demonstrated when William Ole Ntimama's endorsement of Johnson Nchoe for the gubernatorial seat met open resistance. Although the importance and respect accorded by Narok community to the elder statesman was acknowledged by many, it was felt that the choice of Nchoe could serve Ntimama's personal interests, thus maintaining the old political dispensation. For the senatorial seat, although Andrew Leteipa Sunkuli (Independent candidate) had been touted as providing the new crop of leadership, the incessant wrangles for the position with his elder brother, Julius Lekekany Sunkuli, made both of them loose the nomination for the popular URP party ticket to Stephen Ole Ntutu. The Women's Representative position was equally a contest between the old and the new guard: it pitted Agnes Pareiyio (57) and Eunice Marima, wife of the first MP of Narok (60) against the youthful Soipan Tuya, Agnes Shonko and Janet Nchoko.

At the national level, Uhuru Muigai Kenyatta and William Samoei Ruto's Jubilee coalition cast the election contest as "a generational battle". These two political leaders portrayed themselves as a fresh alternative to their CORD rivals.[7] The national political spectrum seems to have been replicated at the local political arena when, in a meeting at their Poroko home, elders from three Maasai clans who convened to arbitrate on who among the two Sunkuli brothers should be allowed to stand for the position of senator, ruled in favor of the younger Sunkuli: this was a complete departure from expectation that Julius, being older and politically more experienced, could have been handed the victory. Yet the elders, on their part, explained that "according to Maasai culture, it is not prudent to send two brothers to war as they could fight each other". Failing to heed the elders' decision, the two brothers ran for the senatorial seat all the same, with the younger Sunkuli running as an independent candidate while the elder one ran on a TNA ticket. Both, however, lost to the elderly Stephen Ole Ntutu who had been handed the prestigious URP ticket on which he won the senatorial seat. As for the gubernatorial seat, the youthful Samwel Kuntai Tunai was handed the URP ticket to run against a host of other contenders: Johnson Nchoe (ODM), Ledama Ole Kina (Independent), Konchela (KANU), Musuni (KNC) and Nkoitoi (WDM-K). In the end Samwel Kuntai Tunai emerged the winner, becoming the first governor for Narok County.

The new generation leadership: Illuminating the national political scene on the local arena

Contrary to the opinion polls conducted just before the March 2013 elections which showed that Narok County was a CORD zone[8] the Jubilee alliance's URP and TNA political parties eclipsed the ODM party in the county to win the Governor and Senate seats and all(except Emurua Dikirr) Parliamentary seats. Additionally, the youthful URP candidate, Rosalinda Tuya (34 years) was elected the county Women's representative. Surprisingly, in the presidential elections (see table 1) Raila Odinga, the Cord coalition presidential candidate, led with over 50% of the county's total votes, followed by Jubilee's Uhuru Kenyatta with slightly over 46%.

Table 1: Presidential results for Narok County, 2013

Presidential Candidate	Karua	Uhuru Kenyatta	Raila Odinga	Peter Kenneth	Ole Kiyiapi	Mudavadi	Dida	Paul Muite
% Vote	0.17	46.38	50.28	1.08	0.81	0.41	0.12	0.05

Source: IEBC, 2013

The aftermath of March 2013 elections in Narok County portrays the proverbial imagery of a community's desire of not "putting their eggs in one basket" or, to put in another way, "killing two birds using one stone". The massive support for Raila Odinga is attributable to his reform policies on land[9] and stand on eviction of mainly the Kalenjin settlers of the Mau forest complex water tower, which sounded politically favourable to the native Maasai inhabitants. Nevertheless, there are clear indications pointing to the fact that this state of affairs is likely to change as demonstrated by the gains[10] made by the Jubilee candidate, whose votes majorly comprise those of the Kikuyu and the Kalenjin in the county.[11] Similarly, the decision by a large percentage of the residents to vote for the presidential candidate, Raila Odinga, while handing massive support to the "lower seat" aspirants from URP party appear paradoxical.[12] This can be explained by the long-standing suspicion and rivalry that has always been prevalent within the locality between the local Maasai and the migrant Kikuyu community. For instance, in the early 1990s, when the constitutional reform debate kicked off, William Ole Ntimama reopened the discussion on majimboism; he also accused Kenya's founding president, the late Jomo Kenyatta, of undermining the independence constitution to favour one tribe and ensure that his people (Kikuyu) dominate the other ethnic groups of Kenya. At the height of the Moi era, violent clashes which broke out at Enoosupukia in Narok County in October1993 led to the eviction of an estimated 5,000 Kikuyu from their farms.[13] When attempts were made to resettle them, the local leadership made it clear that no-one could be allowed back to Narok (Hornsby, 2012). During the one-decade rule by President Mwai Kibaki, efforts to resettle the IDPs on land bought by the government for this purpose met strong opposition from the county residents.[14] People in Narok widely believed that handing the mantle to a Kikuyu president could work against the land rights of the Maasai community.[15]

The election results for winners of County and Parliamentary seats show a landslide victory for the Jubilee coalition (see Table 2 and Table 3). All except one parliamentary seat (Emurua Dikirr) were taken up by the Jubilee coalition, while the winning candidates for Gubernatorial, Senatorial and Women's representative were won by the candidates who contested on the URP ticket; but the elections for the county assembly representatives saw other parties not featuring in the Presidential, Governor and Senatorial positions win several seats (see Table 4).

Table 2: Narok County parliamentary election results, 2013

Constituency	Name	Political Party	Coalition
Kilgoris	Gideon Konchella	URP	Jubilee
Emurua Dikirr	Johana Ng'eno	KNC	Eagle
Narok North	Moitalel ole Kenta	TNA	Jubilee
Narok East	Ken Kiloku	URP	Jubilee
Narok South	Lemein Korei	URP	Jubilee
Narok West	Patrick ole Ntutu	URP	Jubilee

Source: IEBC, 2013

Table 3: Winning candidates for Narok County leaders' seats, 2013

Position	Name	Political party	Coalition
Governor	Samwel Kuntai Tunai	URP	Jubilee
Senator	Stephen Ntutu	URP	Jubilee
Women rep	Soipan Tuya	URP	Jubilee

Source: IEBC, 2013

Table 4: Results for Members of County Assembly (MCA's) vs party affiliation, 2013

Political Party	Seats won
ODM	4
URP	13
KNC	6
TNA	4
WDM-K	1
RBK	2

Source: IEBC, 2013

Again, all winners (except Stephen Ole Ntutu)[16] are young legislators as well as first-time entrants into the political scene. The triumph of the Jubilee coalition in the county, previously dominated by ODM can be explained as follows. Firstly, the URP provided a natural alternative for the community to bring in a fresh leadership, not to mention that its association with Francis Ole Kaparo, a Maasai, led to its appeal to the local community. On the other hand, the TNA/URP merger provided a sole platform on which the Kikuyu and Kalenjin voters in the locality could exercise their right to choose a candidate of their own choice without fear of being reprimanded by their Maasai neighbours. For instance, Moitalel Ole Kenta (a Maasai) received overwhelming support by the mainly Kikuyu voters in the cosmopolitan Narok North Constituency. This scenario presents a positive development in the region as it supports the thesis that "in an ethnically divided society, ethnic affiliations provide a sense of security, trust, certainty, reciprocal help" (Smith, 2009) and provides the pointer to the potential to harness ethnicity for national cohesion.[17] In addition, other factors such as age seem to have played a key role. For example, while Johana Ng'eno, though standing on the little known KNC party in Emurua Dikirr Constituency, received overwhelming support in the vote by the mainly Kalenjin residents to beat URP's David Kipsang Keter.[18]

Conclusion

In the foregoing discussion, we have followed the Maasai voting patterns in Narok County since the re-introduction of the multi-party political system in Kenya in 1992. A striking aspect of the major issues at stake during the 1990s was the desire to safeguard the communities' resources, mainly land coupled with the rapid gain of importance of the ethnicity factor mainly as a result of the opening up of the county and the subsequent influx of non-Maasai voters, more so after the sub-division of group ranches, making land a commodity that could be sold to outsiders. In the subsequent elections, although the restoration of the indigenous communities' rights remained the focus, the simmering poverty levels amid endowment with vast natural resources led the electorate to agitate the need for having a youthful leadership at the helm to captivate a new development agenda in line with the country's current decentralized strategy. Whether the new crop of political leadership will be able to consolidate its position and steer the region to prosperity remains to be seen. On the overall the case of Narok demonstrates the significance of counties not only to the politics of the South-Rift but also to that of the national level. It is also clear that the scenario that unfolded in the region with regard to the just concluded general elections present a window of opportunity for the county to evolve its own unique political culture which will be important for establishing a liberal democratic regime[19] in the region and beyond.

Notes

1   For the first time, the country held a general election under a popularly enacted constitutional dispensation.

2   These comprise the Kipsigis, Gikuyu, Kisii, Luhya, Luo, Somali and the Kamba ethnic groups.

3   *Daily Nation*, January 2, 1998.

4   IED/CJPC/NCCK (1998), Report on the 1998 General elections in Kenya, December 29-30, 1997. Nairobi, Institute for Education in Democracy/Catholic Justice & Peace Commission/National Council of Churches of Kenya.

5   The proposed constitutional draft named after the then Kenya's attorney general, Amos Wako, was put to national referendum on November 21, 2005. The document was unpopular among indigenous groups such as the Ogiek and Maasai, arguing it did not do enough to curb presidential powers.

6   *Daily Nation*, December 31, 2013.

7   *Sunday Nation*, December 30, 2013.

8   Opinion polls conducted in February 2013 indicated that Narok County was a CORD stronghold. This explains why its approximately 253,086 voters out of the county's population of 850,920 were expected to vote overwhelmingly for the coalition.

9   The Maasai have always claimed for redressing their land rights, feeling that migrant communities (mainly Kikuyu) had suppressed them, taken their land and degraded their environment.

10   See the narrow margin as demonstrated by the percentage votes garnered by the two candidates (table1).

11   This will depend on whether the present coalition of URP and TNA parties will continue to hold.

12   Kenyans have been known to vote in a 6-piece system (formerly 3-piece system in which votes are cast for candidates at all levels, from presidential to civic level for a similar party).

13   Akiwumi report on tribal clashes in the Rift Valley.

14   *Daily Nation*, March 19, 2013.

15   Interview with Kosiom ole Lemut, civic ward aspirant, at Olchorro on February 13, 2013.

16   His win can be attributed to the failure by the elder Sunkuli to give way to his younger brother despite the ruling passed by the community elders in favour of the latter.

17   *Daily Nation*, March 20, 2013.

18   During the campaigns, Uhuru Kenyatta's presidential running mate under the Jubilee coalition, William Samoei Ruto campaigned against Ng'eno, who overcame the strong URP wave in Rift Valley to become the first MP for the created constituency by garnering 17,627 votes against Keter 7,819 votes.

19   According to Nabende (2010:107) elections remain the best method for advancing regime change and the manner in which citizens utilize elections to decide the personalities who access power constitutes a core element of democratic governance.

Bibliography

Abdalla, B. *Democratic Transition in Kenya: The struggle from liberal to social democracy.* Nairobi: Development policy and management forum, 2005.

African Union. *African Charter for Popular Participation in Development.* Arusha: African Union, 1990.

Andreassen, B.A. "Bridging Human Rights and Governance: Constructing civic competence and the reconstitution of political order". In *Human Rights and Governance: Building bridges.* The Hague: MartinusNijhoffpublishers,2002.

Chweya, L. *Electoral Politics in Kenya.* Nairobi: Claripress, 2002.

Dahl, R.A. *A Preface to Democracy.* Chicago: University of Chicago Press, 1956.

Elkilit, J. "Electoral Institutional Change and Democratization: You can lead a horse to water but you cannot make it drink". *Democratisation* 6, no. 4 (Winter1999):28-51.

Farrar, C. "Ancient Greek Theory as a Response to Democracy". In *Democracy: The unfinished journey 508 B.C to A.D 1993,* ed. Dunn. Oxford: Oxford University Press, 2008.

Finley, M.I. *Politics in the Ancient World.* Cambridge: Cambridge Press, 1983.

Graaf, D.G.,V.P. Maravicand P. Wagenaar. *The Good Cause: Theoretical perspectives on corruption.* Barbara Budrich Publishers, 2010.

Gill, G. *Free and Fair elections: Inter-parliamentary Union,* Geneva, 2006.

Hornsby, C. *Kenya: A history since independence.* New York: I.B. Tauris&Co, 2012.

Kimberling, W.C. "A Rational Approach to Evaluating Alternative Voter Registration Systems &Procedures". In *RegisteringVoters: Comparative perspectives,* ed. Courtney, J.Cambridge: M.A: Centre for international Affairs, Havard University Press, 1991.

Levy, B. and P. Sahr. *Building State Capacity in Africa: New approaches, emerging lessons.* Wahington D.C: WBI Development Studies, 2004.

Louisie, F. and R. Liebenthal. *Attacking Africa's Poverty: Experience from the ground.* Washinton D.C:The World Bank, 2006.

Martin, R.T.,N.S. Smith and F.J. Stuart. *Democracy in the Politics of Aristotle.* Stoa Consortium, 2003.

Maupeu, H. "Religion and Elections". In *The Moi Succession Elections 2002,* eds. Maupeu etal. Nairobi: Trans Africa Press, 2002.

Mboge, F. and G.S. Doe. *African Commitments to Civil Society Engagement: Areview of eight NPD countries.* African Human Security Initiative, 2004.

Mitullah, W., M.L. Mute and J. Mwalulu. *The People's Voice: What Kenyans say.* Nairobi: Claripress, 1997.

Mute, M.L. and S. Wanjala. *When the Constitution Begins to Flower,* Vol (1). Nairobi: Claripress, 2002.

Omosa, M. et al. *Theory and Practice of Governance in Kenya.* Nairobi: University of Nairobi Press, 2006.

Oyugi, W.O., P. Wanyande and C.O. Mbai. *The Politics of Transition in Kenya: From KANU to NARC.* Heinrich Boll Foundation, 2003.

Republic of Kenya. *Kenya Gazette Supplement No.55. The Constitution of Kenya.* Nairobi: Governmentprinter, 2010.

_____. *Kenya Vision 2030.A globally competitive and prosperous Kenya.* Nairobi: Ministry of Planning and National Development, 2007.

_____. *National Development Plan 1966-1970.* Nairobi: Ministry of Planning and National Development.GovernmentPrinter, 1966.

_____. *Narok County Development Profile 2012.* Nairobi: Ministry of State for Planning, National Development and Vision 2030,2012.

Romdhane, M.B. and S. Moyo. *Peasant Organisations and the Democratisation Process in Africa.* Dakar: CODESRIA, 2002.

Rudebeck, L. *Equal Representation: A challenge to democracy and democracy promotion.* Uppsalla: UppsalaUniversity, 2007.

Salih, M.A.M. *African Democracies and African Politics.* London: Pluto Press, 2001.

Smith, A.D. *Myths and Memories of the Nation.* Oxford: Oxford University Press, 2009.

Society for International Development. *Pulling Apart: Facts and figures on inequality in Kenya.* Society for International Development, 2004.

Suksi, M. "Good governance in the electoral process". In *Human Rights and Good Governance: Buildingbridges.* London: Martinus Nijhoff Publishers, 2002.

Wanjala, S., S.K. Akivaga and K. Kibwana. *Yearning for Democracy: Kenya at the dawn of a new century.* Nairobi: Claripress, 2002.

Wanyande, P. "Democracy and the One Party State. The African experience". In *Democratic Theory and Practice in Africa*, eds. Oyugiet al. London: James Currey, 1988.

World Bank. *Kenya: Country assistance strategy progress report 2004-2008.* Washington D.C: World Bank, 2008.

Kikuyu-Kalenjin Relations in IDP Camps and the 2013 Elections: An Invitation to 'The' Conversation

Susan Mwangi [*]

Introduction

Since 1963, elections in Kenya have been a common albeit a contested phenomenon with groups and individuals aligning themselves on the basis of religion, class, gender and ethnicity to ensure a win or/and retention of power and authority of the ruling group. Of all these, ethnicity, however, though unfixed and often contested, has and continues to be the greatest vehicle through which people and communities are mobilized and identities interrogated as the political elite fight it out in the campaign battlefield. The civil wars in Nigeria, Rwanda, Uganda and Burundi, among others, can be attributed to the contest between ethnic groups over the control of the apparatus of state and government for the allocation of the national pie.[1] The politicization of ethnicity and the use of the 'us' and/against 'them' to denote differences in ethnic identities is also actually articulated in discourses on land as the jargon through which the political processes in Africa are based. In Rwanda, for instance, the genocide revolved around ethnic-cum political identities that were mobilized by Hutu against the minority Tutsi. Ethnicity and politics in Africa generally can thus not be isolated because many times the two dictate who does or who does not ascend to power both at the grassroots and at the national levels.

For the agricultural communities in particular the question of land is not only sensitive and controversial but it forms the basis for (de)mobilization and formation of voting blocks of

[*]   Lecturer in History at Kenyatta University.

especially vulnerable land hungry ethnic communities, with each having a narrative on land ownership to fit their land claims. For such groups, the land disposition initiated by colonialism in the early 19th century plays a major role in the economic and political bargaining power of those concerned. The Kikuyu and the Kalenjin form part of this category. Both live in fertile lands and have equally questioned land utilization and allocation to individuals and groups they claim to be allochtons.[2] Indeed it is on the basis of the land which is often couched in ethnic identities that elections are won or lost by the two communities. Nowhere else is this contestation rampant than in the vast Rift Valley region, an area where colonial alienation of land, redistribution by the Kenyatta government (1963-1978) and re-divisioning by President Moi (1978-2002) continue to inform the history of Kenya's electioneering process. While the Kalenjin claim that the White Highlands were originally their ancestral land, the Kikuyu on the other partly assert that were it not for their sweat and blood, the Highlands would still be unproductive. The later also claim that many of the pieces of land claimed by the Kalenjin and Maasai communities were acquired through a process where the owners sold through a willing buyer-willing seller basis. For them the question of land repossession by either the Kalenjin or the Maasai in the Rift Valley does not indeed arise because according to the Kenyan Constitution a Kenyan can own land or any other property in any corner of the country provided these are authentically owned. It is the authenticity of such ownership, however, that the Kalenjin have contested. They argue that while colonialism played its role in dispossessing the community of fertile parcels, the Kenyatta government hardly considered the community when it was redistributing land after independence. They also note that their pleas to the Kenyatta government to genuinely, redistribute such land fell on deaf ears because the Kikuyu elites always protected land interests through dubious land buying companies majorly owned and run by the same Kikuyu elites (Widner, 1992). While this paper dwells majorly on the merger between TNA and URP and the 2013 elections victory of the two, this merger and emergent relations between the people from the two communities and in particular, those living in IDP camps cannot be understood in a vacuum. Let us now look at the relations of the two communities from a historical perspective.

Pre-colonial and colonial Kikuyu-Kalenjin relations: Some reflections

Apart from the obvious small time clan and neighbour conflicts over animals and land boundaries, pre-colonial relations among and between Kenyan ethnic groups were largely amicable. Communities resolved conflicts with due regard to indigenous conflict resolution mechanisms and often, warring factions were brought together by councils of elders who ensured that justice and reconciliation were, as the hallmarks of the development of any community, achieved. And while we do not deny the possibility of long-lasting feuds among communities, these were however, few and quite dispersed as compared to conflicts that emerged with and after the advent of colonialism in Africa.

In Africa, it has been generally argued that the primary motive of colonialism was economic. Colonialism was exploitative and disrespectful to indigenous boundaries and to indigenous mechanisms of conflict resolution. Itspolicies werebased on capital accumulation which included the exportation of raw materials from their colonies, labour exploitation and transfer through slaves in some areas, taxation of natives and above all the appropriation of African fertile lands. In Kenya, colonial imperialism reached its peak in late 1890s when fertile lands in the Central province and the Rift Valley region were transformed by the British settlers into large scale plantations owned and managed by few foreign landowners. Not surprisingly, to use Franck

Furedi's (1989) words, the impetus behind early resistance movements against colonialism was most discernible in this regionand the politics of land was perhaps the key question dividing Kenya's ethnic sub-nationalismsat and after independence. It has also been argued that the distribution of this scarce resource underlay most of the ethnic rivalries at independence and the division between KANU and KADU between 1960 and 1964 (Throup, 1987). Scholars have argued that much of the alienated lands in the Rift Valley belonged to the pastoral Maasai people, the Nandi, and the Kipsigis communities. In addition, between 1903 and 1907, land was appropriated from the Kikuyu community by the colonial government and the subsequent rapid social and economic transformation emerging out of this alienation, prompted a fierce retaliation battle with the Europeans. The early colonial land policies and most specifically the Crown Land Ordinance of 1902 was also designed with little if any, regard to prior land possessions. The colonial government assumed that the lack of title deeds or inoccupation and lack of cultivation implied no ownership. According to the 1902 land law such land was considered freeland which could be passed over to the Crown at will. It is such land dispossession and disregard to original ownership that disregarded ancestral claims that the political economy of colonialism was founded. The implications for this were and continue to affect the relations between the British and Kenyans, as well as relations among and between different Kenyan communities. Communities became suspicious of their neighbours and identity markers redrawn after colonialism as real or imagined ethnic relations began to be manipulated by African elites in mobilizing for political gains. Among the communities affected by this phenomenon in Kenya were the Kikuyu and the Kalenjin. They began to view and accuse each over land claims and to create imaginary boundaries based on their collective memorizing. Henceforth, competition over land became the fulcrum for political mobilization of the Kikuyu and the Kalenjin.

The increasing number of Kikuyu squatters in White Highlands is another issue that was to have far reaching impacts on the Kikuyu-Kalenjin relations during colonialism. By 1929, the number of squatters had increased tremendously as the colonial administrators pushed thousands of Kikuyu able-bodied men and women to work on their plantations. These squatters had been dispossessed of their land by their kinsmen or by the colonial government. Their numbers, according to Furedi, increased every year and by mid 1930s it was clear that they were not welcome back in Kikuyu districts from where they had originated. The Kikuyulandlord class was indeed hostile towards the squatters because as they claimed they had lost their land rights. They were basically relying on the colonial government to give them land around the Highlands as a reward for their labour or to be offered secure employment. This, as would be expected, was not a welcome move especially from the Maasai, the Kipsigis and the Nandi communities who claimed ancestral ownership of such lands in the Rift valley (Furedi, 1989). Their claims to the Highlands, they argued were based on an assumed right of natives to own and control their homelands. To this group, it was only independence that would drive the Kikuyu back to their original lands in central province. The Kikuyu on the other hand eagerly fought and waited for the granting of independence with the intention, at least in the Rift Valley, to drive out 'foreigners' and take over the lands that they had long cultivated as either squatters or colonial employees. By 1960, the Kikuyu-Kalenjin relations had thus began to sour and KADU, a party that comprised the smaller marginalised ethnic communities, including the Kalenjin, hoped to grant regional governments control over exchange of land and thus effectively block the settlement of such category of landless Kikuyu in the region (Widner, 1991). The situation was to become even worse with independence and the ascendancy of Jomo Kenyatta, a Kikuyu into power. Some IDPs from the Kalenjin communities allege that Kenyatta, together with close members of his now prosperous Kikuyu community bought off the highlands and redistributed them to a clique of rich Kikuyu relatives and cronies – thus heightening the hatred that had been occasioned by the immigration of the Kikuyu into the Rift Valley in the 1920s.[3] The clientelist networks, as Widner observes, became the primary structures of representation, linking Kenyans to the state through political patrons. The Kalenjin secured little at least in terms of land redistribution and state jobs from the Kenyatta government. Their hopes of getting back alienated land were ended with the establishment of land companies headed by Kikuyu elites. The Ministry of Land and Settlement was headed by Kenyatta's allies making it even more difficult for the Kalenjin through their land-buying companies to either purchase land or access loans from the Kikuyu headed financial institutions (Kanyinga, 2009). The unity of Kenyans was thus compromised and the Kikuyu-Kalenjin relations were the worst affected.[4]

The ascendancy of President Daniel arap Moi, a Kalenjin, as the leader of the nation in 1978, was thus a momentous period for the Kalenjin nation. President Moi started his leadership period on a very high note. Apparently he had learnt some fewlessonsfrom his predecessor. He did not wish to antagonize himself or his community and he wished not to present himself as a 'tribalist'. Indeed he constantly stressed the dangers of tribalism to the country's stability denouncing sectionalism (Widner, 1992). He thus went round the country championing for development of the country through improved education, health and improved infrastructure for the nation. His government was, however, to be faced with major challenges especially because he had at His disposal very few land resources to reward and distribute to his allies. The classical connotations of neo-patrimonialism as rewards to clients especially by the use of land were not applicable to President Moi. Land had been given to powerful people in the Kenyatta regime. Indeed even Moi's attempt to restructure the Kenyan state to advance Kalenjin interests was to be done in a slow yet calculated manner. As David Throup notes, the economy was less buoyant, the trebling of the population since independence to 20 million meant that pressure on resources was more intense, but above all Moi faced the insurmountable obstacle of Kenyatta's successful entrenchment of the Kikuyu. Every move that Moi made to reduce Kikuyu hegemony and to dismantle the Kenyatta state thus threatened the stability of his government. He was, however, to succumb to the whims of tribal politics when challenged with the GEMA political and economic wits, dwindling economic fortunes, as well as the 1982 attempted coup that threatened his Presidency. In a resource short polity, Widner notes, the elite find the ethnic idiom useful as a way of sustaining their hold into power and also frustrating the 'others'. President Moi had to ignite the Kalenjin consciousness by portraying them as marginalized and vulnerable group in relation to the Kikuyu who were presented as the 'ethnic others'. Moi astutely began to divert resources from Central Province to the Kalenjin dominated areas as the Kikuyuwere presented as the source of economic and political insecurity. According to Throup (1987), whereas the Kikuyu held 30 percent of cabinet posts throughout Kenyatta's rule, by mid-1980s they had fallen to four full cabinet ministers Kibaki, Matiba, Magugu, and Maina Wanjigi while the number of Kalenjin ministers nearly doubled from 9 to 17 percent. The president also advanced Kalenjin interests through his control of parastatal appointments (Throup, 1987). The impact was frustration. The Kikuyu community had to unite against the Kalenjin onslaught, at least politically and economically. It is in the light of such frustration that the 1992 and 1997 ethnic conflicts in the Rift Valley that saw the emergence of more than 100,000 Kikuyu IDPs and property destroyed were informed. Many Kikuyu IDPs continue to wallow in poverty yet they claim that their ancestral land possessions are in the hands of well-known Kalenjin neighbours. In Molo, Elburgon and Uasin Gishu, many Kikuyu and the Nandi are to date, suspicious of the recent pact made between the Kikuyu headed by Uhuru Kenyatta and the Kalenjin headed by William Ruto. They argue that sustaining such a political deal would require a comprehensive and thorough engagement of elders from both sides. Elders here, they note, should not be politicians but councils of elders comprising elderly people who have lived in the Rift Valley throughout their lives.[5]

President Moi attempted several times without fail to initiate a Kikuyu-Kalenjin dialogue after the 1992/97 ethnic violence. Moi was aware of the economic and political might of the Kikuyu and perhaps to sustain his hold into power, he occasionally used the Kikuyu elite like the late Njenga Karume to bring an end to the ethnic animosity between the two communities. Of course, this was a period when the opposition was vibrant and the Kikuyu were at the epicenter of this dissidence. Moi had to either silence the Kikuyu or bring them close. The former failed and in 2002 a Kikuyu President, Mwai Kibaki, was inaugurated after 24 years of a well-calculated Kalenjin dominance of politics and the Kenyan economy.

Kibaki came to power with a promise of 'de-ethnicising' politics and the economy. He had been voted in by an expectant mass of Kikuyu and non-Kikuyu. Majority of the Kalenjin including the now Deputy President William Ruto had, however, supported Uhuru Kenyatta a handpicked candidate of President Moi. The win by President Kibaki once again left the Kalenjin in the 'political cold' of the 1960s as the Kikuyu's time to eat re-emerged. It would be wrong to imagine that all the Kikuyu or the Kalenjin benefited from the Presidency of one of their own. On the contrary many suffered the pangs of poverty and underdevelopment yet class antagonism within ethnic groups was relegated to the periphery as politicians manipulated real or imagined ethnic narratives to secure public resources for themselves while neglecting the poor even from their communities (Widner, 1991; Kanyinga, 2009).

If the relations between the Kikuyu and the Kalenjin were to be weighed on a scale for comparative purposes, it was thought that the two communities would perhaps never sit for political discussions after the 2007 elections during which period many Kikuyu were killed and displaced from the Rift Valley in an unprecedented manner.[6] It is alleged that majority of those displaced were killed by their Kalenjin neighbours in an attempt to repossess their land and other property. Majority of the Kikuyu left Kalenjin dominated areas and many sought refuge in IDP camps which they created in various parts of Nakuru and Naivasha. Others began to live with relatives or rented houses in urban and peri-urban areas in major Kenyan towns or smaller towns around their homes. The squatter phenomenon was also reintroduced in Central Kenya as returnees squatted at or near their original homelands where they were, obviously, not welcome.[7] A majority of displaced Kalenjin did not opt for displacement camps. They enjoyed little political sympathy and protection because they were viewed as the perpetrators of the 2007/08 PEV. Many thus lived with friends and relatives while others especially in Eldoret, simply returned to their homes after some few days.[8]

It was the unexpected[9] merger of William Ruto's URP party and Uhuru Kenyatta's TNA party at the end of 2012 that, however, saw the relations between the two communities change dramatically. The two renegotiated their identities by calling on their communities to forget their differences and forge ahead for a better Kenya. The drastic circumstances of time and space had become important aspects for negotiating solidarities of the two communities.[10] Thus, rather than seeing each other as enemies, like they had done in the past, the instrumental approach to ethnicity which is based on manipulating ethnic mobilization for material or psychic gain became hardy. The ICC issue was at the centre of this ethnic mobilization. In the year 2012 and 2013 several negotiated pacts were thus signed and adopted in public meetings between the Kikuyu and the Kalenjin 'elders' as a commitment to the unity of the two communities.[11] It is within this backdrop that the Jubilee win should be seen. President Uhuru Kenyatta in his acceptance speech as the Jubilee flag bearer asserted that the coalition would bring to an end 'the era of tribalism' and the animosity between the two communities would be healed.[12] The leaders had decided to create ethnic solidarity to deal with the 'other' political blocks including CORD, Eagle as well as with other political parties. Even candidates from the two communities who presented themselves as presidential candidates outside of the Jubilee coalition were 'othered' in a classic example of how ethnicity was manipulated by the Tutsi and the Hutus in Rwanda. There were no 'mulatoos' during the genocide. One had to belong to either the Tutsi or the Hutu ethnic groups. For Martha Karua and Peter Kenneth, two Kikuyu who sought the presidency of the Republic, their Kikuyuness (primordial attachments to the Kikuyu as a social group) was questioned. It was argued that they were not proper Kikuyu. For Peter Kenneth, for instance, unconfirmed rumours had it that he was supported by a big group of wazungu, a clear indication of his ethnic and primordial affiliation. Martha was simply seen as a spoiler.[13]

Pundits had argued that like other political coalitions forged during electioneering periods, the Jubilee merger would collapse before the elections. They were, however, proved wrong as the two communities (through what Mutahi Ngunyi called the 'tyranny of numbers'[14]) delivered the 2013 elections with a win.

The Kikuyu and the Kalenjin displaced persons in 2012 and 2013

The 2013 Kenyan general elections were held under great tension and expectations especially because they were considered a make or break period for the country. They were held after the 2007-2008 crisis which continued to be a refrain through which electoral campaigns were debated and analysed. The land question under whose banner the 2007-2008 PEV were waged was also revisited. And though considered free and fair by the Supreme Court, the 2013 elections left Kenyans from all walks of life more apprehensive and divided (at least as at 2013). Members of the CORD and Jubilee coalitions in particular had great expectations (for a win) and for this they have been worst hit because the coalitions were formed based on ethnic calculations, where each coalition hoped to win. The CORD coalition consisted of majorly the Kamba and the Luo communities while the Jubilee coalitions comprised of the large Kikuyu and the Kalenjin communities who have since the reign of President Kenyatta fought over claims of land ownership, control and accessibility in the vast Rift Valley areas. It is from these two later communities that majority of the IDPs residing in the larger Rift Valley hailed.

Displaced persons and the 2013 pre-election period

The March 2013 elections were the first one under the new Constitution promulgated in 2010. They were handled by a new IEBC under Isaac Hassan, and the new electronic registration system, though largely faulted after the elections ensured that as many voters as possible registered from and in places outside of their homes, a hitherto unseen phenomenon in Kenya.[15]According to IDPs residing in Nakuru at the time of the research, voter registration of IDPs was largely unsuccessful, at least in terms of the number of IDPs registered.[16] Broad participation of integrated and IDPs living in camps was not realized as was evidenced from our interviews. Some unsettled IDPs in the Pipeline IDP[17] camp and others living in Nakuru town Free Area and Rongai Banita areas, who had managed to locate their identity cards registered in and around primary schools within Nakuru Municipality. Majority of the IDPs, however, reported that they were not able to register as voters because they did not have documents allowing them to register. They alleged that many such documents were misplaced or burnt during the 2008 post-election skirmishes. For those living in camps,for instance, at Pipeline-with about 560 IDPs and Ndefo in Njoro, said that many of their neighbours did not register because they were scared of voting lest the 2007/08 violence re-emerge. This was also the case in Subukia where IDPs from the Pipeline and Mawingu IDP camps were resettled by the government. For this group, mistrust, general indifferenceand fear informed their failure to register and vote in the 2013 elections. This was also captured by IRIN (15 January 2013) when the crew asked one Miss Nyokabi of the Pipeline IDP camp about voting during the March elections. She responded: "How am I expected to participate in another voting exercise if I still have unhealed wounds [as a result] of voting last time?" Others reported that there was little if any civic education regarding registration and the use of the BVR kit further complicated the matter. A group of middle-aged men interviewed sadly reported their suspicion of the use of fingerprints thus:

> The fingerprints were designed in order to verify information regarding who was and who was not a member of the gangs used during the 2008 PEV. Many of us were not willing to give our fingerprints because we were told that those fingerprints would later be used to locate anyone who had engaged in crime in the past. We here in the camp are people from diverse localities who were victims or perpetrators of the 2007-2008 PEV and one can be victimized easily.

Others were scared of the photographs taken during the exercise arguing that the same would be used to track them down if they ever engaged in crime in future. This scenario was also reported in many parts of central province where voter registration apathy had been noted in areas such as Murang'a, Nyeri and Kirinyaga.[18] A group of unregistered women in the Pipeline camp noted that their failure to register was informed by information that went round discouraging people from using the registration machines because they were said to have negative impacts on their future. One woman informed us that they were told that some rays emanating from the machines could cause cancer at a later date.[19] Those not registered were therefore not able or were unwilling to vote.

Another IDP category that did not vote but were registered voters observed that the elections were too close to call. They did therefore did not wish to be associated with either of the two coalitions for fear that if they did they may not benefit from the other side in case their candidate lost. Yet another group of men relocated to farms in Kisima in Njoro and Haji farm in Subukia who had registered at Nairobi Road Primary school near Pipeline IDP camp said they did not vote for fear that supporting Jubilee the dominant party in the region was equal to supporting the Kalenjin who had dislocated them from their farms. This category was bitter with the unity between Ruto and Uhuru.[20] One of them reported that he chose Peter Kenneth over the others. In Eldoret some integrated IDPs from the Kalenjin community told us that they voted for neither Jubilee nor CORD because none of the two big coalitions, in their views,adequately represented their grievances. For them, Musalia was the ideal candidate. When asked if they eventually voted for Musalia they were reluctant to respond. The Kalenjin in particular indicated that, indeed despite the Jubilee wave that swept the Rift Valley, their vote went to the CORD or Musalia because they could not trust a Kikuyu president.[21] By and large, we however, noted that

85 young adults and 50middle aged and elderly people interviewed out of the 150 sampled voted for the 'UhuRuto' coalition.

The above narratives clearly indicate that the IDPs received inadequate voter education awareness especially regarding registration.Many IDPs reported that much of the information they received about the elections was from politicians who constantly promised them that they would resettle them once elected. Some members of the CSOs also briefed the IDPs regarding how to cast their votes and how to tick appropriately. Within the background of elections held under a new Constitution and especially after a post conflict situation, voter education ought to have been conducted in depth. The UN observes that:

> In every election, voter and civic education are necessary to ensure that all constituents – men and women alike – understand their rights, their political system, the contests they are being asked to decide, and how and where to vote. For an election to be successful and democratic, voters must understand their rights and responsibilities, and must be sufficiently knowledgeable and well informed to cast ballots that are legally valid and to participate meaningfully in the voting process.[22]

Marginalised groups in particular should be a target for civic educators. This education should go on throughout the registration, campaign and voting period to ensure that no information by passes those targeted. This appears not to have been the case during the 2013 electioneering period. The IDPs noted that while documents were availed to them many illiterate and busy would be voters were not able to read the same and this greatly disadvantaged them. It was also noted that accessibility to IDP camps was difficult.

The question of land was also (and still remains)central during the campaign period. For the IDPs the land question informed their voting behaviour. Many had been double dispossessed of their lands either in Central in the 1920s or in the 1990s during the Moi regime. The 2007 dispossession was however, the epitome of their misfortunes. Many IDPs who voted the Jubilee coalition noted that they were promised resettlement within a hundred days of the UhuRuto win. The remaining IDPs from the Pipeline camp, as are others all over Kenya, are complaining due to the failure of the Jubilee government to deliver on their promise. IDPs from Nakuru in particular are accusing the government of failing to demarcate land given to them by the Kibaki government in Subukia.[23]

The aftermath and analysis of the Kikuyu-Kalenjin relations

There were mixed reactions among IDPs from the two communities in the camps after the Jubilee coalition won the 2013 polls. Generally, majority of the IDPs were carried away by the euphoria and publicly expressed their hope that the political union of the two communities was an indication of good things to come, meaning a lasting settlement of the land problem and normalization of relations between the two communities. Many Kikuyu, in particular, saw this as the best opportunity to return to their original homes and consequently renegotiate their identity as co-owners of land in the vast Rift Valley. The Kalenjin on their part considered this a good opportunity for their Kingpin and political pointman in the region, Ruto, to seduce Uhuru to renegotiate their lost land back from the Kikuyu without necessarily having to use force.[24] There were however, a section of the IDPs who have learnt the hard way that politicians cannot be trusted. They reasoned that political statements and unions are based on political expediency and vested interests of political bigwigs but not the common good. This group of IDPs argues that if the interests of the politicians change, so would the related social and ethnic arrangements. For the Kalenjin in this category, they in particular distrust the Kikuyu and their argument is that once Uhuru stabilizes the government, he will easily discard Ruto and enrich his community and friends.[25] The Kikuyu in this lot on their part argue that Ruto would not allow them to get back to their lands and that he will issue title deeds to those who repossessedtheir land after the 2007 elections.[26] The IDPs observe that as is the 'norm' in Kenya, ethnic identities will override the interests of their lot and each leader will favour their ethnic group (or those in his economic class) while subtly ignoring, however, the interests of other communities. The communities are therefore captives of their leading politicians.

One thing that is clear about the Kikuyu-Kalenjin relations from the perspective of majority of the IDPs is that the UhuRuto 'union' is conditional. It all depends on how well delicate interests and expectations are handled. To begin with, some IDPs believe that Uhuru and Ruto single-handedly carry the hopes, risks and fears of their respective communities. As long as they remain united, the two communities will be at peace. The following questions therefore beg: What happens after these politicians exit the political scene? Aren't there objective issues that transcend political personalities that strain ethnic relations in Kenya and shouldn't national cohesion and integration be pegged on resolution of these objective issues rather than gratification of the whims and egos of ethnic chiefs?

For a long time, Kenyan politics have depicted individual politicians as more effective in addressing socio-political problems than national institutions. Individuals have overshadowed institutions in resolution of national issues. In fact, individuals threaten, intimidate and even restructure institutions to ensure that their personal interests are safeguarded.[27] Such self-aggrandizement behaviours in some instances, do not in fact consider the depth of ethnic cleavages and in this way the two communities may actually not benefit from the Jubilee government. In the Machiavellian understanding of the relationship between the leaders and the led, the IDPs in both campsargued that it may be a government just like others that have enriched leading politiciansand their cronies while forgetting those who helped them climb the ladder. Self-enrichment in the Kenyan state accounts for the numerous amendments of the independence constitution and the consequent destruction of devolved institutions and the weakening of the institutions mandated to check abuse of power and protection of the common good.

Good-willed powerful individuals may sometimes fight for the common good; and even when this happens, the success of the initiative depends on the plight of such individuals. Most IDPs and Kenyans of all walks of life, often, put their hope in persons rather than institutions. Their hopes rise or die with the rise and fall of such persons. Unless this trend is transformed and institutions rather than individual persons are empowered to transact national business in an impartial manner, the big man syndrome in Kenya will continue and there always will be persons who can hold the entire nation at ransom. This explains why the Kikuyu-Kalenjin relations may depend on what happens to the two leading politicians–Uhuru and Ruto respectively. As noted by Young (2002), leadership is the first condition in managing ethnic diversities in Africa, as evidenced in the example of Julius Nyerere of Tanzania, who put public before private and, though seriously misguided on economic policy, steadfastly willed a nation into existence and built a civic scaffold for a territorial state.

The second condition is the implementation of the constitution and the entrenchment of the constitutional culture in Kenya. The constitution of Kenya 2010 was carefully crafted to strengthen institutions, foster respect for the rule of law and reverse the big man syndrome in Kenya by asserting the rights and obligations of each and every Kenyan.[28] This is a new thing in Kenya. The challenge that is clear to all is that the new constitutional dispensation is being ushered in an environment that is saturated with persons, habits and beliefs that are inclined to the old ways of personalized socio-political arrangements. Clientelism, primordial and instrumental solidarities based on ethnicities, corruption and disorder as instruments for violence have become an integral part of African politics (Chabal and Daloz, 1999). The new institutions must overthrow these old systems and ways of doing things if the good they were intended to bring is to be realized. Land reform, streamlining of the justice system, respect to the rule of law, protection of vulnerable and marginalized persons and groups, including IDPs, effective implementation of anti-corruption policies among other things depend on effective implementation of the constitution in a fair and objective way through the relevant institutions. Resettlement of IDPs in particular should be based on clear and effective profiling of the groups as well as respect for land user and ownership rights in any given part of the country. As Monette (2002) noted, IDPs are not often accurately counted due in part to disagreements over how to define them and the reaction that this may elicit from donors and members of the international communities. It is for this reason that scholars have emphasized that estimates given by governments and their partners may well be conservative and in many cases falling short of the actual number of displaced persons.Displacement and the poor living conditions that accompany it also poses health related problems, insecurity and sexual violence, lack of basic necessities and lack of access to justice. When circumstances allow for IDPs to return home, many remain vulnerable as they attempt to reintegrate into an often hostile environment (USAID, 2004). Many interviewed IDPs noted that while the government has tried to purchase land for them in some parts of the Rift Valley this has not been possible due to hostility from theirwould be neighbours and hosts. And while the Kenyan Constitution has clearprovisions regarding land ownership in any part of the country, the host communities (especially those that were to host the Kikuyu among the Maasai) have often argued that there are many more IDPs that have yet to be settled (Kitale, 2011). Profiling and clear reference to the Constitution is arguably the best and most sustainable basis of national cohesion and integration on which relations between not only Kikuyu and Kalenjin but also every other community in Kenya are to be regulated. However, this reliable foundation is still in its infancy and unless it is well nurtured, it will be futile to lay hope on it.

The third condition has to do with civic literacy. IDPs have witnessed the selfishness and hypocrisy of politicians. To begin with they are currently (July 2013) crying that while they had been promised resettlement within a hundred days, they are yet to be resettled.[29] Those who have been resettled also complained of harsh conditions in their new homes and have been calling on the government to look into their conditions especially in the provision of infrastructural service (schools, health centres and roads).The politicized ethnicity as was observed by the IDPs from both communities has also seen persons who lived happily and peacefully with each other for many years suddenly turned into enemies during election seasons for political reasons. Many talk of no personal grudges against one another. The 'grudges' that are vocalized are generalized and vague, for instance, 'Kikuyu grabbed our land' (this is done by the Kalenjin), or 'Kalenjin are opportunists' (as was said by Kikuyu IDPs).[30] What we noted was that there is lack of specific and actual accusations made before any court of law that would justify such generalizations. This explains why Kikuyu are condemned for the evils or perceived evils of Kenyatta and Kibaki eras while Kalenjin are blamed for the evils of the Moi era. The other communities perceive themselves as innocent victims of these two communities merely because they have not had the opportunity to produce the 'biggest man' in the country. Civic literacy involves critical consciousness that yields some conditions for detachment (at the personal, community and institutional levels).[31]

At the community level, Kenyans need to be detached from irrational ethnic and political party (since they are ethnic based) related biases and generalizations that enhance ethnic solidarity at the expense of alienating other communities. The politicization of ethnicity which has often been blamed for social, economic and political conflicts in many African countries needs to be tackled by both the leaders and the led at all the levels of society. This way, ethnic favouritism that has resulted in many electing a member of their own community for the sole reason of 'eating' would be eliminated.[32] This does not mean demonizing ethnicity but cleansing ethnicity of all its negative elements. National interests should never be sacrificed at the altar of partisan family, ethnic or personal interests. Each individual Kenyan needs to regard him/herself as a citizen with rights and duties as well as responsibilities towards the state of Kenya. This must be regarded as the most valued aspect of one's identity.

At the institutional level, institutions need to be detached from persons occupying them such that the power and authority vested in the institutions is carefully and effectively exercised by individuals entrusted with them without the individuals appropriating the power and authority for themselves and thus abusing public office. The power and authority of the institutions and the respect that goes with it must always be left intact in the institutions even as individuals assume and vacate office. This is because the power and authority belongs to the people of Kenya in particular and humanity in general. Civic literacy as described above is a new thing in Kenya and just like the political and constitutional culture, it needs to be nurtured.

In conclusion, it follows from the analysis above that Kikuyu-Kalenjin relations are personalized and dependent on the whims and wishes of the two leading politicians, Uhuru and Ruto at least for now. Primordial sensations of 'autochthony' in a country with scarce resources concentrated in the hands of a few individuals will always result in conflicts among classes and communities and the two leaders following the new constitution have within the short period that they have been in power attempted to redistribute resources and issue title deeds where they never existed, for instance in Lamu and Mombasa countries. Other areas that need to be dealt with and especially the ASALs, however, still present a challenge that could explode if not handled carefully and diligently. This can, however, change only to the extent that the constitution is effectively implemented and a constitutional culture established accompanied by enhancement of civic literacy in Kenya.

Notes

1   Raila A. Odinga, "What Role Does Ethnicity Play in Africa's Elective Politics?" Posted by African Press International on September 12, 2007.

2   For a well-articulated and detailed analysis of ethnic identities and how they are negotiated in Kenya, see Gabrielle Lynch (2011); on the politics of belonging, see Piet Konings and Francis B. Nyamnjoh (2003) and. Claire Médard (2007).

3   Kiprop Emmanuel, a resident of Rongai in Nakuru, claims to be an IDP because his father's land located at Molo was appropriated by the Kenyatta government and given to one Mr. Thuku from Kiambu in 1965. He insists that land ownership in the Molo, Olenguruone and Elburgon regions are so controversial that the existing title deeds are either fake or they are possessed by people who neither bought nor originally owned these landed spaces.

4   On the relations between the various communities in the Rift Valley during the Kenyatta regime, see Roselind M. Achieng (2005).

5   I interviewed Karanja Njihia in Elburgon in 2009 when undertaking a research on the post-election violence.

6   On the Kenyan 2007 general elections and related violence, see Jérôme Lafargue (2007) and the *Journal of Eastern African Studies* 2, no. 2, May 2008.

7   The Kikuyu returnees were not welcome back after independence and they are not welcome today. Their original homelands are since occupied and title deeds given to new owners. Where were they to go after the 2007 PEV?

8   Prisca Kamungi (2013) gives a detailed account of the reasons why there were few Kalenjin IDPs in camps given by .

9   In the leaked Wikileaks Nairobi Cable No. 39 Sally Kosgey (an ethnic Kalenjin) had expressed doubt that Kikuyu voters in Central and Kalenjin voters in Rift Valley would be willing to set aside the violence suffered at each others hands to form a coalition in 2012.

10 This was a time when the two leaders were facing charges at the ICC for allegedly instigating the 2007 post election violence.

11 The major pact was done at Eldoret's 64 stadium with Ruto and Uhuru mandated with leading the two 'indicted' communities.

12 "Jubilee Alliance Break-Up: What Happens Next?" By Guest Author | December 31, 2012.

13 A Kikuyu, Martha, was considered a spoiler for Uhuru who needed to garner all vote from the Kikuyu dominated regions.

14 See Mutahi Ngunyi and Adams Oloo disagree on the tyranny of numbers part 2. The interview was done by an NTV journalist who hosted the trend on 8 February 2013. He considered the numerical might of the two communities and concluded that there was to be a clear win if the two combined to vote one of their candidates; Uhuru or Ruto.

15 Many Kenyans register in and around their rural aboards.

16 It was not clear how many IDPs registered as voters.

17 Pipeline is an IDP camp created during the 2007 PEV near Nakuru town. It originally hosted close to 2,000 people majority of whom have been relocated to Subukia but about 560 people still live in the camp whose dilapidated tents have left living conditions in the camp unbearable.

18 News 24kenya on December 13, 2012 Rugut: BVR myths unfounded.

19 Interview with a woman identified as Nancy at the Pipeline Camp.

20 This group had been victims of the 1992 and 1997 elections which pitted the Kalenjin against 'outsiders' in the Rift Valley.

21 Interview number 17 on July 23, 2013.

22 www.un/womenwatch/osagi/wps Chapter 5.

23 *The Daily Nation* June 25, 2013 reported that the IDPs nationwide were jittery over non-resettlement despite the 'Uhuruto' promise during the campaign period.

24 Interview with an elderly couple in Rongai, Nakuru.

25 Interview with a Kalenjin young man in Nakuru town. He claims that his family's land was given to a Kikuyu family by Mzee Kenyatta in the late 1960s.

26 Kimari, an IDP at the Pipeline camp. Members of his family have since relocated to Subukia.

27 See Jean-François Bayart(2009); and Patrick Chabal and Jean-Pascal Daloz (1999).

28 The Constitution of Kenya revised edition 2010 published by the National Council for Law Reporting with the Authority of the Attorney General.

29 IDPs from the 2007 PEV were still complaining and protesting that about 1,740 IDPs from 20 camps were still not settled by the government. See *The Standard* Digital, March 6, 2014.

30 Informants noted that many of their grudges simply resurface during electioneering periods and are fueled by politicians who use ethnicity to whip up support.

31 For an in-depth analysis on the conditions of IDPs in camps and new homes, see Lynch (2011); Pavanello, Elhawary and Pantuliano (2010); and Kamungi (2009).

32 For a more detailed analysis of how politicization of ethnicity breeds ethnic favouritism, see Gagnon (1994/95); Miguel (2004); and Daniel Posner (2005).

Bibliography

Achieng', R. *Kenya Reconstructing? Building Bridges of Peace: Post-Conflict.* Münster: LITVerlag,2005.

Bayart, J.-F. *The State in Africa: The politics of the belly.* London: Longman, 1993 Berman, B. *Control and Crisis in Colonial Kenya: The dialectic of domination.* London: James Currey and Athens, Ohio: Ohio University Press, 1990.

Chabal, P. and J.-P. Daloz. *Africa Works: Disorder as Political Instrument.* Oxford: James Currey, 1999.

Furedi, F. *The Mau Mau War in Perspective.* London: James Currey, 1991.

Gagnon, V.P. Jr. "Ethnic nationalism and International conflict: The case of Serbia". *International security* 19, no. 3 (Winter 1994/95): 130-166.

Geschiere, P. and F. Nyamjoh. "Capitalism and Autochthony: The seesaw of mobility and belonging," *Public Culture* 12, no. 2 (2000): 432-53.

Geschiere, P. *The Perils of Belonging: Autochthony, citizenship, and exclusion in Europe and Africa.* Chicago: University of Chicago Press, 2009.

Human Rights Watch. *High Stakes: Political violence and the 2013 elections in Kenya,* 2013. At www.hrw.org

Kamungi, P. "The Politics of Displacement in Multi-Party Kenya." *Journal of Contemporary African Studies,* 27 no. 3 (2009): 345-364.

_____. *Municipalities and IDPs Outside of Camps: The case of Kenya's 'integrated' displaced persons.* The Brookings Institution, London School of Economics, 2013.

Kanyinga, K. "Beyond the colonial legacy: The land question, politics and constitutionalism in Kenya." In *Essays on land law: The reform debate in Kenya,* ed. SmokinWanjala, 45-62. Nairobi: University of Nairobi, 2000.

_____. *The Land Question in Kenya: Struggles, accumulation and changing politics in Kenya,* 2006.

_____. "Land Redistribution in Kenya." In *Agricultural Land Redistribution: Towards greater consensus,* eds. 87-118. Washington, DC: The World Bank, 2009.

Kenya Human Rights Commission. *Killing the vote: State-sponsored violence and flawed elections in Kenya.* Nairobi: KHRC, 1998.

Kitale, C. M. "Internal Displacement in the Kenyan Context: Challenges of justice, reconciliation and resettlement."Unpublished thesis, International Institute of Social Studies, 2011.

Miguel, E. *Ethnic Diversity, Social Sanction and Public Goods in Kenya.* Berkeley: University of California, 2004.

Monette, Z. *The Internally Displaced in Perspective.* The Brookings CUNY Project on Internal Displacement Migration Policy Institute, 2002.

Pavanello, S., S. Elhawary and S. Pantuliano. Hidden and Exposed Urban Refugees in Nairobi; Kenya, HPG Working Paper. *Humanitarian Policy Group. Oversees Development Institute,* 2010.

Posner, D. *Institutions and Ethnic Politics in Africa.* Cambridge University Press, 2005.

Throup, D. "The Construction and Destruction of the Kenyatta State." *In The Political Economy of Kenya.* ed. Schatzberg, M.G. 1987.

Young, C. *Ethnicity and Politics in Africa.* Boston: Boston University Press, 2002.

Widner, J. *The Rise of a Party-State in Kenya: From harambee to nyayo!* Berkeley: University of California, 1992.

An Evaluation of Political Mobilization Strategies Employed by Vigilante Groups in Kisii County during the 2013 Kenyan Elections

Wycliffe Nyachoti Otiso [*]

Introduction

The vigilante phenomenon in Kisii County in Kenya captured public attention in the past decade, owing to the severity of their sanctions and their disproportionate responses to crime and insecurity. Their targets were suspected thieves, murderers and witches. Images of torched huts and suspected offenders drew media attention with such reports grabbing national headlines. Existence of the vigilante phenomenon and links to groups like the Sungusungu are suspected to be involved in political conflicts, especially during the electioneering period. Such involvement was scarcely documented before the publication of the Report of the Commission on Post Election Violence (CIPEV).[1] As a consequence to this publication, possible link between Sungusungu activities and participation in political violence was brought into sharp focus.

Prior to this report, no study has ever established a direct link between Sungusungu and electoral violence in Kisii. Studies emphasized the use of youth groups in settling political contests. In their study, Masese and Mwenzwa (2012) found that gangs and militia like Amachuma associated with political big men had been used to intimidate opponents during political campaigns. They observed that Amachuma was initially formed to protect community interest by supporting Mr. Nyachae, a Cabinet Minister and the political big man from the Abagusii Community. Although it was formed to protect community interests by supporting Mr. Nyachae's presidential ambitions,

* Lecturer at Kisii University, Kenya and PhD candidate in Law and Political Science at Université de Pau et des Pays de l'Adour (UPPA), France

the group later resorted to targeting political competition through intimidation and disruption of political rallies. Such youth groups were viewed as having a natural propensity to be used as agents for instilling fear on political opponents through violence (Anderson, 2002). However, the conduct and outcome of the 2013 general elections in Kisii provide insufficient data to support the understanding that vigilante groups have a propensity to resort to political violence to influence political processes and the outcome of elections. This time there were no reports on the use of Sungusungu in settling political conflicts. This is attributable to changes that occurred during the 2008-2013 electoral cycle. One of these changes is the enactment of the Prevention of Organised Crime Act in 2010. The Act targets the formal character of proscribed groups, and as a result such youth circles have mutated from vigilante to community policing groups. However the state's use of the law as a tool of domination has been ineffective in neutralizing the group's activities. Instead, the group has instrumentalised opportunities within the law to continue operating and exercising political and civic rights like participating in elections (Otiso, forthcoming). Hence the changing activities of vigilante groups in Kisii require us to rethink the understanding of 'law as domination' model as employed by the state (Moore, 2005).

In Kisii, the "former" vigilante group, Sungusungu, has regrouped into the Community Policing Group (CPG). Their change of name into CPG only indicates their formal transformation as their core activities remain the same: tackling crime and insecurity. From the information gathered in Kisii during the 2013 elections there is an ostensible shift in the operation and strategy of Sungusungu to that of participating in the political processes. The groups have changed the mode of accessing decision-making from participating indirectly through big men to participating directly by fronting their own in the electoral process. For instance, the CPG chairman contested for the Kisii Central county ward representative post instead of supporting incumbent political big men. This marked a shift in influencing local politics through non-violent means by directly seeking electoral positions, rather than resorting to the use of violence to influence outcomes of elections of their political patrons. The shift defies conventional assumptions that every electoral cycle in Kenyan politics is characterized by violence that is marshaled by youth vigilante groups at the service of incumbent politicians.

This study examines the changing nature of vigilantism by analyzing their approaches to political mobilization. It looks at nuanced forms of engagement in political processes by the activities of the CPG using Kisii Central Ward as a case study. It also interrogates nuanced political mobilization strategies and the direct participation of the Community Policing Group in elective processes. The decline in political violence during the electioneering period in Kisii is attributable to a marked shift in vigilante activities to non-violent political mobilization discernible from the manner of participation of Sungusungu in 2013 general elections. The changing nature of its operations provides a broader perspective that serves as an alternative to the conventional assumption of armed youth group's predisposition to use violence as their modus operandi. These patterns are in consonance with Pratten's analysis that disputes the "war machines" hypothesis whereby the youth constitute a readily available resource to commit acts of violence. This analysis shows why it is necessary to understand the youth beyond their predisposition to use violence and also appreciate their capability seize opportunities to overcome their state of marginalization.[2]

The study was conducted in Nyaribari Chache Constituency within Kisii Central Ward in Kisii County. Data was collected through observations and open informal interviews because the group under study is a proscribed organization. The exercise took a period of 12 months – some 6 months before elections and 6 months after elections. The observations were mainly done at the polling stations, tallying centers, and political rallies and campaigns.

The paper provides a brief on vigilantism and its contribution to electoral violence. It then examines factual events from the political campaign period culminating into the general elections in 2013 with particular focus on Kisii Central Ward. The study pays attention to the concept of non-violent political mobilization as currently embraced by CPG and evaluates the group motivation to directly engage in political decision-making as opposed to campaigning for godfathers as they did in the past.

Conceptualization: Vigilantism and electoral violence

It is difficult to speak of a universal definition of vigilantism. Rather than focus on a single definition, it is more appropriate to analyze different descriptions of vigilantism and broad commonalities that would encompass all vigilante groups. One such description maintains that vigilantism is "establishment violence" (Rosenbaum and Sederberg, 1974). According to this definition vigilantism consists of acts or threats of coercion in violation of formal boundaries of an established sociopolitical order with the intention of defending that order from some form of subversion" (Ibid.). Fleisher (2000) explains that when the state has been ineffective in protecting existing socio-political order, vigilante groups seek to fill the void in protecting that order by restoring or restructuring existing societal arrangements. Similarly, Plyler (2006) argues that mob justice as a form of vigilantism in the sense that it is a form of social control too. She views vigilante as conservative groups that are dependent on societal values associated with the state because as they operate to restore such values, they themselves are unable to articulate social alternatives with visions different from or independent of the state. However the definitions cited above do not completely fit with the organization and objectives of CPG. A more appropriate definition is provided by Abrahams (1987) who regards vigilantism as a type of self-help initiative by locals in a given area, formed with the common objective of addressing a certain problem, be it political or social. In so far as CPG is concerned, the definition by Abrahams appropriately describes the nature, objective and scope of their activities. This study adopts Abraham's definition to analyze the nuances of CPG in the specific context of Kenya's 2013 Elections. Since the study explores the extent to which CPG employed violence during the 2013 elections, it is also important that we describe the concept of electoral violence before we delve into the factors that led the group's significant shift in the mode of participating in politics.

As we have seen with the term vigilantism, the phenomenon of electoral violence is similarly contested and there exist no scholarly consensus on its precise definition, occurrence and reasons why it should be studied separately from other forms of violence, especially political violence.[3] The study adopts Bekoe's approach that considers electoral violence to be a specific kind of political violence. In his study of the phenomenon in the context of new democracies in sub-Saharan Africa, Bekoe describes electoral violence as a subset of political activities "which is distinguished by its timing, perpetrators and victims, objectives and methods" (Bekoe, 2012: 2). From our understanding of electoral violence it is also important to pose the question: when does electoral violence occur? Straus and Taylor's (2012) approach the study of electoral violence by examining elections six months prior to voting and three more months after the vote. They argue that it is important to study pre- and post-election periods because in most of the times the election day is relatively peaceful. This criterion is useful in the disaggregation of other types of violence that happen around election time as a coincidence. Indeed, as Bekoe cautions, "not all acts of violence around electioneering period constitute electoral violence. Incidents of violence must be related to elections" (Bekoe, 2012). However, this study examines electoral violence for a period of six months after elections in order to cover the period of electoral disputes as provided by the Kenyan Constitution.[4]

Reasons behind CPG shift to political participation

In this section we examine the different reasons that motivated CPG to directly participate in electoral politics rather than continue to influence local politics indirectly through its the established former patronage networks.

Disconnection from patronage networks

During this study we carried out informal interviews with the CPG members and the location leader to find out whether they were in agreement on the decision by the group leader to run for the county ward elections. The CPG leader for the location stated that the group had reached the conclusion that the time was ripe for the group to participate in local political decision-making activities. He stated that the group could only achieve this objective by directly participating in the local politics rather than through patron-client networks because the latter method did not realise tangible benefits to the members. The group wanted to delink itself from such networks owing to unreliability of their former patrons.[5] In the past, CPG relied on the goodwill of political patrons comprising former Kisii Municipal Council councilors to recruit their members for the task of maintaining law and order in the town. However, the relationship between CPG and its patrons only lasted for a while because the political patrons could not keep their promises regarding payment for services rendered.[6] Thus the decision by the CPG to directly seek political posts raises scenarios that require deeper interrogation about the disintegration of these patronage networks and how this affects former clients. A study on the interplay between neopatrimonialism, violence and land tenure systems in Enoosupukia in the 1990s by Scott Matter (2010) found that in neopatrimonial networks, the security of clients, personal access to power and economic resources was dependent on the whims of the patron. The clients were involved in a loose and asymmetrical relationship that carried the risk of getting disconnected at anytime. The result of disintegrated patronage network meant that they were in a vulnerable position and open to further marginalization and domination through both the State institutions – which the former patrons easily accessed –and the law. However, CPG voluntary disconnection from its former patronage network appears to have galvanized the group not to renegotiate a return to their former patronage networks but instead to directly seek access to political power and economic resources. The decision by the CPG to directly get involved in elective politics was well received by the group members without objections.[7] The members were galvanized around the group leader because they were convinced that 2013 elections provided them an opportunity to influence local decision-making given their proven record of having restored security in Kisii County.

The role of the County Assembly in the new dispensation

Prior to enactment of the new Constitution in 2010, the functions of the local government were regulated by an Act of Parliament and the Mayor and heads of departmental committees had a lot of discretion in administering the resources of the municipal council. The ward was represented by a Councilor in the previous system. The public did not rate the position of Councilor highly because of its minor responsibilities and attendant remuneration. However, under the new system the position of the member of County Assembly is for valid reasons viewed to be more powerful than that of a Councilor. The perception that the County Assembly would comprise "honourable members" – who would be the 'equivalent' of a member of National Assembly – was cultivated during the referendum campaigns for the 2010 Constitution and also reinforced by candidates during the 2013 election campaigns.[8] Indeed, the Constitution positions the county assembly as a more robust institution than the former Council Assembly. The County Assembly is entrenched in the Constitution with specified legislative, oversight and approval functions.[9] The desire by the CPG to have some influence in county affairs is in recognition of the vast powers vested in the County Assembly to steer the management of institutions in the exploitation of county resources.[10]

In fact the perception of CPG regarding the power of the County Assembly has been vindicated by the assertion of county assemblies in Nakuru and Kiambu counties. The two assemblies have recently flexed their muscles to an extent of stalling the workings of their county executives. In a brief showdown for supremacy the County Assembly in Nakuru rejected the Governor's nominees and threatened to impeach him for purporting to appoint people of his choice in disregard of a court order. Similarly, the Kiambu County Assembly twice rejected the Governor's nominees to the County Executive and went ahead to impeach the Speaker of the assembly on account that he was the Governor's gatekeeper. While there seems to be a good working relationship between the Kisii Governor and the County Assembly, members of the County Assembly are not precluded from exercising such powers in future to protect their vested interests as it is stipulated in the Constitution and the County Governments Act.

Secondly, the CPG members also realized that it would be difficult to influence the Governor through proxies because the accountability structures under the new Constitution are more rigid compared to those under the old dispensation.[11] Members of CPG were also motivated to seek County Assembly elective posts upon realizing that the new Constitution envisaged members of the County Assembly would playa vital role in the county governance through direct contact with the Governor. They also appreciated the changes that were introduced by the new Constitution especially devolution.

The economic reasons that prompted CPG to participate in elective politics

Chapter 11 of the 2010 constitution contains the economic safeguards for Kenya's devolved units and this played a big role in motivating the CPG to seek political posts in the Kisii County Assembly. CPG stated: "We wanted to increase our influence in the management of county resources".[12] The rationale of establishing county governments is to ensure increased political, economic and social participation by all citizens through decentralization of governance structure. The constitutional language resonates well with CPG's rationale for contesting in ward elections. In particular, Article 174(c) specifies one of the objects of devolution as giving "powers of self-governance to the people and enhance participation of the people in exercise of powers of the State in making decisions affecting them". Article 174 (d) also recognizes "the right of communities to manage their own affairs and to further their development".

Furthermore, Article 203 (2) of the Constitution stipulates that the national government shall not disburse to the county governments less than 15% of all the revenue collected in the county. The intention of CPG to increase their "influence in management of county affairs" was not only in the clamour for political participation but also for economic benefits as members anticipated a huge revenue allocation for Kisii County which did not compare with the meager allocations the government accorded the former Gusii municipality. The Commission on Revenue Allocation had prior to the 2013 General Elections published revenue sharing criteria for all counties which indicated that Kisii would receive the 5th highest allocation nationally. Although the figures were later revised in the 2013/14 financial budget the Kisii County was still allocated a favourable KShs. 5.29 Billion,[13] which was still a sharp increase compared to previous allocations.

Displaying power in the city

The CPG leader puzzled many observers when he opted to vie for the Kisii Central Ward instead of Bobaracho Ward where he hails from though it is only 5 kilometers away for the town centre. It was difficult to determine whether most of the CPG group members were registered in town centre and whether this was a factor arriving at the decision to vie for Kisii Central ward. However, a significant majority of its membership operates their activities in the town centre, and the group also enjoyed popularity among members of the informal sector like hawkers, touts and motorcycle taxi operators. Because CPG enjoyed wide support in the town centre, members felt that their leader would exert more influence in Kisii Central Ward than in Bobaracho Ward. The activities of the CPG including the provision of security, patrols and garbage collection are all done in the town centre, and contesting in the home ward would have pitted the CPG leader against his own clansman which would have complicated his chance of success as clanism is an important factor in Gusii land elective politics. Contests for elective seats in Kisii are an inter-clan affair. Whenever there are more than one leading contestants from the same clan or community, the clan or community initiates negotiations whereby one of the contestants is encouraged to drop his/her ambition in support of the other.[14] Such a negotiated communitarian settlement avoids splitting votes between candidates from the same clan and increases the chances of a clan to clinch the elective post. Ultimately, Mr. Nyangeso emerged the winner by a slim margin over Mr. Ongaki. Mr. Nyangeso comes from the same clan as CPG leader, had he vied for the elections in Bobaracho Ward, members of his clan would have split their votes between the two which would have worked in favour of Mr. Ongaki. In this case, the outcome of the election vindicated the decision of the CPG leader not to vie for election in his home Ward.

The CPG also figured that Kisii Central Ward is more strategic. The ward covers Kisii town centre where the Kisii County headquarters are situated. The County Assembly, the Governor's and County Executive offices are also housed here. The CPG has also its headquarters in proximity to the County headquarters, and consequently its base is in strategically placed in proximity to power. As Green and Butcher[15] argue, proximity to government headquarters is a visible way of displaying power and influence by groups. It is a means of reminding everyone that it is a powerful group and a symbol of the resources it commands. However, it is not only of symbolic but pragmatic importance in that, had he won the election, he would have easily balanced between County Assembly duties and providing leadership at CPG. The CPG administrative headquarters are situated less than one kilometer away from the Kisii County headquarters. This also informs CPG decision not to contest elective seats in Bonchari constituency, which is where CPG was born over a decade ago. Though CPG traces its roots to and remains active in Bonchari constituency, its political operational base has since shifted to Kisii town centre. It is for these reasons that CPG campaigns were concentrated in the town centre. The CPG had the perception that the devolved government priority to the development needs of Kisii Central Ward over the other wards, and hence CPG would gain access to large budgetary allocations to initiate a number of development projects within the ward, and therefore boost its profile, popularity and legitimacy amongst the citizens.

Mobilization of security as a campaign strategy

Judging from the election results, the CPG candidature was well received, even though the CPG leader failed to win the election. There were suggestions that the choice of party (TNA) contributed to attracting cosmopolitan vote especially amongst the large non-Kisii business community represented in the town centre. Further, use of provision of security as the main campaign message seems to have resonated well with the business community. Members of the business community were urged to vote for CPG for the protection of their businesses. As one businessman noted, "In his campaign message, he emphasized that if he was to get elected into office, he was to ensure that every resident of Kisii Town, irrespective of race or ethnic group, was to be accorded full security".[16] The election results show that the campaign message worked to an extent, because the majority of votes for CPG candidate were garnered in the town centre.[17]

This strategy is in tandem with Fourchard's (2012) analysis that depending on context provision, security can be a resource for mobilization of political support depending on the setting and levels of insecurity in a certain area. The CPG leader sought to assure citizens of a safer town centre because he was aware that security was a concern for business community. His "restoration of peace" campaign message however did not appeal to the rural population in Kisii Central Ward because CPG's influence was mainly concentrated in the town centre and waned as one moved towards rural sections of the Kisii Central Ward. In the end the majority of the rural population in the ward voted for incumbent councilor, Mr. Monyenye who eventually won by a small margin. The incumbent put to use his financial clout and his 25 years experience in local politics to capture the seat. But despite the gruesome competition exhibited by the two candidates during the campaigns, there were no incidents of violence at the tallying centre or elsewhere in the ward, after the returning officer announced the results at Keumbu Social Hall on 5 March 2013.

While the desire to directly participate in local elections by the CPG leader may have failed in the Kisii Central Ward, the group strategy to participate in a more indirect form bore fruits in Bonchari constituency. None of the location leaders directly vied for elective posts in Bonchari constituency but they instead opted to support contestants at the constituency and the ward levels. In Bomorenda Ward, for instance, John Ombati was supported by the CPG group and won the seat. At the constituency level, CPG supported John Oroo Oyoka who lost the parliamentary vote to Zebedeo Opore by a margin of 5 votes when the results were announced on 4 March 2013, an election Mr. Oyoka disputed in an election petition citing electoral malpractices. The court ordered a recount of the votes and instead found that Mr. Oyoka was the real winner by 9 votes, and subsequently declared the election of Zebedeo Opore as invalid; the court confirmed

Mr. Oyoka as the Member of Parliament for Bonchari constituency. It is important to note that the advent of Sungusungu in Kisii traces its origin to Bomorenda Ward in Bonchari constituency (Masese and Mwenzwa, 2012).

Even though Mr. Oyoka's victory was slim, it is noteworthy that CPG still wields significant political influence in Bonchari, the area in which it was founded. On a similar note we ought not to dismiss the influence of CPG in its new operational base in Kisii Central just because it lost the ward elections. The results in Kisii Central Ward indicate that the elections were quite competitive. Most significantly is that CPG was able to craft a theme of the need to engage a political process that was devoid of violence throughout the 2013 electioneering period in both Kisii Central Ward and Bonchari Constituency. This marked a shift in political process engagement in Kisii County. But whether the shift will be permanent, inalterable or sustainable will very much depend on underlying factors that are context specific. There is need for further research to interrogate the proximate factors that motivate people or groups of people to engage in violence; the factors should be understood through the political systems, historical contexts and cultural constructions applicable to a specific community in which a vigilante group operates (Pratten and Sen, 2007).

Conclusion

There is an ostensible shift in the involvement of youth groups during election times, which is attributable to several factors. Firstly, there is a change in the mode of participation with every electoral cycle since 2002. In 2002 there were no clear links between youth groups and political violence as compared to the clear implication of vigilante in the 2008 post-election violence. In the 2013 elections, non-violent means to political participation were reflected in peaceful political campaigns both at party nomination and general elections. Secondly there was a tactical change in political mobilization as the CPG abandoned the hitherto patron-client networks for direct participation in politics and sought elective posts in the County wards. The conduct of national elections and subsequent resolution of presidential election dispute, reflect the peaceful atmosphere in which the political process was conducted. The 2008-2013 electoral cycle signals an ostensible acceptance of the need to change the way we conduct our politics. In any case the CIPEV report is explicit that violence should not be the method of choice to resolve political differences and to obtain political power. While the CPG and like youths promise to adopt non-violent means in political participation even at the face of an election loss, it is however unclear whether change in mobilization will be sustained in the current electoral cycle ending in 2017. There is need for further research to interrogate such changes and determine whether they constitute permanent transformation or non-sustainable temporary changes which may not hold whenever the groups get frustrated by political outcomes.

Notes

1   Government of Kenya, Report of Commission on Post Election Violence, Government Printer, p. 34.

2   See analysis in Pratten(2006). Pratten disputes the militia-style "war machines" hypothesis developedby Deleuze and Guattari (see Mbembe, 2003)..

3   The study of electoral violence as a distinct phenomenon has been dismissed because it is an insignificant source of violence and it does not necessarily lead to significant contribution to the level of violence at the national level. Bekoe (2012) reiterates the importance of studying electoral violence even if it is short-term violence, with generally low levels of tension, it has a great impact on state democratization process.

4   Article 105 (2) of the Constitution; Section 85 of the Elections Act.

5   Interview with A, Location CPG Leader, April 5, 2013, Kisii Interview with B, CPG member, February 15, 2013, Kisii.

6   Interview with B, CPG member, February 15, 2013, Kisii.

7   Interview with A, Location CPG leader, April 5, 2013, Kisii; however, it was unclear from the interview whether it was the personal decision of the leader to seek direct political participation that was endorsed by the group or the whether the decision originated from the group.

8   Observations made at political rally held in Kisii Municipal Stadium, February 28, 2013, Kisii.

9   Articles 185(1), 185 (2), 185 (3) and 185 (4) of the Constitution of Kenya 2010 and Chapter III of the County Governments Act.

10   Article 185 (4) of the Constitution of Kenya, 2010.

11   Interview with C, May 2, 2013, Kisii.

12   Interview with A, Location CPG Leader, April 5, 2013, Kisii.

13   CRA Revenue Recommendations for Financial Year 2013/14;retrieved from www.crakenya.org/publications

14   Interview with R. Otundo, Elder, December 11,2012.

15   Greene, J. and J. Butcher 'Proximity and Power' The American, May 8, 2008;retrieved from www.american.com/archive/2008/may-05-08/proximity-and-power

16   Interview with D, businessman, May 6, 2013, Kisii.

17   Out of the 18,304 of the registered voters within Kisii central ward, the polling stations within town- Gusii County hall, Gusii municipal hall, Kisii primary, Nyanchwa primary, Gusii stadium and Masongo, had 11,195 registered voters, which constitutes 61% of the total votes.

Bibliography

Abrahams, R.. "Sungusungu: Village Vigilante groups in Tanzania." *African Affairs* 86, no. 343 (1987): 179-196.

Bekoe, D. Ed. *'Voting in Fear: Electoral Violence in Sub-Saharan Africa'*. Washington D.C. United States Institute of Peace Press, 2012.

E. Masese and E. Mwenzwa. "The Genesis and Evolution of Sungusungu Vigilante group among the Abagusii Ethnic Group of Kenya." *Elixir Social Science* 42, (2012): 6485-6492.

Fleisher, M. "Sungusungu: State-sponsored village vigilante groups among Kuria of Tanzania." *Africa* 70, no. 2 (2000): 209-28.

Fourchard, L. "New name for an old practice: Vigilantes in South-western Nigeria" *Africa* 78, no. 1 (2008): 16-40.

_____"Politics of Mobilization for Security in South African Townships" *African Affairs* 110, no 441 (2011): 607-627.

Government of Kenya. *Commission on Revenue Allocation Revenue Sharing Recommendations for Financial Year 2013/14*. Available at www.crakenya.org/publications

Government of Kenya. *Report of the Commission on Post Election Violence.* Nairobi: Government Printer, 2008.

Government of Kenya. *The Constitution of Kenya 2010* Nairobi: Government Printer, 2010.

Government of Kenya. *County Governments Act.* Nairobi: Government Printer, 2010.

Government of Kenya. *Elections Act 2011.* Nairobi: Government Printer, 2011.

Greene, J. and J. Butcher. "Proximity and Power". *The American,* May 8, 2008. Retrieved from www.american.com/archive/2008/may-05-08/proximitty-and-power/last.

Heald, S. "State Law and Vigilante in Northern Tanzania." *African Affairs*105, no. 419 (2005): 265-283.

Matter, S. "Clashing Claims: Neopatrimonial Governance Land Tenure Transformation and Violence at Enoosupukia Kenya." *Political and Legal Anthropology Review* 33, no. 1 (2010): 67-88.

Mbembe, A. "Necropolitics" *Public Culture* 15, no. 1 (2003): 11-40.

Moore, S. "Certainties Undone: Fifty Turbulent Years of Legal Anthropology, 1949-1999". In *Law and Anthropology: A Reader,* ed. S. Moore. London: Blackwell Publishing, 2005.

Pratten, D. "The rugged life: Youth and Violence in Southern Nigeria." In *Violence and Non-Violence,*' eds. P. Ahluwalia, and Bethlehem, R. Ginio. New York: Routledge, 2003.

Pratten, D., and A. Sen. "Global Vigilantes: Perspective on Justice and Violence." In *"Global Vigilantes,"* eds. D. Pratten and A. Sen, 1-21. London: Hurst, 2007.

Plyer, M. "Keeping the Peace: Violent justice, crime and vigilantism in Tanzania." In '*Violence and Non-Violence,*' ed. P. Ahluwalia, 124-140. New York: Routledge, 2003.

Rosenbaum, H. and P. Sederberg. "Vigilantism: An Analysis of Establishment Violence", *Comparative Politics* 6, no. 4 (1974): 541-70.

Straus, S. and C. Taylor. "Democratization and Electoral Violence in Sub-Saharan Africa." In *Voting in Fear: Electoral Violence in Sub-Saharan Africa,* ed. D. Bckoc, 15-38. Washington D.C. United States Institute of Peace Press, 2012.

New Constitution, Odingaism and the State of Internal Democracy in Orange Democratic Movement and its Effects on the 2013 Elections in Kenya

George Odhiambo Okoth [*] and Gordon Onyango Omenya [*]

Introduction: Historical development of parties and party systems

Parties that exist in political societies today may be authoritarian or democratic; they may seek power through elections or through revolutions; and they may espouse ideologies of left, right or centre, or indeed, disavow political ideas altogether. However, what is important is that the development of political parties and the acquisition of a party system have been recognized as a mark of political modernization in the contemporary world (Heywood, 2002). Since their formation, political parties have served as training ground for politicians, equipping them with skills, knowledge and experience, and offering them some form of career structure, albeit one that depends on fortunes of the party. Political parties have also been the means through which societies set collective goals and in some cases ensure that they are carried out. Parties play this role because in the process of seeking power, they formulate programmes of government through conferences, election manifestos and conventions.

According to Castles (1986), apart from these attributes, criticism of political parties is certainly not new. This author was fiercely critical of parties and factions, believing that they would promote conflict and destroy the underlying unity of society. He was also concerned that, as collective bodies, parties necessarily suppress freedom of thought and the politics of individual

---

[*]   Lecturer at Jaramogi Oginga Odinga University of Science and Technology.

[*]   PhD student at Université de Pau et des Pays de l'Adour (France) and Lecturer at Pwani University.

conscience. Modern concern about politics, however, stems from evidence of their decline as agents of representation and as an effective link between government and the people. Evidence of the contemporary crisis of party politics can be found in a decline of both party membership and partisanship as well as in the rise of antiparty groups and movements (Sartori, 2005). This can be explained by the perception that parties are tainted by power, ambition and corruption, and that they have suffered as a result of general disillusionment caused by the growing inability of governments to deliver on their promises. They are also seen to have failed to articulate the aspirations and sensibilities associated with post materialism or generated by postmodernism (Heywood, 2002)

Party democracy is therefore a process that has grown over time and refers to a form of popular rule that operates through the agency of party as democratic institution (Mair, 1990). There are two views about how this can be achieved. In the first case, party democracy can be realized through institutionalization of principles of intra-party democracy. This process sees political parties as democratic agents that disperse power within them and evenly. This implies, for instance, that there should be broad participation in the election of leaders and a prominent role for conferences and conventions in policy formulation (Randal, 2002). In the second model, democracy dictates that policy-making power should be concentrated in the hands of party members who are elected and therefore publicly accountable (Kartz, 1994). However, some argue that if this process is not checked, a wide and even dispersal of power within the party may lead to the tyranny of non-elected constituency activists.

Looking at Kenya's political parties, Elischer (2008) argues that Kenyan political society had been consistently divided along ethnic lines. At least at the aggregate level of political parties, two of the country's dominant ethnic cleavage lines are the divisions between Luo and Kikuyu and between Kalenjin and Kikuyu. With Kenya's independence, the ruling party KANU emerged victorious with the idea of having a unitary and centralized system of government, which also embraced capitalism both as an economic and political ideology. The political elites were to govern Kenya with this ideology up to 1966 when Jaramogi Oginga Odinga came up with his socialist idea, which led to his breakaway from the postcolonial Kenyatta government. Although this split was ideological, it was also viewed as ethnically driven. The paper uses the dynamics of political developments in the early post independent Kenya to analyse how and whether ODM as a political party has managed to nurture its democratic ideals in the run up to the 2013 General elections.[1] It gives a brief background of party politics and the driving force behind the formation of various parties within the Kenyan political arena. The paper also interrogates the ideological and philosophical leanings of Raila Odinga and assesses whether his ideological leanings had any influence in the senatorial, gubernatorial and parliamentary elections within ODM as a party especially in Nyanza Province.[2]

The origin and development of ODM

Orange Democratic Movement (ODM) is the leading political party in Kenya, and a successor of a former grassroots people's movement bringing together different parties to oppose the 2005 Kenyan Constitutional Referendum. The name ORANGE originates from the ballot cards in the referendum, in which a 'Yes' vote was represented by a banana and a 'No' vote by an orange. Thus the parties claim successorship to those who did not support the referendum at the time (Nyanchoga et al, 2008).

In the Constitutional Referendum of 2005 the 'No' vote which ODM campaigned for won out with 58.12% of Kenyans voting down the proposed constitution, granting victory to the Orange team. Following the rejection of the constitution, President Kibaki dismissed the entire cabinet. ODM responded by calling for immediate general elections, claiming that the Kibaki regime had lost its mandate as a result of the referendum. Kibaki's government resisted this. ODM then emerged as a major opposition party along with KANU, and even organized a number of rallies throughout the country asking for elections and a new constitution amongst other demands (Nyanchoga et al, 2008: 56)

As the General Elections of 2007 progressed, Uhuru Kenyatta of KANU pulled out of the ODM coalition in July 2007 and went ahead to endorse President Kibaki's re-election. This was soon followed by a split of the party into two factions in mid-August 2007, the Orange Democratic Movement Party of Kenya (ODM), and the Orange Democratic Movement Kenya (ODM Kenya), as a result of internal rivalry with Kalonzo Musyoka. Raila Odinga, Musalia Mudavadi, William Ruto, Joseph Nyagah and Najib Balala defected and took over the ODM party (Keverenge, 2007). ODM held their elections for presidential candidate on consecutive days at the Kasarani sports complex in Nairobi. On September 1st, 2007, Raila Odinga defeated Ruto, Mudavadi, Balala and Nyagah for the ODM mantle. He then faced president Kibaki in the 2007 general election representing ODM. Kibaki was declared winner of the elections in circumstances that were described as "highly questionable" by various observers both local and international ones. This declaration triggered widespread violence as scores of people protested against the Electoral Commission's to hurriedly swearing-in of Kibaki as the President late in the evening at the Nairobi state house. ODM won 99 out of the 210 seats in Parliament and together with its affiliates, the party constituted about 110 Members of Parliament therefore becoming the party with the majority members in the House.

Death and by-elections

Soon after the swearing in of the members of the 10th Parliament, the party received a setback when it lost two Members of Parliament in a span of one week through brutal attacks. Mellitus Mugabe Were, the Embakasi MP was shot at close range outside his home in Nairobi while David Arap Too (MP for Ainamoi) was shot dead by a police officer in Eldoret town. ODM managed to recapture the Ainamoi seat which was won by Mr. Too's brother Benjamin Lang'at. The party however lost the Embakasi seat to Ferdinand Waititu of PNU. Unfortunately, as the party was campaigning in Ainamoi, it lost two of its very influential members in a plane crash, the Roads Minister Kipkalya Kones (Bomet) and Home Affairs Assistant Minister Lorna Laboso (Sotik). The two were the main campaigners for the ODM candidate in Ainamoi.

The party's strength was later displayed when it recaptured both seats left vacant by the demise of Hon. Kones and Hon. Laboso through Mr. Kones widow, Beatrice Kones and Dr. Joyce Laboso, a sister to Lorna Laboso. In May 2009, ODM lost Shinyalu MP Charles Lirechi Lugano who succumbed to illness. The seat was recaptured through Justus Kizito Mugali. The party won the Bomachoge Parliamentary seat through Simeon Ogari which was previously held by FORD-People's Joel Onyancha, a PNU affiliate. ODM continued to perform well in consequent by-elections. Following the passing of the political parties act, ODM held its internal elections in late December 2008 with Prime Minister Raila Odinga emerging as the party leader, and Industrialization Minister Henry Kosgey as party chairman. The elections made sure regional and gender representation was taken into account and addressed.

Regardless of these internal and external challenges, ODM was formed on the platform of championing for democratic reforms and accountability in political administration. It was committed to reforming the state by instituting nationhood through collective participation of citizens in governance. These ideals have been clearly defined by its mission statement and vision in the 2013 party constitution which stated its commitment 'to win and maintain power through democratic means and to use such power to ensure economic and political empowerment of all Kenyans'. The party's vision also envisages a 'united and prosperous modern Kenya founded on popular democracy and social justice'. Contrary to these principles, before the 2013 elections, the party was afflicted by internal challenges in the dispensation of democratic ideals. Part of the specific challenges faced included non-inclusive candidate selection procedures and poor conflict management mechanisms.

Some have argued that the party has been run as a personal kingdom and is devoid of anything that is akin to a membership-based organization. Advocates of internal party democracy within the party have been alienated and pronounced 'enemies within' the party. Critics of the party have also argued that before the 2013 elections, the party systematically abused her institutional statutes and became a pillar of authoritarian rule, building her support through clientelism and patronage.

Ideology or ethnicity: Which way for Raila?

Erikson & Tedin (2003) defines ideology as a "set of beliefs about the proper order of society and how it can be achieved". Specific ideologies crystallize and communicate the widely (but not unanimously) shared beliefs, opinions, and values of an identifiable group, class, constituency, or society (Freeden, 2001; Knight, 2006). Ideologies also endeavor to describe or interpret the world as it is – by making assertions or assumptions about the human nature, historical events, present realities, and future possibilities and to envision the world as it should be, specifying acceptable means of attaining social, economic, and political ideals. Different ideologies represent socially shared but competing philosophies of life and how it should be lived (and how society should be governed).

Philosophers and social scientists have, however, long disagreed about whether to embrace a critical, even judgmental tone in describing and analyzing ideologies or, alternatively, to adopt a more value-neutral posture (Jost et al., 2008b; Knight, 2006). The former, more critical tradition descends from the writings of Marx & Engels (1846/1970), who regarded ideology (in contrast to science) as a potentially dangerous form of illusion and mystification that typically serves to conceal and maintain exploitative social relations. Along these lines, (Mannheim, 1936: 55) depicted certain ideologies as "more or less conscious disguises of the real nature of a situation". Habermas (1989), too, treated ideology as a form of "systematically distorted communication", and this characterization remains common in certain circles of social theorists.

But also, an ideology is a more or less coherent set of ideas that provides the basis for organized political action, whether this is intended to preserve, modify or overthrow the existing system of power. It is against this background that Raila's beliefs and philosophy on a democratic rule and social justice leading to a fair and equitable representation and leadership is examined. The history of political parties and their ideologies can be traced to the immediate post-independent Kenyan government.

Kenya became independent on 12 December 1963 and became a republic in the following year. President Jomo Kenyatta, who was the head of the Kenya African National Union (KANU), became Kenya's first president. A small but significant leftist opposition party formed in 1966, the Kenya People's Union (KPU), was led by Jaramogi Oginga Odinga, a former vice president and Luo elder. There followed three years of political harassment and detention of party leaders. The KPU was banned and its leader detained after political unrest related to Kenyatta's visit to Nyanza Province when he went to open the New Nyanza General Hospital on 25 October 1969. No new opposition parties were formed after 1969, and KANU became the sole political party. President Kenyatta was not excited about the hospital, since it was built with Soviet money and seen as Odinga's project. This was the genesis of ideological wars between Kenyatta of KANU and Odinga of KPU seen as a conduit for socialist ideologies in Kenya. Moi's regime also flourished on a one party system after Kenyatta's death in 1978. Moi's regime became more authoritative and dictatorial and did not allow any liberal opinion to be aired. During his reign, a number of politicians were detained without trial for opposing his rule while a number of them went into exile in different countries. Under this kind of environment social justice and democracy as an ideology could not prevail (see Ogot, 2006; Cohen, 2004).

Party competition was legalized in Kenya in the late December 1991 after several decades of one party rule under the Kenya African National Union (KANU). Immediately afterwards, the opposition formed the Forum for the Restoration of Democracy (FORD), whose leadership set up incorporated representatives of all major communities. A few months into its formation, the FORD split into FORD-Asili and the FORD-Kenya as its two main leaders, Jaramogi Oginga Odinga (Luo) and Kenneth Matiba (Kikuyu) failed to overcome their respective ambitions to become the FORD's presidential candidate. Subsequently both the FORD-Asili and FORD-Kenya rapidly developed into parties representing Kikuyu (FORD-Asili) and Luo/Luhya (FORD-Kenya) interests, which were evident in terms of their leadership, set up as well as their electoral support (Throup and Hornsby, 1998).

The FORD-Kenya further disintegrated as its Luo and Luhya wing fought viciously over its leadership. The Luo wing under the leadership of Raila Odinga eventually defected to form the National Development Party (NDP) whose support was confined to the Luo dominated areas of Nyanza Province. Simultaneously the FORD-Kenya declined to a party whose outreach was reduced to Luhya leader and followers.

In addition to FORD, the Democratic Party (DP) emerged also in the late 1991 as a breakaway faction from KANU under the leadership of Mwai Kibaki and John Keen. At its formation the DP included Kikuyu elites but also smaller communities such as the Kamba, the Meru, or the Maasai. As the Ford and later FORD-Kenya, the DP was equally unable to stay united. Feeling marginalized by the dominance of Kibaki's personality and his wealthy Kikuyu entourage, John Keen from the Maasai as well as Charity Ngilu and Agnes Ndetei from the Kamba left the party, while Keen and Ndetei defected back to KANU, Charity Ngilu took over the Social Democratic Party (SDP) which had hitherto been unknown to the wider Kenya populace and transformed it into a party which openly advocated Kamba interest. Thus due to their ethnic factionalism and ethnic rivalry, the Kenyan democratic opposition had reached a situation of almost complete fragmentation into several (mono) ethnic parties by early 1998 (Elischer, 2008).

On the governing benches, at the time, the KANU showed ethnic bias in favour of the Kalenjin community of president Moi as well as in favour of the many smaller communities such as the Maasai, the Turkana and the Samburu (Elischer, 2008).

In 1997 NDP was formed and thereafter in 1998 merged with KANU. The NDP highlighted that the New KANU represented first and foremost a unique opportunity for the Luo people to regain power. Later on Raila fell out with KANU and Moi. A significant number of the New KANU leaders under the leadership of Raila Odinga decided to break away from the KANU over the issue of a Kikuyu presidential candidate and defected to the Liberal Democratic Party (LDP). The LDP then merged with National Alliance Party of Kenya (NAK) in order to form the National Rainbow Coalition (NARC). The NARC proved to be the first and so far only nationwide alliance, which managed to include all of Kenya's major ethnic groups without falling apart before Election Day (Ndegwa, 2003).

However, as early as two weeks in Kibaki's presidency, initial tensions became visible between the different ethnic wings which made up the NARC (Kadima and Owuor, 2006). The NARC Kikuyu MPs for example voted for fellow Kikuyu opposition parties when it came to the selection of prestigious chairmanship position of Parliamentary Committees. Kibaki himself appointed several ministers closely associated with Kenyatta's former hawkish Kikuyu elite including Njenga Karume and John Michuki. The deteriorating relationship between them and the rest of the NARC came to a final end over Kibaki's refusal to initiate constitutional reforms, which would have seen the creation of strong executive Prime Minister.

In the eventual referendum that was held in 2005 in which the executive powers of the president were strengthened in the infamous (Amos) Wako Draft (constitution), Raila Odinga's led group voted 'No' against the government proposed constitution which was viewed as an embarrassment to the Kibaki government. Kibaki followed swiftly by sacking all the cabinet ministers who campaigned against the proposed constitution. Raila Odinga and Kalonzo Musyoka were the main losers in this sacking. This in turn led to the formation of the Orange Democratic Movement led by Odinga and eventually the Party of National Unity led by Kibaki (Elischer, 2008). Although the split had a clear ethnic dimension, it brought to the fore some ideological and philosophical standpoint of Raila Odinga.

Raila's philosophy has been anchored on his desire to see a democratic Kenyan society free from authoritarian and dictatorial rule. He believes in constitutionalism and a devolved system of government where resources are enjoyed by the people and not by individuals. His ideas on social justices also envisages a free Kenya where people are at liberty to enjoy their freedoms of speech, assembly, press and the ability to chose a leader of their choice. Babafemi (2006) argues that the indignity of seeing his father detained without trial and his KPU opposition party banned, and the oppressive nature of the past regimes shaped Raila's decision to go into politics and to fight to rectify the wrongs he felt his family, Kenyans and those who fought for democratic freedoms suffered. His struggles, beliefs and ideology have therefore always revolved around liberating the oppressed from repressive regimes so that they can enjoy their civil and political rights. All these freedoms, Raila believed, could only be achieved through reforming and reviewing the Kenya's constitution.

Odingaism ideology and the 2013 elections

The people of Kenya ushered in a new Constitution in the year 2010 which changed the country's constitutional order. The major change was that the country moved from a parliamentary system of governance to a presidential system of governance. It was believed that the impact of the Constitution would be felt during the electioneering period of 2013. In this new constitutional dispensation, new elective positions were created. These positions included the post for the senator, governor, county representative and women representative. Unlike, the old constitutional order, the new constitutional dispensation barred presidential candidates and their deputies from seeking any parliamentary seat. This, in essence meant that in case a presidential candidate fails to clinch the presidency then he/she had to be 'out' of politics for the next five years. In this context, therefore, the fundamental question would be whether the new Constitution would undermine the presidential ambitions of Raila Odinga leading to the collapse of Odingaism or whether it would sustain Odingaism with Raila becoming the president. But what is Odingaism as an ideology? To answer this question, we need to trace the family and political background of Raila Odinga within the concept of the role and the position of his father within the members of his Luo community.

In defining Odingaism, it is important to highlight some historical facts about the philosophical ideas surrounding it. Murunga (2003: 47) observes that the obsession with the Odinga family is cultural. Indeed, among the Luo, the *Ker* (teacher) was the ultimate moral or spiritual leader. This leader was also a *japaro* (thinker) who had been elevated to the status of *Ramogi* (the Moses of the Luo). The name 'Jaramogi' means the disciple of Ramogi; it was the name given to Oginga Odinga, Raila's father, not by himself but by the consensus of the community in 1954. This fact alone underlined and continues to legitimate his leadership of the Luo. As Oruka explained,

> ... From time to time in history a person of great moral insight and courage comes to the scene and by communal consensus assumes the role of Ker. Once one is declared a *Ker* it is considered to attract a curse if anybody is at war with him or her. A *Ker* is hardly ever formally elected. There can be a hierarchy of *Ker* and there are generally persons who play the role of *Ker* in their particular clans or districts. But usually there is the ultimate *Ker* who is seen as the torchbearer of *Ramogi*, the dominant ancestor of the Luo. Odinga as Jaramogi has played this role since the early 1950s (Oruka, 1992: 28).

Jaramogi Oginga Odinga was installed as Ker in 1954. This installation explains why the Luo have considered Odinga worth their support. The excellent leadership of Odinga in business and politics and his figure as the leading Luo politician all provide reasons why the Luo installed faith in him. It should be remembered that Raila Odinga was not just Oginga Odinga's favored son; he was also active alongside his father in the politics of dissent against the oppressive and authoritarian regimes of both Kenyatta and Moi. For this, he unofficially took over the leadership of the Luo after the death of his father, though not in the status of Ker this time. This dissent against political oppression and authoritarianism informed Raila's ideology and philosophy of social justice, liberalism and political freedom of the masses anchored in the ideology of social democracy.

Odingaism is used to refer to the unrelenting faith and belief that the Luo and other non-Luo have in Oginga Odinga and his son Raila. Odingaism is unlike any other ideologies in Kenyan politics because it rotates around a personality whose stature in his society and beyond gives him the unreserved trust of the followers. Similarly, Odingaism is unlike any ideology in Kenya because the cultural logic of its origin has fused with his personality to produce a form of authority hardly possessed by many other leaders in Kenya, including Kenyatta and Moi. What distinguishes Odingaism from others is that it is grounded on real authority; it is not crafted around a hawkish evocation of a carefully orchestrated personality cult (Schatzberg, 2001: 23). Such personality cults are what both Kenyatta and Moi tried to build but Odingaism is of a different nature. Its legacy has a long-standing basis that even with the death of Jaramogi Odinga, his successor Raila Odinga has been able to continue to marshal and get unreserved ethnic and non-ethnic Luo followers (see Murunga, 2003: 51). The idea of Odingaism illustrates the sense in which ethnic men of power, or boss men, control popular voice and community decisions. The effect of this works well if the boss man is tolerant and is able to direct the energies of his following to constructive end like Odinga did for the Luo Thrift and Trading Corporation (LUTATCO). LUTATCO was based on Jaramogi Oginga Odinga's economic ideology for the economic empowerment of Africans against the capitalist colonial settlers (Atieno-Odhimabo, 1976; Odinga, 1967).

Thriving on Odingaism, Raila Odinga has been able to consolidate the Luo and non-Luo ethnic support base to his advantage. He has been able to mutate from the principles, philosophy and ideologies of his father who operated along the lines of socialism. Raila has embraced social democracy both as a political philosophy and ideology. Guided by the values and principles of social democracy and the humanness of the African traditional societies, Raila has been particularly concerned about the oppressed, the poor, inequity in the distribution of public resources and the voiceless majority. His unrelenting fight for social justice for all and participatory democracy earned him three detentions without trial during the 24 years of Moi's rule. This handed the Odinga family lots of sympathy from Kenyans who believed in change and reform. Mr. Odinga was seen as the one who would spearhead the necessary reforms within the country. Proponents of social democracy never rejected liberal values and recognized their importance for workers. However, they formerly declared that political freedom was a precondition of the social freedom and the political rights alone were not enough for the social emancipation, and therefore, the political freedom had to be extended to the social issues. Freedom creates opportunities but without social rights, the political freedom can never be universal. Hence, taking it as a single system of principles "freedom-social justice-solidarity became an axiom of the social democracy" (Acharya, 2003). Raila believes in these ideologies, however, within the African context these ideologies sometimes become too difficult to achieve because of the ethnicised nature of politics. However, he used his philosophy based on the ideology of social democracy to increase the democratic space within Kenya's political arena which has ensured freedom of speech, association, assembly, equality and the rule of law. This has been realized by putting the existing governments in constant check and accountable to the people of Kenya. Odingaism, therefore, is a special brand of 'political-isms' that refers both to the exceptional hold which the Odinga's, and especially Raila, have over the Luo. To his followers, Raila epitomizes a symbol of political freedom and a liberator that Kenyan masses have been hitherto denied in the past successive authoritarian political regimes (De Smedt, 2009). It is this ideology that Raila has tried to inculcate and nurture in his ODM party. This paper also examines if these ideologies drive the ODM party operations and politics.

Knowledge of the contents of intra-party democracy

Our informants' understanding of intra-party democracy (IPD) was not well developed or explained. This was attributed to the lack of basic education by the party on issues of governance as service to party members. However, there was general understanding of the role of political parties in linking ordinary citizens to government. There was also good knowledge of political parties as organizations that contest elections and engage in other public activities designed to influence policies in government. Political parties were also viewed as elite-owned instruments for seeking and maintaining political power with formal machinery or structures found at all levels of political activity-national, regional, district, constituency, ward, all the way down to the grassroots.

For the case of ODM, IPD was explained through four critical elements. In the first case, IPD was a process of popular participation and consultation at all levels on party matters as well as freedom of expression to criticize party leadership. The second most important aspect noted was that IPD reflects on adherence to the party constitution. Thirdly, informants felt that a party is internally democratic if its members are able to influence vital party decisions. And fourthly, most respondents identified issues of transparency and accountability and regular free and fair elections in party nominations as the main indicators of internal party democracy. However in regard to the ratings of the various interpretations of IPD, popular participation and consultation at all party levels and on all matters, and freedom of expression to criticize party leadership were identified as the major indicators that should define internal democracy in ODM.

In regard to this understanding of IPD, most party officials interviewed observed that the party performed poorly in terms of adherence to the basic tenets of democracy because decision making in the party was not based on a deliberative and participatory process among party members seen as equals. The decisions were also not guided by party constitutional procedures and regulations while the party leader lost control of the decision making process in the party once he became Prime Minister and delegated it to elites. In reference to the Iron Law of Oligarchy formulated by Michels (1962) it was suggested that the party favored domination by a few (elites) in which case the participatory or democratic structures were unable to check the manipulation of elites but only disguise them. Within the framework of Michels' ideas, elite groups in ODM like in any party were acknowledged for their specialisation, expertise and better organisational skills. However compared to the ordinary members of the party they dominated the rank and file of the party while the party members remain disposed to accept subordination and venerate them. According to a former Member of Parliament and close ally of Raila Odinga, Hon. Gor Sungu, "Raila became a different man, meeting him became a nightmare for many of his close friends". This suggests that the party leader killed the process of consultation or was selective in his associations, often ignoring those with whom he may have developed weak or poor relations.

Denis Kodhe also observed in *The Standard* newspaper that the party leader was burdened by the task of administration as the Prime Minister as well as the challenges of striking a power balance in the coalition arrangement which was linked with policy inconsistencies. He was therefore not fully in charge of the party:"Raila seemed to have lost his knack and surrounded himself with handlers and advisors who cared less about the future than their personal development". Kodhe states that:

> The rain started beating Odinga and ODM party immediately after he became the Prime Minister in the Kofi Annan negotiated Grand Coalition government in 2008. From there on, the situation has been downhill all the way, until sometime last year (2012) when most members of his 'Pentagon' team deserted him to join or form other political outfits (*The Standard*, March 15, 2013).

The deliberative and participatory processes hitherto nurtured through the representative symbol and organ of the party (pentagon) was systematically relegated together with Raila's compatriots in the struggle. The able critics in the party like Hon William Ruto, Musalia Mudavadi and Najib Balala who contributed in sustaining internal competitive democracy were also replaced with individuals who could not sell their agenda in their respective constituencies or counties, let alone campaign for his election as president.

Some of the close allies and advisers who are said to have been allowed to influence party policies included personalities like Medical Services minister and secretary general of the party Prof. Anyang' Nyong'o. Together with many others, this team served to isolate some of the lieutenants in the Pentagon, forcing them to abandon ship. Lawyer and author Miguna Miguna, Raila's legal and constitutional advisor, was one such casualty who was sacked for writing an opinion questioning the integrity and capability of Isaack Hassan, the IEBC chairman.

Candidate selection processes

Other reasons given to indicate that the party was not democratic include the imposition of parliamentary candidates on the electorate, even though the party held some kind of primary elections in February 2013. Yet, the nomination dates were pushed close to the Interim Elections and Boundary Commissions deadline (IEBC) in order to control defections. According to IEBC calendar, the parties were supposed to do their nomination between 4 January 2013 and 17 January 2013,and to submit the final list of names on 18 January 2013.Most of the parties chose to have the nominations on the last day, i.e. 17 January 2013 in order to prevent losers from defecting and contesting in other parties.

The ODM nominations were administered by an ODM National Election Board (NEB) which was however undergoing a hurried reformation after Odinga, on 19 September 2012, took steps to bolster the democratic credentials of the board which was previously perceived as weak and partial. This was in response to heated criticism of the ODM's contested nomination of Augustino Neto for MP for Ndhiwa. By overhauling the membership of the NEB and insisting that: "Our nomination process for various electoral positions in the coming general election must be flawless", Raila sought to give aspirants across the country faith that they will have a fair opportunity to win the ODM ticket if they join or remain in the party. However, this seemed to have been primarily motivated by the desire to avoid defections to other parties and, to a lesser degree, the need to make absolutely certain that there was no risk of a party split in the run-up to the presidential campaign.

This re-emphasis on internal democracy was confirmed by the new NEB, which issued the following statement:

> The Board is currently reviewing the roadmap for holding fair, transparent and democratic elections and nominations. The Board affirms that the nomination process will be fully transparent, inclusive and participatory. Every ODM member who wishes to run for any post will have the freedom to stand and every voter will have the right to vote for the candidate he/she wishes to nominate and elect. Finally, NEB assures candidates that there

shall be no direct nominations. The playing ground will be even and non-compromised (*The Standard*, Tuesday, September 25, 2012).

Contrary to the spirit of this statement by the National Elections Board, on 17 January 2013 ODM primaries failed to take off in nearly all the constituencies save for Karachuonyo, Rarieda, Nyakach, Kasipul Kabondo and Suna East; and plans to hold repeat polls the following day also suffered serious logistical challenges before collapsing. But even in the five constituencies where elections were held, only former Rarieda MP Nicholas Gumbo secured the party's ticket to run in the 4 March 2013 General Election. Analysts have argued that the anger by the party supporters degenerated into a protest vote against ODM nominees in favor of its partners in CORD as well as possible withdrawal from voting Raila as their preferred president.

Earlier on, on 5 January 2013, CORD affiliate parties through a Joint Election Board announced that it would conduct joint nomination exercise for all elective posts in the coming general election. Besides setting up a joint Election Board, CORD also formed an Appeals Board to deal with disputes arising from the nomination which were expected to be highly contested and potentially divisive. In effect, according to this arrangement, the candidates from ODM, Wiper Democratic Movement (WDM), FORD-Kenya, CCU, KADU-Asili, Kenya Social Congress, TIP, Mkenya Solidarity Movement, United Democratic Movement and Peoples Democratic Party would have to work extra hard to secure the coalitions ticket for the March 2013 elections. Nomination for Governor, Senator, Member of Parliament, Women Representative and Member of the County Assembly (Ward Representatives) would be by universal suffrage through secret ballot on 17 January 2013 (*The Standard*, January 6, 2013). However, on 8 January 2013, Raila Odinga announced that CORD had shelved the joint nomination strategy and adopted a new plan that blends party primaries in some regions with what it called 'negotiated democracy' in other areas. According to the alliance leaders, the team embraced a blend of measures that included allowing parties to nominate candidates to compete in its stronghold areas, hold joint nominations in cosmopolitan areas and give room for negotiated democracy in swing vote areas (*The Standard*, January 9, 2013). But, this plan was not to be as each party went ahead and conducted its own nominations. This came about as a result of the small parties within the coalition citing domination by the bigger parties in the coalition.

Flaws in the ODM party primaries started to be evident when ODM aspirants in Migori raised the red flag after the ODM party decided to reserve the Migori senatorial seat for the Kuria community during the 'Isebania Declaration' which gave the position of the senate to the Kuria people, a minority in the Migori County dominated by members from the Luo community. In this declaration attended by Raila Odinga, the seat was preserved for the former Kuria MP Wilfred Machage, thereby violating the party nomination rules and guidelines of free and fair nominations devoid of direct nomination. This did not auger well for other party aspirants for the same senatorial position from Migori who had already invested and paid over KShs. 250,000 as nomination fee to the party for the senatorial seat (*The Standard*, December 5, 2012).

Stakes were higher in some areas like Karachuonyo where former MP James Rege was declared winner by the returning officer after beating his main challenger Adipo Akuome with a 3,000 margin but the party offered its nomination ticket to Mr. Donny Opar who had trailed the front runner from the tail end. Mr. Rege is quoted as saying:

I am shocked that my name is missing from the list published in the IEBC website. I won in broad daylight. I am surprised that fraud of this magnitude is being meted out on me," complained Mr. Rege (*Sunday Nation*, January 27, 2013).

His main challenger, Mr. Akuome, moved to Vice-President Kalonzo Musyoka's party, Wiper, to face off with Mr. Opar in Karachuonyo constituency. In Nyakach where former MP Polynce Ochieng lost the fight for the party ticket, ODM nominated Nairobi businessman Aduma Awuor, forcing Mr. Ochieng to flee to Wiper while another candidate, Mr. Erick Ouma, secured Cyrus Jirongo's Federal Party of Kenya ticket while in Kasipul, Mr. Were Ongondo secured a TIP ticket and notified his supporters of the change. Former Migori MP John Pesa, who won the contest in Suna East, was tongue tied after he learnt that his rival, Mr. Junet Sheik Mohamed, had secured the party ticket following an order from a prominent party official. However, by Friday, Mr. Mohamed's certificate was yet to be signed. John Pesa complained to the *Sunday Nation*:

I was declared winner. I was not anticipating these games until Friday when I realized that my name was missing from the IEBC list. I don't understand who is doing this to me and why I am being fought", Mr. Pesa told the *Sunday Nation*.

Instead of providing reasons for these challenges, Mr. Bett the ODM director of elections blamed local leaders and former MPs for conspiring to disrupt the party's logistical planning for a proper poll. This again confirms the fact that party institutions were not respected by some leaders or that clear rules and policies regulating the elections process were not in place.

This was the scenario in Kisumu Town West Constituency and Kisumu Town Central Constituency. In Kisumu Town West, Mr. Olago Aluoch who was defending his parliamentary seat on an ODM ticket had to decamp to Ford Kenya after he was defeated in the bungled party primaries by Rozah Buyu popularly known as Dwasi. However, Mr. Olago Aluoch went against the grain to defeat Rozah Buyu of ODM on a FORD-Kenya ticket to the dismay of the locals in an area which is an ODM stronghold. Generally, the way nominations were carried out ignited violent demonstrations across Nyanza province. The sight of agitated voters chanting anti-Raila slogans amid claims of poll rigging in the Orange primaries in Nyanza was a rare sight. So, too, was that of protestors threatening to decamp to rival Uhuru Kenyatta's coalition (*The Standard*, January 27, 2013). It is, therefore, evident that since Raila was more focused on the presidency, he did not want to 'get involved' in local nomination process which could have painted him as a tribal chief while he was playing national politics.

Although Kenya has a sizeable African middle class, ethnic cleavages have more often than not stifled the reformist agenda. Campaigns for office openly appeal to ethnic allegiance. All the major political leaders draw most of their support from their particular ethnic strongholds. Needless to say, this dynamic has diminished the importance of both ideology and social questions as bases on which to distinguish between parties (and their leaders) (Mutua, 2008: 22). Cohen and Kanyinga (2002: 131) observe that the territorial space of tribe is not merely some historical or geographical given within which the political interplay of the local and the national takes place. While particular places have acquired an inherent economic and social meaning, territoriality has increasingly become a source of political power. Strategies, including violence, to politically controlled contested territorial spaces have been an integral part of sustained attempts to maintain political and, thereby, give shape to the identities from which the political content of the local is lately derived.

According to Nyong'o (*The Standard*, January 6, 2013), the litmus test for democracy in political parties is not based so much on whether or not they hold primaries but whether they conduct themselves in accordance with rules and regulations formulated by their members, accepted by them and exercised without favor among all members. That is why democratic elections are often defined as struggles over rules of the electoral game before they become struggles over elections themselves. Democracy does not mean that all forms of methods adopted in a competitive election must be the same. All it means is that the competitive process must be open enough to allow for multiple choices that can produce ideas and leadership in the use of state power for democratic and good governance following the elections. Although Nyong'o's arguments are practical in western democracies, these arguments fall short of expectations within smaller democracies, like Kenya, where election rules and regulations are just followed in paper.

Odingaism in the gubernatorial and senatorial race in Siaya and Kisumu counties

Other cases of concern that demonstrated abuse of party institutions were reflected in the senatorial and gubernatorial elections. The battle for the Siaya County senate, a county where Raila Odinga emanates from, threatened to divide ODM party right in the middle. The race attracted two stalwarts, former Lands minister and Raila's key strategist, Mr. James Orengo and Former Finance assistant minister and Raila's elder brother Dr. Oburu Odinga. The competition between these two ODM members created two factions in the Orange Party, although all of them drummed up support for their party leader, Raila Odinga (*The Star*, February 1, 2012). In this race, ODM ministers and MPs aligned themselves either on Orengo or Oburu's side while some chose not to support either. Those who chose to be neutral did so because they did not know the premier's (Raila's) position, a sign of not wanting to antagonize the premier thereby rubbing him the wrong way (Otieno, 2013). This is evidence of politicians who are not ideologically grounded but whose survival in politics depends on Odingaism and party leadership. Ministers from Western province and MPs from Nyanza province were sharply divided over whom between the two leaders should run for the seat. Former Planning Minister and the current governor for Kakamega, Mr. Wycliffe Oparanya and his then Local Government counterpart Paul Otuoma allied themselves to Oburu Odinga and Orengo respectively. Oparanya on a campaign trail for Oburu in Gem constituency in November 2012 asked Orengo to shelve his ambition, saying Oburu was the most senior and experienced leader who could be entrusted with Siaya county leadership.

However, the former cabinet Minister in charge of sports Paul Otuoma, campaigning for Orengo in Alego Usonga (part of Siaya County), argued in favour of Orengo by asserting that Orengo deserved the position because of his legal background to help Raila Odinga implement the new constitution. MPs Fred Outa (Nyando) and Nicholas Gumbo (Rarieda) also threw their weight behind Oburu, while Martin Ogindo (Rangwe), Jakoyo Midiwo (Gem- a cousin to Raila) and Edwin Yinda (Alego Usonga) supported Orengo. Although, Raila's position on this race was not clear, his proverbial response was that 'when a child cries for a razor he should be given'. Both the contenders for the senatorial seat, however, vowed that only the people of Siaya would decide who between them would become their senator. Although other contenders for the seat like Joe Donde and Gideon Ochanda were also in the race, their candidature did not prove problematic as that of Oburu and Orengo (*The Star*, February 1, 2013). In addition to the competitive party primaries that characterized the ODM nominations, other factors other than ideology and ethnicity also played a key role in determining who would go to the senate.

For instance, in Siaya County, ODM as a party had to try the principle of negotiated democracy in order to accommodate the competing candidates and to avoid fallout from the party. This arrangement saw Dr. Oburu Odinga step down for Mr. James Orengo. Oburu argued that his rivalry with Orengo was dividing the party and that is why he agreed to shelve his ambitions after consultations within the party and instead run for the governor's post in Siaya (*Daily Nation*, December 18, 2012). In this negotiated democracy, Oburu stated that "We therefore, decided that the two big seats be divided between the two regions of the county", that is, senator for the greater Siaya (consisting of Siaya, Ugenya and Gem Districts) and governor for the greater Bondo (consisting of Bondo and Rarieda districts). In this deal both Orengo and Oburu agreed to support each other for the senatorial and gubernatorial seats respectively (*Daily Nation*, December 18, 2012). With this negotiated democracy, James Orengo went ahead and clinched the Siaya senatorial seat on an ODM ticket.

However, efforts by the ODM leadership to negotiate a deal which saw Finance assistant minister Dr. Oburu Oginga bow out of the race for the senator's seat appeared to have hit the rocks after other gubernatorial aspirants refused to play ball. Signs that the deal may not work emerged during a rally at Ugunja trading centre on 29 December 2012 in Ugenya constituency when efforts by Lands minister James Orengo to market Dr. Oburu Oginga for the governor's seat backfired after residents openly showed their support for his challenger, Mr. William Oduol. Attempts by Gem MP Jakoyo Midiwo to tell residents that the decision to have Dr. Oginga run for governor's seat had been reached by all MPs from the county and endorsed by Prime Minister were met with boos from the residents who kept on chanting Mr. Oduol's name who also warned the party against giving his opponent a direct nomination. The deal was seen as undemocratic seat sharing (*Sunday Nation*, January 6, 2013). These private settlements brokered by owners of political parties deny the party rank and file their democratic right to nominate their candidates. Second, they deny parties the right and deserving candidates. Third, they derail and defeat democracy and the ideologies that parties stand for (*Sunday Nation*, January 9, 2013:18). The democratic principles and ideologies that the ODM stood for were therefore put on trial and relegated to the periphery.

Odinga's brother Dr. Oburu Oginga subsequently lost the Siaya governorship primaries to William Oduol in a controversial contest whose results were nullified after being contested by Mr. William Oduol. Mr. Amoth Rasanga was then handed the nomination certificate (*Sunday Nation*, January 27, 2013). Dr. Oburu Oginga and his sister Ms Ruth Adhiambo Odinga, who had sought the ODM ticket to vie for the positions of governor in Siaya and Kisumu counties respectively, however, argued that they were victimized because of their family name: Odinga. Viewed from a different perspective, the rebellion and riots that characterized the candidature of both Ruth Odinga and Oburu Oginga and the subsequent announcement of their victories in the gubernatorial races in Kisumu and Siaya respectively symbolized a rebellion against the Odinga dynasty, something that was unheard of in Luo Nyanza an indication that Raila Odinga's influence during the party primaries was at its lowest. Their candidature was seen as an attempt by the Odinga family to impose candidates on the electorate (*Sunday Nation*, January 27, 2013). Dr. Oburu was denied the ODM certificate by the party's elections board after his opponent, Mr. William Oduol contested the results announced by the returning officer (*Sunday Nation*, January 27, 2013).

Although both Oburu and Oduol were denied nomination in favor of Amoth Rasanga, Mr Franklin Bett, the Chairman of the ODM Elections Board, argued that they found it impossible to determine the clear winner of ODM's nominations in Siaya County. There was violence in the region as evidenced by reports of the returning officers being beaten and some kidnapped (*Saturday Nation*, January 26, 2013). Mr Bett argued that the party turned to article 3.1 of its constitution to decide the way forward. The article gives the party's National Elections Boards the leeway to pass the responsibility to the National Executive Committee in situations where its dispute resolution team is unable to come with a solution. But what did this portend for Raila? The argument is that Raila found himself in an in-between position which put him in a delicate situation as far as his principles, ideas and family issues were concerned. He had to embrace democratic ideals and social justice that he has always believed in at the expense of family issues.

Despite the mythical grip that Jaramogi's family has kept on the politics of Luo Nyanza, his first born son, Dr. Oburu Odinga lost his bid for the Siaya gubernatorial seat on a CORD ticket. This is something that could never have been thought of before and also considering that Dr. Oburu Odinga has for 19 years served as the MP for Bondo riding on Odingaism. Another scion of Jaramogi and sister to the former Prime Minister Raila Odinga, Ruth Odinga, who had expressed interest in becoming the first governor of Kisumu also bowed out of the race following a bitter dispute as to who between her and Jack Ranguma won the Cord ticket (*The Star,* January 26-27, 2013). Jakoyo Midiwo, a first cousin of Raila got a direct nomination even after being beaten by a new comer Elisha Odhiambo. Allies of Raila such as outgoing Rangwe MP Martin Ogindo, immediate Nyakach MP Pollyns Ochieng were also floored in the nominations by newcomers (*The Star,* January 26-27, 2013). The same confusion and lack of party primaries informed by ideologies also characterized the Kisumu senatorial and gubernatorial seats.

In Kisumu, the senatorial seat attracted ODM secretary general Prof Anyang' Nyong'o and Ochola Ogoda. Mr. Ochola Ogoda however allayed fears that Prof Nyong'o was using his position as the Secretary General of the party for his own advantage. In the run up to party primaries, pressure was mounting on Prof Anyang' Nyong'o to step down over a conflict of interest (*Sunday Nation*, January 6, 2013). His stepping down according to his opponents would ensure a level playing field by ensuring free and fair primaries. The Kisumu County senatorial nomination was marred by delays in delivering voting materials alongside other logistical problems. Some polling stations like Osiri did not receive voting materials and the voters ended up voting two days after the official days of the party primaries (Origi, 2013). Although, this contravened the new Elections Act, which set deadlines for the party primaries, the IEBC accepted the name of the nominees after their deadline had passed.

In a controversial nomination process which was disputed by Mr. Ochola Ogoda, the ODM national board decided to give its secretary general Nyong'o the nomination certificate following a decision in his favor by the ODM dispute resolution committee. Ogoda and Nyong'o had disagreed over the Kisumu senatorial election (*The Star*, January 26-27, 2013). Later on, Ogoda accepted the decision by the ODM dispute resolution committee to give Nyong'o the nomination certificate for the senator elections and vowed to support him. Considering that Kisumu is an ODM stronghold, many residents believed that Nyong'o clinched the ticket because he did not have a strong challenger (Otieno, 2013). An ODM ticket was almost an automatic ticket to the upper house (senate) for any aspirant whether at the senatorial, gubernatorial or parliamentary levels. In the general elections, Prof Nyong'o floored his only opponent from TNA. It was, however, not an easy ride for the two contenders for the Kisumu gubernatorial seat.

In the Kisumu gubernatorial seat, which pitted Jack Ranguma and Ruth Adhiambo Odinga who were the main contenders, chaos erupted during the party primaries with the declaration of Adhiambo Odinga as the winner of the Kisumu County gubernatorial race. This win was seen as a way of the Odinga's family trying to impose one of their own on the Kisumu people who considered Ruth Odinga as an outsider. Indeed she hails from Bondo and is married in none of the three Kisumu clans (Kisumo, Kajulu and Kano-Kolwa). Owiyo (2013) a Kisumu resident retorted that 'we shall vote for Raila as a president but he should leave us to choose whoever we want for the other races (senator, gubernatorial and parliamentary seat - malokuro to wamiye, pinyka to owenwa). But again through a negotiated democracy, Jack Ranguma carried the ODM ticket for the gubernatorial race while Adhiambo Odinga was appointed as the deputy governor. Having tested the waters and the public mood, Raila denied any role or involvement in the nominations and said that he was prepared to work with those chosen by the people. His appeal for a six piece voting for ODM candidates during his last campaign in Kisumu also fell on deaf ears as people went ahead and elected Olago Aluoch as the MP for Kisumu Town West on a Ford Kenya ticket. This election was challenged in court by the ODM loser Roza Buyu. However, the court upheld the election of Olago Aluoch. Other non-ODM candidates also won various seats through other political parties' tickets within the CORD alliance. The six-piece voting pattern meant that only ODM candidates were to be voted in at all levels without regard to their development record. The six-piece suit voting pattern is suffocating, cumbersome and impractical in the current climate. Many voters may have decided on their presidential candidate but felt free to choose candidates for the other seats from any party, a person who is able to deliver change (*Saturday Nation*, January 26, 2013).

It was therefore observed that the failure of the primary nominations in ODM in 2013 was as a result of an attempt to ensure the re-election of the party's incumbent MPs some of whom upgraded to contest the senatorial and gubernatorial seats. Consequently, the existing internal procedures were seriously flouted resulting in confusion and division. In the TNA and URP, such incidences were limited and, the parties' electoral performances were comparatively impressive and with limited controversies. According to some observers the 2013 ODM primary elections resulted in increased independent candidates and defections in Luo-Nyanza than any other party due to "lack of transparency and intra-party democracy".

Time and again, Raila has favored his close relatives for top Government positions and recently, for elective posts. He perfected the art of Odinganisation, just like the Kikuyu ruling class Kikuyunised key government posts. It could be argued that some Luo members silently carried forward memories from the sham ODM nominations in December 2012 to March 2013, and punished Raila for imposing his siblings Oburu Oginga and Ruth Odinga and cousin Jakoyo Midiwo on them, yet they had been resoundingly voted out in their various counties. For the first time ever, Raila was booed at some rallies when he was accompanied by his bunch of Luo MPs that voters had rejected at the nominations, yet through biased petitions by the ODM Elections Board, became winners, while the true winners were declared losers.

Existence and influence of institutional arrangements in political parties

In assessing the types and influence of institutional arrangements within ODM, we asked the informants if they had knowledge of rules and regulations which guide the functioning of their party. Most informants did not have any information. However, party convention was considered the most relevant institutional arrangements above all others. Knowledge of the party constitution was also weak. This probably served to explain why leaders in the party often disregarded the need to consult with their members when they settled to form or opted out of coalitions. Furthermore, the findings revealed an acute information deficit mainly among officials at district level regarding constitutional rules.

For some informants, Party slogans were in some instances mistaken or perceived as rules. In explaining this degree of ignorance among party officials, it was explained that this process is partly perpetrated by the culture of secrecy around, and monopoly for party information by the political elites. It is important to conclude from these findings that a good relationship between the party leaders and members has been difficult to secure in the absence of adequate knowledge of existing party rules and documents such as constitutions. In order to enhance internal party democracy in the party, it is important that party officials, leaders and members be fully acquainted with these documents.

Informants at the constituency party offices indicated "respect for the party leaders" as a very fundamental institution, but observed that such an informal institution has been exploited to ensure uncritical acceptance of decisions of the elite. In most cases the informal institutions have worked in favor of the patronage power relations.

Intra-party democracy and party funding

Within the context of intra-party financial management, this component sought to establish, key sources of party funding, who controls the allocation of party resources in the party, the level of transparency about sources and allocation of party finances and the correlation (if any) between the source of party funding and control of party agenda. The findings showed that ODM party gets most of their funding from three major sources: private funding by their leaders, Parliament, and foreign donations. Membership contributions were not indicated as a source of party funding. Fundraising activities and interest groups contributions were also noted as sources of funds

Most of the informants said that the party gets its finances privately from the party leadership and from contributions from members of parliament. Informants also noted that NEC controls the allocation of party resources. Others indicated that the party president/leader domineers in the control of party resources. These findings are indicative of limited intra-party democracy since party members are not an important source of party funding, probably due to acute poverty levels in Kenya. This undermines intra-party democracy in the party due to the absence of transparency and accountability.

The responses also revealed that the party just like other parties is not transparent at all. Political experts held that there is no financial transparency virtually across all parties. There is a lot of secrecy surrounding sources and allocation of party resources as well as undisclosed party funders. Because the party leader and close allies are the key private funders to the party, the sense of political patronage has dominated the party.

From these results it can be concluded that private funding mainly by party presidents and a few elites limits membership control over the party activities. Finally, the fact that party elites particularly presidents/chairpersons wield more control than the National Executive Council (NEC) and members in the allocation of party resources provides them with the authority to control party agenda. Thus, pervasive patronage and clientelistic relationships and networks have become coercive forces in the party. It can be concluded that the limited transparency and accountability on one hand, and strong control of party agenda by party presidents/elites disadvantages party members in the sense that it limits free participation. Hence, institutional arrangements governing party funding and accountability have insignificant impact on elite behavior to the detriment of intra-party democracy.

Conclusion

With the General Election now over, it is now time to critically examine factors that negatively and positively steered politics in the Luo community during the past decade. It is also important to project the way forward for this ethnic group and the ODM party, since its leader Raila Odinga is currently not an elected politician. Odinga would have been viewed as a great leader whose political strategy, personality and vision have not only enabled him to introduce constructive and institutionalized reforms, but such a form of deliberative political thinking would have portrayed him as a charismatic champion for change and meritocratic politicization of the nation. However, Raila Odinga became a victim of the new Constitution (2010) that he had passionately campaigned for. The new Constitution (2010) effectively locked out Raila Odinga from the centre of power. He could not join the legislative assembly as the new Constitution (2010) constitutionally barred him from becoming a Member of Parliament. This used to be the case before the new Constitution came into being since Kenya followed a purely parliamentary system of governance.

The newly elected Luo legislators should move away from the 10-year mode of politicking to an economic development mode. It is true that Kibaki reneged on his signed 2002 MOU with Raila and was later alleged to have stolen his presidency in 2007. However, Luo Nyanza has been associated with politicking and eventually, the goal of securing Raila's presidency was thwarted by the Supreme Court verdict which put a stay on the election of President Uhuru Kenyatta thereby legitimizing his presidency. There is need for ODM to go back to the drawing board and reassess itself with a view to finding solutions to their internal democratic problems.

Organizational theory was used to examine the state of internal democracy in ODM. Proponents of this theory argue that it is better to view political parties as 'living systems', because they are human organizations with internal and external structures that define their operations (Michel, 1962). The theory emphasizes that just as all living systems, a political institution due to external and internal interactions must undergo structural changes and if they cannot learn and adapt to these environmental dynamics, their systems may disintegrate. As such, political parties must adapt in accordance with survival and other needs such as re-election and gaining support among the electorate (Avnon, 1995).

A major aspect of political organizations/party according to this theory is their leadership. This is critical to their success because the institutional leader is able to weld members of the organization into a committed polity, with a great sense of identity, purpose and commitment (Masime, 2010). Political party leadership therefore has the obligation of ensuring that vital institutional interests, that keep members' vision and aspirations in focus, are in tandem with political interests and intrigues that characterize the political environment in which they operate. In this context, institutional values and practices should not be at cross-purposes with democratic norms and values, but rather complement each other.

Organization theorists also emphasize that both interests and power in a political party are shaped by institutions and not by political elites. Internal party organization and orientation therefore influence the choices and interests of parties, such that it is not just the political leaders that should be the focus of reform, but also structures, such as ensuring election boards work (Diamond, 1994). Institutional processes such as decision-making in political parties are therefore critical in the analysis of behavioral traits of an institution as they are the source of decisions and institutional outcomes. How decisions are made in political organizations will invariably influence their stability and success in achieving their goals (Scarrow, 1996).

Drawing from this theory, the following are suggested ways of improving the state of democracy in ODM.

(i) Leadership of the party should be separated from national leadership and those holding elective political offices should not hold party offices. The party should have executive officials to manage and organize party activities.
(ii) Party leadership should ensure that vital institutional interests, that keep members' vision and aspirations in focus, are in tandem with political interests and intrigues that characterize the political environment in which they operate.
(iii) The party must undergo structural changes and learn to adapt to the ever changing political dynamics, otherwise their systems may disintegrate.

Notes

1 In order to provide a substantial reflection on the status of intra-party democracy in the party, this assessment was based on five elements of formal party institutions; knowledge of the contents of intra-party democracy; the existence and influence of institutional arrangements in ODM; candidate selection processes in the party; party funding and the theoretical paradigms that inform the party's administration and democratic practice.

2 The study was carried in Kisumu and Siaya Counties of Kenya's Nyanza Province. Non-probability sampling techniques like purposive and 'snowball' sampling were used to select key informants for collection of qualitative data while secondary data was collected from party documents, general review of media reports and commentaries on party activities. The informants were drawn from different backgrounds namely party officials/leaders, party members, the general public and political experts and activists.

Bibliography

Acharya, M. *Why Social Democracy for Nepal*. Nepal: Tankan Prasad Acharya Memorial Foundation and Freiderch Ebert-Stiftung, 2013.

Avnon, D. "Parties Laws in Democratic Systems of Government". *The Journal of Legislative Studies* 1, no. 2 (1995): 283-300.

Babafemi, B. *Raila Odinga: An enigma in Kenyan politics*. Nairobi: Yintab Books, 2006.

Barnes, S.H. "Party Democracy and the Logic of Collective Action". In *Approaches to the Study of Party Organization,* ed. Crotty, W.J. Boston: Allyn and Bacon, 1968.

Basedau, M. and A. Stroh. *Measuring Party Institutionalization in Developing Countries: A new research instrument applied to 28 African political parties*, GIGA Working Papers No. 69, 2008.

Castles, *The Future of Party Government* Vol. 1,1986.

Cohen, A. *Urban Ethnicity.* London: Routledge, 2004.

Cowen, M. & K. Kanyinga "The 1997 Elections in Kenya: The politics of communality and locality". In *Multi Party Elections in Africa*, eds. Cowen, M &L. Liisa. New York: James Curry, 2002.

De Smedt, J. "No Raila, no Peace!' Big man politics and election violence at the Kibera grassroots". *African Affairs* 108, no. 433 (2009): 581-598

Democracies. *Party Politics* 8, no. 1 (2002):5-29.

Diamond, L. and R. Gunther (eds.) *Political Parties and Democracy.* Baltimore, Md: Johns Hopkins University Press, 1994.

Elischer, S. "Do African Parties Contribute to Democracy? Some findings from Kenya, Ghana, and Nigeria", *Africa Spectrum* 43, No 2 (2008): 175-201

Erikson, R.S, & K.L. Tedin. *American Public Opinion.* New York: Longman, 2003.

Freeden, M. *Reassessing Political Ideologies.* London: Routledge, 2001.

Gumbe, L. Strengthening Cord, May 2013.

Habermas, J. *The Theory of Communicative Action*, Volume Two. Boston, MA: Beacon, 1989.

Heywood, A. *Politics*. Palgrave Macmillan U.K, 2002.

Jost, J.T, B.A. Nosek & S.D. Gosling. "Ideology: Its resurgence in social, personality, and political psychology". *Perspect. Psychol. Sci.* 3, (2008b): 126–36

Kadima, D & F. Owuor. "The National Rainbow Coalition". In *The Politics of Party Coalition in Africa*, ed. Kadima, D. South Africa: Konrad Adenaver Foundation, 2006.

Katz, R. and P. Mair. *How Parties Organize.* London, 1994.

Keverenge, S. "Political Party Formation and Alliances: A case of Kenya". A thesis proposal presented to School of Social and Human Studies, Atlantic International University, 2007.

Kuenzi, M. and G. Lambright. "Party System Institutionalization in 30 African Countries". *Party Politics* 7, no. 4 (2001):437-468.

Mair, P. *The West European Party System*, A comprehensive account of parties and party systems in Europe. Oxford: Oxford University Press, 1990.

Mannheim, K. *Ideology and Utopia*. New York: Harvest Books, 1936.

Masime, K and P. Oesterdiekhoff. *Institutionalizing Political Parties in Kenya*. Nairobi: Masime & Oesterdiekhoff Stiffung (FES).

Michels, R. *Political parties: A sociological study of the oligarchic tendencies of modern democracy*. New York: The Free Press, 1962.

Murunga, G. "Ethnicity, Community Relations and Civil Society in Contemporary Kenya: Trends and field experience", *Ufahamu - A Journal of African Studies* 29, no. 2&3 (2003): 1-65.

Mutua, *M. Kenya's Quest for Democracy: Taming Leviathan*, Kampala: Fountain Publishers, 2008.

Ndegwa, S. "Kenya: 'Third time lucky'". *Journal of Democracy* 14, no. 3(2003): 145-158.

Odhiambo, A. "'Seek Ye First the Economic Kingdom': A history of the Luo Thrift and Trading Corporation (LUTATCO) 1945-1956". In *Economic History and Social History of East Africa*, ed. Ogot, B. A. Nairobi: Kenya Literature Bureau, 1976.

Odinga, O. *Not Yet Uhuru*. London: Heinemann, 1967.

Ogot, B.A. *Decolonization and Independence in Kenya*. London: James Curry, 1995.

Oruka, H.O. *Oginga Odinga: His philosophy and beliefs*. Nairobi: Initiative Publishers, 1992.

Panebianco, A. *Political Parties: Organization & power*. Cambridge: New Rochelle, 1988.

Sartori, G. *Parties and Party Systems. A framework for analysis,* Colchester: ECPR Press, 2005.

Scarrow, S.E. *"Politicians Against Parties"*. *European Journal of Political Research,* (1996):298-309.

Throup, D. & C. Hornsby, C. *Multi-Party Politics in Kenya,* USA: Ohio University Press, 1998.

Weissenbach, K. "Political Party Assistance in Transition. The German 'Stiftungen' in sub-Saharan Africa". In *Promoting Party Politics in Emerging Democracies,* eds. Peter Burnell & André Gerrits. Special Issue of Democratization 17, Issue 6 (2010)(forthcoming).

Widner, J. *The Rise of a Party State in Kenya*. Berkeley: University of California, 1992.

Luo Women Voters/Aspirants and the New Constitutional Dispensation in the March 2013 Kenya Elections: The case of Siaya and Kisumu Counties

Mildred A.J. Ndeda [*]

Introduction

Women are slightly over fifty per cent (50%) of world population but occupy only twenty per cent (20%) of political positions. According to Andrea Wikham, they are less than 10% of the world's leaders and of the 193 member states of the UN, only 21 have either a female Head of State or of Government. Hence despite decades of enfranchisement, only a small fraction of political representatives around the world are women (Wickham, 2013). Given this state of affairs it is clear that women's participation in politics as either voters or aspirants is crucial because first and foremost everyone should have the right and opportunity to be a political representative. There are also a number of benefits that could accrue with female participation in politics. For instance given their nature as primary caregivers in households and communities they have the capacity to advocate strongly for both women's and children's issues. Wikham asserts that in countries with more women in parliament and government there is a tendency to have more equitable laws and social programmes and their budgets also tend to benefit women, children and families better (Ibid). Further evidence shows that countries with greater gender equality (in all spheres, labour, politics, education etc.) have higher GNP (Gross National Product) per capita. This is like the impact of women's leadership in the corporate world in terms of improved business performance. Empirical evidence also shows that greater female representation in parliament lowers the level of corruption. As Michelle Bachelet, Executive

* Professor of history at the Department of History of Jaramogi Oginga Odinga University of Science and Technology, Kenya.

Director of UN Women stated: "When more women are leaders, decisions better reflect and respond to the diverse needs of society. As I have learned: When one woman is a leader it changes her. When more women are leaders, it changes politics and policies".[1]

In most African countries, the marginalization of women has continued since pre-colonial and colonial era. As Parpart and Staudt (1989) point out, the state served as a vehicle for elite male interests and in the process enhanced and extended men's power, leaving women with limited avenues for participation in politics. Similarly Chazan (in Parpart and Staudt, 1989) asserts that the state policies towards women remained discriminatory and coercive as a result of which women have played minimal roles in statecraft in Africa. Due to their exclusion, the constitutional and legal status of women's participation in all levels of governance is regarded as key indicator of the level of any country's democracy. The gendered quality of such a country would be marked in its institutions, such as the cabinet, parliament, judiciary, army, and civil service. This exclusion leads to the conclusion that women constitute a historically oppressed and marginalised group despite their value as individuals with creative solutions, contributions and whose concern for cohesiveness in society would contribute to the quality of life (Mama, 1991).

The participation of Kenyan women in leadership and governance has a long history. Since Kenya's independence in 1963, women have tried to effectively participate, alongside men, in governance and decision-making in all aspects of public life. But in the first five decades since independence, progress towards women's access to formal political leadership positions was slow due to structural obstacles which include: the deeply embedded patriarchal socio-cultural values; undemocratic institutions and policy frameworks and low levels of civic and gender awareness.

In 1963 the long-standing issue about gender resurfaced in Kenya with the key question on the role of women in the new political dispensation. Women's issue was captured during the second Lancaster House Conference of 1962 by Priscilla Abwao (2002: 7) who intimated that Kenyan women were "not asking for a special position for ourselves" but that in the new dispensation they would be "treated as equal partners in the new society which we are creating, as well as the endeavours to create that society" (Ibid). But Kenyatta's government did not fundamentally change the colonial system and its structures (Savage and Taylor, 1999: 70) that overlooked women's participation in governance and leadership. That government did not address issues of gender and failed to integrate women's issues into the national agenda. Women were therefore denied the chance to develop initiatives and gain political voice. Instead the political culture of Kenya in the 1960s and 1970s comprised violence, intimidation, detention, and police harassment causing most women to keep off politics (Nasongo and Ayot, 2007: 164-196). The majority only participated as voters, dancers and mobilisers during campaigns/elections, in preparation and distribution of food in meetings and leafleting (Kabira and Wasamba, 1998). Thus, between 1964 and 1969, there was no woman Member of Parliament (MP) in Kenya. In November 1969, the first woman was elected into parliament and one more nominated (Waiyego, 2004). Therefore, of the total number of elected legislators between 1969 and 1974, women formed 0.56% and 5% of nominated members (Ibid).

In the 1970s, public awareness of the importance of women's issues increased, partly fostered by the United Nations Decade for Women (1976-1985) which culminated in the United Nation's

Women Conference in Nairobi in 1985 and other International Women's Conferences (Mexico, Copenhagen and Nairobi Women's Conferences). During that decade the number of women members of the Kenyan parliament increased. Julia Ojiambo became an Assistant Minister for Culture and Social Services, the highest office in the government ever held by a woman since independence. Other women members of parliament included; Phoebe Asiyo, Winfred Nyiva Mwendwa, Grace Onyango, Eddah Gachukia, Jemima Gecaga, Philomena Chelagat Mutai and Anarita Karimi (Wamalwa, 1991: 245-253).

The wave of democratization in the 1990s opened up political spaces and Kenyan women,led by the women's movement seized this political opportunity (Ibid). This period also saw the formation of new gender based lobby groups (Nzomo, 1997: 97) that influenced political parties to integrate gender in their agenda and programmes. But given that Kenya's multi-party politics was characterised by ethnicity (Choti, 2005), most women identified themselves with their communities rather than gender.[7] Despite this, the first multi-party elections in December 1992 still reflected the big effort of the women's movement to empower female voters and candidates. Over 40 women were elected councillors in 1992 as compared to 20 in 1983 while 6 were elected to parliament compared to 2 in 1983.[3] Three years later, in May 1995, Nyiva Mwendwa was appointed to head the Ministry of Culture and Social Services. She was the first female full cabinet minister in independent Kenya.

During the second multi-party elections in 1997 women were more prepared and visible than they had been in 1992 but still only four women were elected to parliament[4] and five were nominated out of a total of 12 seats, which was only 4.0% representation (Ibid). Most women voters at grassroots level remained susceptible to manipulation and this undermined their freedom of choice in the elections. The 2002 elections in Kenya were significant because they were the first transitional elections. The election year was characterised with much political activity and women also engaged in this hence in 2002, 44 women were nominated out of the 1,037 parliamentary candidates. At the local government level, only 380 women were nominated out of the 7,008 candidates competing for a total of 2,093 seats (Ibid).

The overall performance for women in Kenya however, improved during the same period as shown in table 1:

Table 1: Women in parliamentary elections since independence

Women representation in Parliament, 1963-2007 Parliament	Period	Women elected	Women nominated
First	1963-1969	0	0
Second	1969-1974	2	1
Third	1974-1979	6	4
Fourth	1979-1983	5	4
Fifth	1983-1988	3	2
Sixth	1988-1992	2	2
Seventh	1992-1997	7	6

Eighth	1997-2002	9	4
Ninth	2002-2007	10	8
Tenth	2007-2008	16	6
Total	60 37		

Source: Ministry of Gender and Sports, February 2008.

In relations to Table 1, women's performance in parliamentary electoral politics in the first decade of independence was marginal but there was a gradual increase in the number of women MPs up to 2002. 1997 elections were the only exception to this trend marked by a drop in the women's performance in electoral politics (Nzomo, 2003: 17-33). In 1997only nine women were elected out of the 220 members of parliament (MPs) (Njenga, 2007). In the 2002 elections the number of female MPs increased to 18 out of the 222 members of parliament. This still fell below the United Nations target of 30% representation of women in politics and the Beijing Platform for Action (in 1995), where all governments ratified equal participation of women and men in decision-making bodies (Ibid). During the 2007 general elections of the 2,548 candidates fielded 269 (10.56%) were women.[5] Of the 210 elected members of the National Assembly 15 (7.12%) were women.[6] The number of women in the tenth Kenyan parliament was 22 or 9.8 % of the 224 members. Evidently the gender imbalance in Kenya's political playing field continue to widen given that the male political ideology continues to define the standards of evaluation of women's political performance and participation.

In the first General Election under the 2010 Constitution it seemed that the space could be opened for an increased number of women to vie but finally, of the 290 MPs, only 16 women were elected. Granted, the Constitution provides for 47 women representatives from the counties. Women's performance in the 2013 polls cannot be discounted, given that it accounts for some 25 per cent of the 67 women who have been elected to Parliament since 1963.[7] The 11th Parliament, therefore, brings on board the largest number of women to have ever sat in the House. This was an improvement over the previous parliament which had only 9.85% (one of the lowest in the region) but a far cry from the minimum one-third called for in the new constitution. Both the Carter Centre and the European Union's Observer Mission highlighted the disappointing number of women candidates in their preliminary reports on the election.[8] The vast western region of Kenya elected only six of the 16 women MPs – four of them from Rift Valley. Out of the 47 counties, no women were elected as governor or senator. In the 2013 general elections women winners upped the proportion in that body to 64 out of 349 seats or 18.3%.

It raises serious questions about why almost 30 years after Kenya hosted the third UN Conference on Women and nearly two decades after the famed Beijing conference, Kenya continues to perform so poorly in the vital area of women in political leadership. Nyanza and Western provinces performed particularly badly, sending only two women to the National Assembly, namely the former nominated MP Millie Odhiambo, who won the Mbita seat, and newcomer Mary Emaase of Teso South. Even with the guaranteed 47 women representatives, Kenya has not met the constitutional threshold of no more than two-thirds of public office holders being of the same gender and as stated in Kweyu's (2013) article. "...we are far short of the 117 [women required] and we are aware that the House shall be unconstitutional".

Given that women account for slightly over 50 per cent of the voters, why do they continue to lag in elective politics? Why does Kenya lag behind East African Community partners like Tanzania that has 126 women in their 350-member Parliament; Uganda (135 out of 386); Burundi (32 of 105 Lower House and 18 of 41, Upper House); and Rwanda (45 of 80, Lower House and 10 out of 26 Upper House)? Kenyan women have come a long way in penetrating the political male-dominated world. Kenya's political history has recorded great women who went through many difficult and humiliating conditions to fight for equality and participation in politics at both the local and national levels. Thus to respond to these issues a local level situation has been chosen to analyse women as voters and aspirants. The two localities of concern are Kisumu and Siaya counties.

Kisumu County covers an area of 2,085. Sq. Km and has 5 Local Authorities (Municipal Council of Kisumu, County Council of Kisumu, County Council of Nyando, County Council of Muhoroni and Town Council of Ahero) whose administrative capital is Kisumu Town.[9] It is famed for its association with Lake Victoria which contributes a very large part to the economy given its support of the fishing and fish processing industry.[10] Agriculture is also a common economic activity with sugar and rice irrigation industries. Kisumu County borders Vihiga to the North, Nandi County to the North East, Kericho County to the East, Nyamira to the South, Homa Bay to the South West and Siaya to the West. The population of Kisumu is 968,909, (Male – 48.9 %, Female – 51.1 %). The number of constituencies is six (2010) (Kisumu Town East, Kisumu Town West, Kisumu Rural, Muhoroni, Nyando and Nyakach). The registered voters in 2013 were 336, 174. Jack Ranguma, Anyang' Nyong'o, and Rose Nyamunga were elected as governor, senator and women representative, respectively in the Kisumu County during the 2013 elections.

Siaya County on the other hand covers an area of 2,530.5 Sq. Km. It has seven Local Authorities[11] whose administrative capital is Siaya town. It has a population of 842,304 (Male – 47 %, Female – 53 %). The number of Constituencies (2013) is five.[12] The number of registered voters was 285,696. The existing resources include agricultural land, fisheries, indigenous forests; rivers, timber and the main economic activities/industries are subsistence farming, livestock keeping, fishing, rice farming and small-scale business. The elected leaders during the 2013 elections are Cornel Rasanga Amoth (Governor), James Orengo (Senator), and Ombaka Christine Oduor (women representative).

Women and politics in the new constitutional dispensation in Kenya

Until the March 2013 general elections women's political representation stood at 9.8% compared to Rwanda's 56.3%, South Africa 42.3%, Tanzania 36% and Uganda's 35%. However, the new constitution, approved in August 2010, enshrined within it women's rights captured mostly within the Bill of Rights section. The Bill of Rights guarantees the right to equal treatment for women and men.This includes the right to equal opportunities in political, economic, cultural and social spheres; the right to be free from discrimination on the basis of sex and several other characteristics. The Bill of Rights also specifies that "the State shall take legislative and other measures to implement the principle that not more than two-thirds of the members of elective or appointive bodies shall be of the same gender".[13]

The new Constitution had various gains for women in Kenya which included the entrenchment of the principle of Affirmative Action, the 1/3 representation of either gender in elective positions, 47 women each elected by registered voters of the counties, 12 nomination special seats for youth, People With Disabilities and Workers, a third (6) of which would be for Women Representation in the National Assembly (Rugene, 2013). This Constitution (2010) recognizes women's social, economic, cultural and political rights in all institutions of governance including political party structures and other organs of decision making. It has ensured that women would no longer be marginalized in the public arena.

According to this constitution the devolved government must have female representatives for the National Assembly, the Senate and County Assembly. The National Assembly has a total of 349 members i.e. 290 elected members, 47 women county representatives and 12 nominated members. Within the Senate, there are 18 slots for women, 12 nominated by political parties according to their proportion of the Senate, 1 representing youth and 1 People with Disabilities, i.e. 18 women of 67 members is 26.9%. Included are also 7 Members appointed by parliament from among its members of whom at least 2 must be women, 1 nominated by political parties and 1 woman experienced in public affairs but not nominated by Members of Parliament.[14] The County Assembly includes 47 elected members from each of the counties and nominated members appointed by the parties. In fact political parties were required to ensure that for every three party members presented to vie for political office, one had to be a woman, and if she failed to be elected, a woman must be nominated by the party.[15]

Evidently this Constitution opened the space for women to participate in leadership and decision-making, through the provision of minimum gender quotas for all elected and appointed bodies. The use of constitutional or legal quotas has proved effective in advancing women's political participation in regions like the Scandinavia and Latin America. Perhaps that is why Chief Justice Willy Mutunga emphasized: "With this initiative, Kenya joins other countries in the region using constitutionally reserved seats to enhance women's political participation". These new provision were put to the test during the March 2013 general elections.

Despite these provisions, the previous parliament failed to pass measures to implement the principle that at least 117 (one third of the 349 seats) members of the new parliament would be women and instead voted to delay the implementation until 2015. Although logically the goal seemed unattainable while still maintaining the rights of political parties, candidates and voters, this was a disappointment for Kenyan women.[16] Moreover while the constitution allowed for nomination of women through the party list only a few political parties had entrenched the criteria for nominating women and determining their ranking on the party list by the time of the March 2013 elections. The process of deciding who to include in the party list could easily be abused by party officials by selecting their cronies or accepting favours as a basis for inclusion and ranking on the party lists. It was therefore significant for parties to develop rules and regulations for identifying and nominating deserving persons to the party lists. Otherwise political parties would face many disputes if inclusion on the party lists is not participative and/ or seen to be fair.

The 4 March 2013 election implemented the devolved government defined in the constitution through a new county structure. Some power and resources thus shifted from a centralized national government to the new 47 counties. However since the elections the power shift has been contested vehemently by the various centres of power. Each county has a governor, a county assembly with representatives from each ward, and a senator in the newlycreated national Senate. Seven women candidates vied for a governorship in an effort to make history as the first governors of their respective counties and all were defeated. In the Senate race, all 19 women candidates seeking to be among the 47 elected to the House lost their contests.[17] About 300 women competed for the 47 seats reserved for them in the counties, while 156 battled for constituency parliamentary seats against male opponents.[18] This was a sharp fall on the 269 who contested the last ballot in 2007. A total of 16 women were elected as Members of the National Assembly in the general elections despite a myriad of challenges to their candidatures.

Most of the women elected to the 11th parliament were in the Jubilee alliance and they included Rachael Nyamai (Kitui South), Joyce Laboso (Sotik), Mary Wambui (Othaya), Grace Kipchoim (Baringo South), Mary Emase (Teso South), Alice Wahome (Kandara), Naomi Shabaan (Taveta), Cecile Mbarire (Runyenjes), Terris Tobiko (Kajiado East), Esther Murugi (Nyeri Town), Alice Wambui (Thika Town) and Esther Gathogo (Ruiru). Those elected through the CORD Coalition included Millie Odhiambo (Mbita), Jessica Nduku (Kibwezi East), and Regina Ndambuki (Kilome).

Some of the hurdles that faced women in the 2013 elections included social culture. It was perhaps the greatest setback given Kenya's patriarchal society with most communities still clinging to the traditional perception that men are leaders with women portrayed as lacking vital leadership qualities. Such long-standing cultural beliefs have been held by men and women alike. The colonial system with its patriarchal tendencies strengthened the African structures by introducing the public and domestic sector that emphasised women' domain as the domestic sphere particularly in the rural areas while men became part and parcel of the public sphere where they were used as labourers in the urban and settled areas. Colonialism thus dictated that women's place was in the home and were therefore not expected to indulge in activities that removed them from the domestic sphere, and women who were considered independent women created by the very system through the process of urbanisation and schooling, who tribal associations sought to control. This paradigm has been used by male chauvinists to frustrate women's efforts to aspire for political leadership. Such stereotypes have specifically been used to lock women candidates out of parliament. Many Kenyan communities, including the Luo, still believe that men should lead and so men have control over all social, political and economic spheres. Even among the more educated and cosmopolitan youth, these attitudes are deeply engrained. As one aspirant Risper Akinyi Pete who contested for Deputy Governor's seat in Kisumu County noted, "Stereotypes that women cannot lead still reigns in the region and a time has come that this must be changed in order to achieve vision 2030. Emerging from a region where men are believed to be the only leaders, it is hard to win the confidence of the electorate to vote for women" (Gwengi, 2013). Any woman who goes to the contrary is viewed as rebellious, one of loose morals and is often alienated by the community.

Culture change does not happen overnight. With passage of the new constitution it is clear that Kenyans' vision for the future includes greater gender equity. For women who vied for political office it is painfully clear that implementation of that vision is a distant reality. As one woman observed, Women were disadvantaged in the concluded elections because of cultural barriers and financial constraints to mount campaigns. There was also propaganda used by some male aspirants to the effect that women should not be given positions because they had the women representative seat.

She added that since political parties in Kenya are ethnic based instead of ideological, some women, new to politics, started their campaigns too late because of confusion over the political parties to run on. Combining politics and 'child-rearing'/family life has also been a challenge because most women cannot balance both private and public life. Women candidates, running campaigns and shouldering domestic responsibility are particularly overworked and likely to burn out in addition.

Apart from society's negative attitude towards women's leadership, the financial resources required to launch a competitive campaign automatically exclude many women from participation. The financial constraints that many women interested in politics face compared to their male counterparts bar them from contesting, thereby making their political potentials go unnoticed.[19] But even for those women able to pay the prohibitive nomination fee, a host of other hurdles present themselves (Gathigah, 2013). A member of the E.U. Observer Mission mentioned in a newspaper interview that all female candidates indicated campaign financing was a significant issue. They received little or no support from their political parties. Additionally, a spokesperson for the Coalition of Violence against Women in Kenya argued that "the risk to women in the search for public office was still very high".[20]

Their financial constraints began with qualification for the party nominations, which required payment of the equivalent of 1,700 dollars. In addition to this, finances are crucial in political campaigns at all levels. A campaign team right from the preliminary levels needs transport(getting vehicles, fuelling them to facilitate mobility, and branding), food, regalia and insignia that profile the candidate. They also need t-shirts, pens, pencils and caps. Running a campaign in a rural constituency is very expensive since the constituencies are huge and not well served by roads, telephones, electricity and other infrastructure available in the urban areas. Then there are the expectations for hand-outs from the electorate. According to Achieng', hand-outs given by politicians will always create a lot of insecurity and economic constraints: "It is unwise to exchange one's vote for as little as KSh. 50. We should think of long term issues".

Awuor who was running for the senatorial seat in Siaya responded to the challenges she would face as follows:

> The biggest challenge I see is probably not having the needed financial resources to get me to be able to get my message to all expected 400,000 plus voters. The other challenge some people have told me several times is that I'm going to fight Oburu and Orengo who are said to be unbeatable and the favourites. The challenge in this case is not these two candidates but to get the voters to understand that the elections are not about the two leaders but about them. To understand that I'm not interested in fighting the two candidates and that my energy will be directed toward fighting poverty, hunger, illiteracy and diseases in Siaya County and Kenya. The other challenge is that as a woman many say this is impossible. The best thing that ever happened is to see the Mission Impossible movies. Every step I make I approach it knowing this is not an easy task. I approach it knowing they are tasks that have to be done for the families whose children do not get secondary education to aspire to be like these men and have to get education that these men have not provided them the last 5 years. In one year after election I will lead the goal for all children in Siaya and Kenya to have 12 years of education.[21]

The political parties' structures are also male-dominated and therefore discriminative against women. It becomes challenging for women to voice themselves or to take leading positions. Most of the parties nominate men to vital positions during elections meaning that limited numbers of women politicians hit the campaign trails and those few who do so rarely address public rallies because such campaign rallies are often male-dominated.[22]

Given that an individual's education level is a crucial determinant to one's engagement and participation in a democratic process, the women's inability to read and write has been one of their weakest points.[23] Some communities have also failed to educate the girl child; she is often married off early as the boy child goes to school. Consequently, most women are not just ignorant of their rights and what belongs to them but they are also not economically empowered. Such ill-educated women grow up with the mentality that generally women are not good enough hence it becomes impossible for a woman bearing such perceptions to support another qualified woman, including voting for her.

Media coverage on the successes of women politicians and potential contenders is limited compared to their male counterparts. Women politicians expressed various challenges that they faced when dealing with the media. According to Media and Communication specialists from Maseno University Naomi Senda, women felt discriminated by the media because they often did not understand the operations of the media. Moreover for the aspirants to gain the confidence of the media they needed to package their message well. However, women expressed fears that their opponents sometimes used media to destroy them. They also noted that media sometimes solicited money from aspirants in order to publish or broadcast stories (Gwengi, 2013).

Few women in Kenya harbour illusions of entering politics due to widespread use of violence. Given that a great deal of the election outcome is determined by bribery, outright hostilities, harassment, intimidation, blatant discrimination, threats and intimidations, an uneven playing field and a largely unsympathetic public, women invariably fail to secure the kind of support that is won through violence (both physical and psychological) and coercion (Gathigah, 2013). Moreover, men campaign and lobby at night. A woman is not expected to do so hence a woman aspirant might go to bed thinking that her position in the party is secure, only to wake up to new realities in the morning after men have kept their night vigils. Women who defy these political traditions face threats of rape, and other forms of bodily harm, verbal abuse and derogatory words. This violence on the campaign period and Election Day made many potential women candidates to keep off politics.[24] There were instances when the candidates were attacked together with their supporters. In some cases the supporters were even raped (Oywa and Wangui, 2007:6). Violence against women in the Western region of Kenya is rampant even without the elections. It is only enhanced during the elections.

Professor Jacqueline Oduol, a former aspirant, described the negative judgements made when women moved into the often judgmental public eye of politics. She said, "You will be made ridiculous. You will be made invisible, and you will be burdened with guilt and shame. Expect double punishment, and to have information withheld from you".[25] Women politicians also alluded to this when they stated that the campaign period was most challenging and most unpleasant part of the electoral process because that was when their femininity and gender identity was questioned. For example women candidates were questioned not on their ability or capacity to lead but on their moral aptness for political office. For women the focus would be on their marital status, sexuality, to the whereabouts of their children and husbands. Marital status is an issue commonly used for penalizing women in politics worldwide. As one American Senator, Barbara Mikulski, lamented, women who run for office can never win on this issue "If you are married, you were neglecting him. If you were widowed, you killed him. If you were divorced, you did not keep him. And if you were single, you couldn't get a husband anyway" (Branden, 1996: 6 in Choti, 2005). The Kenyan Human Rights Commission documented examples of "youth shouting obscenities at women [candidates], manhandling them, and tearing their clothes, stones being thrown". They further stated that those who support the women candidates also faced intimidation and sometimes "their husband's wrath".[26]

Male-dominated parties interfered with the political space offered to women by Article 81(b) which stipulates that not more than two-thirds of the members of elective public bodies shall be of the same gender. This means that environment of the 2013 elections was still not enabling because women remained under attack from male opponents and even society. When Vesca Kangongo presented her bid to vie for the gubernatorial seat in Uasin Gishu County in Kenya's Rift Valley region, her rivals swore that the governor of the region "would be anything but a woman".[27] This statement was echoed across the country and consequently only a handful of women run for tickets of top seats.

The culture of violence and rigged elections has persistently interfered with women's participation in electoral politics, especially in Nyanza. Because of retrogressive cultural practices, the two Gusii counties of Kisii and Nyamira have never elected a woman to Parliament since independence. And in Luo Nyanza, no woman has been elected MP between 1997 and 2012, a situation attributed to violence during party nominations and elections. The fear of violence and lack of resources and voter education had conspired to ensure that only five women were running for the various positions in Siaya County. This was evident when a majority of the men who spoke to the House Committee on Implementation of the Constitution in Siaya, Migori and Homa Bay on ways to ensure election of more women in the 4 March elections opposed the gender balance requirement. They stated to the committee chaired by Mandera Central MP Abdikadir Mohamed in Homa Bay that "Women are yet to show by action that they are capable leaders beyond verbally saying that 'they can",[28] Mrs Margaret Omondi, who sought the ODM endorsement for the Ugenya parliamentary seat, wanted the party leadership to "walk the talk" and support women leaders by ensuring clean nominations free of violence. Mrs Omondi, a former Nairobi director of education, and secretary-general of the Kenya National Commission for UNESCO, was pitted against Mr Steve Mwanga, lawyer David Ochieng and businessman Chris Karan.[29]

Women had the potential to utilize their numerical advantage and mobilization skills at the community level to garner seats as MPs, Governors, Senators and County assembly representatives in the general elections.[30] One of the challenges was the type of information that grassroots leaders had, for instance that women could only vie for the reserved women representative seats and not for the competitive and the 'most-eyed' seats for governors, senators and county assembly representatives. It can be stated that the power play and the yearning for resource control in the political parties which are controlled by men made it hard for women members. This led to apathy among voters who lacked interest and concern on issues relating to women and surprisingly these also included women who are sometimes viewed as their own enemies. Voters have not made the situation any better. On the campaign trail they demanded bribes which made it difficult to address the real issues. Such rural women continue to be viewed as housekeepers and homemakers by their societies and the thought of them leading is 'absurd'.

In the light of these challenges what can be done for women? According to Anne Njenga the success of women in politics in Rwanda, Liberia, Sweden and South Africa shows that there are many strategies women can use to gain power. She states that women in Kenya could call for the implementation of affirmative action to increase their participation in decision-making bodies and should also unite and actively participate in nation-building activities.[31]

One of the most tried and tested ways of increasing women's participation in the political arena is quotas. Quotas can be effective at three levels (Wickham, 2013). The first level is political candidacy – quota systems at this level mandate that from the pool of aspirants, a certain portion must be female. The second level is nomination – quotas (either legal or voluntary) ensure that a certain percentage of nominated candidates on a political party's ballot must be female. The third level is election – certain seats in a political body are 'reserved' and can only be filled by women (Ibid).

Wickham further intimates that the nations that rank top in terms of female representation in government use some form of quota system to ensure female participation. Rwanda is a striking example of such nations. In 1995, Rwanda was ranked 24th in the world in terms of female representation but in 2003, after introducing a quota system it took first position. Countries such as Argentina, Iraq, Burundi, Mozambique, and South Africa have also experienced similar improvements in the participation of women. Although quotas have their shortcomings given the huge barriers to women's participation in the public sphere, quotas alone can close such gaps as one of the simplest ways to begin to level the playing field. However their effectiveness may also be determined by the improvements in education for girls and women, better access to healthcare and childcare for mothers and families.

Without taking quotas into account the creation of Women's Rep positions in Kenya might mean that women will tend to vie for that position and are therefore less likely to compete for other roles. This trend can only be averted with the creation of support programmes that tackle issues of culture, access and education.The quota system should be merged with the increase in confidence for women and transformation of cultural features that have led to the subordination of women. It may be of particular importance that all the features of the modified electoral system was understood and party leaders equipped on how to implement some new provisions in the constitution and legislation. Effective voter contact strategies needed to be taken into account with the candidates and managers, to ensure that each team understood the importance of voter identification and conducting other related activities prior to Election Day. Hence the 2013 quota system had counterproductive effect because apart from the women representative vote and nominations, the number of women aspirants was lower than in 2007.

With all of these gains in store for women of Kisumu and Siaya counties and given that the 2010 Constitution was not yet fully implemented, were women and particularly at the grassroots aware of the opportunities presented? Did they know how they could be vigilant and proactive in the monitoring and implementation processes, which would have made it possible for women to win by their votes? But what was the opinion of grass roots women voters regarding women participation in leadership and the barriers to women's running for office? Would women vote fellow women? Were there risks that women would face? Were the campaigns of women leaders issue-based, especially around performance, accountability and delivery of services that impact on the welfare and empowerment of the most vulnerable sectors in their communities?

Women voters and aspirants in the 2013 Elections in Kisumu and Siaya counties

Before the 2013 elections it was common knowledge that Nyanza and Western provinces had the highest number of women who had declared interests in various elective positions, which included vying for senator and governor for their respective counties. This was reiterated just before the 2013 general elections by Leo Odera Omollo[32] when he reported the possibility that more women leaders in Nyanza would contest the elections against seasoned male politicians. He stated that for the first time in Kenya's political history Luo-Nyanza witnessed several high profile women leaders take their men compatriots in several parliamentary, senate, county and civic positions during the March 2013 general elections. A new political dimension, which seemed to favour women representatives, was slowly cropping up. The ground seemed to be getting fertile and yawning for a change in favour of women over men.

Among these women was the Nominated MP Millie Odhiambo who was aspiring to be the MP for Mbita; Adhiambo Odinga (sister to Prime Minister Raila Odinga) aspiring to be Kisumu governor; Agnes Awuor (a former Nun) the aspiring senator in Siaya County; and Professor Collete Suda, a senatorial candidate for Migori county. The women leaders in the region who appeared to be the favourites of the electorate included those who had excelled in the academic fields, past exemplary services to the community.

The women leaders tipped to clinch seats included Mrs Rose Buyu – a Nairobi based business woman who in 2007 gave the incumbent Kisumu Town West MP John Olago Aluoch a run for his money and almost ousted the outspoken Kisumu lawyer. Popularly referred to by her peers as "Dwasi" (female cow) Buyu seemed favoured to win the election in the newly realigned Kisumu Town West, which covered most parts of Kisumu rural locations, and which exclude Kisumu Central constituency which covered the Central Business Distinct (CBD) and peri-urban areas of Nyalenda, Pand-Pieri, Airport, Kibuye, Industrial Areas and Milimani Estate.

The newly created Kisumu Central constituency did not seem to favour the incumbent John Olago Aluoch. The MP was also a stranger in the choice to defend his seat in Kisumu Town West constituency due to several factors. Although actively participating in parliamentary debates and contributing a lot on most issues of national importance, Aluoch appeared to have burned the bridges between him and the Town's population, especially those who voted for him in 2007. He was blamed for having favoured non-indigents and appeared to have side-lined members of the indigent Jo-Kisumu people. He also faced myriad of accusations that he had filled all the important posts in the CDF (Constituency Development Fund) with outsiders, especially people from Southern Nyanza and Siaya regions.

Mrs Buyu hailed from around Holo market in Kisumu West location and was a member of the influential family of the late Mr Radiak, a former sales and marketing manager with the Kenya Breweries Limited. Her home of birth is Sakwa, Bondo and her late father, Mzee Patrick Onyango Ochang' was not only a close friend of the late Jaramogi Oginga Odinga, but also one of the first African pioneers in big businesses in Kisumu City long before independence.Due to their long-standing family tie with the Odingas dating back to 1950s she was commonly referred to as the Prime Minister Raila Odinga's sister. By the time of the elections she had made major inroad in nearly all the rural locations, turning up with hefty donations during fund drives for important community socio-economic projects but despite all her effort she did not clinch the seat.

Kisumu County had a number of women vying for various positions. Kisumu County also lead in the number of women who showed interest in the governor's seat. This seat attracted three women aspirants who sought the Orange Democratic Movement (ODM) ticket, namely Ruth Adhiambo Odinga, Atieno Otieno, a lawyer, and agriculturalist Rhoda Otieno Ahonobadha. No woman showed interest in the senator's seat (Ouko, 2012). The following women competed at the nomination level: Women Representatives Kisumu (3): Rose Nyamunga, Anyango Millicent Abundho, and Dorine A. Atieno; National Assembly Kisumu County (7); Kisumu East Constituency (2): Mary Atieno Anyango, and Irene Odhiambo; Kisumu West Constituency (2): Caren Atieno Amonde, and Rosa Buyu; Kisumu Central Constituency (0); Seme Constituency (0); Nyando Constituency (1): Mary Odhiambo; Muhoroni Constituency (0); Nyakach Constituency (2): Anyango Pollyns Ochieng', and Olive Achieng Okal; County Reps Kisumu (16): Mary Odhiambo, Monica Aluoch, Farina, Millicent A. Mbadi, Caren A. Wema, Mary A. Mbula, Felgona A. Otieno, Monica Aluoch, Rose A. Juma, Lynette C.A. Muga, Pamella A. Milama, Millicent A. Adino, Pamella A. Omino, Priscah A. Misachi, Rose Akinyi Ngutu, and Farida A. Salim. Their entry into the political arena would have diminished the mentality that Kenyans seem to have of women leadership and encourage more women to come out in big number to join politics. However it is unfortunate that women often become their own worst enemies and pull down what they are supposed to nurture and protect.

The race for election of the first Siaya County women representative attracted a host of aspirants, but only three won party nominations and subsequently cleared by the Electoral Commission to run. However, according to Action Aid that hosted a workshop for women aspirants in the county, 53 women were interested in elective politics. Two of these women had shown interest in the governor's seat but only one survived the race for a while.[33]

Siaya also had her fair share of female aspirants. The following contested in various capacities: Governor Siaya (2): Nellie Okwiri, and Monica Oduor; Senator Siaya (1);Women Rep Siaya (2): Omwamba Violet, and Emilly Awita; National Assembly (5); Ugenya Constituency (3): Omondi Jane Damarice, Mary Apiyo Omondi, and Jane Omondi; Ugunja Constituency (0); Alego Usonga Constituency (1): Maslister A. Oudia; Gem Constituency (0); Bondo Constituency (0); Rarieda Constituency (1): Benter Opande; County Representatives Siaya (13): Dosline Nyakore, Grace A. Otieno, Dolrosa E. Otieno, Margaret A. Achola, Rosemary A. Ogutu, Mildred D. Atieno, Jessica A. Oluoch, Sylvia A. Migaya, Jael A. Jaoko, Dolly Edith Otieno, Rose Angule, Lilian A. Arigi, and Nadhifa Y. Hamisi.

In Siaya, Awuor faced Lands Minister James Orengo and Finance Assistant Minister Oburu Oginga. She made it clear that "she is the bridge to the change for which Siaya County has been yearning." Awuor, with her doctorate in political science, seemed to have what it took to join the non-level playing field but before she knew it she was out of the contest. When Agnes Awuor Ogeng'o was asked, 'why do you want to represent Siaya County in the Senate? She responded:

> I want to represent Siaya because I believe and I am convinced that Siaya County is in need of new leadership. I believe we need new ideas and a new debate. We cannot continue with stories of corruption and public funds that could have benefited many in Siaya had they been used wisely. When I look at Siaya community I see people with drive, focus, purpose and energy but lacking the right leadership. The few years I have been blessed to be abroad have opened my mind to see things better and more clearly and I feel it is my duty to give back to my community through service. Lastly Siaya is a great county with a great history, a great people which can be shaped to have better schools, better hospitals and better modern settlements.[34]

Women county representatives for Siaya and Kisumu who won were Ombaka Christine Oduor, and Rose Auma Nyamunga. There was only one woman elected Member of Parliament (MP) in Nyanza region namely Millie Akoth Odhiambo of Mbita. In Mbita constituency, she took part in the race against her close cousin Phares Ogweno Ratego, an executive with an NGO in Nairobi. Odhiambo who had made a name for herself as a firebrand and formidable debater in the tenth Parliament was one of Prime Minister Raila Odinga's troop soldiers. Her rising popularity with youths and women in Mbita could have caused the Immigration and Registration of Persons Minister Gerald Otieno Kajwang' packing to contest for the Homa-Bay County Senate seat instead of defending his Mbita parliamentary seat which he had held since 1997. The election battle between Odhiambo and Ratego in Mbita was one of the toughest election ever witnessed in the area featuring two prominent members of one family.

In the parliament that ended by March 2013, there was no elected female MP from Luo Nyanza. In Luo Nyanza, politics for long remained the preserve of men. The only Luo woman elected in the tenth parliament was Elizabeth Ongoro and this came through Kasarani – a metropolitan constituency in Nairobi – while Millie Odhiambo was an ODM nominatedMP. Given such circumstances the recurring question was whether women politicians from Luo Nyanza would break the jinx and emerge victorious selected MPs in the 2013 elections. Was patriarchy at the forefront of hindering Luo women from holding positions of power, and specifically parliamentary power?

A close analysis of women participation in politics in Luo Nyanza showed that the last time the Luo community elected a woman MP wasin 1992 when Phoebe Asiyo became Karachuonyo Member of Parliament in the first multi-party elections on a FORD-Kenya ticket then under Jaramogi Oginga Odinga. Before that she was also elected MP in 1979 and 1988. After her retirement in 1996, there was no elected female MP from Luo Nyanza until 2013 general elections. During the 1997 elections, all MPs from the region were men and the same trend repeated in 2002 and 2007 elections.

As already indicated since independence, Luo Nyanza had only been represented by three women, namely Grace Ogot (Gem), Grace Onyango (Kisumu) and Phoebe Asiyo (Karachuonyo). There are a composite of reasons behind poor ratings of women parliamentary aspirants in Luo Nyanza. The first major reason is the observation that women have always been considered world over as their own enemies in other words they do not vote for their own gender. It has been evident in Kenyan politics that women rarely vote for fellow women. The majority of women in the region prefer voting for male aspirants because they believe parliament and politics is a male preserve. This mind set is advised by patriarchy, a social system in which the male is the primary authority figure central to social organization and the central roles of political leadership, moral authority, and control of property, and where fathers hold authority over women and children. It implies the institutions of male rule and privilege, and entails female subordination.

Historically, patriarchy has manifested itself in the social, legal, political, and economic organisation of a range of different cultures. The term was used to refer to autocratic rule by the male head of a family. However, in modern times, it more generally refers to social systems in which power is primarily held by adult men.

All forms of feminism define patriarchy as an unjust social system that is oppressive to women. As feminist and political theorist Carole Pateman writes, "(t)he patriarchal construction of the difference between masculinity and femininity is the political difference between freedom and subjection" (Pateman, 1988: 207). In feminist theory, the concept of patriarchy often includes all the social mechanisms that reproduce and exert male dominance over women. Feminist theory typically characterizes patriarchy as a social construction, which can be overcome by revealing and critically analysing its manifestations (Tickner, 2001: 1197-8). Thus feminists define it as a gendered power system and a network of social, political and economic relationships through which men dominate and control female labour, reproduction and sexuality as well as define women's status, privileges and rights in a society. It is a successful system because those who gain this privilege are often unaware of it and therefore inadvertently perpetuate the ill treatment of the people in this society whose suffering is the fulcrum upon which this society turns.

The argument here is that the patriarchal nature of the Luo has shaped and perpetuated gender inequality to the extent of allowing male domination and female subordination in all sectors including politics. This has been fuelled by the socialization process hence to amend the situation may require re-socialisation process. Patriarchy must be seen as social construction and women must also learn how culture imprisons them. The majority have accepted the statusquo and simply recognize politics as a dirty game requiring tough qualities which, according to them, women lack. Only if such attitudes are dismantled can women aspirants continue the struggle for representation and the women voters to actually vote in women.

Secondly, there is the problem of high-level poverty amongst women which interferes with their participation in politics as aspirants. As women voters they are easily bribed by rich candidates. The problem of buying of voter's cards by agents of unpopular but wealthy male candidates has made it impossible for female aspirants from the region to win elections. In Luo Nyanza, few women have the kind of financial resourcestodishtothepoor. The politics of gonya, which means "pay me" or "release me with some cash", has always worked negatively for female aspirants. The youth always demand payments before casting their votes under the pretext that once MPs clinch their parliamentary seats, they quickly retreat and do no longer interact with the public. The gonya concept was rampant in the 2013 campaigns and some campaigners were held hostages until they gave money to those who attended their meetings. Women voters in Rarieda for example moved from one campaign meeting to another because of the expectation to get some cash from the aspirants. This means that women voters voted for reasons other than the appropriateness of the vying politician for the specific post.

The third determinant of success is the placement of the individual in the politically correct party. Luo Nyanza has been a one-party region since the reintroduction of multiparty elections in 1992. In 1992 Ford Kenya was the correct party to vie from in Luo Nyanza then in 1997 it was National Democratic Party, in 2002 it was Liberal Democratic Party (LDP) and ODM in 2007. Anybody contesting in a party ticket perceived to be incorrect never even got opportunity to hold campaign rallies. It is only in 2013 that it was possible for candidates from other parties within the Coalition for Reforms and Democracy (CORD) to vie. Still this means there were other party tickets that would not be acceptable in Nyanza.

Another key problem has been the male-dominated party nominations' fiasco in Nyanza. In the 2007 elections, in Luo Nyanza, women aspirants had to migrate to smaller and peripheral political parties in order to receive nomination certificates for elections after they were locked out in ODM nominations. The consequence of such a move is that women aspirants lost voter hype and attention when they moved to small parties which lacked popularity in the region. In the 2007 elections, no female aspirant was nominated to run on an ODM ticket, leading some determined female aspirants to contest in other parties and ended up with dismal performance. Such female candidates included Monica Amolo (Ndhiwa), Elizabeth Ogolla (Rangwe), Esther Dwalo (Rangwe), Consolata Yambo (Gwassi), Agnes Okong'o (Rongo), and Rosa Buyu (Kisumu Town West). This means that the 2013 general elections were keenly watched in relations to the position and participation of women. Moreover it was the first election after the 2010 Constitution opened political and other spaces for women. Luo Nyanza was again dominated by ODM with only a few people migrating to other parties but within the CORD Alliance. Would women be given a chance to win parliamentaryseatsandreap from what was previously a male domain? Evidently women did get the chance to vie, but in Siaya and Kisumu only the two women representatives got the chance.

The basis for the political advancement and better representation of women is there. Women make up some 60 per cent of the voting population in Kenya which surely should provide a platform from which more women can reach elected positions. But it was uncertain whether all had registered as voters and whether those registered would actually vote in the 2013 election. Whether registered or not in the countdown to the 4 March 2013 elections, it was obvious that women would get into that polling booth and vote for men only in all the various positions. The bothersome question is the motivation behind women voting for men.

Luo women voters responded to situations in a similar manner to their male counterparts as reported by Gemma Jones, anthropologist, and J. Omondi, candidate for ward representative in rural Luo land.[35] They state that during the nominations for the 2013 general elections in Nyanza for the ODM primaries, a new Luo saying was coined in the village: Okbichaloni, or 'things are not what they seem to you". Specifically, this refers to the idea of being thoroughly convinced that your understanding of a situation is clear and correct, yet finding in the final reckoning that tables have turned. The villagers were simply intimating that everyone would be affected by this okbichaloni at some point. The primaries were marred by disorganization, constantly changing deadlines and rumours of dirty tricks by some candidates. And there was general despondency even among the villagers including women. However on the election date the voter turnout proved that people were committed to voting. With this village buzzword in mind, Omondi recalled an occurrence on his campaign trail.While on his way home on the day preceding the primaries, Omondi, with his ODM party cap on, was stopped by a group of women. They greeted him with pomp and grandeur with "go sigala gala" – a celebratory cry – clapping and dancing. They presented to him their developmental issues (lack of water, matches, and small business opportunities) which culminated in their promise to vote for him because of his favourable leadership qualities. One woman inquired about his polices to which he retorted that "(s)ince you will vote for me I will give everyone here a lot of money that is my policy". Whereas most of the women accepted this, one challenged him that in spite of financial provisions he still needed to have a plan for the future. At this point, Omondi revealed that he was aware that this group was not expecting or waiting for him because this village was not part of his ward and they were actually not familiar with each other. This was a group of women merely interested in the finances Omondi could give as a result of their seemingly verbal commitments. Omondi gave the women food for thought when he stated: "Someone like me could be your husband or son. What if they were running because they see a need and they want to help? When you lie to them, it is the same as those politicians you complain of who fail to fulfil their election promises". He was basically stating that the women were made of the same stuff as those they chose to lead them and that for them political expediency caused them to seek money under any pretext.

Evidently there were many different motivations for voting, which only become clear in hindsight and perhaps not even then. He concluded that discussion about policy and other issues was more of an entertainment gimmick during the campaign process. This idea was reinforced when he saw those who had sworn to vote for him lining up behind their clan-man during the aborted primaries. There are possibilities that money extensively determined who was voted for and this implied that even a "settler" in the area (non-indigene) or a mad man could be voted in if he had the cash supply. But it also turned out to be about loyalties and wrangles at the level of clan, sub-clan and even family. Evidently both men and women failed to see the intersection between voting and area development. The phrase okbichaloni has ever more resonance. Things never quite look what you think they are. From afar, this portrays a bizarrelywarped image of the day-to-day life of ordinary Kenyans. In this, the villagers coining the term okbichaloni to describe the ever-changing election story seem miles ahead in their thinking. Perhaps the women aspirants were also not expecting what they got because at the back of the mind of the women voters this concept ran strong and they were not going to break the Luo patriarchy to vote women into leadership. Women are normally the bearers of culture and for cultural change to occur women must be transformed in their thinking patterns. Patriarchy is one of the core features of Luo culture and therefore cannot be changed during the electioneering period. It is a long-term task for both men and women to undertake with great commitment before the election process will have a mixture of genders vying and winning.

Conclusion

Although Kenya is a democracy with a vibrant civil society, which holds periodic and predictable, at times, controversial elections, Kenya's performance on women's representation has been dismal. Women have not fared well in elective politics in the successive post-colonial General Elections since 1963. Kenya's first parliament did not have even a nominated women representative. Although Mrs Grace Onyango would be elected in the second General Election, in 1969, to represent Kisumu town constituency, women have not fared well in the successive General Elections, despite the increasing number of women candidates for both civic and parliamentary seats.

The Constitution of Kenya 2010 spelt out a new dawn of gender equality. The implementation of the one-third gender principle was requisite for this equality to become a reality. But this gender principle was not implemented in the March 2013 elections. The national Assembly which had 16 women elected out of 290 members was well below the one-third rule. Moreover after the elections the failure to implement the principle has slowed down the gains of women. To date assessment of most appointments made demonstrates that the government is slow in attaining the one-third threshold.

Perhaps two main reasons accounts for women's exclusion from higher elective offices: Kenya's patriarchal culture and electoral system. Kenya's political contests requires an enormous outlay of social capital, yet the processes of economic, cultural and political capital accumulation still favour men more than women. Moreover, the electoral system has not only engendered an overly adversarial political contest, but also a violence-prone electioneering, which favour men. Kisumu and Siaya counties are but a reflection of most of Kenya.

Notes

1   Remarks by UN Women Executive Director Michelle Bachelet at the Australian Parliament House, Australia, August 23, 2012. More at: http://www.unwomen.org/en/news/stories/2012/8/un-women-executive-director-michelle-bachelet-addresses-parliamentarians-in-australia/#sthash.TSK1K1wq.dpuf

2   Weru, G. "Special Report" *Daily Nation*, Nairobi Kenya, August 23, 1995 AWC, "A Journey of Courage"

3   Ibid.

4   The 200 members House.

5   Women's Shadow Parliament—Kenya 2008, 9; Commonwealth Observation Mission 2008, 16.

6   Women's Shadow Parliament—Kenya 2008, 9.

7   Kweyu, D. "Why Kenyan Women Perfom Below Par in Elective Politics", *The Nation,* March 23, 2013.

8   Ossmann, K. *Kenyan Elections 2013: Peaceful Prevention and Community Reporting Project*

9   Dane, L. Risks more *Kisumu County Facts and Details,* My Aspirant my Leader: your County edition.

10 Ibid.

11 Town Councils of Bondo, Ukwala, Ugunja, Yala, county councils of Siaya and Bondo and Municipal Council of Siaya.

12 Alego-Usonga, Ugunja, Bondo, Gem, Rarieda and Ugenya.

13 Ossmann, op.cit.

14 Rugene, N. "Record number of women".

15 Ibid.

16 Ossmann, op.cit.

17 Ibid.

18 Rugene, op. cit.

19 Njenga, op.cit.

20 Ossmann,op.cit.

21 Awour, "Senate Aspirant of Siaya & Diaspora Representative Speaks!", July 30, 2012, Jamhuri Team.

22 Njenga, op.cit.

23 AWC, A Journey of Courage

24 See also Jabatiso, J. "Women candidates fall to gender bias", *East African Standard,* December 27, 1997.

25 (CREAWs UN Women project and launch of the updated Women Candidates in Kenya training manual)

26 Ossmann, op.cit.

27 Gathigah, M. "Women Navigate Political Minefield".

28 Njeri, "Women aspirants".

29 Ibid.

30 It should be noted that during the 2010 referendum women electoral registration was lower in Nyanza in comparison with high level in Central (Kikuyu) provinces.

31 Njenga, op.cit.

32 Leo Odera Omolo, "Kenya: More women leaders in Nyanza will contest the March 2013 general elections", *blog.jaluo.com/*?p=27502 in Kisumu City.

33 *Standard Digital,* Thursday February 14, 2013. - See more at: http://www.sierraleonetimes.com/index.php/sid/212577633/cat/c1ab2109a5bf37ec#sthash.bsW8U5Hd.dpuf

34 Awour, op.cit..

35 *Gemma Jones, anthropologist and J. Omondi,* Kenya Decides 2013 – Part 3 – Aborted primaries muddy the local elections in rural Kenya. http://ruvr.co.uk/2013_03_05/Kenyan-election-politics-or-tribalism/ https://www.youtube.com/watch?v=JnlMcQ_6uQg

Bibliography

Abwao, P. "Memorandum on Behalf of African Women to the Kenya Constitutional Conference in London, February, 1962." Cited in Atsango C. "Two Steps Forward, One step Back: Women and constitutional reform 1997–2002". *FIDA Annual Report* 2002, p.7 http://www.1web.co.ke/fida/reports/fidaannualreport 2002.pdf.

Branden, M. *Women Politicians and the Media.* Lexington: University Press of Kentucky, 1996.

Chazan, N. "Gender Perspectives on African States". In *Women and State in Africa,* eds. J.L. Parpart and K.A. Staudt. London: Lynner Rienner, Boulder, 1989.

Choti, C.O. "Gender and Electoral Politics in Kenya: The Case of Gusii Women, 1990-2002". Unpublished PhD Diss., Clark Atlanta University, 2005.

Commonwealth Observation Mission. *Report of the Commonwealth Observer Group for the 2007 General Elections in Kenya,* January 17, 2008 http://www.thecommonwealth.org/shared_asp_files/GFSR.asp?NodeID=174448

European Union Observation Mission. Kenya *Final Report: General elections December 27,* 2007, April 3, 2008 http://www.eueomkenya.org/Main/English/PDF/Final_Report_Kenya_2007

International Idea "Kenya" IN *Voter Turnout,* 2009.http://www.idea.int/vt/country_view.cfm?CountryCode=KE

Interparliamentary Union. *"KENYA: National Assembly",* 2008http://www.ipu.org/parline/reports/2167_E.htm

Gathigah, M. "Women Navigate Political Minefield in Kenya", *Inter Press Service Nairobi.* January 25, 2013.

Jabatiso, J. "Women candidates fall to gender bias", *East African Standard,* December 27, 1997.

Kabeberi, N. "Statement by Njeri Kabeberi as captured in Dorothy Kweyu: Why Kenyan Women Perform Below Par In Elective Politics", *The Nation,* March 23, 2013.

Kweyu, D. "Why Kenyan Women Perform Below Par in Elective Politics", *The Nation,* March 23, 2013 at 19:44.

Mama, A. *Women Studies and Studies of Women in Africa during the 1990s.* Dakar: CODESRIA, 1991.

Nasong'o, S.W. and T.O. Ayot. "Women in Kenya's Politics of Transition and Democratization". In *Kenya: The Struggle for Democracy*, eds. E.R. Murunga and S.W. Nasongo, 164-196. Dakar: CORESRIA, 2007.

Njenga, A.W. Ass. Secretary, Narc-Kenya Scandinavia. Published by African Press in Norway, Apn, africanpress@chello.no on April 12, 2007

Nzomo, M. "Taking Stock – Women's Performance in Kenya's Parliamentary Politics in the 2002 General Elections." *In Perspectives on Gender Discourse: Women in politics.Challenges of democratic transition in Kenya*, ed. M. Nzomo, 17-33. Nairobi: Heinrich Ball Foundation, 2003.

Nzomo, M. "Kenyan Women in Politics and Public Decision-Making." In *African Feminist: The politics of survival in sub-Saharan Africa,* ed. Mikell Gwendolyn. Philadelphia: University of Pennsylvania, 1997.

Omolo, L.O. "Kenya: More women leaders in Nyanza will contest the March 2013 general elections" *blog.jaluo.com/*?p=2750, Kisumu City

Ossmann K. *Kenyan Elections* 2013. Peaceful prevention and community reporting project, 2013.

Ouko J. O. "Why Kenyan Women Must Fight For Their Political Rights. Voices of Justice for Peace, Regional News by Onyango C."October 10, 2012.

Oywa, J. and B. Wangui. "How Sexism locked women out." *Gender AGENDA Election Platform.* November 21, 2007.

Parpart J. L. and K.A. Staudt, eds. *Women and the State in Africa.* London: Lynner Rienner, Boulder, 1989.

Rugene, N. "Record number of women in the political race". *Kenyan Elections 2013: Peaceful prevention and community reporting project.* March 3, 2013.

Savage, D.C. and C. Taylor. "Academic Freedom in Kenya." *Canadian Journal of African Studies* 25, no.2 (1999): 310.

Wanjiku, K. and P. Wasamba. *Reclaiming Women's Space in Politics.* Nairobi: Centre for Gender and Development, 1998.

Waiyego S. M. "Engendering Political Space".Unpublished MA Thesis, Kenyatta University. 2004.
Weru, G. "A Journey of Courage." Special Report. *Daily Nation,* August 23, 1995.

Wickham, A. "Women in Politics. The Irish and Kenyan cases". From Countdown to Kenya February 27, 2013.

Women's Shadow Parliament-Kenya."The Elusive Quest for Women's Empowerment in Electoral Politics: A Synopsis of the 2007 Electoral Year". In *Second Rapid Assessment and Gender Audit of Electoral Processes in Kenya (Raga II).* 2008. http://womenshadowparliament. org/downloads/Elusive_Quest_for_Women%27s_Empowerment_in_Electral_Politics.pdf

The Election Commission and the Supreme Court: Two new institutions put to the test by elections

Marie Wolfrom [*]

Introduction

Kenya's new Constitution, adopted in August 2010, arose from the embers of the 2007-2008 post-election violence (PEV) and sought to avoid a repeat of that bloody episode, in particular by strengthening accountability and enhancing the independence of the Judiciary. The genesis of the document had started years earlier with several drafts, notably the one drafted from 2002 to 2005 by constitutionalists at the Bomas of Kenya.[1] The final version also drew on the Kriegler Commission[2] report, an uncompromising analysis of the contested December 2007 general elections (IREC, 2009).

During a peaceful referendum, two thirds of Kenyans voted in favor of the constitution. This constitution specifies several electoral process measures adapted from the Kriegler Report recommendations. These include a new and independently nominated electoral board, the Independent Electoral and Boundaries Commission (IEBC), and a Supreme Court composed of seven justices empowered to resolve presidential election-related disputes.[3] The 4 March 2013 election put to the test these two institutions for the first time in particularly complex circumstances: six simultaneous elections of national and local officials were to take place that day.

[*]   Freelance journalist and Masters holder from Sorbonne University, Paris, France. This article was originally published in French under the title "Commission électorale et Cour suprême kényane à l'épreuve du scrutin : Deux nouvelles institutions fragilisées" DOI: 10. 3917/afco. 247. 0053 (*Afrique Contemporaine*, n° 247, Élections Kenya, © De BoeckSupérieurs.a., 2013 1re édition, Fond Jean-Pâques 4, B-1348 Louvain-la-Neuve).

Did these institutional reforms actually foster improvements in electoral administration? According to Robert Pastor, "the absence of independent ECs [electoral commissions] is likely to lead to 'flawed' elections, but the establishment of independent ECs is not sufficient to assure successful elections. The ECs must also be perceived as independent and competent" (Pastor, 1999:18).

In terms of security, the situation has been far better. Although violent acts did occur, in particular in the months leading to the votes, they remained very localized and sporadic, and in no way commensurate with the massacres and massive displacements of 2007-2008. Despite this progress, the IEBC and the Supreme Court –which had held a record high public-confidence rating before[4] Elections day – ultimately disappointed many Kenyans. Doubts hover over the integrity of IEBC: several audits still seek to clarify the otherwise obscure conditions for tenders and procurement of election materials. The commission also faces doubts about its competency and professionalism, given the failure of all the expensive electronic systems it had set up in the name of transparency and fairness, the missing electoral forms and modified registries, and the underwhelming response of election officials toward the malfunctions.

The Supreme Court ruling seemed to favor political concerns over legal ones. Under strong pressure from both camps – namely, the Jubilee coalition of Uhuru Kenyatta and William Ruto as opposed to Raila Odinga and Kalonzo Musyoka's CORD coalition – the judges shielded their reasoning from scrutiny, undermining their appearance of authority. Their final decision was criticized as lacking depth or a solid legal argument.

The present article will explore the process that led to this end result – thus showing how the constitutional reforms intended to bring transparency and credibility to the electoral process in Kenya eventually failed to bring about their stated goals. It does so by drawing upon daily first-hand observations of the situation in Kenya during the entire electoral period, from voter registration to the Supreme Court's validation of the presidential election outcome. A selection of newspaper articles, along with interviews conducted after the elections with electoral experts, jurists and election workers – notably the IEBC chairman, Ahmed Isaack Hassan – complement these observations.

A new "independent" electoral commission, the IEBC

The Electoral Commission of Kenya (ECK)[5] that presided over the December 2007 elections did not survive the cataclysm that followed: more than a thousand people killed and 600 000 displaced. Although reports and scholarly works have shown that politicians had orchestrated most of the violence, the electoral commission – utterly overwhelmed and manipulated – suffered the greatest loss of credibility. The Kenyan parliament dissolved the ECK at the end of 2008, dismissing all its members from commissioners down to technical workers. However, the commission did not entirely deserve its fall from grace; after all, it had organized the 2002 presidential elections, considered by many as Kenya's most transparent elections ever, and the 2005 constitutional referendum. However, President Mwai Kibaki's hurried and unilateral appointment of several commissioners just before the December 2007 election – in violation of political balance rules – sounded the ECK's death knell.

Kenya had no electoral commission for five months until the creation of the Interim Independent Electoral Commission of Kenya (IIEC) in May 2009, which was established by a 2008 amendment (Art 41) to the Constitution. The IIEC, chaired by attorney Ahmed Isaack Hassan and comprising eight other commissioners,[6] moved into the ECK's former premises and started its work afresh. It required a completely new secretariat and personnel; by law, it could hire no one who had worked for the preceding commission.

One of the commission's first tasks was to create an entirely new voter registry, removing the 1.2 million phantom electors signaled in the Kriegler Report.[7] The IIEC conducted voter registration from the end of March to the beginning of May 2010 for a total of 12.4 million, clearly fewer than the more than 14 million registered during the 2007 elections. It also ran early tests on a biometric voter registration and identification system in 18 electoral districts. On this basis, the IIEC successfully organized the August 2010 constitutional referendum, which took place without disruption nor any dispute over the result: 67% voted in favor.

Article 88 of Kenya's constitution provided for a new electoral commission, named the Independent Electoral and Boundaries Commission (IEBC). The IEBC Act, approved by Parliament in June 2011, set out the means of selecting and nominating commission members. Breaking with the overtly political appointment practices of previous commissions,[8] the Act stipulates a selection committee of seven members.[9] It is these members who audition candidates and recommend several of them to the head of state, who then consults with the Prime Minister. The latter nominates the commission chairman and eight commissioners. The National Assembly must approve all nominees.

This method of nominating members was aimed at ensuring the IEBC's independence, but did not really achieve its goal. Indeed, politics insinuated itself in endless, out-of-view backroom deals from the choice of the selection committee members to the lawmakers' approval of the commissioners. Within the Kibaki-Odinga coalition government, negotiated under international pressure to end the political crisis,[10] each camp carefully pushed forward its own pawns. The electoral commission's independence vis-à-vis the government is a key factor in the elections' credibility (Mozaffar, 2002); however, ensuring its genuine independence remains a vital concern. Many experts consider that Kenya's commission, rather than having a veneer of independence, would do better to return to openly political appointments of commissioners, with half given to the government and half to the opposition. As a legal expert declared, "This would not be an independent commission, but it would be a balanced one" (anonymous, author interview, May 8, 2013).

All of the IIEC commissioners were candidates for a second term. Despite Ahmed Isaack Hassan's appeal for more continuity, only he and two IIEC commissioners were retained in the IEBC. Hassan would later opine that this lack of continuity had adversely affected the organization of the 2013 elections (Ahmed I. Hassan, author interview on April 26, 2013).

In November 2011, the IEBC commissioners were officially sworn in. They immediately began preparations for the general elections, which seemed to present special complexities. Unlike in previous contests, voters would have to vote, on Election Day, for six different positions instead of three previously: president, senator, representative, governor, local councilor and women's National Assembly representative. Holding six elections simultaneously seemed a great challenge.

In fact, a European observer noted, "To my knowledge, that has never been done in Europe" (EUEOM, 2013). The IEBC pushed back deadlines because of the difficulty of this task; some members of Parliament, who did not want to shorten their term in office, engaged in delaying maneuvers. Although the new Constitution had envisioned elections in August 2012 (later planned for December 2012),[11] the IEBC finally set the date for March 2013 to allow more time for organization.

In compliance with Article 89 of the constitution, the IEBC first had to increase the number of electoral districts from 210 to 290. The Kriegler Commission had recommended redrawing constituencies whose number of voters was either too high or too low.[12] Then the real preparations for the elections began with the registration of political parties[13] and requests for tenders of electronic materials. After a successful 2010 pilot project for electronic registration in 18 districts, the IEBC proceeded with a new biometric registration system, using digital fingerprints and photographs to curb fraud. "And, after changing the electoral districts, we had to let voters register in the polling station of their choice", explained Immaculate Njenga Kassait, IEBC director of voter registration (Immaculate Kassait, author phone interview, April 30, 2013).

That is when the problems began. To this day, observers cannot tell whether these were due to inexperience, incompetence or willful sabotage. Disorganization plagued the tenders-request process for biometric voter registration kits. Commission members could not agree among themselves, and ended up cancelling the bidding process and opting to register voters manually. The Kenyan government rejected their decision, preferring to make a government-to-government deal with Canada for election materials. The two countries finally signed a contract at the end of September for 15,000 registration kits manufactured by Safran Morpho, a French company. It delivered the kits at the end of October and in early November.

Because of the delay, the IEBC had only one month to register voters, between November 19 and December 18, 2012 deadline. To make up for lost time, it ordered 5,250 more biometric devices than the 9,750 originally planned. In the end, the IEBC utilized 15,000 biometric voter registration kits in approximately 25,000 voter registration centers. This generated a huge cost overrun and a commensurate controversy.[14] The commission set a goal of registering 18 million people; it quickly became apparent that it could not reach that objective in the allotted time. Many Kenyans put off registering, either out of apathy or because they misunderstood the process, given that the IEBC had shortened its voter education materials and sent them out late. In some peripheral regions, voter registration kits arrived several days after the starting date. Nomadic herders who had travelled dozens of kilometers to register refused to come back at a later date (Ongiri, Odonga and Jenje, 2012). On the Kenyan coast, the Mombasa Republican Council (MRC), an autonomous movement that had called for an election boycott, appears to have deterred some potential registrants. Many young people were unable to obtain the required identity cards, and rumors that political parties were buying up identity cards to prevent certain voters from registering began circulating, These rumors, particularly widespread in the slums of Kisumu, seemed aimed at deterring certain segments of voters from registering at all.

On 18 December 2012, the IEBC announced that it had registered 14.3 million citizens and published provisional statistics for each electoral district on its website. The commission felt the registration drive had been successful given its short timeframe. However, in light of the financial and technical means deployed – much higher than in previous registrations – the drive fell well short of mobilizing the estimated 22 million eligible voting-age citizens. Moreover, the IEBC had registration of neither prisoners nor most of the Kenyan diaspora.[15]

To reduce the likelihood of the type of fraud seen in 2007, the IEBC announced that electronic identification devices would identify voters at their polling stations. Moreover, it also planned to use an electronic results transmission system to facilitate the immediate release of provisional results. Upon completing their counts, polling station officers would use a secure mobile phone network to send results to the national election center at the Bomas and to the 290 electoral districts and 47 counties. Electronic transmissions would, in theory, allow for a check on manually filled-in forms. This was meant to provide an additional level of security, especially given the alterations to forms that had been seen in the past. The IEBC then vaunted this apparently airtight process in the press. It even challenged hackers to try breaking into the transmission system, by way of demonstrating its complete effectiveness.

Unfortunately, on Election Day, this edifice crumbled like a house of cards. Despite internal criticisms and warnings from the commission's own IT director, the IEBC belatedly purchased identification kits from the South African company Face Technologies; these kits arrived too late for the commission to train all election workers in their use. By Election Day, many polling stations had not yet received their kits, or could not use them correctly because they lacked fully charged batteries or appropriate passwords. This caused delays, with polls opening after the planned 6:00 a.m. hour in many constituencies. Many voters had waited in queues since 3:00 a.m.; often they had come in trucks chartered by political parties. In most cases however, a later closing hour made up for the late opening, since everyone still waiting at 5:00 p.m. – the official close of polling – was supposed to be allowed to vote.

Given the lack of working identification kits, most polling stations opted to manually record voters, using a paper registry provided by the IEBC. The means used to organize these lists – whether alphabetically by first name or by surname – remain a mystery, since the IEBC has never made the lists publicly available. During the ensuing debates at the Supreme Court, it will appear that different types of paper registries had been used on Election Day, thereby casting doubts on their credibility. In some polling stations, election workers had voters queue up alphabetically by first name; in others, by last name. These differences created much confusion; some voters waited many hours in one queue before realizing they should have waited in another.

As promised, at 6:00 p.m., the IEBC began announcing the provisional voting results that had been transmitted directly from polling stations, even though some were still open for people to vote. However, the electronic transmission system, intended to increase transparency by sending closing totals for broadcast on all television stations, struggled to meet its commitment. As the Carter Center[16] noted, "The information displayed was often inaccurate, displaying sums that did not match numbers on the screen" (Carter Center 2013: 4). "The unreliability of the data displayed through the tabulation process undermined public trust in the IEBC" (Carter Center, 2013: 6). Strangely, the gap in votes between the two presidential candidates, who were running head-to-head, varied only slightly, whereas the results differed greatly between regions, an obvious symptom of voting along ethnic lines.[17]

The provisional results also showed a very high percentage of rejected ballots[18] – some 300,000 of the 40% of votes published on 5 March, or about 7% of all ballots.[19] At first, the IEBC did not include these rejected ballots in their calculations of candidate vote shares, placing Uhuru Kenyatta above the 50% threshold. The Coalition for Reform and Democracy (CORD) officially lodged a protest against the commission, putting forward that Article 138(4) of the constitution states that "all the votes cast"[20] must be counted whether valid or not. On the evening of 5 March, Ahmed Isaack Hassan announced that the rejected ballots would be included in percentage calculation, provoking anger among the Jubilee coalition of Uhuru Kenyatta and William Ruto. The Carter Center criticized this decision: "This last-minute interpretation of the definition of 'votes cast'…should have been taken well in advance and shared with stakeholders in order to avoid the confusion that followed this decision on such a crucial issues" (Carter Center 2013, 4). It seems that the commission acted casually or hurriedly: as its chairman has since admitted (Ahmed Hassan, author interview, April 26, 2013), it did not wait for the legal advice it had solicited before announcing the change. Its interpretation of "all votes cast" would later be contested before the Supreme Court.

On the evening of 5 March, the IEBC chairman acknowledged the failure of the electronic transmission system; it had supplied a trickle of early results before completely breaking down in the morning. He then summoned election directors from 290 electoral districts to Nairobi in order to tabulate ballots manually.

A long wait began for all Kenyans, who saw themselves plunged into something of a repeat of 2007. Election officials verified the results of each district at the Bomas of Kenya central election center, and then read the results live on television. On seeing how long the tabulation was taking, the media preached patience, but tensions rose when some district-level election managers took several days to arrive in Nairobi. Election officials accused agents from the political parties of disruptive behavior – excluding them, as well as local and international observers, from the tabulation room. The Carter Center "regrets the IEBC decision to confine party agents and observers to the gallery of the national tally center, making effective observation impossible" (Carter Center, 2013: 7).

Even before the results were announced, it quickly became apparent that the CORD coalition was dissatisfied with the balloting and tabulation process, and that it intended to file a complaint. Anyang' Nyong'o, one of CORD's campaign managers, sent more than a dozen letters to the IEBC to protest irregularities, apparently without receiving a reply. All of these letters, clearly designed to make CORD's position known before any hearing, appeared in CORD's submission to the Supreme Court on 16 March. During a press conference at the Serena Hotel on Thursday[7] March, Kalonzo Musyoka, fellow candidate of Raila Odinga in the CORD coalition, demanded that the electoral commission stop the tabulation and start over, by publishing the official reports coming out of the polling stations, the Forms 34, rather than Forms 36 that show aggregated results at the constituency level. The outgoing Vice President presented three main arguments to justify his request: (1) the failure of the electronic voter identification kits in, he claimed, "more than 80% of the country" or, according to the electoral commission, in about half of the polling stations; (2) the failure of the electronic transmission system that was supposed to prevent fraud but which he said caused "tainted counts"; and (3) the IEBC's refusal to allow CORD's electoral agents[21] to observe the ballot tabulations at the electoral center in the Bomas.

The election commission circumvented Musyoka's demands, and on Saturday March 9, announced Uhuru Kenyatta's victory with 50.07% of votes, 8,000 above the 50%-plus-one threshold required to win the first round of voting. Two hours later, in a speech before the media entitled "Democracy on Trial" (Odinga, 2013), Raila Odinga denounced "another biased election" with questionable results, comparing it to December 2007. However, in this statement broadcasted live on television and radio, and eagerly awaited by all Kenyans fearful of new violence, Odinga weighed his words to avoid inflaming his audience:

> "Any violence now could destroy this nation forever. That would not serve anyone's interest… we would have readily conceded if IEBC had attempted to deliver a reasonably honest election," Odinga declared before announcing his legal complaint. "We have a new independent judiciary in which we in CORD and most Kenyans have faith. It will uphold the rule of law, and we will abide by its decisions… Let the Supreme Court determine whether the result announced by IEBC is a lawful one."

The Supreme Court's dilemma

Given the increasingly tense situation, Chief Justice Willy Mutunga stated that the Supreme Court was ready to handle any electoral petition brought forward. The looming Supreme Court trial looked to be a great test for the new institution that had only published one ruling on gender parity in Parliament. As with the electoral commission, the Court's seven members had gone through a rigorous selection process in 2011. They had been auditioned by the five-member Judicial Service Commission (which included the former president of the Law Society of Kenya, lawyer Ahmednasir Abdullahi), and the Commission had passed their nominations to outgoing President Mwai Kibaki and Prime Minister Raila Odinga. The coalition agreement stipulated that Kibaki and Odinga had to agree on the candidates; Parliament eventually confirmed their selections.

The process was an unprecedented exercise in transparency. The hearings were broadcast live and almost entirely transcribed in the following day's newspapers. However, despite the strict process set out in the new constitution, intended to avoid all accusations of nepotism or favoritism, the Supreme Court nominations could not avoid controversy entirely. As with the IEBC, the desire to achieve an ethnic and political balance sometimes overshadowed a careful examination of competencies. "Justice Philip Tunoi was chosen because there had to be a Kalenjin and he was the best of the bunch," claimed a legal expert and observer of the judiciary (anonymous, author interview on May 7, 2013). Another legal expert added: "We ended up with intellectuals who lacked judicial experience and judges who lacked an intellectual dimension" (anonymous, author interview on May 10, 2013).

The choice of Chief Justice proved particularly thorny. Willy Mutunga, known for his unimpeachable integrity, quickly appeared to be the favorite. A lawyer by training, he was a militant reformer who had long fought for constitutional changes and expansion of political parties; he was also a famous activist who had been imprisoned in the 1980s. However, his candidacy met with some opposition. Some judges feared a purge of those discredited by accusations of incompetence and corruption. Others mocked Mutunga's frequently changing religious beliefs – successively Animist, Protestant and Catholic before his conversion to Islam. They also criticized his turbulent private life, including two divorces and two children born out of wedlock. Some made fun of his diamond-encrusted left ear and his stance in favor of gay and lesbian rights. When Mutunga was questioned about his earring during his hearing, he explained that he wore it in homage to his ancestors, and that he was not homosexual. In 2011, the legislators finally nominated Willy Mutunga as Chief Justice; they also nominated

Nancy Baraza as his deputy and Keriako Tobiko as Director of Public Prosecutions (DPP). The executive branch presented the three as a take-them-or-leave-them team; this maneuver meant that the highly-contested[22] Keriako Tobiko rode to the strategic position of DPP on the back of Mutunga's and Baraza's popularity. Nor did other justices receive unanimous approval. Njoki Ndung'u, a former legislator, was considered too political because of her participation in Mwai Kibaki's PNU party campaign in 2007. Mohammed Ibrahim was almost excluded (he had been criticized for being too slow in making rulings on the cases before him) from the bench before finally being cleared in January 2013.

In October 2012, Nancy Baraza was suspended and then forced to resign after mistreating and insulting a security guard who, nine months earlier, had tried to inspect her purse at a mall entrance. Lady Kalpana Rawal replaced Baraza, but too late to for confirmation by a Parliament that would dissolve before the elections.

In March 2013, therefore, six justices[23] rather than seven examined the validity of the three petitions filed with the Supreme Court. This raised some questions about how to reach a majority decision: Did the Chief Justice wield a dominant vote? What would happen if the Court were split three-to-three? An answer came quickly: in the event of a tie, Kenyatta's victory declaration would prevail. Those contesting his victory had to convince at least four of the six justices.

To avoid a power vacuum (or conversely, a situation like Ghana's, where President John Dramani Mahama had been sworn in despite a still-pending petition in the courts), the new Kenyan constitution provides for a tight timeframe in the event of a disputed presidential election. According to Article 140, the parties have seven days from the official announcement of results to lodge a complaint. The Supreme Court in turn has two weeks to hold hearings and make a ruling from which there is no appeal. As with the American model, in the interim the election winner becomes the president-elect and prepares his or her transition into office with the help of the outgoing president, who expedites current business. However, the constitution does not define the conduct of these parties in the event that the Supreme Court receives a petition contesting the results; this caused much discussion, particularly about whether a president-elect in a contested election might receive confidential information about the country's security. On these grounds, the CORD coalition harshly criticized meetings that Uhuru Kenyatta held with the chief of staff and the head of Kenya's intelligence agency.

The time restrictions played a significant role in the petition. Many lawyers thought the timeline was too short for those making the complaint. Given the complexity of gathering evidence, many electoral documents were unavailable on 9 March, when the election results were published. The CORD coalition had to summon the IEBC before the High Court before they could obtain a copy of the election proceedings.

Although some lawyers have since proposed extending the deadline to 45 or even 60 days, the timelines cannot be modified without a constitutional amendment. This means that political parties and their candidates would be well advised to prepare for cases of suspected fraud in advance, by gathering as much data as possible when the elections start. CORD's leaders clearly had not done this; they tacitly admitted that they had not deployed agents to all polling stations, unlike the opposing Jubilee camp's faultless organisation. Lacking agents in certain locations, particularly in the Central and Rift Valley regions, CORD was unable to make a parallel ballot tabulation that would have allowed it to challenge results polling-place-by-polling-place, a deficiency that would weigh heavily upon its petition.

Meanwhile, Jubilee spent KShs. 3.5 million (Nesbitt 2013) on a call center, hosted by Kencall, to centralize the results submitted by its agents in 33,000 polling stations. This allowed the Kenyatta-Ruto camp to announce provisional results on Thursday, 7 March to a limited few; these results were very close to those announced by the election commission two days later. Tweets disseminated the so-called record participation rate of 86%[24] starting on the night of Monday 4 March 4– five days before the IEBC's official announcement. This occurred even though some polling stations were still open at the time; to this day, no one knows whether it was simply a coincidence or not.

A three-week judicial marathon followed the 9 March announcements. Time was short for both the plaintiffs and the defense. They hired the country's most prestigious lawyers for what promised to be a historic and unprecedented trial,[25] one entailing a crucial and uncertain outcome. The IEBC engaged a record 20 lawyers.[26] Its chairman, Ahmed Isaack Hassan, employed more than three defense attorneys for himself; one, Ahmednasir Abdullahi, had helped select the sitting Supreme Court justices in 2011, during his tenure on the Judicial Service Commission. This placed the justices in a somewhat awkward position and gave Ahmednasir Abdullahi a psychological upper hand which he used during the auditions.[27] The process also saw ethnic favoritism, as nearly every plaintiff and defendant hired an attorney from his own ethnic community: Uhuru Kenyatta employed Fred Ngatia, William Ruto hired Katwa Kigen, and Raila Odinga engaged George Oraro.

Strong external pressure was put on the Court,[28] especially on Chief Justice Willy Mutunga; some told him he should withdraw because of his past support for Raila Odinga's candidacy (News Time 2013; Associated Press 2013). It was assumed by some that he would side with civil society, given that he was "one of their own." Nazlin Umar, a political activist and 2007 presidential candidate, verbally attacked the Chief Justice on the first day of hearings (25 March) in an obvious effort to intimidate him. On an unprecedented live television broadcast of the arguments, Umar accused Mutunga of bias toward the Prime Minister. Interestingly, Umar had found a front-row seat among the lawyers in an area that required a special identification badge, despite the draconian security measures taken for the trial.

Three election petitions were filed with the Supreme Court. The CORD coalition and the Africa Center for Open Governance (AfriCOG) demanded the invalidation of the election results, on the grounds that they were not free and fair as required in Article 81(c) of the constitution. These petitioners especially criticized the inexplicable variations between the number of registered voters on 24 February – the date the voter registry was published – and the number used on Election Day. They also criticized the failure of all the electronic verification and transmission systems, the differences between the results reported by polling stations on the Forms 34, and the results aggregated at the constituency level on Forms 36.

In addition, two of Kenyatta's supporters filed a petition to overturn the IEBC's decision to count rejected votes in the tabulation of results. At the start of arguments, the Court ordered verification of Forms 34 and 36 from 22 polling stations and a recount of all forms from all 33,000 polling stations.

On the other hand, the Court dismissed a CORD affidavit that offered new evidence, ruling that CORD was too late in filing it and had done so without the Court's permission. The Court also dismissed a request from AfriCOG asking for an audit of all the manual voter registries used on Election Day. The Court did allow Attorney General Githu Muigai to participate in the trial as an amicus curaie, or friend of the Court, but refused to grant the same status to Yash Ghai, one of the fathers of the Kenyan constitution, whom the defendants considered too partisan.

After four days of intense arguments, the Court announced its verdict at the end of the day just before Easter, on 30 March. Willy Mutunga announced briefly and without explanation the panel's unanimous decision confirming Kenyatta's narrow victory, while excluding the rejected ballots from the count – a ruling that shocked the plaintiffs. George Oraro, a courteous and usually calm lawyer, stood up to leave the room upon hearing the Chief Justice's first words, before sitting down again. The losing side was more disturbed by the justices' unanimity than by the failure of their petition. They may have questioned whether it was real unanimity, or a political decision to maintain the country's cohesion.

The Supreme Court ruling angered some, provoking demonstrations in Kisumu and in the Kawangware slum in Nairobi; a strong police presence nipped these protests in the bud. Raila Odinga announced that he would respect the judges' decision even as he signaled his disagreement with their ruling, claiming that "Kenyans lost their right to know what really happened".

Although criticism remained muted before publication of the Supreme Court's detailed judgment, an uproar ensued after the ruling appeared on 16 April, two days late. Contrary to tradition, the judges neither read nor summarized the 113-page ruling aloud before the Court (TheStarKenya 2013). Several civil-society lawyers rose up in arms, submitting opinion pieces to the press and calling the judgment "lazy" and "casual" (Murunga, 2013; Maina, 2013; Ongoya, 2013). They especially criticized the Court's use of dubious Nigerian jurisprudence, and railed against the rejection of the supplemental evidence tardily submitted by CORD's attorneys. Furthermore, the Court, for all intents and purposes, ignored the findings of the ballot recount it had ordered, despite the fact that the new tabulation revealed several mistakes and internal errors in the IEBC's published election results.[29] Although the Court acknowledged some imperfections, it found that the petitioners did not succeed in showing how these errors drastically affected the election results; in this, the Court set a very high threshold for the evidence required to challenge presidential election outcomes. The Court directed its only criticism toward the IEBC's tender-award and procurement process, recommending an investigation.

Chief Justice Willy Mutunga seemed shaken by the avalanche of attacks in the media and on social networks, and by his weak public support. He defended himself on his Facebook page, asking Kenyans for "justice for the Supreme Court" and denying accusations of corruption. His knee-jerk reaction surprised many and was considered a sign of weakness (Otieno, 2013). In May, the Supreme Court published an addendum to its ruling that corrected several errors without changing the substance (Nation Media Group, 2013). While this step may prove valuable for legal purposes, inasmuch as the ruling will be used in future Court decisions, it further weakened the institution's image of infallibility.

Conclusion

The elections passed peacefully for the most part, although some Kenyans still question the outcome. Was justice sacrificed on the altar of peace? Given the scale of the errors and the doubts cast on its results, how could so many watchdogs – international observers as well as the High Court – have concluded that the election had been free, fair and transparent? Are such irregularities inevitable? If so, must Kenyans resign themselves in perpetuity to accepting imperfect election results?

Most accepted the situation, wanting to get on with their lives as quickly as possible. Others found that the elections left a bitter aftertaste. Many Kenyans felt keenly disappointed in the IEBC and Supreme Court, feeling that both had betrayed their hopes for solid and reliable institutions.

Once again, the 2013 Kenyan elections showed that institutional reforms are a necessary but insufficient condition for legitimating the electoral process. Without political will to implement the legal reforms, Kenya's elections may long remain open to doubts. It seems a shame that the courts failed to prosecute electoral infractions committed in plain sight across the country, such as vote rigging and voter intimidation. Nor did the courts pursue voters who registered multiple times, despite the commission's assurances that it would prosecute such offenses.

Since the elections, the IEBC has been audited; if these investigations uncover proof of irregularities, the commission's image will be further tarnished. DPP Keriako Tobiko, complying with a Supreme Court recommendation, has ordered an inquiry into the commission's procurement activities.

In July 2013, former Prime Minister Raila Odinga threatened to boycott all future large elections the IEBC might organize in the future, demanding that the commission undertake fundamental reforms. According to him, the IEBC is "the most corrupt and inefficient electoral commission in the history of this country" (Mosoku, 2013). To date, government and lawmakers have yet to respond or take a position, and their ultimate position will generate further questions. Will authorities draw lessons from 2013 that lead to major repercussions, as occurred in 2008? These might include the ouster of some commissioners,[30] or even the creation of a new electoral commission if investigations find proof of serious or criminal offenses. Or will a coalition of lawmakers with common political interests protect the electoral commission's current leadership?

The Supreme Court's situation poses more of a paradox. While the public retains trust in the institution, albeit an eroded one, some segments of civil society do not; they remain disturbed by what they perceive as Willy Mutunga's betrayal. Rare shows of support for him have not counterbalanced the many criticisms that have appeared in the press; the Chief Justice revealed his consequent hurt and worry through a public – and surprising – statement on Facebook.

It is hard to tell if this episode has permanently tarnished Mutunga's credibility. The Supreme Court remains a young institution and Kenyans give it the benefit of the doubt. However, they will closely examine this Court's future decisions to see if it will adopt a progressive stance in the spirit of the constitution, or a more conservative one along the lines of its first two decisions. One may also wonder whether the high burden of evidentiary proof required will deter future losing candidates from petitioning the Court.

The IEBC must not take shortcuts in reviewing its procedures for requesting tenders, hiring and training election workers, and educating the public. It should also learn from its technology failures.[31] The electoral commission needs a push to look into these matters; so far it has distinguished itself by a lack of self-doubt. By continuing debates about the 2013 elections, civil society has attempted to impel the commission toward change. Two Kenyan nongovernmental organizations, AfriCOG and Inform Action, set up an Internet site called "The People's Court" – effectively thumbing their noses at the electoral commission. The site collects eyewitness voter accounts of election proceedings, and analyzes voting statistics and the Supreme Court ruling.

Kenyans, especially the winning party's members, have repeatedly and forcefully called for the country to turn the page on the elections and move forward. Questioning Kenyatta's first-round win appears futile; however, it seems crucial to ask how to improve the electoral process by 2017, in order to prevent the errors and irregularities observed in 2007 and 2013, and to avoid permanently discouraging voters' participation.

Notes

1 The Bomas of Kenya, a cultural centre on the outskirts of Nairobi, is often used for conferences.

2 The Kenyan government established and officially named the Independent Review Commission (IREC) in February 2008 to investigate implementation of the December 2007 general elections. The IREC was later renamed after its president, Johann Kriegler, a former judge from South Africa.

3 According to Article 163(3a) of the constitution, the Supreme Court has "exclusive" authority to resolve all disputes arising from presidential election results.

4 According to an Ipsos Synovate poll published at the end of February 2013, 89% of Kenyans had confidence in the IEBC and 72% trusted the Supreme Court. At the end of June, according to the same polling institute, only 32% had high confidence in the IEBC and 34% in the Supreme Court.

5 The ECK was chaired by Samuel Kivuitu, who admitted on 2 January 2008 that he did not know if Mwai Kibaki had truly won the December 2007 presidential election.

6 Each commissioner represents one of Kenya's eight provinces. They were nominated by a parliamentary select committee, approved by the National Assembly and appointed by the President in consultation with the Prime Minister.

7 The National Bureau of Statistics estimated that 1,733,000 registered voters died between 1997 and 2007, but the ECK had only erased 513,000 names from the voter registry. According to the Kriegler Commission, 1.2 million deceased voters remained in the registry used in 2007.

8 Robert A. Pastor (1999) distinguishes five types of electoral commission: an election office within the government; an election office within a government ministry but supervised by a judicial body; an independent election commission manned by experts and directly accountable to Parliament; a multiparty election commission, composed of representatives of all political parties; and a non-partisan election commission, composed of distinguished individuals proposed by the president and legislature, such as Kenya's IEBC.

9 Taking care to maintain political balance, the President and Prime Minister may each nominate two committee members. Mwai Kibaki chose Mwanyengela Ngali and Marion Mutugi, while Raila Odinga nominated Ekuru Aukot and Rosa Akinyi Buyu. Judge Isaac Leanola from the Judicial Service Commission, Irene Keino from the Kenya Anti-Corruption Commission, and Sophie Njeri Moturi, from the Association of Professional Societies of East Africa, together nominated the remaining IEBC members.

10 A power-sharing agreement was made on 28 February 2008, after more than a month of tough negotiations under the guidance of Kofi Annan, former United Nations General Secretary.

11 In January 2012, the High Court ruled that the elections had to take place within 60 days of Parliament's termination, 14 January 2013, unless the coalition in power ended prematurely.

12 In 2008, the Kriegler report criticized the constituencies' imbalances, noting that Embakasi population was 351% above the average, while Lamu East represented only 18% of the average.

13 58 parties registered within the 90-day legal limit.

14 The purchase contract ballooned from KShs. 3.9 to 9.6 billion, provoking controversy: "The Government Loses Billions in BVR Deal" (Menya, 2012).

15 An estimated 2.5 million Kenyans live outside the country. Only 2,637, living in the nearby countries of Burundi, Rwanda, Tanzania and Uganda, were able to register to vote. Prisoners had been allowed to vote in the 2010 referendum, but the IEBC did not make this possible in the 4 March election, despite a High Court ruling authorizing such votes.

16 The main goals of the Carter Center, a foundation created by former American president Jimmy Carter, include defending human rights, resolving conflicts peacefully, and observing elections.

17 In Kenya, constituents traditionally give priority votes to representatives of their ethnic group. Thus Uhuru Kenyatta garnered 93% of the votes in the Central region, essentially populated by Kikuyu, his ethnic group. Raila Odinga gained more than 86% of vote in the Nyanza region where Luo predominate.

18 Rejected ballots are unmarked, marked in error or put in the wrong ballot box. They should not be confused with "spoilt ballots", which are tossed before being put in a ballot box.

19 The number of rejected ballots ultimately fell to 108,975 in the official results, or 0.88% of votes cast. This seems low for such a complex election; the percentage of rejected ballots in the 2010 "yes-no" referendum stands at 2.4%. The IEBC justified it as a computer error that multiplied the number of rejected ballots by eight during the electronic transmission, without convincing the losing side, who perceived this as numbers manipulation.

20 Article 138(4) states: "A candidate shall be declared elected as President if the candidate receives more than half of all the votes cast in the election; and at least twenty five per cent of the votes cast in each of more than half of the counties".

21 In violation of international procedures, local and international election observers were also asked to leave the tabulation room. They were relegated to a gallery where it was impossible to see anything. The Carter Center and the European Union Election Observation Mission criticized this in their report on election proceedings.

22 A High Court petition was filed against his nomination in June 2011, and rejected in May 2012.

23 Willy Mutunga, Philip Tunoi, Jackton Ojwan'g, Mohamed Ibrahim, Smokin Wanjala and Njoki Ndung'u.

24 Several political pundits questioned this percentage, since participation rates in the presidential elections of 2007 and 2002 only reached 69% and 57.18% respectively.

25 In 1992 and 1997, complaints had been filed against the election and re-election of Daniel arapMoi. At the time, the judiciary was so politically captured that it rejected the pleas for procedural reasons.

26 The lawyers cost KShs. 360 million; as of early August 2013, this remained unpaid, infuriating the attorneys (Nation Media Group 2013).

27 Abdullahi insisted that the Supreme Court itself was "being tested," comparing it to a "crawling baby".

28 On 20 February, Mutunga gave a press conference to discuss a threatening letter he had received from the mysterious "Mungiki Veterans Group". He complained that he had been prevented from taking a plane to Tanzania on February 14 because of a memorandum from Francis Kimemia, the head of Kenya's civil service.

29 A team of analysts working for the Supreme Court found significant discrepancies in the counts of five of the 22 polling stations. The team also found many missing or faulty forms 34 and 36 across all stations. However, the magistrate's registry, which was supposed to show the justices the results of the analysis, was presented in a summary fashion that minimized the problems.

30 Some call for the ouster of Chairman Hassan, who personally cast doubts on Raila Odinga in his affidavit, accusing him of inability to acknowledge electoral defeat.

31 The IEBC's identification and transmission systems did work perfectly during Makueni's partial senatorial election on 26 July 2013. This led the IEBC to congratulate itself, and the losing party in the presidential elections to wonder yet again about the system failures in March.

Bibliography

African Elections Database (AED) (for chart of voter registration trends)

Carter Center."The Carter Center Finds Kenya Election Results Reflect Will of Voters". *The Carter Center International Election Observation Mission to Kenya.* Nairobi, April 4, 2013. p.4. Retrieved from http://www.cartercenter.org/resources/pdfs/news/pr/kenya-tally-040413.pdf

Constitution of Kenya (2010). *Constitution of Kenya Article Nos. 81(c), 88, 89, 140, 184(4).* Nairobi: National Council for Law Reporting. 2010. Retrieved from http://www.kenyaembassy.com/pdfs/The%20Constitution%20of%20Kenya.pdf.

European Union Electoral Observation Mission (EUEOM) 2013. Press conference in April 2013.

_____. *Final Report of the EU Election Observation Mission in Kenya,* Nairobi, May 2013.

_____. *Preliminary Statement,* Nairobi, March 6, 2013.

Independent Review Commission [Kriegler Commission] (IREC 2009). *Final report on the 2007 Elections in Kenya.* Nairobi: Ministry of Interior and Coordination of National Government. 2008. Retrieved from http://kenyastockholm.files.wordpress.com/2008/09/the_kriegler_report.pdf

International Crisis Group. "Kenya After the Elections". *Africa Briefing* no. 94, May 15, 2013

Kenya Elections Database (KED) (for chart of voter registration trends) Kenya Supreme Court, April 16, 2013.

Lafarge, J. *Les élections générales de 2007 au Kenya.* Paris: Karthala, 2008.

Maina, W. "Verdict on Kenya's presidential election petition: Five reasons the judgment fails the legal test". *The East African,* April 20, 2013.

Menya, W. "Government loses billions in BVR deal". *The Star,* November 3, 2012. Retrieved from http://allafrica.com/stories/201211030644.html.

Mosoku, G. "CORD will not contest future polls if IEBC is not reformed, former Prime Minister Raila Odinga says". *The Standard,* July15, 2013. Retrieved from http://www.standardmedia.co.ke/?articleID=2000088429&story_title=raila-boycott-threat-in-protest-over-iebc.

Mozaffar, S."Patterns of Electoral Governance in Africa's Emerging Democracies". *International Political Science Review* 23, no.1 (2002): 85-101.

Muhumuza, R., and J. Straziuso. "Election dispute big test for Kenya's top judge". *The Associated Press,* March12, 2013. Retrieved from http://bigstory.ap.org/article/election-dispute-big-test-kenyas-top-judge.

Murunga, G. "Supremacy of the Supreme Court did not show through on first big test". *Daily Nation,* April 19, 2013.

Nation Media Group."IEBC under siege from lawyers over KShs. 360 million petition bill". *Daily Nation,* August3, 2013. Retrieved from http://www.nation.co.ke/News/politics/Lawyers-threaten-to-sue-IEBC-over-fees/-/1064/1936322/-/3vyidj/-/index.html

Nation Media Group. "Poll team ignored advice on vote kit". *Daily Nation,* March 18, 2012. Retrieved from http://www.nation.co.ke/news/politics/IEBC-bought-faulty-kits-despite-warning/-/1064/1722994/-/f26ogyz/-/index.html.

Nation Media Group. "Top Court corrects error in poll ruling". *Daily Nation,* May19, 2013. Retrieved from http://www.nation.co.ke/news/politics/Top-court-corrects-errors-in-poll-ruling/-/1064/1857440/-/ltpmbiz/-/index.html

Nesbitt, N.A. Contract signed on February 27, 2013 between Market Race and Uhuru Kenyatta's The National Alliance (TNA) party.

Newstime Africa. "Will Chief Justice Willy Mutunga cosy relationship with Raila Odinga affect the outcome of the election petition?" *newstimeafrica.com,* March21, 2013. Retrieved from http://www.newstimeafrica.com/archives/31301

Odinga, R. "Democracy on trial: a statement on the elections in Kenya by the Reforms and Democracy coalition". Nairobi, March 9 2013. Retrieved from http://www.nairobiwire.com/2013/03/democracy-on-trial-full-statement-by.html.

Ongiri, I.O., P. Odonga and B. Jenje. "IEBC says registration problems are minor". *Daily Nation*, November22, 2012. Retrieved from http://www.nation.co.ke/News/politics/IEBC-says-registration-problems-are-minor/-/1064/1626302/-/d08q72z/-/index.html.

Ongoya, E. "The Supreme Court was too casual in its ruling on presidential petition". *Daily Nation,* April29, 2013.

Otieno, O. "CJ Mutunga must accept his new image and move on". *Daily Nation,* March4, 2013.

Pastor, R.A. "The role of electoral administration in democratic transitions: implications for policy and research". Democratization 6, no. 4 (1999): 1-27. Retrieved from http://www1.american.edu/ia/cdem/pdfs/roleelectoraladministration.pdf.

The Star Kenya."Supreme Court: Full judgment on election petition". *The Star Kenya,* April 16, 2013. Retrieved from http://www.scribd.com/doc/136198180/Supreme-Court-Full-judgement-on-election-petition-April-16-2013.

"The Grassroots Are Very Complicated": Marginalization and the Emergence of Alternative Authority in the Kenyan Coast 2013 Elections

Ngala Chome [*]

Introduction

After the re-introduction of multi-party politics in the 1990s, anxieties about future political possibilities on the Kenya Coast have generally driven various individuals and grassroots organisations into making appealsfor regional unity and regional autonomy, including a much publicised secessionist demand on the run-up to the 2013 general elections (Willis and Chome, 2014; Willis and Gona, 2012). These individuals and organisations (e.g. the Mombasa Republican Council, the Coast People's Forum and the Mijikenda Council of Elders) have not only imagined and spoken for a wider Coastal political community (Wapwani, meaningpeople of the Coast) but have from time to time made clear their dissatisfaction with Members of Parliament (MPs) representing Coastal constituencies in the National Assembly; they claimed that the MPs have failed in addressing the 'marginalisation' of the Coast region from national politics and key institutions of governance at the political centre.

In 2010 and 2013– that is, between the promulgation of a new constitution and the general election–these discussions assumed a central place in coastal and to an extent, national politics.

[*] Commonwealth Shared Scholar for the year 2013-2014 at the Center of African Studies, University of Edinburgh and BIEA fellow. This article was originally published in French under the title "Marginalisation politique et politisation des structures alternatives de pouvoir dans la province de la côte au Kenya : Analyses des dynamiques électorales et des pouvoirs politiques locaux" DOI: 10.3917/afco.247.0087 (*Afrique Contemporaine*, n° 247, Élections Kenya, © De Boeck Supérieur s.a., 2013 1re édition, Fond Jean-Pâques 4, B-1348 Louvain-la-Neuve).

The Mijikenda Council of Elders Association (MICOSEA) highlighted the frustrations that the "indigenous" people of the Coast had had with their formal political representatives; arguing that disunity amongst Coast leaders had undermined the region's influence on the national political stage and thus had marginalized it. This included an affront onthe educated 'sons' and 'daughters' of coastal "natives", who – according to the self-proclaimed "elders" of MICOSEA, and other individuals claiming to speak for organizations such as the Malindi District Cultural Association (MADCA) and the Mombasa Republican Council (MRC) – have "forsaken" their uneducated ethnic kin in their flight to the capital Nairobi, or into the diaspora. This discourse rejecting formally elected representatives and the educated elite also speaks to a longer historical narrative along the Kenyan Coast – one that rejects a Kenyan state perceived to have devastated the economic and cultural futures of its "native peoples". This discourse underpinned the politics of the MRC, a secessionist group that demanded coastal independence on the grounds of political marginalization by the central government (Willis and Gona, 2012).

These recent developments in Coastal politics are not very new. Political marginalisation has been the central and overriding theme animating politics on the Coast Region since the late colonial era. It has also been the focus of a modest but growing academic scholarship (e.g. Stren, 1970; Mazrui, 1997; Mazrui, 2000; Meilink, 2000; Gona, 2008). This chapter interrogates the role of political marginalisation in shaping political consciousness along the coast of Kenya and the consequences for electoral politics in the 2013 general elections. In particular, the chapter examines the politicisation of alternative structures of authority under the context of the marginalisation of Coastal MPs on the national political stage by mostly MPs from upcountry[1] regions between 2002 (at the end of the Kenya African National Union rule and dominance) and the 2013 general-elections. During this period ethno-regional coalition building and negotiation – a key feature of Kenyan politics – became much more contentious. As Lynch (2006: 49) has observed, "he negotiation of ethno-regionalism [became] inexorably intertwined with common perceptions of how political representation and redistribution actually works". Following in this precedent, the perception by most who consider themselves as indigenous to the Coast that their MPs had failed in the negotiation of a Coastal political community and its interests (Gona, 2008); explains why various individuals with other forms of authority (educated, religious, traditional) took it upon themselves in speaking on behalf of the people of the Coast – leading to the emergence of what I refer to as alternative authority in Coastal politics.

The perceived marginalisation of the former Coast Province by the Kenyan state is not only read from the low status of Coastal politicians in national politics but also from the poverty and the low socio-economic levels of those considered as 'indigenous' to the Coast. However, there exist different readings of marginalisation amongst the imagined community of the people of the Coast. For most Mijikenda, marginalisation is expressed as a loss of ancestral land (to both Arab and up-country communities) and is rooted in conditions of serious impoverishment and social exclusion; "finding themselves on the lowest rung of the ladder of capitalism and feeling like outsiders in most national political proceedings" (McIntosh, 2009: 37). For Arabs, encroachment on land and privilege acquired during the colonial period, and the perceived threatening of Islamic institutions by the predominantly Christian upcountry groups forms the main reading of this marginalisation (Willis and Chome, 2014). Indeed, these feelings of marginalization and apparent political weakness on the national political stage have led others in describing the Coast Region as the least national in terms of power, influence and orientation (Mazrui, 2000).

The result of this overall marginalization is that Coastal MPs have become a quintessential class of privileged elites – one that may wield much power, but have little authority; one that may enjoy great economic influence but little political acceptance. The contention is that since Coastal MPs have a relatively weaker anchorage in Kenya's political economy (compared to their Kalenjin, Luo or Kikuyu counterparts), they cannot effectively provision neo-patrimonial ethnic structures that seem to give politicians elsewhere in Kenya the much needed political legitimacy. This serves to constrain their wider legitimacy amongst those considering themselves as being from the Coast. In examining this discourse of marginalisation and how it interacts with ideas of political representation and legitimacy on the Coast (and the consequent politicisation of alternative authority structures), the chapter engages with a wider literature on African politics and specifically on the nature and role of institutions of political representation.

Most significantly, as I will argue, the strategic marginalisation of coastal MPs in the national sphere has weakened the legitimacy of formal political representation on the Coast Region, and of national politics in general. This in turn has enabled the emergence of an alternative space, with alternative political authority structures; these have sought – with varying degrees of success – greater respect and recognition, and wider legitimacy. A disclaimer is given: that these alternative spheres of authority, despite seeking and attaining enough space during 2010 and 2013 in local electoral politics, were seriously curtailed in influencing political outcomes due to the existence of multiple fault lines of race, ethnicity, business competition and personal rivalry, which divide the imagined community of the people of the Coast. To illustrate its main assumptions, the chapter will examine the case of the Mijikenda Council of Elders Association, the Coast Professional Forum and the Mombasa Republican Council.

In addition, the chapter will briefly highlight the politicisation of the Church in Mombasa during 2010 and 2013. Concerned with rising political activism among those who consider themselves 'indigenous' to the Coast Region, the traditionally apolitical Christian community (predominantly up-country and chiefly resident in Mombasa) became politically active and involved during the 2013 general elections. However, the latter can also be considered part of an emerging wider pentecostalisation of politics in Kenya (Deacon and Lynch, 2013).

The chapter proceeds as follows: the first section of the chapter considers the main discussions regarding representative politics in Africa, arguing that neo-patrimonial literature continues to be relevant in the understanding of Kenyan politics in general and of the Coast in particular. In this way, the pressure from the grassroots by MPs to be responsive to clientelistic demands is causing a politicisation of alternative authority structures since MPs find themselves constrained– due to a lack of resources caused in turn by a marginalisation from national political structures. The second section discusses the main political trends on the Coast from 2002-2013 by offering a contextual background to the emergence of alternative authority during the 2013 elections which will be considered in the third section of the chapter.

Patronage politics and the institution of the Member of Parliament

The nature and role of African political institutions, and in particularly that of the Member of Parliament, has been the subject of much academic debate in Africanist political science. The main question has been whether political institutions in Africa, seen and described as neo-patrimonial, can endure. However, after withstanding a raft of reforms and interventions (structural adjustment, decentralisation, and democratisation) a number of analysts (e.g. Orvis, 2006; Lindberg, 2010) have sought to explain the durability of African political institutions that nonetheless remain neo-patrimonial – especially with the normalisation of multi-party elections in much of the continent.

The idea, that "political clientelism is endogenous to its own existence" (Lindberg, 2010: 117) inherently assumes that neo-patrimonial structures will wither in the face of increased institutionalisation of political power in Africa (Posner and Young, 2007) and of decreasing wealth for furnishing patron-client relationships between voters and their representatives. To address this analytical problem – which priviledges a Western liberal democratic tradition that does not attach strong material and personal imperatives to political processes – Lindberg (2010) argues that in addition to the formal functions of Members of Parliament in Africa (legislative, representative, monitoring the executive etc.) a more informal role –the role of dispensing patrongae to constituents in terms of private and collective goods – should also be taken seriously. The contrast is that, while in Western liberal democracies the electorate expects politicians to 'deliver the goods' in terms of a promised public policy, law or adherence to a certain ideology, in much of Africa, where single-member district representation is also common, voters have continued to judge the performance of their parliamentarians mainly by their capacity to bring development projects to their constituents (Barkan, 1975).

Migdal (1988) offers a more apt characterization of political institutions in general that is useful to an understanding of the role of the institution of Member of Parliament in Africa. In his examination of political institutions, Migdal (1988) argues that the mobilisation of power, in addition to structuring and constraining it, is a crucial element of political institutions and a key to their endurance. The contention is that the ability to mobilise power is related to the ability to deliver key components of people's "strategies of survival," their "blueprints for action and belief" comprising a mix of material resources and systems of meaning –myths and symbols that help explain their place in the world and how they can survive and perhaps prosper within it (Migdal, 1988: 26-27).

In the above context, neo-patrimonialism, i.e. the personalisation of state public goods to sustain personal loyalties between a politician (patron) and a follower (client) and the apparent ethnicisation of these relationships, becomes a central operational logic within which power gains meaning and is legitimated. In African politics, the endurance of political institutions, formal or informal, within or without government, has thus been connected to their ability to provide 'goods of modernity' (school bursaries, construction of schools, roads and slaughter-houses etc.) and in 'linking' the population to the government (Branch and Cheeseman, 2006).

In the context of the above analysis, in Kenya, and in much of Africa, elections have been described as referenda on the performance of individual MPs in obtaining resources for their local community (Barkan, 1979). Therefore, the fact that Coastal MPs are marginalised from access to resources at the disposal of what has been an overly-centralised state – dominated by elites representing other ethno-regions – has meant that their legitimacy in mobilising and speaking for or on behalf of 'Coastals' is largely constrained. In sum, Coastal MPs are expected by their electorate to respond to clientelistic demands and find an effective way to address 'historical injustices' in order to resolve a widespread sense of marginalisation in the region (Gona, 2008). It is under this context that the emergence of alternative authority structures in

Coastal politics is explained. Before doing so, we will turn to the major trends in Coastal politics between 2002 and 2013.

The "loss" of majimbo and the political marginalisation of Coast Region politicians (2002-2013)

In local debates, as highlighted above, a central discursive theme features constant public resentment by Coastal people against Coastal MPs. This relates to the theme of political marginalisation on the Coast, where ordinary citizens considering themselves as belonging in the Coasthave from time to time expressed publicly the disavowal of Coastal MPs, including voting them out during elections or not participating in elections at all. According to Gona (2008: 252), "the elected leadership has failed the Coast because when it came to making hard choices and decisions on issues that they promised in campaigns to address (crucially the land question, perception of marginalization and the quest for equitable distribution of national resources) the leaders have walked away from the people". This proves a strong sense amongst common people on the Coast that problems affecting them would not be solved by their current representatives and especially if no form of strong regional autonomy is attained.

A former system of decentralisation: the quasi-federalist or regionalist form referred to in Kenya's political lexicon as majimbo was therefore widely popular on the Coast and on other regions such as the Rift Valley where domination by other communities, particularly Kikuyu–in land and civil service jobs – has been feared. Majimbo was described as an "alternative vision" of the independent Kenyan state, "a proposal for decentralisation in which six or more provinces comprising independent Kenya would have equal status" (Anderson, 2005: 547). Regionalism was short-lived, deemedby powerful sections of Kenya's ruling eliteas destabilising in its design and "tribalistic" in its intentions. However, the politics and expectations of majimbo, which was meant in its adoption in the 1960s to protect minority ethnic communities against majority ethnic communities (Nyanjom, 2011), continued to influence political consciousness among the Coast people. In particular, the majimbo idea (or regional autonomy) determined how leadership was perceived by voters on the Coast, and functioned as a discursive repertoire embedded with the themes of autochthony, belonging and autonomy. In a nutshell, expectations by Coastal voters are in line with those that were intended with the majimbo project, and this has meant that MPs are expected by their electorate to be responsive to patronage and other kinds of political demands, framed less as patronage, yet imbuing an ethno-regionalist character.

This is important because at the national level, the Coast Region has never had a serious political party and has produced only one presidential candidate, Chibule wa Tsuma, who ran on a Kenya National Congress Party (KNC) ticket in 1992 and came in a distant sixth. Coastal parties such as Shirikisho, Kadu-Asili, and Chama Cha Uzalendo have had little impact either nationally or regionally. This has made the Coast susceptible to parties originating elsewhere. This electoral weakness supplies the context for the Coast's engagement in national politics of transition in 1997-2002, and in opposition politics from 2002-2007 and in 2007-2013, through NARC and ODM successively (see Table 1).

Table 1: Main political parties in Kenya 1997-2013

1997-2002	2002-2007	2007-2013	2013 elections
KANU-government	PNU-government	Coalition Government between PNU and ODM	JUBILEE Coalition
NARC-opposition	ODM-opposition		CORD Coalition

After the 1997 general elections, which saw violent clashes targeting members of up-country communities in a suburb of Mombasa, new Coastal political leaders emerged, including Karisa Maitha and Najib Balala. These politicians became important opposition politicians in the former Coast Province as the country edged towards the general elections in 2002. Within the NARC party, Karisa Maitha and Najib Balala became the Coast's point men, challenging and consequently replacing Katana Ngala and Sharif Nassir, both of KANU. Both Balala and Maitha went on to become important cabinet ministers in Mwai Kibaki's first cabinet (2003-2004) as Ministers for Local Government and Tourism respectively.

Maitha died in office in 2004 and did not see the conclusion of the constitutional review deliberations, widely referred to as the "Bomas Process." Led by Yusuf Abubakar, the 24 Coast delegates at Bomas "demanded that 70% of regional revenue be retained and that control of minerals and ports be left to the Coast jimbo – in their view, a key concession" (Devereux, 2012: 19). The political marginalisation of Coast MPs in national politics would therefore soon begin after their failure to make sure regionalism or majimbo was included in what became referred to as the 'Wako draft' in 2005, named after the then Attorney-General, Amos Wako, who was then the government's point man in the work of revising the document (Kramon and Posner, 2011). The draft would be rejected in a constitutional referendum the same year by 80% of the voters on the Coast Province, second only to voters on the former Nyanza Province, which posted a total of 87% opposed. After the constitutional referendum, President Mwai Kibaki dismissed his cabinet of ministers only to reinstate later what were seen as his loyal backers during the campaigns for the Wako draft. In the 2005 cabinet reshuffle, Najib Balala, the then MP for Mvita constituency, was sacked. Balala had become the symbolic head of the Coast region within the then emerging opposition coalition, the Orange Democratic Movement (ODM) of Kenya, which had led the opposition campaign during the 2005 referendum.

Therefore, after the referendum, the national opposition under ODM decisively captured the former Coast Province due to its earlier opposition to the 'Wako draft' and declared strong support for majimbo. Balala's representation of the Coast within the ODM party did not go unchallenged by Mijikenda politicians – notably Morris Dzoro (Jibana), Anania Mwaboza (Chonyi), and Ali Mwakwere (Digo). All Mijikenda politicians, as a result of their loyalty to Kibaki's government, had been appointed as heads or deputy heads of various ministries in the Government of National Unity (GNU) formed after 2005. They consequently challenged Balala's pretensions as a Coast leader, claiming that he was an Arab rather than an 'indigenous' Coastal, and as such not worthy of the region's leadership. However, these Mijikenda politicians – like Balala in ODM – were not part of the locus of power under the GNU. They also did not command any following in their own constituencies. With the exception of Mwakwere, whose election was successfully petitioned, they all lost their parliamentary seats in the 2007 general elections. When Raila Odinga, the ODM presidential candidate in the 2007 general elections, lost the presidency to Mwai Kibaki, Najib Balala was marginalized within ODM power structures and acquired a more absentee posture in national politics; he kept to matters within his ministry as he eventually moved out of Raila's camp, edging towards the then-emerging camp led by Uhuru Kenyatta and William Ruto, and founding his own party, the Republican Congress (RC), in 2012.

After the 2007 general elections (where, following the National Accord and Reconciliation Act, ODM and PNU each received 50% of government appointments), the coalition's cabinet appointments illuminated the insignificance of Coast politicians within government. Both Ali Mwakwere (then Matuga MP) and Najib Balala (then Mvita MP) were appointed full cabinet ministers. In addition to the appointments of Amason Kingi (then Magarini MP) and Dr. Naomi Shabaan (Taveta MP), the Coast Region received only 10% of the positions in the grand coalition cabinet. In addition, these Coast ministers owed allegiance to their parties and to appointing authorities rather than to their electorate, as demonstrated by their inability to take unified stands on matters that affected the Coast (unlike their counterparts in Central Kenya, Luo Nyanza or the Rift Valley) – as well as by Mwakwere's campaign politics during the Matuga by-election in 2010.

Rhetoric employed by PNU stalwarts and cabinet ministers (such as Beth Mugo and the late George Saitoti) in this by-election almost amounted to the blackmailing of Matuga voters. Campaigning for Mwakwere, they reiterated that Matuga voters, and all 'Coastals' by extension, would lose the bendera (ministerial flag) if they did not send Mwakwere back to parliament, since President Kibaki had allegedly reserved the seat for him. Mwakwere consequently returned to parliament and was re-appointed to the cabinet. Appointing MPs to the cabinet completed (in Kenya's former hybrid system) a presidentialist patronage system foundered on an extensive clientelist network of regional and district-level leaders (Barkan, 1979; Widner, 1994). This meant that the less the number of ministers appointed from a region, the less patronage the region receives from goods controlled by the state.

During the time of the Matuga by-election, the government had endorsed yet again, a proposed draft for a new constitution that introduced new counties on Kenya's geo-political map. The 2010 Constitution's provisions on devolution received mixed reactions on the Coast Region. The fact that they did not include extensive provisions on regionalism – as Coastal delegates had requested at "Bomas" five years earlier – may have contributed to the Coast having the widest turnout-to-registered-voter ratio in the country during the 2010 Constitutional Referendum (KNDR, 2010: 20). This meant that turnout was decisively lower than registration, which suggests that the 2010 Constitution did not sufficiently respond to the expectations that voters had at the time of their registration.

This largely compromise and modest decentralization, that went on to be promulgated as part of a new constitution in 2010, was easily accepted by Coast MPs as they continued to play second fiddle to their up-country counterparts during Kibaki succession politics at the national level. The issues having the greatest effect on those who consider themselves indigenous to the Coast persisted unabated. Low representation in government, land evictions, poor results in national examinations, and the appointment of a Kikuyu managing director at the Port of Mombasa, with plans for port privatization initiated – all instilled concern and lack of trust towards the central government and Coast MPs. The continued absence and silence of Coast politicians on these issues did not improve matters. Therefore, when the MRC coined the rallying call "Pwani Si Kenya'" (the Coast is not part of Kenya), it provided a kind of gestalt "... subordinating the host of grievances and problems that are typically debated on their own basis into a single point" (Goldsmith, 2011: 22). This pulled the rug out from under the feet of Coast MPs claiming to represent Coastal grievances. The emergence of the MRC opened a chapter in Coastal politics in which MPs lost the monopoly to speak about issues that touched the hearts of the populace. It was thus felt that since the death of Karisa Maitha in 2004, no other Coast MP had come close to claiming the title of 'regional patron'. In this case, professionals, in the name of Coast Professional Forum, emerged to feel the gap that existed in articulating Coastal problems.

The Coast People's Forum and other professional associations

Joe Khamisi, a sophisticated and accomplished bureaucrat who also served as MP for Bahari constituency in 2003-2007, founded the Coast People's Forum (CPF) in 2006 (*Daily Nation*, April 4, 2006). After his loss in the 2007 parliamentary elections to Benedict Gunda, he left the organization in the hands of the educated elite of Coast Province. CPF would remain docile until conversations on a new constitutional dispensation resumed under the auspices of the Committee of Experts in 2009-2010. Its major successes have included the organization of the Coast Province Investment Conferences, civic education about the 2010 Constitution to push for its passage in the Coast Region, and successful lobbying for the formation of a Task Force with a mandate to look into the issues of Coastal marginalization.

Its political origins notwithstanding, CPF's stated objectives are civic engagement and the promotion of socio-economic activities (The Constitution of the Coast People's Forum, 2006:1). It also includes an online discussion group called "Wapwani" where the educated coastal elite debate and converse about regional issues. In these discussions and in the CPF constitution, "failure of leadership" in the Coast Region forms a core theme. Combined with the Coast's history of electing parliamentarians of low or questionable educational credentials, the conveners of CPF felt that time had come for Coast Region professionals to unite and engage with the region's political problems.

For a long time, many Coastal professionals had been at the very best apolitical. A class small in number, many of them had worked hard in school and secured important national and international jobs without relying much on political patronage. Their position in Kenya's political economy therefore stands outside the usual dynamic, in which the changing tides of identity politics determine career paths in both the civil service and the private sectors. Since political processes have not directly aided their ascension in either sector – their advancement has often come through sheer diligence in school and the professions – they have also tended to alienate themselves from their communities and grassroots civic programs. The less-fortunate who consider themselves Coast natives or "Coasterians" generally paint the more fortunate and educated elites as unhelpful and selfish; they are seen as not "getting" their kin jobs and the right connections the way their Up-country counterparts supposedly do. The Coast Professional Forum (CPF), in many ways, sought to bridge this gulf.

Coastal professionals, in veiled attacks on their MPs, have also claimed legitimacy – and the right to make statements on behalf of the community – through their educational achievements, credentials that Coast MPs could not match. Most members of the CPF are accomplished university professors, bankers, IT specialists, and university students, clearly differentiated from the caliber of people who represent the Coast Region in the national assembly.[2] After the passage and promulgation of the 2010 Constitution, members of the CPF and its allied associations (such as the Kwale KUU and the Kinango professionals) used their participation in these organizations as springboards for political office. Many also presented themselves for appointments in various constitutional offices. For example, Murshid Abdallah, a Mombasa-based lawyer and member of the CPF, applied unsuccessfully to two constitutional commissions before he was appointed to the National Police Service Commission. Dr. Mohamed Swazuri, a land expert and also a member of the CPF, was appointed Chairman of the National Land Commission. Mohamed Alawy, a former Company Secretary at the Kenya Ports Authority was appointed to the Independent Electoral and Boundaries Commission. Other Coast professionals (as shown in Table 2) who might or might not have been CPF members claimed to speak for Coast residents by virtue of their educational and professional achievements. These professionals also stood for elective seats, particularly for the newly-created position of county governor during the 2013 elections

Table 2: Coast professionals who vied for political office

Name	Professional Career	Contested Political Office
John Mruttu	Former Managing Director of Kenya Pipeline and Oil Refinery	County Governor, Taita Taveta
Jacinta Mwatela	Former Deputy Governor, Central Bank of Kenya	County Governor, Taita Taveta
Suleiman Shahbal	Chief Executive Officer, GulfBank	County Governor, Mombasa
Abdallah Mwaruwa	Former Managing Director, Kenya Ports Authority	County Governor, Mombasa
Ibrahim (Babangida) Khamis	Career Banker	County Governor, Mombasa
Hassan Omar Sarai	Former Vice-Chairperson, Kenya National Human Rights Commission	Senator, Mombasa County
Prof. Gabriel Katana Gona	Professor at Pwani University College	Governor, Kilifi County
Naomi Sidi	Former Deputy Managing-Director, Kenya Airports Authority	Women Representative, Kilifi County
Salim Mvuria	Former Manager, Plan International	County Governor, Kwale County
Mohamed Mwachai	Former Permanent Secretary	County Governor, Kwale County

In all these contests, professionals ran in direct confrontation with former Coast MPs. This led to a competition between a "new" kind of politics that invoked professional and managerial efficacy and an "old"p politics that appealed to the affective side of representation, based in identity and membership. This does not mean that the "new politician," steeped in a professional/managerial image, did not also make appeals to those less interested inefficacy. As Martin Sheffter (1994) has argued, politicians with access to state resources (those he called "internally mobilised") were more likely to eschew programmatic appeals in favour of clientelism, while outsider politicians, whodo not benefit from such access, were more likely to adopt programmatic appeals as the only viable strategy to gain the support of significant segments of the population. This was epitomized by the Mombasa contest for the Senate seat between Hassan Omar and Ramadhan

Seif Kajembe, and that between Suleiman Shahbal and Hassan Joho for the governor's seat (*Daily Nation*, January 9, 2013).

Many voters were drawn to the polls by more proximate political competitions; fivenew local-level seats were created in the 2010 Constitution (Willis and Chome, 2014). This explains the higher voter turnout for the general elections in 2013 compared to 2007 (Table 3). However, compared to the rest of the country, voter turnout in the Coast Region remained low, indicating a higher level of voter apathy (Table 4). Supremacy wars emerged between wealthy candidates, echoingrivalries in business circles in Mombasa; some candidates used violence and intimidation. "New politics" candidates, Suleiman Shahbal, Hassan Omar, Sureya Hersi (a county women's representative candidate in Mombasa) and Awiti Bolo (then a Nyali parliamentary candidate and now an MP) forged a united front to call for peaceful elections. Omar, Shahbal and Bolo were singled out for personal attacks during the campaigns by alleged supporters of Hassan Joho, a seasoned politician.

Table 3: Voter registration and turnout trends in the Coast region 1992-2013

Year	Registration	Voter Turnout	Voter turnout as % of total registration
1992	640, 140	316,147	49.4%
1997	782, 179	407,449	52%
2002	879,741	370,611	42%
2007	1,178,627	602,868	51%
2013	1,164,083	817,209	70.2%

Source: Electoral Commission of Kenya and Independent Electoral and Boundaries Commission.

Table 4: A comparison between Coast region and Central region voter turnout

	Estimated Total Population	Registered Voters	Voter Turnout	Turnout as % of total registration	Turnout as % of total population
Kiambu County	1,623,282	860,716	785,735	91.3%	48.2%
Former Coast Province	3, 325, 507	1, 164, 083	817, 209	70.2%	24.6%

Source: Independent Electoral and Boundaries Commission.

After their politicization – caused by but also driving the delegitimisation of formally elected representatives –coastal professionals had therefore sought to make their presence felt in local electoral spaces, with varying degrees of success and unity. In Kwale, when CPF brokered a deal between the Digo-dominated Kwale KUU and the Duruma-dominated Kinango professionals associations to share county positions equally amongst the county's ethnic groups, ethnic sentiments won and the talks collapsed. The Kinango professionals, citing Digo domination, rejected the deal and formed an alliance with the Kamba community in Kwale; they voted as a bloc for Salim Mvuria, who won the governorship of the county.

Even as the delegitimisation of formal representatives led to the politicisation and emergence of the coastal educated elite as a conscious class, one with self-appointed community and political roles, the Coast residents strong disaffection with national politics persisted (Willis, 2013). It remains to be seen how the relationship will shape between the region's county governments, where professionals gained some seats, and the national government in the context of fulfilling the "Coast Agenda." It is likely that the coastal populace will turn their interest more toward the working of county governments, as marginalisation of their MPs in national political arenas continues unabated.

The Mijikenda Council of Elders Association (MICOSEA)

The Mijikenda Council of Elders Association (MICOSEA) was formed in 2004 solely for political functions, seeking to "offer guidance" to the Coast Region's politicians.... MICOSEA differs from CPF on two grounds. It is based on traditional rather than educational primacy and has stricter criteria for membership: it speakssolely for members of the Mijikenda community. Modeled on the lines of the Mijikenda Union (formed in 1945 and disbanded in 1980), MICOSEA sought to exploit or foster a sense of "Mijikenda Unity" – a somewhat spurious unity in light of the actual disarray amongst Mijikenda politicians and their low status in national politics. The Mijikenda identity is itself a classic case of ethnic invention (Willis, 1993; Willis and Gona, 2013). The term originated with a group of mission-educated civil servants in the 1940s, and spread with the subtle support of colonial authorities; its success depended on the cultural affinities of the groups in question (Willis and Gona, 2013). Current historiographies – accepted as truth, taught in schools and "verified" by repetition – base this unified and discrete Mijikenda identity in a history of shared migration from Singwaya – a tradition which did not in fact exist before the twentieth century (Willis, 1993).

An early success of the new Mijikenda identity came in the late 1950s and early 1960s, when it was politicized in a nervous Coastal politics of autochthony against Arabs and Swahilis (Salim,1971). The Mijikenda identity wasalso politicised during the 'Likoni clashes' in 1997 (Mazrui, 1997). Equally, it became harder to mobilize the Mijikenda politically after the death of Ronald Ngala in 1972 (Gona, 1990), and again after Karisa Maitha died in 2004. This was mainly as the result of the inability by formal political representatives representing Mijikenda constituencies to confer status upon the Mijikenda since their marginalisation in national politics reduced their access to the state's largesse and related, intangible benefits of identity.

Given the broad lack of identification with formal state institutions, traditional authorities have gained significance among the coastal Mijikenda on juridical matters around socio-cultural issues. Here, they exercise considerable influence. From time to time, they have also been appropriated by politicians to legitimise their elected offices. Therefore, taking on specific political functions, MICOSEA sought to "bring back unity". This was a strategy to mobilize the Mijikenda, who would then dominate Coastal politics and bargain effectively at the national level. MICOSEA faced one major challenge from the outset – a lack of funds. One of its grand initial strategies (which failed during the run-up to the 2007 general elections) was to spur Mijikenda voter registration in Mombasa in order to elect Mijikenda MPs to all of Mombasa's constituencies. The last time this strategy had worked was during the 1974 general elections, when the Giriama Union East Africa mobilized Mijikenda voters from Mazeras to register in Mombasa West (now the Changamwe and Jomvu constituencies) and vote for its vice-chairperson, Ferdinand Mwaro.

MICOSEA's only major success came in soliciting funds from Kamlesh Pattni, the architect of the infamous Goldenberg Scandal and his KENDA party; the funds purchased one bulldozer for each of the nine Mijikenda groups, to be used in agriculture. Also with Kamlesh Pattni's support, MICOSEA sent some of its members to a meeting with former Libyan President Muammar Gaddafi in Libya in late 2010. Gaddafi promised money, but the Libyan crisis that deposed him intervened; in the meantime, Pattni had become the Chair of the House of Traditional Leaders.

After the promulgation of the 2010 Constitution, Patrick Birya, the chairman of the Mijikenda Youth Association under the auspices of MICOSEA, planned an event to announce the Mijikenda's endorsement of the former managing director of Kenya Ports Authority, Abdalla Mwaruwa (a Digo technocrat), in the 2013 Mombasa gubernatorial elections. That support followed the lines of MICOSEA's initial grand-strategy during the 2007 general elections, which, of course, had not succeeded. When Mwaruwa lacked the funds to support the endorsement event, Birya opportunistically approached Suleiman Shahbal (an Arab businessman and technocrat), who had just colourfully announced his interest in the governor position. Eventually, the Mijikenda Youth Association "endorsed" Suleiman Shahbal in early 2011 at a ceremony held at the Sheikh Khalifa Bin Zayed Hall in Mombasa. Shahbal went on to pick a Mijikenda running-mate, Emmanuel Nzai (a Mijikenda technocrat), and Birya used his accrued networks to become the national organizing-secretary of Uhuru Kenyatta's party, The National Alliance (TNA). Notwithstanding the importance of the traditional elders' legitimacy as shown through its continued appropriation by political leaders, MICOSEA's disintegration into a host of other organizations did not help its electoral influence; it often gave way to money and political expediency while failing to mobilize the Mijikenda vote.

The MRC: Just another political association?

A year after the formation of MICOSEA, a new and more potent organisation announced its appearance in Kenya's Coast Region. The "Republican Council" addressed a letter to Queen Elizabeth II that "set out, at considerable length, the multiple grievances of the Coast Natives" (Willis and Gona, 2012: 15). The list was familiar enough: "poor education access, the domination of Up-country people in public-sector jobs, the "grabbing of huge chunks of Coastal land" by Kenyatta and others" (Willis and Gona, Ibid). Referring to the Zanzibar Protectorate Agreement of 1890, the group claimed (inaccurately, on numerous grounds) that the treaty;

> "provides a road map and a wholesale politico-administrative package" under which the Kenya Colony colonized by the British Governors, and the Coastal Protectorate (also known as Kenya Protectorate) colonized by the Arabs under Arab sultans, were to be two independent territorial entities with definite territorial boundaries and full and equal constitutional rights…[…] And that since the 2004 "Bomas draft" of a new Kenyan constitution — a draft that would have addressed Coastal grievances — had been sabotaged by the "land grabbers," therefore "we, the Coast Protectorate Natives, denounce the citizenship of Kenya," and "the Coastal Protectorate, known as Mombasa, is declared a Republic of Mombasa from now – and is under the authority of the Republican Council".

The letter (Republican Council to Your Majesty, Queen of the United Kingdom, 2005) was signed by Omar Mwamnuadzi and twelve others, including H. R. Nzai. This group would not achieve substantive publicity until February 2012, when government security officers attempted to arrest its members at a local video bar in Likoni, Mombasa, and a clash ensued. By this time, calling itself the Mombasa Republican Council (MRC), the group claimed to have registered about 80,000 members.

Re-emerging in an environment marked by particularly strong feelings of apathy, hopelessness and disillusionment with the promise of national politics, the secessionist message of the MRC appealed to many Coast residents. This rejection of the Kenyan state also accompanied a rejection of Coast MP's who, acting largely as clients of national politics, have generally failed to keep campaign promises when required to make hard choices on Coastal issues. Crucially, they have failed to address the land question, perceptions of marginalization, or the quest for equitable distribution of national resources (Gona, 2008). The MRC letters and citations of agreements, which continued to circulate along the Coast until the time of the 2013 elections, were the MRC leadership's attempt to appropriate documentary knowledge and present a distinctive challenge to state legitimacy (Willis and Gona, 2012).

The MRC's popularity, while varying between parts of the Coast, has exceeded anything claimed for decades by any local political association. Justin Willis (2013) argues that the MRC provided the distinctive character of the 2013 elections in the Coast Region. The overall effect was that the leaders of the MRC, as astute grassroots mobilisers and efficient orators, had gained wide respect and recognition amongst self-identified Coasterians. They were quick to distance themselves from Coast MPs. While expressing his frustrations about the grassrootsresponse to the MRC secessionist calls (by leaders such as Omar Mwamnuadzi and Rashid Mraja), which bypassed the rational approach of the Coastal educated elites in CPF, one informant reiterated that "the grassroots are very complicated" (Interview, March 2013). What the latter might not have appreciated, however, is the extent to which the 'grassroots', frustrated by their feeling a decline in their status in Kenya – had come to distrust their elected officials and the calculated jargon of formal politics.

The government responded by banning the MRC. The ban was lifted on 30 July 2012 by a three-judge panel; but the government responded by banning the organization yet again. A month after the government's re-banning of the MRC more than 20 people were reportedly killed in attacks in Kaloleni, Mtwapa and Kwale. On 4 October, five people, including the bodyguard of the then-Fisheries Minister Amason Kingi, were killed in a remote village in Mtwapa when armed assailants interrupted a meeting he was addressing (Benyawa and Masha 2012). The motive and identities of the attackers were unknown, but suspicion immediately fell on the MRC. Reports indicated that one of the assailants shouted the MRC's separatist slogan, *Pwani si Kenya!*. The next day, the government issued a statement threatening the leadership of the MRC with dire consequences. At this time, the government added another layer of accusations – the MRC was planning to disrupt that year's national examinations on the Coast Region. The MRC leadership distanced itself from these accusations and all the attacks, claiming that the gang had no links with MRC, but were individuals hired to commit the crimes so that blame would fall on the group. The government did not explain how the visible leadership of the MRC (in this case, Mwamnuadzi, Mraja and Nzai) could muster the financial and organizational ability to pursue all the activities allegedly linked to them.

However, on 14 October, the government's crackdown on the MRC began, and more than 40 alleged members of the MRC were arrested. The MP nominee, Sheikh Dor was also arrested after he intimated in an interview that he would fund the MRC if they approached him. Interestingly, the then-Makadara MP, Gideon Mbuvi Sonko, (incidentally born and raised in Kwale), bailed the MRC leaders out of jail, asking them to go and preach peace – and they agreed.

Conspiracy theories abounded, questioning the source of all these attacks. The most prevalent claimed that the attacks were organized to discourage voter registration and actual voter turnout, so as to favour the Jubilee Coalition, which had minimal support along the Kenyan Coast (Chanji, 2012). The incoherent nature of the MRC idea made it vulnerable to appropriation in other quarters, by actors who could use its popularity for their own gains. As a result, on the night before the election, separate yet similarly executed attacks occurred in different parts of the Coast Region, leading to the death of 10 security officers and a number of other people.

Overall, the MRC idea, otherwise expressed as disaffection with national politics and with formal officials, became the ultimate symbol delegitimizing formal leadership in the Coast Region, giving rise to the significance of alternative authority structures, during the 2013 elections. In this context, the MRC was not merely another political association, but was also a form of political consciousness, one appealing to many who identify as Coasterians. As a result, among those considered indigenous, the MRC presented itself as a spontaneous reaction against marginalization that is seen by many at the Coast to be caused by the up-country communities and the passive reaction of Coastal MPs.

In the urban centers, men from across Kenya have competed for jobs, working for the municipality, for the railway, and most of all, on the docks, with Coastal natives claiming primacy and feeling threatened (Willis and Gona, 2012). In the rural areas – mostly in Kilifi, Kwale, Tana-River and Lamu – contestations over claims to land based on indigeneity/autochthony have always been used against those based on settlement schemes. These have led to conflicts that pit peasant families that consider themselves as indigenous to the Coast against up-country residents from Central, Eastern and Western Kenya. Due to the predominance of up-country groups within the Christian community, chiefly based in Mombasa, the debates and discussions initiated by conversations about and around the MRC and Pwani si Kenya also took on a religious note. The formation of the Mombasa Church Forum after the 2010 constitutional referendum and the subsequent emergence of the Pwani Church, which I will consider shortly, attest to this.

Christians and Coasterians

The interdenominational Mombasa Church Forum, led by Reverend Wilfred Lai of the Redeemed Gospel Church, actively campaigned for voter registration in Mombasa.For instance, it organised a registration rally in late 2012, when the MRC's call for an electoral boycott was at its zenith. Additionally, the Mombasa Church Forum did not advocate for secession. On the other hand, the Pwani Church described itself as a confederation of Christian churches of "indigenous coastal peoples," and asserted its support for the Mombasa Republican Council as a "spontaneous coastal people response to the long-standing grievances of the coastal people against the government of Kenya and … up-country immigrant communities" (Willis and Gona, 2012).

Concern in the Christian community increased in late 2012, when two churches were burned in Mombasa following the brutal murder of a firebrand Muslim cleric, Sheikh Aboud Rogo. The fact that that the two main contenders for the Mombasa gubernatorial race, Suleiman Shahbal and Hassan Joho, were Muslim, also concerned the Mombasa Church Forum. A governor-candidates' debate organized by the MCF saw Mombasa Christian leaders seeking assurances from Suleiman Shahbal that he would not turn Mombasa into a Muslim-Middle-Eastern enclave, as some accusations would have of him. A few days after the debate, the Mombasa Pentecostal Church endorsed its "Christian" candidate, the unaffiliated Tendai Mtana Lewa, the only other Christian in the race. He managed to garner about 10,000 votes.

Conclusion

This chapter has argued that Coast residents' disaffection related to the political marginalisation of Coast MPs at the national level has contributed to the emergence of alternative authority structures that, in turn, posit contending visions of primacy and legitimacy. As this article has shown, the authority of elected officials has been contested by alternative forms of politics and legitimacy. It remains to be seen what the role of these alternatives will become with the introduction of government devolution. As already noted, some of them (MICOSEA and CPF) tried to steer local outcomes during the 2013 general elections, in Mombasa and Kwale respectively. Most importantly, the Coast Region's experience in the 2013 elections highlighted the failure of the elected to articulate a political community. In a country whose most salient political features include ethnic and regional brokerage, this added to the indigenous Coast residents' feeling of political marginalization and their missing opportunities for participation. This explains the emergence of the MRC, CPF and MICOSEA, low voter participation rates, and the formal political representatives' inability to mobilize the the Coast natives.

Notes

1   Part of Kenya's political lexicon meaning 'not of the Coast'.

2   The most noted example is that of the Likoni MP, Masoud Mwahima, a primary-school drop-out.

Bibliography

Anderson, D. "Majimboism: The troubled history of an idea". In *Our Turn to Eat: Politics in Kenya since 1950,* eds. D. Branch, N. Cheeseman and L. Gardner, 23-52. Berlin: Lit Verlag, 2012.

Bienen, B. Kenya: *The politics of participation and control.* Princeton: Princeton University Press, 1974.

Barkan, J.D. "Legislators, Elections and Political Linkage". In *Politics and Public Policy in Kenya and Tanzania,* eds. Barkan, J.D. and J.J. Okumu, 64-92. New York: Praeger Publishers, 1979.

Barkan, J.D. "Bringing Home The Pork: Legislative behaviour, rural development and political change in East Africa". In *Legislatures in Development,* eds. Smith, J. and L. Musolf, 265-288. Durham, N.C.: Duke University Press, 1975.

Benyawa, L. and J. Masha. "MRC terror on Minister Kingi". *The Standard Digital* (October 5, 2012). Retrieved from http://www.standardmedia.co.ke/?articleID=2000067669&story_title=MRC-terror-on--Minister-Kingi.

Branch, D. and N. Cheeseman. "The Politics of Control: Understanding the executive-bureaucratic state, 1952-1978". *Review of African Political Economy* 33, no. 107 (2006): 11-31.

Chanji, T. "MRC's agenda not very clear". *The Standard Digital,* October 11, 2012. Retrieved from http://standardmedia.co.ke/index.php/ads/sports/InsidePage.php?articleID=2000068196&story_title=MRC%E2%80%99s-agenda-%E2%80%98not-very-clear%E2%80%99

Devereux, F. "From Majimbo to Mwambao: Kenya's coastal politics and the threat of secession". Unpublished MA thesis, University of Oxford, 2012.

Deacon, G. and G. Lynch. "Allowing Satan In? Moving towards a political economy of neo-Pentecostalism in Kenya". *Journal of Religion in Africa* 43 (2013): 108-130.

Goldsmith, Paul. *The Mombasa Republican Council Conflict Assessment: Threats and opportunities for engagement.* Nairobi: Kenya Civil Society Strengthening Programme, 2011.

Gona, G. "A Political Biography of Ronald Gideon Ngala". Unpublished MA thesis, University of Nairobi, 1990.

_____. "Changing political faces on Kenya's coast, 1992-2007". *Journal of Eastern African Studies* 2 (2008): 242-253.

Kramon, E. and N.P. Daniel. "Kenya's New Constitution". *Journal of Democracy* 22, no. 2 (2011): 89-103.

Lindberg, S. "What Accountability Measures Do MPs in Africa Face and How Do They Respond? Evidence from Ghana".*The Journal of Modern African Studies* 48 (2011): 117-142.

Lynch, G. "Negotiating Ethnicity: Identity politics in contemporary Kenya". *Review of African Political Economy* 33 (2006): 107.

Mazrui, A. *Kayas of Deprivation, Kayas of Blood: Violence, ethnicity and the state in Coastal Kenya.* Nairobi: Kenya Human Rights Commission, 1997.

_____. "The Kenya Coast: Between globalization and marginalization". In *Kenya Coast Handbook: Culture, resources, and development in the East African littoral,* eds. Hoorweg, J., D. Foeken and R.A. Obudho, xxi-xxvi. Munster, Hamburg, and London: Lit Verlag, 2002.

McIntosh, J. "Elders and Frauds: Commoditised expertise and politicized authenticity among Mijikenda". *Africa* 79, no. 1 (2009): 35-52.

Mwajefa, M. "Mombasa set for big battle for party tickets with the arrival of coalitions". *Daily Nation* January 9, 2013. Retrieved from http://www.nation.co.ke/News/politics/Mombasa-set-for-big-battle-for-party-tickets/-/1064/1660774/-/o5i5v8/-/index.html.

Nyanjom, O. "Devolution in Kenya's New Constitution". Society for International Development. *Constitution Working* Paper 4, (2011): 1-30.

Onsarigo, C. "Joho cleared for Mombasa governor race". *The Star* January 31, 2013. Retrieved from http://www.the-star.co.ke/news/article-105276/joho-cleared-mombasa-governor-race.

Orvis, S. "Bringing Institutions Back to the Study of Africa". *Africa Today* 15, no. 2 (2006): 95-110.

Posner, D.N. and J.Y. Daniel. "The Institutionalization of Political Power in Africa". *Journal of Democracy* 18 (2007): 126-40.

Salim, A.I. "The Movement for 'Mwambao' or Coast Autonomy in Kenya, 1956-63". In *Hadith 2, Proceedings of the 1968 Conference of the Historical Association on Kenya,* ed. Ogot, B.A., 212-228. Nairobi: East Africa Publishing House, 1971.

Shefter, M. *Political Parties and the State: The American historical experience.* Princeton, N J: Princeton University Press, 1994.

South Consulting. *The Kenya National Dialogue and Reconciliation (KNDR) Monitoring Project*, 8th Review Report. Nairobi, Kenya, 2010.

Stren, R. Factional politics and central control in Mombasa, 1960-1969. *Canadian Journal of African Studies* 4, (1970): 33-56.

Widner, J. *The Rise of a Party-State in Kenya: From 'Harambee' to 'Nyayo',* Berkeley: University of California Press, 1992.

Willis, J. *Mombasa, the Swahili and the Making of the Mijikenda.* Oxford: Clarendon Press, 1993.

_____. "What can the Kenya Coast tell us about the 2013 elections"? *African Arguments* (April 4, 2013). Retrieved from http://africanarguments.org/2013/04/04/what-can-the-kenyan-coast-tell-us-about-the-2013-elections-%E2%80%93-by-justin-willis/.

Willis, J. and G. Gona. "Pwani C Kenya? Memory, documents and secessionist politics in coastal Kenya". *African Affairs* 112, no. 446 (2013): 48-71.

Willis, J. and N. Chome. "Marginalization and Political Participation on the Kenya Coast: the 2013 elections". *Journal of Eastern African Studies* 8, no. 1 (2014): 115-134.